Pioneers of Personality Science

Autobiographical Perspectives

STEPHEN STRACK, PhD

BILL N. KINDER, PhD

EDITORS

SPRINGER PUBLISHING COMPANY

New York

For our parents,
Ralph D. and Grace Naylor Strack
Rodney P. and Juanita Altizer Kinder

Copyright 2006 by Springer Publishing Company, Inc.

Springer Publishing Company, Inc.
11 West 42nd Street, 15th Floor
New York, NY 10036-8002

Acquisition Editor: Sheri W. Sussman
Production Editor: Richard Rothschild, Print Matters, Inc.
Composition: Compset, Inc.

Library of Congress Cataloging-in-Publication Data

Pioneers of personality science: autobiographical perspectives/[edited by] Stephen Strack, Bill N. Kinder.
    p. cm.
Includes bibliographical references and index.
ISBN 0-8261-3205-7
    1. Psychologists—Biography. 2. Personality—History. I. Strack, Stephen. II. Kinder, Bill N., 1946-

BF109.A1P56 2005
155.2′092′2—dc22
[B]
                                                                            2005054060

06 07 08 09 10 5 4 3 2 1

Printed in the United States of America by Bang Printing

Contents

Stephen Strack, PhD is Assistant Director of Training at the VA Ambulatory Care Center in Los Angeles, and holds faculty appointments at Aliant International University, Los Angeles, and Fuller Graduate School of Psychology in Pasadena, CA. As a graduate student at the University of Miami he worked with Theodore Millon, the later Robert N. Meagher, Jr., and Catherine Greene. Since receiving his Ph.D. in 1983, Dr. Strack has continued to work in the area of personality theory and assessment. He has published 3 edited books and over 40 articles and chapters. He is a Fellow of the American Psychological Association and Society for Personality Assessment and a Board member of the Millon Institute for Advanced Studies in Personology and Psychopathology.

Bill N. Kinder, PhD is professor of psychology at the University of Florida (USF) in Tampa, and former editor of the *Journal of Personality Assessment* (1993–2002). After completing his PhD in clinical psychology from the University of South Carolina in 1975 he was a resident and instructor at the University of Texas Medical School in Galveston, before joining the faculty at USF. He is a Fellow and former Secretary of the Society of Personality Assessment. He has published widely in the areas of personality assessment and various aspects of human sexuality.

Contributors

Jack Block, PhD
1395 Rifle Range Road
El Cerrito, CA

Arnold H. Buss, PhD
Department of Psychology
Seay Hall
The University of Texas
Austin, TX

James N. Butcher, PhD
Department of Psychology
University of Minnesota
75 East River Road
Minneapolis, MN

Richard Dana, PhD
Regional Research Institute for
    Human Services
Portland State University
P.O. Box 751
Portland, OR

Leonard Handler, PhD
Department of Psychology
University of Tennessee
310C Austin Peay
Knoxville, TN

Robert R. Holt, PhD
P.O. Box 1087
Truro, MA

Wayne H. Holtzman, PhD
Hogg Foundation for Mental Health
The University of Texas
Austin, TX

Samuel Karson, PhD
6737 Fairfax Road
Chevy Chase, MD

Bill N. Kinder, PhD
Department of Psychology
University of South Florida
4202 East Fowler Avenue
Tampa, FL

Paul M. Lerner, PhD, ABPP
P.O. Box 800
Camden, ME

Jane Loevinger, PhD
6 Princeton
St. Louis, MO

Joseph Masling, PhD
Department of Psychology
SUNY/Buffalo
Buffalo, NY

Theodore Millon, PhD, DSc
IASPP
5400 SW 99th Terrace
Coral Gables, FL

Edwin S. Shneidman, PhD
11431 Kingsland Street
Los Angeles, CA

Stephen Strack, PhD
VA-LAACC (116B)
351 East Temple Street
Los Angeles, CA

Norman Sundberg, PhD
Department of Psychology
University of Oregon
Eugene, OR

Irving B. Weiner, PhD
13716 Halliford Drive
Tampa, FL

Marvin Zuckerman, PhD
1500 Locust Street, Apt. 4013
Philadelphia, PA

Foreword

Biography as history teaches us that stories of people's lives often chronicle the course of events. Like many other histories, the history of personality assessment can be richly told by tracing the careers and contributions of its pioneers. Customary scholarship presents person-focused history by writing *about* the pioneers—who they were and what they did, what influenced them to pursue the professional course they chose, and how the products of their efforts influenced those who came after them. Steve Strack and Bill Kinder have proceeded otherwise in preparing this volume, by inviting personal accounts written *by* pioneers in personality assessment.

These invitations have resulted in the present compilation of autobiographical accounts of the personal and professional lives of 15 major figures in personality assessment. These accounts provide captivating glimpses of the individual life paths of these influential psychologists and offer illuminating perspectives on the people, ideas, and events that have shaped this psychological specialty. *Pioneers of Personality Science* will bring pleasure to readers who treasure biography as history and a wealth of information to psychologists who value the study, teaching, and practice of personality assessment.

Irving B. Weiner, PhD
University of South Florida
Tampa, Florida

Preface

The second half of the twentieth century may be viewed by future psychologists as a period of unparalleled growth for personality theory and assessment. Although serious study of the subject matter had begun by the mid-1930s (Allport, 1937; Lewin, 1935; Murray, 1938; Stagner, 1937), it was the impetus of World War II that brought personality study to center stage (Pervin, 1990). The war effort focused researchers' attention on armed forces selection issues and standardized testing, while the enormous psychological casualty rate created the need for more treatment providers. The latter necessitated the creation of clinical psychology training programs throughout the country, which were staffed primarily by personality psychologists. The war also highlighted social influences on personality behaviour; for example, the authoritarianism that was evident in the societies that started the fighting. After the war the public wanted to know why and how otherwise intelligent people could be shaped to support wholesale human destruction, and by the late 1940s personality psychologists were prepared to provide some answers.

To test the waters we put together two sets of essays that highlighted the early work of Timothy Leary (Strack, 1996) and the contributions of Theodore Million (Strack, 1999). The success of these endeavors led us to propose a more comprehensive set of autobiographical articles that appeared later.

The history of personality psychology since then has been fast paced, breathtaking, controversial and, at times, exasperating. The attractiveness of this topic to young men and women entering graduate school after World War II ensured ample brain power for the burgeoning field. Many of the best and brightest professors were working in the area, and personality psychology held the promise of being a royal road to understanding not just behavior, but the full complexity of the human being as well. Possessing optimism and a variety of impressive theories, post-World War II personologists shed light on many behaviors, attitudes, symptoms, and traits, and helped define a strong role for personality in related fields such as developmental, social, and clinical psychology. However, the competitive spirit of these pioneers sometimes made the academic environment seem more like a boxing ring than a place for dispassionate inquiry. The controversies in the 1950s over idiographic versus nomothetic assessment, clinical versus statistical prediction, response sets, and the real-world validity of objective and projective personality test results made for lively debate, but also made the field look "a mess" (Blake & Mouton, 1959, p. 226) to some observers.

The 1960s and 1970s saw some of the enthusiasm of post-World War II personology fade away. Continuing controversies caused some of this, but there were other, perhaps more important, factors including the increased interest by psychologists in advances made in the behavioral, cognitive, and social areas of the field. During this time, personality as an explanatory concept was given little importance by many academics, causing some to believe that the field was dying out (Carlson, 1975).

Nevertheless, by the 1980s, personology had regained strength as psychologists turned their attention to affect and motivation, the development of new theories of the self, advances in health psychology, and Axis II of the *Diagnostic and Statistical Manual of Mental Disorders* ([DSM–III], 3rd ed.; American Psychiatric Association, 1980), which asked practitioners to consider the role that personality played in the diagnosis and treatment of psychiatric patients. The 1980s also saw major developments in personality assessment, partly spawned by the advent of personal computers (Megargee & Spielberger, 1992), as well as by the birth of a new journal, *Psychological Assessment*. With enthusiasm for the field increasing, it seemed as though personology was in the midst of a renaissance (Millon, 1984).

In the 1990s, the health and vitality of personality psychology could be seen in the increased membership in the Society for Personality Assessment (SPA), the surge of research that caused the *Journal of Personality Assessment* (*JPA*) to increase its number of issues from four to six per year in 1991, and the appearance of the journal *Assessment* in 1994, whose mission was to "present a new voice in an increasingly diverse and expanding field" (Archer, 1994, p. iii). On examining issues of the top journals during this period, readers will note the intense scrutiny given by investigators to personality disorders; factorial approaches to individual differences, including the five-factor model; projective assessment; and interpersonal aspects of personality.

Although the scientific achievements of the men and women who dominated the field of personality during the last 50 years are well documented in the pages of its journals and related books, there is a dearth of information on the lives of many of these pioneers, including the forces that helped shape their contributions. Therefore, in the interest of illuminating the persons—and personalities—of some of these individuals, we set our sights on publishing a series of personality autobiographies in *JPA*.

We began with a list of prominent personologists nominated by ourselves and others in the field. We invited these men and women to submit journal-length (25–35 typed pages) manuscripts that included information about their personal background (childhood and early adulthood), but focused primarily on the people and events that impacted their most important contributions to the field. We encouraged creativity and asked that they include anecdotes and photographs whenever these would help make their histories come alive.

The second series, titled *Personality Autobiographies*, was inaugurated in *JPA* in January 2002, and now includes contributions by over 20 individuals. Since the first of these articles was published, the series has become more popular than we had imagined. We have been told by scores of readers that they value the articles for their historical perspective, as well as for the intimacy and warmth they convey about the individuals writing them. We have been asked by readers to compile the autobiographies into book form so that people outside SPA can have an opportunity to learn from them.

This book is a response to their request. In coordination with *JPA* and its publisher, Lawrence Erlbaum Associates, Inc., we have gathered together 15 autobiographies by pioneers in personality psychology that were previously printed in journal form. The authors were given an opportunity to update and expand their articles, and to include a selected bibliography of their most important scientific contributions to the field. Many of the authors took this opportunity to include new material that could not be published in the journal. Some asked to include new photographs. Thus, the readers of this volume will not only enjoy the convenience of having 15 autobiographies within a single cover but they will also be treated to updated information and a concise bibliography from each contributor, to make their own research easier.

We decided to order the autobiographies alphabetically by the authors' last names to avoid the invidious comparisons that sometimes arise with choices based on the nature of the contribution (theoretical versus empirical) and area of (or extent of) influence. Our relatively neutral choice was made easier by the recognition that each of them made contributions in several areas over periods of decades. Some had to overcome immense personal hardship or break through social boundaries to succeed, while others struggled against professional bias and the zeitgeist of their era. All persevered to find a voice for their immense talents and curiosity about *what makes people behave the way they do*. The diversity of their accomplishments is manifest and worth honoring, but our own tendencies toward compulsiveness (or conscientiousness) repelled the idea of random assignment.

In the tradition of *A History of Psychology in Autobiography* (Murchison, 1930, 1961; Lindzey, 1989), a series begun in 1930 by Carl Murchison and E. G. Boring, and later nurtured by Gardner Lindzey, our long-term goal is to publish additional volumes as more pioneers of personality science report on their lives in progress. We hope that readers will continue to share our love and enthusiasm for the history of personality theory and assessment as revealed by these men and women who forged the way.

Stephen Strack
Los Angeles, California

Bill N. Kinder
Tampa, Florida

REFERENCES

Allport, G. W. (1937). *Personality: A psychological interpretation*. New York: Holt, Rinehart, & Winston.

American Psychiatric Association. (1980). *Diagnostic and statistical manual of mental disorders* (3rd ed). Washington, DC: Author.

Archer, R. P. (1994). Editorial statement. *Assessment, 1*, iii–iv.

Blake, R. R., & Mouton, J. S. (1959). Personality. *Annual Review of Psychology, 10*, 203–232.

Carlson, R. (1975). Personality. *Annual Review of Psychology, 26*, 393–414.

Lewin, K. (1935). *A dynamic theory of personality*. New York: McGraw-Hill.

Lindzey, G. (Ed.). (1989). *A history of psychology in autobiography, Vol. 8*. Englewood Cliffs, NJ: Prentice Hall.

Megargee, E. I., & Spielberger, C. D. (Eds.). (1992). *Personality assessment in America: A retrospective on the occasion of the 50th anniversary of the Society for Personality Assessment*. Mahwah, NJ: Lawrence Erlbaum.

Millon, T. (1984). On the renaissance of personality assessment and personality theory. *Journal of Personality Assessment, 48*, 450–466.

Murchison, C. (Ed.). (1961). *A history of psychology in autobiography, Vol. 1*. New York: Russell & Russell. (Original work published in 1930.)

Murray, H. A. (1938). *Explorations in personality*. New York: Oxford University Press.

Pervin, L. A. (1990). A brief history of modern personality theory. In L. A. Pervin (Ed.), *Handbook of personality theory and research* (pp. 3–18). New York: Guilford.

Stagner, R. (1937). *Psychology of personality*. New York: McGraw-Hill.

Strack, S. (Ed.). (1996). Special series: Interpersonal theory and the interpersonal circumplex: Timothy Leary's legacy. *Journal of Personality Assessment, 66*, 211–307.

Strack, S. (Ed.). (1999). Special series: Millon's evolving personality theory and measures. *Journal of Personality Assessment, 72*, 323–456.

CHAPTER 1

My Unexpected Life

Jack Block
University of California, Berkeley

PROLEGOMENON

Since adolescence, I have been interested in why people turn out the way they do. There is both fortuity and over-determination in the way lives eventuate over time. I have been keenly aware, afterward, of such factors in my own life and, consequently, I have been motivated to study and to understand personality development and its vicissitudes.

Within that overarching concern, I have had a number of more specific theoretical, methodological, and empirical interests: the concepts of ego-control and ego-resiliency as central structural variables of personality; self concept, identification, and ego identity; the role of affect and emotion in influencing behavior; the differential behavioral effects of various environmental contexts; sex-role and socialization patterns; individual differences in the understanding of various kinds of metaphor (linguistic, pictorial, and affective); the understanding and improvement of observer evaluations of character structure; the understanding and improvement of experimental procedures to assess personality; the proper evaluation of personality change; developing an entirely general, assumption-free and sensitive method for estimating the number of statistically significant findings to be expected by chance; recognizing and responding to the relation-obscuring effects of data outliers; programming and development of a psychology-oriented data processing and statistical package of computer programs; active engagement in literature debates regarding the "consistency-inconsistency" of personality and the "continuity-discontinuity" of personality development; theorizing regarding a systems theory of intra-psychic functioning, of how anxiety comes about and how such intense stresses are kept or brought within bounds; and advancing the methodology and actual practice of longitudinal inquiry. I am aware that the preceding list represents a wide range of scientific activities—too wide perhaps.

ORIGINS

I was born on April 28, 1924, in Bay Ridge, Brooklyn, New York. Horses still pulled wagons in those days. My father, an immigrant from Lithuania, died when I was 14 months old, so I was reared by my single mother, an immigrant from Belarus, along with two older sisters. My father had been a jeweler and, after his death, my mother continued his jewelry store. She was an intelligent but uneducated, necessarily survival-oriented woman who had come to America as a mid-adolescent, working in the garment trade for a dozen years until she married my father. In so many ways, she was typical of that aspiring-immigrant time but, even within that context, she was also and especially a woman of valor, resourcefulness, and quiet but indisputable love.

Important to her and to me were her three sisters and three brothers (my aunts and uncles), and—to a subsequently diminishing extent as our lives diverged—their families. There was much visiting among us, but it also seemed to me that my mother's house (and our large backyard) was central to the extended family, both during the time when my grandparents lived with us and thereafter. We lived behind the jewelry store and in a railroad apartment above.

I grew up as a favored youngest child, the only male, with curly hair, non-athletic, plump, surrounded by women—mother and two sisters. As it was recognized that I was without a masculine model, I was on many Saturdays apprenticed to three older male cousins (the Shapiro boys, on my father's side), learning to throw and catch the culturally-required hard baseball. They helped me markedly and memorably toward self-esteem, toward masculinity, and an awareness of the larger political, social, and economic world—its injustices and ailments. (Elliott, the eldest cousin, years later introduced me as a volunteer helper but also as a learner in the Bellevue Psychiatric Ward. Even later, when Elliott became principal at a tumultuous, difficult school in Harlem, his tribulations and achievements were memorialized in an eloquent book by Nat Hentoff.)

My first school in Brooklyn was PS 2, with a school yard a city block long and an alley wide. I did well in grade school, skipping a couple of years, and becoming a great patron of the public library. One never purchased books then, if only because one could not afford to. When I was age 10, we moved to a nice, private house in Bensonhurst, where I went to Shallow Junior High School, had an Eskimo husky dog, and still read much. In the middle 1930s, after my mother was granted a highly desirable liquor sales license, we moved again, to the Yorkville section of Manhattan, then the center of the Nazi-oriented and culturally influential German-American Bund. I finished junior high school at age 13, of a typical enough size for my age but nevertheless surrounded by much taller, less inquiring, and Jewish-scape-goating 15-year-olds.

For several years, family life had been busy and anticipations were optimistic. Prohibition had just been revoked and my mother's liquor store loomed prosperous. But a vain uncle aroused alcohol authorities by his implied claims of her owning (illegally) multiple licenses, with the result that my mother's license was revoked. We became penurious through her efforts to reverse the license decision. Then she tried and failed with a ladies' undergarment shop, and in desperation took on an 80-room "residence club" located in Harlem (121st St. and Lexington Ave.). The phrase "residence club" was a euphemism for a non-boarding house wherein single individuals lived separately but in a number of slightly modified apartments. I tended the building's furnace and did sundry other maintenance tasks.

Upon the advice of a teacher, I enrolled in Stuyvesant High School rather than the now-defunct but then progress-quickening Townsend Harris High School, to slow my academic acceleration. I quite properly was considered unready psychologically to graduate so early. I do not remember doing exceptionally well in high school except in writing. Well enough but not distinctively so. I read a lot, much on muckraking works, many utopias. I became a lifelong socialist upon reading Edward Bellamy's *Looking Backward* (1888). Achieving most of my adult growth during these high school years, I made the swimming team, and graduated at age 16, earning a scarlet S, rimmed in blue, centered on a white sweater. I did not attend my high school graduation.

Upon my graduation, my mother after several years living up in Harlem, unhappily running that large and stress-inducing rooming house, moved us all to Long Beach, Long Island, out of the New York City legal limits. My mother became a highly-esteemed caretaker of young mothers just returned from the hospital with their new babies. My older sisters, then in their twenties, were around but largely involved in their own lives.

After high school, like others in my ethnic generation, I was oriented toward a college degree. My only further academic possibility, given my means, was to attend a New York City-funded college. But I was no longer a New York City resident. Providing the necessary and sufficient city address of an aunt, I enrolled, I suppose unethically, at Brooklyn College. I commuted to college via the Long Island Railroad, an arduous daily chore. I quit after one unhappy year and bad grades. During the next year, I worked at a gas station, as a lifeguard, a furniture mover, and was a vocational student in metal milling school. I purchased for $10.00 a Chevrolet convertible, frantically waved down on the road to the local junkyard. And I played a lot of ping-pong at the community center.

I then returned to Brooklyn College, now living with a college friend in a minimalist Flatbush apartment. I remained diffuse, with a double major—in American studies and psychology—but I also became an athlete, being on the swimming and wrestling teams (in my senior year, because of my relative size I even was drafted onto the football team, becoming the first campus 3-letterman). I was also involved in endless, intense political discussions. Because of my extreme myopia, I was never accepted by the military. My grades continued to be lousy, I was on academic probation for a year, and graduated with the lowest Grade Point Average (GPA) of anyone I have subsequently encountered in academic life, i.e., a GPA of 2.23.

For my American studies major, I did a lot of reading and writing (on Friedrich Hayek and the issue of equality versus freedom). In my psychology major, I had courses with Dan Katz, subsequently the well-known social psychologist; Hy Witkin, of Rod-and-Frame fame; Ed Girden, the then-noted experimentalist; and Abe Maslow, the personality guru (and actualizer-promiser, who made a play for the lovely, all-American girl I was then dating). I never received an A grade in a psychology course although I did in math and American studies. I did not attend my college graduation. I worked summers in various Catskill resorts as a waiter, earning appreciable funds for the next academic year.

Well into my senior year in college, I decided to become a psychiatrist, which required attending medical school. Consequently, I needed the medical school prerequisites in order to apply. Prior to my imminent (not eminent!) graduation, I could only take the first half of the required two semesters of inorganic chemistry. But in order to apply promptly to medical school, I still needed to successfully complete the second half of inorganic chemistry, two semesters of organic chemistry, and a semester of quantitative analysis.

For the summer of 1945, I enrolled in both of the two successive and intensive summer sessions taught at New York University (NYU), using my true, not unusual name but deliberately providing two different addresses. I hoped the use of similar names but different addresses would expedite my enrollment in these courses. During the first summer session, under the one address, I took the first half of organic chemistry and, under the second address, I took its prerequisite, the last half of inorganic chemistry. My ruse was not discovered until the final days of the first summer session. However, since I was doing well, my deception was pardoned. I did well in the second summer session also, compiling a gorgeous GPA of 4.0 over the entire summer.

WORKING TOWARD A PhD

In fall 1945, I was interviewed for a NYC medical school and was promptly rejected. Temporarily aimless, two conjoining influences then captured me: my girlfriend had taken a job in the Mayo Clinic nursery school at Rochester, Minnesota, and a good friend was trying to get me into the University of Wisconsin, claiming I could be accepted even though the semester there had already started. Because Rochester was relatively close to Madison, I had my transcripts sent to the University of Wisconsin. NYU sent mine very quickly, and on its basis alone, I was accepted into the Madison graduate psychology program. My embarrassingly mediocre Brooklyn College transcript arrived much, much later, in mid-December, and caused graduate office consternation. But I was doing well in my Wisconsin graduate courses, and was allowed to continue. I owe my subsequent professional career to the differing efficiencies of the NYU and Brooklyn College administrative offices. Most likely, I would not have been accepted at Wisconsin had my Brooklyn College transcript been forwarded promptly. Incidentally, my Rochester girlfriend necessarily returned to New York and we ultimately broke up.

At Wisconsin, I took the usual courses for graduate students, many of them dry or to me of trivial psychological relevance. But I learned much from a year-long home seminar given by Norman Cameron, a gentle, wise psychiatrist-psychologist, who was eloquent regarding the strange but indisputable logic underlying psychopathology. I also imbibed a good deal of information about academic clinical psychology from Ann Garner Magaret, a new, young professor recently arrived from Stanford University, insistently scientific in her approach. During one summer, I was a bemused and amused attendant in the monkey labs of Harry Harlow but never took a course with him. For valuable clinical experience, I worked as a VA trainee at Mendota State Hospital, near Madison, under Dr. Sol Garfield and saw varieties of psychopathology beyond my ken. Perhaps accidentally and certainly curiously, I hit it off with brilliant, witty David Grant, an experimentalist who also taught statistics and who was encouraging of a clinical student who had wandered into his quantification course. I had responded to one of his assignments in an unusual way that he deemed clever, and his responsiveness heartened and enlivened me. The only graduate student I recall from my Madison days is Len Eron, of subsequent television and aggression research fame. I learned to drink coffee at all hours, moved in leftist circles, and even (because of my borsht belt kitchen experience) organized a dinner for inspiring Norman Thomas, perennial socialist presidential candidate and 149 others. I earned an MA in 1946, and stayed on a bit at Wisconsin, meanwhile industriously applying again, without success, to medical school. But by early 1947, I had become restless. "Go West, young man" seemed a personal directive.

My eldest sister with her new family had settled near Los Angeles, and I thought it would be supportive (of me) if I were in school nearby. In my geographic innocence, I thought Stanford was close and so, to maximize probabilities when I applied to Stanford Medical School for 1947 admission, I requested that, were I to be rejected, I be considered for the Stanford Psychology Department as well. Sure enough, I was turned down by the medical school but was accepted for the psychology graduate program. It was only then that I learned that my sister lived 450 miles from Palo Alto. In anticipation of attending Stanford, I worked the prior summer as a waiter and barwaiter in the Catskills, again saving all my money for school.

I arrived at Stanford and found that tuition fees significantly drew down my funds. I earned a room in a dog-and-cat hospital on El Camino Real by cleaning kennels and helping with pet surgery over weekends. I pedaled my old bike down Palm Drive to the University each morning and back in the evening. I breakfasted on tangerines plucked by climbing a tree in the Inner Quad, then adjourning to the old Student Union for a glazed doughnut and a plastic cup of steaming black coffee, played a lot of basketball, haunted the journals room of the library, ate some kind of dinner often at Walgreen's lunch counter; had knee surgery as a delayed consequence of my football days, was hermit-like, and did not get into San Francisco at all during my first year at Stanford. I duly observed that Stanford was not quite the place for leftist talk.

Brilliant Ernest (Jack) Hilgard taught the required course on learning theory. I still remember seeking him out with an ill-formed idea I had. He casually took my half-baked conception, permutated and explored its possibilities, and turned it all back to crestfallen me, who no longer wanted the notion. Paul Farnsworth was informative, gossipy, and slyly funny on the history of psychology; calvinistic Calvin Stone instructed us on his conception of comparative psychology; Donald Taylor sternly communicated an experimentalist's ethos; reserved, quietly shrewd, and elegant Maud Merrill James together with young, recently arrived Frances Orr provided clinical instruction; an inexperienced Howard Hunt lectured didactically on psychoanalysis; energetic Lloyd Humphreys furthered my methodological understandings. And eminent psychological statistician Quinn McNemar—supportive and understanding beneath his acerbic manner, and the best practicing clinician with graduate students—communicated deep understanding of methodology and its absolute necessity. I also took a wonderful year-long medical physiology course with disabled Victor Hall of the Med School (I topped all the enrolled medical school students, required to take the same course, but, alas, applying yet again to Stanford Med School, I was turned down once more). And I had most stimulating times with sociology professor Richard LaPierre and visiting sociology professor Louis Wirth of Chicago.

As my second year at Stanford began, I had tuition money only for one final quarter, so I went to see Howard Hunt, director of the clinical program, to tell him I would have to be leaving. He casually informed forlorn and desperate me that I could join a number of my fellow graduate students already serving as VA clinical psychology trainees. This was a position I had earlier applied for because it served my psychological interests and was generously (even extravagantly) subsidized by the Veterans Administration in the postwar period. I was elated by this new possibility because it meant I could afford to remain at Stanford and could even live somewhat graciously.

Clinical psychology was new, even unlikely at Stanford, seeking to define and transform itself after the war. It was the élan of the clinical students to be both clinically oriented and also to academically outdo the psychology graduate students focusing on "hardnosed," "experimental" psychology. Our motivation was such that we indeed did better. I served for two years at the Menlo Park VA Psychiatric Hospital—a great learning experience that also permitted much scholarship, training, and research at the Stanford campus nearby. And graduate student discussions.

An unusually good group of graduate students was at Stanford during this postwar era, partly because of the return of veterans keen to renew their education. Fellow graduate students that I well remember were chipper Dick Bell known later for his emphasis on the bidirection of effects in socialization; Gerry Blum, who created the Blacky Test as an operationalization of psychoanalytic psychosexual theory; Harold Raush, a good friend interested in formalizing interaction; Paul McReynolds, who both historically and conceptually integrated diverse aspects of clinical psychology; Wayne Holtzman, who created an interesting alternative to the Rorschach Test; Hal Stevenson, later an active contributor to cultural factors in developmental psychology.

And, all important, vivacious, eager, resourcefully bright, and most attractive Jeanne Humphrey.

I had met Jeanne when we had both started at Stanford in 1947, she coming from Reed College after wartime service as an ensign with the SPARS having attended Oregon State, where she achieved the unusual distinction of failing in home economics while simultaneously making the dean's list for academic achievement. She had been accepted at Harvard's graduate school but was lured by the ambience of Stanford.

In the nature of things, we took a number of courses jointly, and found we both were excited by reading Kurt Lewin and psychoanalytic theory. We talked, we argued, and we discovered that we danced very well together, and decided to try an ambitious joint thesis exploring some Lewinian ideas we had extrapolated into psychoanalysis regarding what we called ego-control and ego-resiliency. We worked long and hard the academic year of 1949–50, and became imbued with the conceptual unity that seemed to underlie seemingly diverse behaviors. And, we also became imbued with each other. In a number of ways, we followed our graduate themes throughout our subsequently fused careers (e.g., Block & Block, 1951; Block, J. H., & Block, J., 1952, 1980). We married in 1950, shortly after I wrote my thesis (Block, 1950) and received my PhD. I did not attend the formal ceremony to receive my graduate degree.

Jeanne, needing some additional courses, wrote her thesis (Block, J. H., 1951), earned her PhD in 1951, and was promptly hired as an instructor at Stanford for 1951–52. For a number of years, her considerable energies centered mostly on bearing and rearing our four offspring—Susan Dale, Judith Lynne, David Lewis, and Carol Anne—while I sought to further my career in psychology. But she still found time and stamina to hold several ad hoc, flexibly-scheduled psychological positions, investigating the psychosomatics of childhood asthma (for which she later received the Hofheimer Award of the American Psychiatric Association) and the nature of physicians multiply accused of malpractice. But in the main, caring for our children kept her from a full-time career in psychology until the early sixties.

When I received my doctoral degree, I was informed by a UC San Francisco psychology professor on the admissions committee of the UCSF Medical School that he could arrange my medical school acceptance. By then, however, suddenly so close to my long-sought career goal (and recently married), I had the soul-searching recognition that so much of medicine and psychiatry consisted of practicing the status quo rather than advancing it. So, I opted to remain a psychologist because of the field's intrinsic intellectual interest for me.

The Stanford scuttlebutt among the graduate students at the time was that if one wanted to live in the Bay Area (as we all had come to wish), it was necessary first to go to the East or Midwest in order to establish a career that would justify returning. With this understanding, many reluctantly left Palo Alto (and subsequently never returned). But, after receiving my degree, I necessarily had to linger in the Bay Area at least a year, awaiting Jeanne's degree completion.

ESTABLISHING A CAREER

With my brand-new PhD, I took a position in 1950 at Langley Porter Clinic, with Dr. Jurgen Ruesch, a research psychiatrist. Our research theme was interpersonal communication (e.g., Block, 1952; Block & Bennett, 1955). Also joining the research team were Gregory Bateson, the well-known anthropologist-generalist, and Weldon Kees, a serious and accomplished poet, writer, and filmmaker. It was a stimulating group and I was multiply influenced.

Centrally, I read William Stephenson (e.g., 1953) on Q-methodology, was intrigued by his approach, seeing however some problems and possibilities different from those he had envisaged. I thought Stephenson viewed Q in almost cosmic and unverifiable terms whereas I valued the essentials of the approach in a more plebian way, as becoming, with some modifications and specific recognitions, a reasonable way of objectifying and making comparable otherwise non-comparable clinical descriptions. I even then had developed much faith, yet unsupported, in the value of clinical formulations. Although I had no ultimate trust in any single clinical description, I had a good deal of respect for the consensus reached by a number of clinicians. However, clinical descriptions were (and, sadly, still largely are) unsystematic, idiosyncratic, and therefore largely unusable for research and analytical purposes. I considered that Q-methodology could provide a tenable way to permit (nay, "force") clinicians to express their personality formulations within a generally sufficient but standard language together with a standard "grammar" (the fixed frequency distribution), thus achieving a commensurateness among the formulations offered by various clinicians.

I spent a good deal of time creating what I thought might be a sufficiently comprehensive set of Q-items describing personality and, separately, person-to-person interactions (Block, 1962, 1990). In one study, I gathered Q-sorts from a central person and the 26 individuals constituting her relevant social matrix (e.g., her mother, ex-husband, boss, colleague, secretary, babysitter, and so forth). Data collection was an arduous task, as was the data analysis in those pre-computer days. Not surprisingly, several styles of interaction evidenced themselves, instructively, for both the target person and the individuals in the social matrix.

After two years at Langley Porter Clinic, I was invited to move to a part-time position in the recently established Institute for Personality Assessment and Research (IPAR) at the University of California at Berkeley, becoming full time there in 1953. IPAR was a derivative of the derring-do wartime OSS, and I was excited to be on the staff. There was the director, Donald Mackinnon, a New Englander who had been in the personality section of Office of Strategic Services (OSS): Richard Crutchfield, a social-perception psychologist from Swarthmore; Harrison Gough, a young, hyperactive Minnesota PhD who focused on the MMPI and his less offensive variant, the California Psychological Inventory; Frank Barron, a Berkeley doctorate with novel-writing ambitions, and myself. Also associated with IPAR on a part-time basis were R. Nevitt Sanford, a psychoanalytically oriented psychologist, and Robert E. Harris, chief psychologist at Langley Porter Clinic, a quiet but acute person. I also met Ravenna Mathews Helson, then a graduate student but subsequently a long-term and interestingly productive colleague. This was another stimulating group, with many assessment goals evaluating such target groups as graduate students, Air Force jet pilots, significant published writers, architects, and medical student applicants.

I merged well with IPAR for the next four years or so. Carrying through the same research paradigm characterizing the earlier theses of Jeanne and myself, I studied individuals whose self-esteem was too high and those whose self-esteem was too low in contrast to individuals with intermediate self-esteem. I also studied individuals who were confident of their decisions, even when confidence was unwarranted, and individuals who remained uncertain even when decision confidence was clearly warranted, contrasting both groups with a third group of individuals who adjusted their decision confidence as a function of the objective obviousness or unsureness of a decision (Block & Petersen, 1955; Block & Thomas, 1955). I studied the personality implications of different reactions to partial reinforcement. I evaluated fathers' attitudes toward child-rearing and the characterological implications of different degrees of parental restrictiveness (Block, 1955a). I embarked on a multifaceted study of emotion—the phenomenology of different emotions, across genders and across cultures (Block, 1957c), the study of heightened versus flattened affect and appropriate versus inappropriate affect as reflected by skin conductance while watching an emotion-laden movie, a synesthetic version of the semantic differential, and a study of the characterological qualities of "good" (undetectable) liars and "bad" (readily discernible) liars (Block, 1957b). I also studied accuracy of person prediction as a function of the target being judged and the person doing the judging (Block & Baker, 1957). I learned to both value and question personality inventories. And with a stern visage and interior qualms, I conducted stress interviews of Air Force officers, medical school applicants, and others.

Methodologically, I carried through various studies on the Q-method, regarding the implications of forcing judgment, considerations involved in gradually generating a personality-descriptive Q-set generally agreed upon by clinicians as sufficient, on the relation between ipsative and normative data, and I demonstrated that aggregated or consensus judgments were readily replicable and also were reliably superior in prediction accuracy to even the best (usually non-replicable) individual judgments (Block, 1955b, 1956, 1957a).

As perhaps a response to this youthful flurry of activity, I was invited by Robert White in 1956 to come to Harvard, on one of their five-year assistant professorships. Deep familial introspection resulted, with some ambivalence and uncertainty about our remaining in Berkeley—Jeanne and I and our multiplying kids liked Berkeley very much; we had good local friends; with sweat equity, we had built a house (with the loving craft of Jeanne's father, a Portland building contractor); and there lurked in us a wistful hope that I could some day land a faculty position at Berkeley. We both recognized that the established rule against nepotism precluded Jeanne from an academic position.

In 1956, while struggling to conceptualize personality in a way susceptible to moment-to-moment research, I thought of dynamically changing personality (or ego) structure via various drugs. I had read *The Doors of Perception* by Aldous Huxley (1954) and been most intrigued by the experiences described so vividly therein. Because of my experimental interest in modifying ego structure (but also no doubt for other, over-determined reasons), I arranged to imbibe a proper dosage of mescaline at UC San Francisco Hospital under the supervision of the chairman of the pharmacology department. At this time, the effects of psychedelics were largely unknown in America except for the slim Huxley volumes and a few articles in the psychiatric-psychological literature, so my experience was of interest not only to me but also to Gregory Bateson and a couple of psychologists who observed me under the influence of mescaline.

My experience was profound. At the start, I was more than a little anxious about what I was letting myself in for. As the mescaline took hold, I felt intensely vulnerable; for instance, the joshing from a psychologist-friend that ordinarily I would respond to with repartee impressed me as hostile, hurtful, and warranting suspicion. As the powerful effect deepened, I was panicky before the flood of perceptions and thoughts that assailed me. But then, as the effect no longer intensified and even seemed to be ameliorate, the experience became something to be relished and attuned to, something cosmic and religious in a Zen-like way, indeed "a cleansing of the doors of perception." I returned to ordinary reality phenomenologically restructured. Flashbacks of this "trip" recurred for some time. My profound experience with mescaline suggested to me that if the leaders of America and the Soviet Union were to jointly have a psychedelic experience, the dangerous tension between the two superpowers would seem cosmically unimportant and thus end.

Along about this time, an academic position in personality psychology became available in the Berkeley Psychology Department. Don Mackinnon, director of IPAR, proposed that Frank Barron and I share the position, a move that would provide secure academic credentials for both of us while we continued to function at IPAR. However, after some argument, the department selected me for a full-time tenured position as an associate professor. Frank soon left IPAR for an advantageous full professorship at UC Santa Cruz, then in its early days. I was informed a year or so after taking the position that the debate within the conflict-ridden department regarding Mackinnon's proposal had been decided not by my sterling personal qualities but rather because I was perceived as more likely to be independent of Mackinnon's influence. So it goes. . . .

The summer prior to my first academic year, 1957, I prepared an endless and obsessive series of handwritten notes, outlines, and ideas. I had never really taught before and worried I would run dry during the course of a lecture. But for such an emergency, I invented a tolerable excuse—I would simply say the lecture had to be cut short that day because I had to take one of my small children to the pediatrician. With that potential excuse conveniently in my memory, I was no longer chronically anxious when lecturing. It eventuated that I never in my career became speechless during lecturing and my initially prepared notes served me for some time. For several years, being low man on the academic totem pole, I taught three of the four courses required for all graduate students in my section of our split department.

The Berkeley Psychology Department was a riven place when I entered it, and for many years thereafter. After so much internecine fatigue, there finally was a consensual but not friendly understanding that overt hostilities were simply too time consuming. Not uniquely, I evolved into a reluctant lone wolf. Being a primo don was a widespread survival technique because, otherwise, one became a vassal of those faculty members uninhibited about being a primo don. Although I was relatively friendly and open with psychology colleagues at other universities, within my department and the institutes I was associated with, I learned through sad experience to worry about academic power plays and backbiting. Although nominally I was a member of the personality group of the department, I connected as much or more with colleagues in the clinical and developmental groups. In our own research over the years, Jeanne and I tended to invite and mentor clinical graduate students as our research assistants.

In my new position, because of my continuing interest in drug effects and with nominal supervision by a psychiatrist at Kaiser Hospital, I invited about 30 lay people into the mescaline situation after first assessing them in a number of ways. A benign and psychologically supportive environment proved crucial for their positive psychedelic experience, as it seemed to me that anticipatory anxiety both delayed and restricted the profound appreciation of the perceptual phantasmagoria rushing at one during this drug-induced state. I might also mention, as a historical note, that my IPAR colleague, Frank Barron, learning of my earlier psychedelic immersion, self-administered some peyote to gain his own experience, and went on to introduce psychedelics to Timothy Leary, who soon thereafter arrived at Harvard from Berkeley. The subsequent cultural ramifications of the use of psychedelics by Leary and his confreres in the sixties and seventies are well known.

However, I full well recognized that the experimental use of drugs to modify personality structure could only provide anecdotal information and that within a public or even a private university it was prudent to focus my energies elsewhere. So, for several years, I attended to my burgeoning family, to teaching, to playing tennis, to engaging in political advocacy, and to sprinkling into the psychological literature some perhaps useful and interesting research.

Turbulent times arrived at Berkeley in the early 1960s. The Free Speech Movement (FSM) erupted when a bureaucratic vice-chancellor arbitrarily ruled that a segment of the campus walkway historically employed for political purposes could not be so used for the same. There was immediate student reaction, at first polite and discursive, but subsequently challenging the authorities. Soon, the idiotic, un-American, Washington war on Vietnam replaced the FSM as a campus and area focus, leading to activists' involvement in the 1968 presidential election. My family—Jeanne, myself, and our kids—were all caught up in the cascade of political events. We supported the FSM, rallied against the Vietnam horror, and did precinct work for Senator and poet Gene McCarthy. We had evolved comfortably into Berkeleans. And we had purchased a handyman's special—a larger and latently attractive house in which our kids grew up, and which I still inhabit.

THE INSTITUTE OF HUMAN DEVELOPMENT
LONGITUDINAL STUDY

In the late 1950s I became aware of the longitudinal Berkeley Guidance Study (BGS), a longitudinal study, that had been well underway by Jean Walker Macfarlane at the Institute of Child Welfare (soon to be renamed the Institute of Human Development, or IHD). I thought the Q-sort method in conjunction with the personality Q-sort items I had earlier developed could be useful for Macfarlane's study, especially for the impending further adult assessment. Macfarlane was an old-fashioned and somewhat accidental clinical psychologist, quite obviously not oriented toward empirical research. She was not especially receptive to my forwardness at the time, but several years later I learned that she had indeed adopted my Q-approach, casually and confusingly rewording a number of the Q-items that I had carefully developed, though she had applied the method only partially. I could only shrug.

Meanwhile, I had become friendly with Harold Jones, then director of IHD. Harold was a prestigious figure, a former president of the SSRC, and soon to retire. My psychophysiological study on externalizing and internalizing had found results intrinsically related to a favorite finding of Jones some 25 years earlier. We were both intrigued. He and his wife Mary (famous in the 1920s for her work on phobic desensitization with Watson) were friendly to Jeanne and me and our children, inviting us all to their home.

At the Institute, the Ford Foundation had awarded a large grant for an assessment of all three IHD subject samples (the Oakland Growth Study of the Joneses, the Berkeley Guidance Study of Macfarlane, and the small Berkeley Growth Study of Nancy Bayley), the researchers then in their mid-thirties. I felt too distanced from the enterprise to intrude upon the several already-present Institute research planners, but I did see many of the Jones's subjects in a psychophysiological procedure. Later, because I had come to realize that it was impossible to manipulate ego structure experimentally in ethical ways, because I had become aware of the longitudinal studies and the obvious power of the longitudinal idea, and because Harold Jones was very encouraging, I was primed to accept his invitation to temporarily join IHD.

There was a joyful retirement party for Harold and Mary before they flew off to enjoy Paris where, sadly, he died hours after landing.

For the summer of 1960, I was asked to serve as acting director of IHD since I was the only relevant academic senate member available. I had embarked on and finished a book entitled *The Q-sort Method in Personality Assessment and Psychiatric Research* (Block, 1961). It presented a method and rationale for commensurate assessment and evaluation of psychiatric and non-psychiatric patients. Many problems in observation were believed to be eliminated or minimized by the method—systematic and completeness of description was assured as well as fully comparable rather than idiosyncratic usage of the underlying continuum. The method, its rationale, and the recommendations I offered for research practice have been widely adopted over the years by many investigators, and the book's recommendations remain especially relevant over 40 years since its initial publication. During this period, I also used the opportunity to learn more about the three diverse longitudinal studies located at IHD and their research potential. Some of my tentative explorations into the data seemed confirmatory and seriously whetted my interest in the longitudinal material.

At IHD at this time, however, all the longitudinal studies were in the doldrums. This was not my view alone. With respect to the three longitudinal samples, Harold Jones was gone, Jean Walker Macfarlane was about to retire, Nancy Bayley, progenitor of her own tiny sample, had left for Santa Cruz and no longer was a factor. The Ford Foundation-supported follow-up assessment had been completed in a catch-as-catch-can way during the later 1950s and subsequently the analysis and interpretation of the significance of the studies had languished. Funds had expired, the Institute was being criticized within the University, and national research review committees were not inclined to provide supporting grants. An especially powerful and influential criticism of longitudinal inquiry attributed to Lee Cronbach had been leveled: "Longitudinal studies issue promissory notes which are never redeemed." The new IHD director, upon his accession, promptly proposed closing down the longitudinal studies and redirecting the Institute.

It was in this context that I prepared a research application to NIMH for a necessarily large research grant. After a scrupulous site visit by agency representatives, the grant was approved. My plan and research design entailed organizing the available archival material and insisted upon partitioning data and information into three fully independent dossiers for each IHD participant. By doing so, any subsequently obtained relationships between these separated time periods would be logically clean rather than "contaminated" by prior knowledge about the participants. Because information and data for the subjects were often disparate and incomplete, I applied the Q-sort method to each available subject at three different time periods, with multiple and different clinical Q-sorters being permutatively invoked for each of the three periods of a given subject; in this way, commensurate data were "made" for each subject. I also unified the Macfarlane and Jones samples to help rise above the statistical smallness of each sample—the Bayley sample was simply too small and special to consider.

Ultimately, I worked on this study for nine years, obsessively immersed in myriad details and responding to myriad requirements of the enterprise: with a brilliant programmer, Eleanor Krasnow, I was closely involved in the design of a complex, integrated set of computer programs necessary for the data processing and statistical analysis of the new and varied IHD data; I was involved in the psychometric construction and evaluation of various sets of archival material to see if internally consistent, psychologically sensible scores could be derived as a precondition for subsequent use of these data to establish longitudinal relations; I collected more data from the Macfarlane subjects to increase the sample's comparability with the Jones sample; I monitored closely the quality of the many Q-sortings by clinicians on which the study depended so heavily; and I planned and evaluated all the many and diverse data analyses.

Organizing this effort was no small or solitary or short task. In its first phase (ending in mid-1965), I was aided appreciably by Norma Haan, an M.A., who had been employed as an interviewer for the Ford follow-up, and who helped supervise much of the Q-data generation. Judith Casoroli resourcefully did all the many tasks and chores that can be demanded of a research assistant. My wife, Jeanne, and two other clinicians did environmental history interviews, codified by a separate EQ-set of the study participants.

In 1963–64, sabbatical time having accrued, we spent the academic year in Oslo, Norway, where our children attended Norwegian schools. Jeanne returned actively to psychology by developing her Child Rearing Practices Report, administering it within the four Scandinavian nations, in England, and in the United States. In Norway, I worked on another book (see response sets below). Back in Berkeley, the laborious process of systematically Q-sorting all the subjects according to logically pre-arranged sets of sorters went forward.

Having returned fully to the psychology department at Berkeley, I necessarily wrote and happily received NIMH research grants to complete the study. The information accumulated over the many years of the IHD longitudinal study was gone over carefully and subjected to various quality controls. The resulting data then were subjected to a variety of analyses, in particular a longitudinally dynamic, time-spanning typological analysis of personality development for males and, separately, for females in order to discern different paths of life. The emerging developmental types demonstrated life continuity for some individuals and life change for others but always a coherence of development. The book, *Lives Through Time* (LTT), appeared in 1971, integrating and reporting the relationships found. The research design and methodology used in LTT in the 1960s has continued to be followed by the Institute in their subsequent assessments.

OUR ONGOING LONGITUDINAL STUDY

In 1968, with my work on LTT drawing to a close, and with my wife, Jeanne, bringing a body of her own research on student activism and gender roles to completion, we sought a confluence of our careers which, of necessity, had been progressing too separately. While she was having and preoccupied with our children, I had emphasized—though not exclusively—securing my career. When she had turned again to being a full-time psychologist in 1963, as the children became more self-sufficient, she too had been absorbed in the challenge of establishing herself as an independent psychological scientist. Of course, during all these years, besides being helpmeets, we had been mutually influencing each other's work and thinking—she introduced me to broader and softer issues; I made her own work more rigorous. Thus, we complemented, supplemented, and potentiated each other. But we had not had the opportunity to work together directly and we wanted to. Jeanne had just received an NIMH Research Scientist Development Award because of her productive research and was freed for a long enough time to explore her own thinking and research themes. I was already securely tenured and thus also freed.

Accordingly, and for reasons having to do with our personal conceptual interests and what we judged to be important research needs of the field, we formulated plans for our own longitudinal study. We saw many opportunities to improve upon the largely unplanned, unsystematic, and accidental IHD longitudinal studies. We wished to commit our own research errors rather than try to rectify or be forced to live with data from studies initiated by others with different interests and orientations. And we felt we were both old enough yet young enough to embark on our own longitudinal venture.

Hence, the 1969 initiation of the Block and Block (1973) longitudinal study was a deliberate career investment, intended to permit the developmental study of our concepts of ego control and ego resiliency, the study of sex role development and of gender differences, the study of self percepts over time, the study of parenting styles and their consequences, among other concerns. The powerful logic of the longitudinal method had impressed us both as being incontestable; the psychological issues that we could study were intellectually exciting and personally meaningful to us; previous longitudinal projects were unable to respond to these contemporary concerns, and the idea of a jointly-nurtured, jointly-managed research enterprise was reinforcing. And so this major effort was begun.

In central ways, the longitudinal study, once embarked upon, shaped (indeed, controlled) our subsequent lives as psychologists. To begin, we formulated a list of research criteria: we would do an intentional, well-grounded longitudinal study; we would make public and communicable to our peers just what was done, how observations were made, how categories or numbers were generated, and how conclusions or implications were drawn; we would go on for a long time, from early childhood on through adolescence into adulthood; we would have a sample of reasonable and continuing size, of both sexes, seen at a number of developmentally aptly-selected times; we would have a conceptual integrating rubric rather than be blandly or blindly eclectic; we would be closely psychological in our approach rather than work only with distal epidemiological indices; we would be comprehensive, intensive, systematic, and scientifically contemporary in our coverage; we would manifest methodological craftsmanship; we would try to be innovative and au courant as we went along; and we would be alert to the inevitable problems of sustaining the quality of the enterprise over the long period of time required. Taken altogether, this was an adolescent, grandiose ambition. I will not say we achieved all of these desiderata (indeed, I would wish to be the first one to criticize our enterprise; as John von Neuman once remarked informally, "in order to maximize n functions, when n equals or is greater than 2, you have to be very lucky"). Therefore, I will leave to others the assessment of how well my wife and I achieved our goals in a decade.

Longitudinal study is frequently urged but seldom tried if only because a 10-year project is not a tenure project. It feels like wrapping an albatross around your neck, putting a monkey on your back, mounting a tiger, and grabbing a bear by its tail—all at once. Because time is unstoppable, the pressures are incessant and in ways beyond mention in formal publications or talks (e.g., a lovely Saturday afternoon spent with Jeanne making curtains for an experimentation-fitted mobile home while Jack is laying its carpeting). Before we were through evaluating the implications of one assessment, we had to plan for and ready another. If we were to maintain funding, papers and chapters needed to be written and they needed to be impressive. It was not easy.

We began with 128 three-year-olds, 64 girls and 64 boys, who were intensively assessed (10 to 16 hours) at ages 3, 4, 5, 7, 11, 14, 18, 23, and, less intensively but materially, at age 32. Assessments were unique in insuring that quite independent data sources were employed (Life history-data, Observation-data, Test-data, and Self report-data, i.e., LOTS of data!). Assessments have included observations by multiple observers, videotaped interviews, laboratory procedures galore, a wide array of self-report procedures and questionnaires, and the collection of life data relating to school, family, and environmental happenings, and so on. At age 23, we have 104 subjects; at age 32, we have 92. To insure "clean" findings, assessors used during one assessment were never involved in a second assessment. The parents of these subjects also were assessed at various times in various ways. I shall not detail the rationale, design, subsequent implementation, products, and implications of our longitudinal venture. But it is an observation rather than an act of self-praise to suggest that no other sample in psychology has been so closely and protractedly assessed, in so many ways, over a span of three decades.

Tragically, Jeanne was swept away by pancreatic cancer in December 1981. I was devastated, and still am, by the loss of my intimate and intellectual partner. Always lurking in the subtext of a longitudinal study is an awareness of life's inescapable uncertainties. After all her work planning and seeding and tending the garden, and with all her anticipation, she was suddenly not around for the harvest.

And harvesting is what my collaborators and I have tried to do. Not enough, not fast enough, but a good deal nevertheless. The longitudinality of our data has brought new and, I believe, important recognitions. For the first time, the ramifying constructs of ego-control and ego-resiliency were studied longitudinally, with implicative results. We have shown that ego-control is remarkably rank-order consistent from early childhood to early adulthood, a period of 30 years, for both sexes, thus replicating in two separate and different samples (e.g., Block J. H. & Block, J., 1984; Block & Robins, 1993; Kremen & Block, 1998; Westenberg & Block, 1993). We have shown that, in boys and young men, ego-resiliency is remarkably rank-order consistent from early childhood to young adulthood. However, for girls and young women, there is not a longitudinal continuity of resilience. This absence of consistency cannot be attributed to methodological problems or chance fluctuations; we have strong evidence from various of our data sources indicating that a significant psychological restructuring occurs in girls as they approach and reach puberty, a transmogrification we do not yet understand although we have attempted to focus on this phenomenon. We have attractively systematic data on just which character qualities are relatively consistent over time and which are relatively ephemeral or situationally influenced. We were able to largely identify at age 3 the individuals who 15 years later would become drug abusers; we examined different patterns of drug usage, noting the differences between frequent drug-users, drug-abstainers, and experimenting drug-users (Block, Block, & Keyes, 1988); we could find early antecedents in childhood of subsequent depression in the early 20s (e.g., Block & Gjerde, 1990; Block, Gjerde, & Block, 1991); we demonstrated that many of the findings attributed to divorce could be seen instead prior to the fact of divorce (Block, J. H., Block, J., & Gjerde, 1986; Block, Block, & Gjerde, 1988); and so on. We have reported aspects of family values and family interactions that antedate and likely influence various behavioral propensities (e.g., Block, J. H., Block, J., & Morrison, 1981).

Many additional findings likely remain hidden in our files, but others will have to seek them out. A prime mover or two is now again needed to carry on, nurture, and perhaps realize the later potential of the results of our study. Although a lifetime must pass before a longitudinal study truly identifies a person's coherencies and themes, we have moved along an appreciable, and most significant, portion of the life path. At the outset of a new millennium, there is still a good deal more to observe and analyze.

Jeanne and I certainly were the prime movers of the study. But scientific colleagues have been involved in our longitudinal inquiry as well: David Harrington and Anna von der Lippe in the seventies, Per Gjerde, David Funder, Dan Ozer, and Michiel Westenberg in the eighties, and Adam Kremen and C. Randall Colvin in the nineties. And a host of graduate students as research assistants over the years, with the expected turnover no matter how good they were. In quite another category but at a level most necessary for sustaining and enhancing our project was Suzanne Manton, our administrative assistant for many years. Without her resourceful help, this effort certainly would have faltered during the adolescence and early adulthood of the participants, especially when I was catastrophically distraught and enervated following the loss of my personal and professional partner.

SOME ANALYTIC DETOURS
Estimating Chance Significance
In 1955, the University at Berkeley installed its first electronic computer, an IBM 701 with a 4K memory (!), card reading input, and output printed on an accounting machine. I had read about these new-fangled, potentially revolutionary electronic marvels and had an ambitious idea for which they seemed eminently suited.

At this time in psychology (and even a half century later), there was appreciable concern about the issue of calculating "chance significance" as the baseline against which empirical findings could be compared. I had come to realize that contemporary and classical methods of estimating chance significance were premised on statistical assumptions unrealistic to an unknown extent. They presumed that multiple significance tests (as, for example, when comparing the responses of two groups to the many items in a personality inventory) would lead to 5% of the contrasts being statistically significant at the 5% level of significance, 1% at the 1% level, and so on. But this presumption was based on two unquestioned and untested assumptions: that each statistical test was independent of every other statistical test and that the distribution of scores for each variable (or item) was bell-shaped (or for items, split 50–50) rather than severely skewed. I knew that both of these assumptions were empirically flagrantly incorrect. There remained the continuing problem of truly ascertaining the baseline of chance significance; however, the solution was mathematically intractable for any data set and, moreover, if achievable, would vary as data sets varied.

My own effort at a solution was triggered by my memory of demonstrations in an elementary statistics course. Therein, and quite typically, all of the students were required to repetitively flip, say, eight coins, duly recording the number of heads and tails each time. The instructor showed that the sets of coin flips, when summed, approximated with increasing and ultimate precision the results predicted by working out the existent formula for the binomial distribution. We were suitably impressed by the economy of inference afforded by this mathematical approach; we had not really needed to laboriously flip all those coins. All we needed was the formula. Except that the formula or other available formulas made assumptions which in many empirical contexts simply and importantly did not apply.

The thought struck me that with the miraculously fast (for its time) calculating speed of the 1955 IBM computer, one could effortlessly and endlessly, in effect, go back to just tossing coins. One did not need mathematical statistics as a basis; one could allow the computer to run on iteratively to ultimately generate the required sampling distribution. Ordinarily, one evaluates whether one's empirical data meet the assumptions underlying a statistical model so that one can then use the model for inference. Instead, I recognized that, by iteratively and rapidly resampling or coin-flipping one's actual empirical data, one could create a tailor-made chance sampling distribution from and for the particular data set. This empirically-derived sampling distribution would uniquely incorporate all the unspecifiable and mathematically intractable characteristics of one's data and thus provide a fully justifiable basis for inference regarding the consequentiality of a particular data analysis.

So, I set about to use computer speed, very much enhanced since, to empirically determine from actual data sets, with all their variance-covariance aberrations—and without any mathematical assumptions whatsoever—just what percentage of MMPI item analyses of typical samples reach the nominal level of 5% or 1% or whatever.

In absolute computer coding (this was well before assembly language, compilers, Fortran, etc.), I wrote a program that included a cascading random number generator to divide an actual sample into two chance-defined groups of individuals, and tested for their degree of difference with respect to their MMPI responses, a typical kind of analysis at the time. Via computer iteration, I did this several thousand times, summing the results. It proved to be the case that, because of the appreciable correlation among many MMPI items, and because many MMPI items are responded to in preponderantly skewed ways, somewhat less than 2% of the items achieved significance at the nominal 5% level, a finding quite discrepant from conventional interpretation. I subsequently generalized this approach in a variety of research contexts, to multiple t-tests, to correlations, and to evaluating the difference between correlation matrices.

This empirical approach to estimating chance significance was finally, though reluctantly, published in *Psychometrika* in 1960; its publication had been delayed because its non-mathematical nature did not seem appropriate for a formula-oriented journal. This general approach was later independently developed and extended by Julian Simon in his "resampling" work (1969) and further elaborated by Efron (1979) in what was called "the bootstrap method," a name that has become catchy. The "resampling" approach has become quite important in recent years.

The Bandwagon of Response Set

During the first part of the 1960s, the notion of the response set was the most popular research topic in personality psychology, dominating the journals. Response sets had been presented as vitiating the validity of self-report questionnaires such as the MMPI. The view had been advanced, forcefully and repetitively, that individuals in responding to personality inventories based their responses on acquiescent response tendencies and/or on what was socially desirable; responses to questionnaires did not have the psychological meaning imputed to them. Many had leaped aboard this scientific bandwagon of a reigning artifact, and a thousand corroborating articles had appeared demonstrating that a response set interpretation alone was a sufficient explanation of the empirical results supposedly offered by inventories.

I certainly had my own criticisms about existing inventories and questionnaires but thought they had surprising validity as well. Reflecting in Oslo and relying on the dependable reliability of the Norwegian and American postal systems, I went on to unconfound response set from meaning, separated acquiescence from social desirability, and was able to demonstrate how a seemingly tenable response set interpretation had come about as an accidental artifact of the way extant inventories had unthinkingly been constructed. I also showed how even when an acquiescence response set was eliminated, previous relationships remained and that "social desirability" necessarily had a substantive psychological interpretation. This unconfounding plus some unusual, multiply replicated and substantial validity demonstrations gave what was considered to be a complete explanation and refutation of the phenomenon. After my book, *The Challenge of Response Sets* (Block, 1965), appeared presenting my reasoning and evidence, there suddenly was an abrupt cessation of interest by psychologists (including myself) in the proposed artifactual conclusion. I had become a world expert on a topic in which no one subsequently was interested anymore.

The Bandwagon of Personality Inconsistency

Although the 1970s were mostly taken up by the press of our longitudinal work, I made time to involve myself in the seminal topic of the decade, the issue of the consistency-inconsistency of personality. Prior to Mischel's (1968) influential critique, I had already published a conceptual article entitled "Some Reasons for the Apparent Inconsistency of Personality" (Block, 1968). Mischel's book, when it appeared, did not impress me at the time as especially important. When his critique began to become the received view in the field, I was among the first to counter its gloomy message. My widely circulated 1975 paper entitled "Recognizing the Coherence of Personality," part of which was published as "Advancing the Psychology of Personality: Paradigmatic Shift or Improving the Quality of Research?" (Block, 1977), proved to be helpful in setting a different perspective on the Mischelian conclusions. With the logical and psychological argument regarding studies purported to demonstrate inconsistency, the introduction of needed psychometrics, and many kinds of empirical data—including findings from our longitudinal study as well as from LTT—I made a case for the coherence of personality over time and many kinds of situations (Block, 1981). It was important to do so, I thought, given the ideological temper of the times.

For the last two decades or so, the idea of personality consistency has been again accepted and is again being actively promulgated. Mischel and other early believers in the empirical absence of deep personality consistency have come to acknowledge important personality and behavioral coherence and continuities. However, they have chosen to recharacterize their reasoning in terms different enough so that the underlying coherence they too have observed may not seem evident. In my most recent book, *Personality As an Affect-Processing System* (Block, 2002), I consider analytically their most recent conceptualization.

SUNDRY CRITIQUES OF PSYCHOLOGICAL RESEARCH

Because of my methodological training, the nature of my psychological interests (and my personal bent), I have invested much of my academic time in proffering various analytical critiques that appear to have had appreciable impact. Thus, in addition to my concerns with psychology's bandwagon themes of response set and personality inconsistency, I have created various tempests—large and small—with regard to a variety of claims in the psychological literature. Specifically, I have questioned various prevalent or faddist movements as the once remarkably popular "reflectivity-impulsivity" concept and its easy but invalid operational measure in developmental psychology (Block, J., Block, J. H., & Harrington, 1974), the widely promulgated as inexorably-founded Five Factor view of personality (Block, 1995), the social psychology counter-intuitive (and erroneous) claim that "positive illusions" foster mental health (Block & Colvin, 1994; Colvin & Block, 1994), the "act frequency approach" as collecting untenable inventory information (Block, 1989), the "semantic similarity" argument as fallacious when confronted by empirical data (Block, 1977a; Block, Weiss, & Thorne, 1979), and the remarkable number of false positives "diagnosed" by a nominal "psychoticism" scale (Block, 1977b, 1977d). Altogether, a salmagundi of criticism that I hope has been leavening.

INFLUENCES ON MY PSYCHOLOGICAL VALUES

Many psychologists have shaped me through the years though I cannot even begin to remember or cite them all. Mention of a scant half dozen must therefore suffice here. In scattered order, I owe much to the trenchant mind of Paul E. Meehl; the psychometric, as well as the psychodynamic writings of Jane Loevinger; the quiet acumen of Robert W. White regarding the coherence of personality; the deep recognitions by John Bowlby regarding the human need for attachment; the clinical insights of David Shapiro into neurotic styles; and the widely-unappreciated psycho-system efforts of Norbert Bischof.

THE EMERITUS YEARS

During the 1990s, my health severely faltered. I had had multiple life-interrupting hip surgeries, beginning in 1969. During 1984–86, I had an especially difficult orthopedic experience, being first hospitalized for four months with an infected hip joint implant, then living without any hip joint at all on one side for 16 months and with massive daily penicillin infusions. When my bone infection was presumed gone and I was again deemed suitable for hip joint replacement, I had the surgery. Always, I had recovered reasonably well from these medical procedures, but in 1998, I had open-heart surgery to replace a leaking aortic valve and recovered slowly. Then, in mid-2000, after experiencing an ever-increasing ataxia, a benign tumor pressing on my spinal cord was diagnosed as the source of my staggering gait and I underwent spinal cord surgery. The surgery left me fundamentally disabled, unable to walk, and with insufficient, neurologically weakened hands.

Nevertheless, or perhaps because, of the solitude enforced on me by my disability, I completed an earlier started, overly ambitious theoretical book on a systems view of personality. The book, *Personality As an Affect-Processing System*, appeared in 2002. It is certainly inadequate in a number of ways, but I suggest that it may be integrative of a number of personality phenomena. Within it, I propose that two concepts closely akin to ego-control and ego-resiliency are to be found in the empiricism offered by many investigators and that the concepts, when systematically elaborated into perceptual and action modes, can be seen as underlying a number of interesting phenomena. I consider it a noble failure at attempting an approach that was both daunting and premature. I anticipate that the readership will be limited but completing the book seemed personally necessary to me.

CODA

Psychology has enormously expanded its scientific reach in the last half century. During this time, however, it has seemed to me that psychologists have tended to become ever more specialized. In recent years, many impress me as having turned away from the psychological approaches having relevance for our lives as they are led or experienced. For example, although I appreciate and cheer on the accelerating neuroscientific emphasis within psychology and recognize that when we finally understand "the left brain interpreter" said to organize experience, psychology will have advanced enormously. Until that happens in the distant and dim future, the recognition should continue that, although the mind is indeed a function of the brain, the two cannot be made coordinate; there still exists a logical chasm involving context and meaning between these two levels of observation.

I continue to appreciate the view of psychological science that nomothetically focuses on general laws, with little concern for the implication of individual differences ("nuisance variance"; Block, 1993, 1995). But, as Underwood (1975), the premier experimental psychologist of the mid-twentieth century observed, nomothetic findings may well require resorting to the "crucible" (his term) of evaluation via individual differences in order to achieve a proper understanding of the underlying processes involved.

I have often used and enjoyed the esthetics of controlled experimentation or elegant research designs as preferred methods for achieving causal understanding of a phenomenon. And I am somewhat uneasy and uncertain when studying variation and covariation in the natural, uncontrolled world. However, when the orthogonalizing requirements of a research design also entail procedural artificiality and ecosystem unrepresentativeness, I would rather study the conditions actually influencing behavior and experience in the natural world, and learn to tolerate the attendant ambiguities.

I am attracted, as all of us are, to the study and analysis of psychological phenomena that are conveniently and quickly accessible. There is no necessary connection between the importance of a psychological problem and the convenience or time required to study that problem. Nevertheless, the preoccupation of psychologists with short-term, conveniently researchable questions may mean neglect of important psychological understandings discernible only over long periods of time. Thus, the study of particle physics is of fundamental importance but has little to say about plate tectonics, because of the profound differences in their focus and time scales. Similarly, I suggest that short-term, convenient approaches to psychological issues may generate useful recognitions but have little to contribute to a developmental understanding of the perceptions, behaviors, and experiences constituting the domain of personality psychology. One cannot see a mountain with a super collider.

All of this is by way of saying that the idea of scientific method is not tied to a particular content area or to a particular strategic presumption or to a particular analytical approach or to a particular scale of measurement. The scientific method continues to apply in more naturalistic, less controllable, extended time-scale domains, although its form and rules of inference may change. Astronomy, geology, meteorology are all serious and important but not neat sciences; systematic observation and theory-building also characterize these sciences, although they are not especially experimental in nature.

So it is with the study of personality development, the psychological science that educes the conditions and consequences of personality change, that evaluates the similarities and the differences in the way the life course is followed, that studies the adaptive functions, common and different, by which individuals respond to and from their changing world and changing self-recognitions, which tries to explain why people turn out as they do.

SOME PERSONAL RECOGNITIONS

I own up to a personal reactivity that both furthered my intellectual career and attenuated my professional career. I tend not to simply shrug at popular positions or matters with which I fundamentally disagree. I was and am a contrarian.

Early on, I was diffident. But as I gained in knowledge and thought, I gradually became more self-confident (although I believe the field of psychology is generally too receptive to assuredness and assertion per se, though not always wisely) and intolerant of what I perceived as insufficiency in my field. Accordingly, as the fields of personality and developmental psychology moved on, I was not indifferent to a number of issues or movements with which I centrally disagreed; instead, I reacted. My written disagreements were close critiques, perhaps too often unnecessarily fierce ones. In my later years, I tended to be viewed as an unapproachable curmudgeon. According to my own self-image, I was more approachable and less formidable than colleagues and students presumed.

Looking back now at the life I have traced out, I look for commonalities in what I have sought to influence and the influences in my own life. It seems to me that I have been focused in my psychological career on methodologically strengthening the often-frail, affirmative findings that scientific psychology commonly issues—an effort that seemed entirely consonant with my personal values and aspirations to help move the science and the world toward better and clearer understandings. Thus, there is a common factor underlying my emphasis on commensurateness in Q, to insure the consensuality and validity of clinical views; my methodological digression to estimate chance significance more truly, so as to be more confident of the believability of substantive findings; and the prolonged, consuming investment by Jeanne and myself to reliably ascertain life paths—these were all meaning conserving (but not conservative) positions. Rather than centering on a kind of naïve nihilism (as was exemplified by multiple demonstrations of seeming response set or of the apparent absence of personality coherence), I have almost reflexively tried for a more advancing, cumulating, consequential psychology. I suggest that these lines of effort coherently derive from my adolescence-formed political-humanistic-scientific concerns. I have aspired to do something meaningful in my professional life, to ask important questions, to use serious science to answer them, to in small but indisputable ways better psychological understanding of lives.

Although not conventionally identified as a theorist, I have covertly had my own speculations about the nature of personality along the way. I have been restrained in expressing them (except, primarily, for my 1982 paper on assimilation-accommodation and my 2002 theoretical book). By and large, I have focused on psychologically interesting empiricism and on improving method. Why this personal inhibition about speculative theorizing? Excessive concern for rigor and avoidance of conceptual blarney, certainly. But perhaps too because of an early-ingrained tentativeness coming from being a first-generation, unapprenticed son. I have viewed myself as thrust, untrusting and unmodulated, into a world in which I had to warily learn on my own, and imperfectly, much of what others readily, unthinkingly, assimilate from their surround.

How do I weigh the other influences on my life? The cultural tides in which I swam were turbulent, often with an undertow of anti-semitism but also permitted me to reach unimaginable academic shores. Given my worrying childhood and adolescent anticipations, my life has proven to be intellectually engaging, culturally rich, and materially provident. But the primary centering and affectively sustaining influence on my adult life was Jeanne, my partner intellectually, in family, and most personally. In the last twenty-odd years without Jeanne, I have been able somewhat to continue the legacy we created together, and to watch our children become productive and prideworthy. And I have learned the lessons taught by illness and vulnerability. Regarding the world, I subscribe to the adage of Italian socialist, Antonio Gramsci: "pessimism of the intellect, optimism of the will."

REFERENCES

Bellamy, E. (1888). *Looking backward*. Boston: Ticknor.

Block, J. (1950). *An experimental investigation of the construct of ego control*. Unpublished doctoral dissertation, Stanford University, Stanford, California.

Block, J. (1952). The assessment of communication, II. Role variations as a function of interactional context. *Journal of Personality, 21*, 272–286.

Block, J. (1955a). Personality characteristics associated with fathers' attitudes toward child rearing. *Child Development, 26,* 41–48.

Block, J. (1955b). The difference between Q and R. *Psychological Review, 62,* 356–358.

Block, J. (1956). A comparison of the forced and unforced Q-sorting procedures. *Educational and Psychological Measurement, 16,* 481–493.

Block, J. (1957a). A comparison between ipsative and normative ratings of personality. *Journal of Abnormal and Social Psychology, 54,* 50–54.

Block, J. (1957b). A study of affective responsiveness in a lie-detection situation. *Journal of Abnormal and Social Psychology, 55,* 11–15.

Block, J. (1957c). Studies in the phenomenology of emotion. *Journal of Abnormal and Social Psychology, 54,* 358–363.

Block, J. (1960). On the number of significant findings to be expected by chance. *Psychometrika, 25,* 369–380.

Block, J. (1961). *The Q-sort method in personality assessment and psychiatric research.* Springfield, IL: C. C. Thomas. (Reprinted by Consulting Psychologists, Palo Alto, California, in 1978).

Block, J. (1962). *The California Q-set.* Palo Alto, CA: Consulting Psychologists.

Block, J. (1965). *The challenge of response sets: Unconfounding meaning, acquiescence and social desirability in the MMPI.* New York: Appleton-Century-Crofts.

Block, J. (1968). Some reasons for the apparent inconsistency of personality. *Psychological Bulletin, 70,* 210–212.

Block, J. (1971). *Lives through time.* Berkeley, CA: Bancroft.

Block, J. (1977a). Advancing the psychology of personality: Paradigmatic shift or improving the quality of research? In D. Magnusson & N. S. Endler (Eds.), *Psychology at the crossroads: Current issues in interactional psychology* (pp. 37–63). Hillsdale, NJ: Lawrence Erlbaum.

Block, J. (1977b). The Eysencks and psychoticism. *Journal of Abnormal Psychology, 86,* 653–654.

Block, J. (1977c). An illusory interpretation of the first factor of the MMPI. *Journal of Consulting and Clinical Psychology, 45,* 930–935.

Block, J. (1977d). The P-scale and psychosis: Continued concerns. *Journal of Abnormal Psychology, 86,* 431–434.

Block, J. (1981). Some enduring and consequential structures of personality. In A. I. Rabin, J. Aronoff, A. M. Barclay, & R. A. Zucker (Eds.), *Further explorations in personality* (pp. 27–43). New York: John Wiley.

Block, J. (1982). Assimilation, accommodation, and the dynamics of personality development. *Child Development, 53,* 281–295.

Block, J. (1989). A critique of the Act Frequency Approach to personality. *Journal of Personality and Social Psychology, 56,* 234–245.

Block, J. (1990). *The California Q-set* (CAQ-90, revised form). Palo Alto, CA: Consulting Psychologists.

Block, J. (1993). Studying personality the long way. In D. C. Funder, R. Parke, R. C. Tomlinson-Keasy, & K. Widaman (Eds.), *Studying lives through time: Approaches to personality and development* (pp. 9–41). Washington, DC: American Psychological Association.

Block, J. (1995). A contrarian view of the five-factor approach to personality description. *Pychological Bulletin, 117*, 187–215.

Block, J. (2002). *Personality as an affect-processing system*. Mahwah, NJ: Lawrence Erlbaum.

Block, J., & Baker, B. O. (1957). Accuracy of interpersonal prediction as a function of judge and object characteristics. *Journal of Abnormal and Social Psychology, 54*, 37–43.

Block, J., & Bennett, L. (1955). The assessment of communication, III. Perceptions and transmission as a function of the social situation. *Human Relations, 8*, 317–325.

Block, J., & Block, J. H. (1951). An investigation of the relationship between intolerance of ambiguity and ethnocentrism. *Journal of Personality, 19*, 303–311.

Block, J., & Block, J. H. (1973). *Ego development and the provenance of thought: A longitudinal study of ego and cognitive development in young children*. Progress report to the National Institute of Mental Health, University of California, Berkeley (in mimeograph; 92 pages, single-spaced).

Block, J., & Block, J. H. (1981). Studying situational dimensions: A grand perspective and some limited empiricism. In D. M. Magnusson (Ed.), *Toward a psychology of situations: An interactional perspective* (pp. 85–103). Hillsdale, NJ: Lawrence Erlbaum.

Block, J., Block, J. H., & Gjerde, P. F. (1988). Parental functioning and the home environment in families of divorce: Prospective and concurrent analyses. *Journal of the American Academy of Child and Adolescent Psychiatry, 27*, 207–213.

Block, J., Block, J. H., & Harrington, D. M. (1974). Some misgivings about the Matching Familiar Figures Test as a measure of reflection-impulsivity. *Developmental Psychology, 10*, 611–632.

Block, J., Block, J. H., & Keyes, S. (1988). Longitudinally foretelling drug usage in adolescence: Early childhood personality and environmental precursors. *Child Development, 59*, 336–355.

Block, J., & Colvin, C. R. (1994). Positive illusions and wellbeing: Separating fiction from fact. *Psychological Bulletin, 116*, 28.

Block, J., & Gjerde, P. F. (1990). Depressive symptomatology in late adolescence: A longitudinal perspective on personality antecedents. In J. E. Rolf, A. Masten, D. Cicchetti, K. Neuchterlein, & S. Weintraub (Eds.), *Risk and protective factors in the development of psychopathology* (pp. 334–360). New York: Cambridge University Press.

Block, J., Gjerde, P. F., & Block, J. H. (1991). Personality antecedents of depressive tendencies in 18-year-olds: A prospective study. *Journal of Personality and Social Psychology, 60*, 726–738.

Block, J., & Kremen, A. M. (1996). IQ and ego-resiliency: Clarifying their conceptual and empirical linkage and separateness. *Journal of Personality and Social Psychology, 70,* 349–361.

Block, J., & Petersen, P. (1955). Some personality correlates of confidence, caution and speed in a decision situation. *Journal of Abnormal and Social Psychology, 51,* 34–41.

Block, J., & Robins, R. W. (1993). A longitudinal study of consistency and change in self-esteem from early adolescence to early adulthood. *Child Development, 94,* 909–923.

Block, J., & Thomas, H. (1955). Is satisfaction with self a measure of adjustment? *Journal of Abnormal and Social Psychology, 51,* 254–259.

Block, J., von der Lippe, A., & Block, J. H. (1973). Sex-role and socialization patterns: Some personality concomitants and environmental antecedents. *Journal of Consulting and Clinical Psychology, 41,* 321–341.

Block, J., Weiss, D. S., & Thorne, A. (1979). How relevant is a semantic similarity interpretation of personality ratings? *Journal of Personality and Social Psychology, 37,* 1055–1074.

Block, J. H. (1951). *An experimental study of a topological representation of ego-structure.* Unpublished doctoral dissertation, Stanford University, Stanford, California.

Block, J. H., & Block, J. (1952). An interpersonal experiment on reactions to authority. *Human Relations, 5,* 91–98.

Block, J. H., & Block, J. (1980). The role of ego-control and ego-resiliency in the organization of behavior. In W. A. Collins (Ed.), *The Minnesota Symposia on Child Psychology* (Vol. 13, pp. 39–101). Hillsdale, NJ: Lawrence Erlbaum (Wiley).

Block, J. H., & Block, J. (1984). A longitudinal study of personality and cognitive development. In S. Mednick, M. Harway, & K. M. Finello (Eds.), *Handbook of longitudinal research: Vol. 1. Birth and childhood cohorts* (pp. 328–352). New York: Praeger.

Block, J. H., Block, J., & Gjerde, P. F. (1986). The personality of children prior to divorce: A prospective study. *Child Development, 57,* 827–840.

Block, J. H., Block, J., & Morrison, A. (1981). Parental agreement-disagreement on child rearing orientations and gender-related personality correlates in children. *Child Development, 52,* 965–974.

Colvin, C. R., & Block, J. (1994). Do positive illusions foster mental health? An evaluation of the Taylor and Brown formulation. *Psychological Bulletin, 116,* 3–20.

Efron, B. (1979). Bootstrap methods: Another look at the jackknife. *The Annals of Statistics, 7,* 126.

Funder, D. C., & Block, J. (1989). The role of ego-control, ego-resiliency, and IQ in delay of gratification in adolescence. *Journal of Personality and Social Psychology, 57,* 1041–1050.

Huxley, A. (1954). *The doors of perception.* New York: Harper.

Kremen, A. M., & Block, J. (1998). The roots of ego control. *Journal of Personality and Social Psychology, 75,* 1062–1075.

Mischel, W. (1968). *Personality assessment*. New York: John Wiley.

Simon, J. (1969). *Basic research methods in social science*. New York: Random House.

Stephenson, W. (1953). *The study of behavior: Q technique and its methodology*. Chicago: University of Chicago Press.

Underwood, B. J. (1975). Individual differences as a crucible in theory construction. *American Psychologist, 30*, 128–134.

Westenberg, M., & Block, J. (1993). Ego development and individual differences in personality. *Journal of Personality and Social Psychology, 65*, 792–800.

SELECTED BIBLIOGRAPHY

Books

Block, J. (1961). *The Q-Sort Method in personality assessment and psychiatric research*. Springfield, IL: C.C. Thomas. (Reprinted by Consulting Psychologists, Palo Alto, California, in 1978).

Block, J. (1965). *The challenge of response sets: Unconfounding meaning, acquiescence and social desirability in the MMPI*. New York: Appleton-Century-Crofts.

Block, J. (1971). *Lives through time*. Berkeley, CA: Bancroft.

Block, J. (1990). *The California Q-set* (revised form). Palo Alto, CA: Consulting Psychologists.

Block, J. (2002). *Personality as an affect-processing system*. Mahwah, NJ: Lawrence Erlbaum.

Journal Articles and Book Chapters

Block, J. (1952). The assessment of communication, II. Role variations as a function of interactional context. *Journal of Personality, 21*, 272–286.

Block, J. (1955). The difference between Q and R. *Psychological Review, 62*, 356–358.

Block, J. (1956). A comparison of the forced and unforced Q-sorting procedures. *Educational and Psychological Measurement, 16*, 481–493.

Block, J. (1957). A comparison between ipsative and normative ratings of personality. *Journal of Abnormal and Social Psychology, 54*, 50–54.

Block, J. (1957). Studies in the phenomenology of emotion. *Journal of Abnormal and Social Psychology, 54*, 358–363.

Block, J. (1957). A study of affective responsiveness in a lie-detection situation. *Journal of Abnormal and Social Psychology, 55*, 11–15.

Block, J. (1960). On the number of significant findings to be expected by chance. *Psychometrika, 25*, 369–380.

Block, J. (1961). Ego identity, role variability, and adjustment. *Journal of Consulting Psychology, 25*, 392–397.

Block, J. (1962). Some differences between the concepts of social desirability and adjustment. *Journal of Consulting Psychology, 26*, 527–530.

Block, J. (1963). The equivalence of measures and the correction for attenuation. *Psychological Bulletin, 60*, 152–156.

Block, J. (1968). Personality measurement. *International Encyclopedia of the Social Sciences* (Vol. 12, pp. 30–37). New York: Macmillan.

Block, J. (1968). Some reasons for the apparent inconsistency of personality. *Psychological Bulletin, 70*, 210–212.

Block, J. (1977a). Advancing the psychology of personality: Paradigmatic shift or improving the quality of research? In D. Magnusson & N. S. Endler (Eds.), *Psychology at the Crossroads: Current issues in interactional psychology* (pp. 37–63). Hillsdale, NJ: Lawrence Erlbaum.

Block, J. (1980). From infancy to adulthood: A clarification. *Child Development, 51*, 622–623.

Block, J. (1981). Review of J. Loevinger, Scientific Ways in the Study of Ego Development. *Contemporary Psychology, 26*, 245–246.

Block, J. (1981). Review of O. G. Brim, Jr., & J. Kagan (Eds.), Constancy and change in human development. *Contemporary Psychology, 26*, 746–750.

Block, J. (1981). Some enduring and consequential structures of personality. In A. I. Rabin (Ed.), *Further explorations in personality* (pp. 27–43). New York: John Wiley.

Block, J. (1982). Assimilation, accommodation, and the dynamics of personality development. *Child Development, 53*, 281–295.

Block, J. (1989). A critique of the Act Frequency Approach to personality. *Journal of Personality and Social Psychology, 56*, 234–245.

Block, J. (1990). Biography of Jeanne Humphrey Block. In A. N. O'Connell & N. F. Russo (Eds.) *Women in Psychology* (pp. 40–48). New York: Greenwood.

Block, J. (1990). Review of Michael Rutter (Ed.), Studies of psychosocial risk: The power of longitudinal data. *Human Development, 33*, 321–324.

Block, J. (1993). Studying personality the long way. In D. C. Funder, R. Parke, R. C. Tomlinson-Keasy, & K. Widaman (Eds.), *Studying lives through time: Approaches to personality and development* (pp. 9–41). Washington, DC: American Psychological Association.

Block, J. (1995). A contrarian view of the five-factor approach to personality description. *Psychological Bulletin, 117*, 187–215.

Block, J. (1995). On the relation between IQ, impulsivity, and delinquency: Remarks on the Lynam, Moffitt, and Stouthamer-Loeber interpretation. *Journal of Abnormal Psychology, 104*, 395–398.

Block, J., & Baker, B. O. (1957). Accuracy of interpersonal prediction as a function of judge and object characteristics. *Journal of Abnormal and Social Psychology, 54*, 37–43.

Block, J., & Bennett, L. (1955). The assessment of communication, III. Perceptions and transmission as a function of the social situation. *Human Relations, 8*, 317–325.

Block, J., & Block, J. H. (1951). An investigation of the relationship between intolerance of ambiguity and ethnocentrism. *Journal of Personality, 19*, 303–311.

Block, J., & Block, J. H. (1981). Studying situational dimensions: A grand perspective and some limited empiricism. In D. M. Magnusson (Ed.), *Toward a psychology of situations: An interactional perspective* (pp. 85–103). Hillsdale, N.J.: Lawrence Erlbaum.

Block, J., Block, J. H., & Harrington, D. M. (1974). Some misgivings about the Matching Familiar Figures Test as a measure of reflection-impulsivity. *Developmental Psychology, 10*, 611–632.

Block, J., Block, J. H., & Keyes, S. (1988). Longitudinally foretelling drug usage in adolescence: Early childhood personality and environmental precursors. *Child Development, 59*, 336–355.

Block, J., Buss, D. M., Block, J. H., & Gjerde, P. (1981). The cognitive style of breadth of categorization: The longitudinal consistency of personality correlates. *Journal of Personality and Social Psychology, 40*, 770–779.

Block, J., & Chang, J. (1960). A study of identification in male homosexuals. *Journal of Consulting Psychology, 24*, 307–310.

Block, J., & Colvin, C. R. (1994). Positive illusions and wellbeing: Separating fiction from fact. *Psychological Bulletin, 116*, 28.

Block, J., & Gjerde, P. F. (1990). Depressive symptomatology in late adolescence: A longitudinal perspective on personality antecedents. In J. E. Rolf, A. Masten, D. Cicchetti, K. Neuchterlein, & S. Weintraub (Eds.), *Risk and protective factors in the development of psychopathology* (pp. 334–360). New York: Cambridge University Press.

Block, J., & Gjerde, P. F. (1986). Distinguishing between antisocial behavior and undercontrol. In D. Olweus, J. Block, & M. Radke-Yarrow (Eds.), *Development of antisocial and prosocial behavior: Research, theories, and issues* (pp. 177–206). New York: Academic.

Block, J., Gjerde, P. F., & Block, J. H. (1986). Continuity and transformation in the psychological meaning of category breadth. *Developmental Psychology, 22*, 832–840.

Block, J., Gjerde, P. F., & Block, J. H. (1986). More misgivings about the Matching Familiar Figures Test as a measure of reflection-impulsivity: Absence of construct validity in preadolescence. *Developmental Psychology, 22*, 820–831.

Block, J., Gjerde, P. F., & Block, J. H. (1991). Personality antecedents of depressive tendencies in 18-year-olds: A prospective study. *Journal of Personality and Social Psychology, 60*, 726–738.

Block, J., & Kogan, N. (1998). Parental teaching strategies and children's cognitive style. *International Journal of Educational Research, 29*, 187–204.

Block, J., & Kremen, A. M. (1996). IQ and ego-resiliency: Conceptual and empirical connections and separateness. *Journal of Personality and Social Psychology, 70*, 349–361.

Block, J., Levine, L., & McNemar, Q. (1951). Testing for the existence of psychometric patterns. *Journal of Abnormal and Social Psychology, 46*, 356–359.

Block, J., & Petersen, P. (1955). Some personality correlates of confidence, caution and speed in a decision situation. *Journal of Abnormal and Social Psychology, 51*, 34–41.

Block, J., & Robins, R. W. (1993). A longitudinal study of consistency and change in self-esteem from early adolescence to early adulthood. *Child Development, 94*, 909–923.

Block, J., & Thomas, H. (1955). Is satisfaction with self a measure of adjustment? *Journal of Abnormal and Social Psychology, 51*, 254–259.

Block, J., & Turula, E. (1963). Identification, ego control and adjustment. *Child Development, 34*, 945–954.

Block, J., von der Lippe, A., & Block, J. H. (1973). Sex-role and socialization patterns: Some personality concomitants and environmental antecedents. *Journal of Consulting and Clinical Psychology, 41*, 321–341.

Block, J., Weiss, D. S., & Thorne, A. (1979). How relevant is a semantic similarity interpretation of personality ratings? *Journal of Personality and Social Psychology, 37*, 1055–1074.

Block, J. H., & Block, J. (1980). The role of ego-control and ego-resiliency in the organization of behavior. In W. A. Collins (Ed.), *The Minnesota Symposia on Child Psychology* (Vol. 13, pp. 39–101). Hillsdale, NJ: Lawrence Erlbaum (Wiley).

Block, J. H., Block, J., & Gjerde, P. F. (1986). The personality of children prior to divorce: A prospective study. *Child Development, 57*, 827–840.

Block, J. H., Patterson, V., Block, J., & Jackson, D. (1958). A study of the parents of schizophrenic and neurotic children. *Psychiatry, 21*, 387–397.

Caspi, A., Block, J., Block, J. H., Klopp, B., Lynam, D., Moffitt, T. E., & Stouthamer-Loeber, M. (1992). A "common-language" version of the California Child Q-set for personality assessment. *Psychological Assessment, 4*, 512–523.

Colvin, C. R., & Block, J. (1994). Do positive illusions foster mental health? An evaluation of the Taylor and Brown formulation. *Psychological Bulletin, 116*, 3–20.

Funder, D. C., & Block, J. (1989). The role of ego-control, ego-resiliency, and IQ in delay of gratification in adolescence. *Journal of Personality and Social Psychology, 57*, 1041–1050.

Funder, D. C., Block, J. H., & Block, J. (1983). Delay of gratification: Some longitudinal personality correlates. *Journal of Personality and Social Psychology, 44*, 1198–1213.

Kogan, N., & Block, J. (1991). Field dependence-independence from early childhood through adolescence: Personality and socialization aspects. In S. Wapner & J. Demick (Eds.), *Bio-psycho-social factors in the field dependence-independence cognitive style across the life span* (pp. 177–207). Hillsdale, NJ: Lawrence Erlbaum.

Kremen, A. M, & Block, J. (2002). Absorption: Construct explication by Q-sort assessments of personality. *Journal of Research in Personality, 36,* 252–259.

Kremen, A. M., & Block, J. (1998). The roots of ego control. *Journal of Personality and Social Psychology, 75,* 1062–1075.

Shedler, J., & Block, J. (1990). Adolescent drug use and psychological health: A longitudinal inquiry. *American Psychologist, 45,* 612–630.

The author (1987, on sabbatical at Harvard)

With wife Jeanne H. Block (1975, at a conference in Sweden)

With Ravenna Helson and Harrison Gough (the early 1970s, in Berkeley)

From left: Lew Goldberg, Jerry Wiggins, Jane Loevinger, Jack Block, Doug Jackson (1991, at conference in Palm Springs)

Jeanne and Jack Block (1978, at a longitudinal study participants' party)

CHAPTER 2

Pathways

Arnold H. Buss
The University of Texas at Austin

When you come to a fork in the road, take it.
—Yogi Berra

When you reflect back on your life, you may be able to see when you might have traveled in one direction or another, or whether fate had placed you on one path or another. Thus, where I was born and grew up was determined by a choice my father made in the early 1920s. He was an assistant cameraman, making silent movies on Long Island, New York. Seeking bluer skies, the film company went to Hollywood. If my father had gone with them, I would have grown up in California, but he stayed and I was born in 1924 in Brooklyn. What follows are forks in my road, paths taken, paths not taken, facets of my identity, and some final comments.

My childhood warrants only brief comment. My parents were loving, and my memories are pleasant. I read a lot and enjoyed table games and cards. And I played many different ball games, which eventually led to occasional (and modest) success as an adult in intramural handball, racquetball, and tennis. I was promoted ahead in elementary school and graduated from junior high school at the age of 13.

Thus, I was two years ahead of my schoolmates and started college at the age of 16. I attended a small all-male college on the Bronx campus of New York University, and I commuted on subways 1½ hours each way from Brooklyn. The students were mainly premeds, prelaws, predents, and engineers. I was a premed who was supposed to follow in the footsteps of a distant cousin, the hero of our extended family. My motivation was weak and my study habits, poor; I was not mature enough for college.

In my junior year, during World War II, I was drafted into the army and sent to basic training to become a medic. I wound up in an infantry regiment, trained to give first aid on the front lines. Then I was transferred to the vene-real disease ward of a base hospital, where I learned first hand about diseases best not described. Subsequently, the war started to wind down, and I was transferred to a hospital ship unit being formed. After Germany surrendered, our ship sailed to France and England repeatedly, each time returning with sick and wounded.

I entered the army as a green youngster who had lived at home and never been more than 30 miles outside of New York City. I had been in school for most of my life and was accustomed to people who cared for me. From my first days in the army I learned that no one else especially cared about me, that I had better obey orders, and that the response to being told I made a mistake was, "No excuse, sir." Like many in my generation, I had to grow up fast. And I did bond with other soldiers and made some lasting friendships.

At one of the camp libraries, I discovered books by Sigmund Freud, whose works were both fascinating and arcane. I decided to become a psy-chologist, which then and now meant clinical psychologist to a layperson.

I reentered civilian life with newfound motivation and with decent work habits. I finished college in a year and two summers. My decision about which graduate school to attend was based mainly on how close I could come to East Lansing, Michigan, where my future wife was attending college. Neither Michigan nor Michigan State would accept me. Who knows what my profes-sional career would have been like if I had been accepted by the University of Michigan, whose clinical psychology faculty was then psychoanalytic in orientation. But that was a path not taken.

GRADUATE SCHOOL

In 1947 I wound up in an adjacent state, at Indiana University, with no idea of the excellence of its faculty. The chairman was B. F. Skinner, with whom I took a class in my first year. He told us we did not have to buy his approach, but for the sake of communication we would use his vocabulary. I soon dis-covered that his concepts were embedded in his vocabulary so that we were voicing his brand of radical behaviorism. It was great to sit at the feet of one of the giants of twentieth-century psychology. I could see a sphere of applica-tion for his concepts, but radical behaviorism was too extreme for me.

One of my professors was W. N. Kellogg who, with his wife, had home raised a chimpanzee. Another couple, the Hayes's, subsequently home raised a chimpanzee named Vicky, and they visited Indiana University in 1948. They were trying to get Vicky to talk. She did manage some consonants but no vowels; hence the word *cup* came out without the *u*. Another graduate student tried to give her some items from a performance IQ test, but Vicky kept climbing on furniture and would not pay attention; I have tested pre-schoolers who did that.

Years later I was introduced to one of the signing chimpanzees at the home of Trixie and Al Gardner in Reno, Nevada. The Gardners taught me a couple of signs, and when I signed, the chimp excitedly replied with lots of signs, making me feel ignorant at being unable to respond. Given the publicity on subsequent research with chimps by others, we need to recognize the Gardners' (Gardner & Gardner, 1969) pioneering research as opening up the area of language in primates.

Another of my professors was R. C. Davis, an important physiological psychologist (that's what they were called then) who studied brain and behavior before the modern electronic revolution. I had classes with J. R. Kantor, whose interbehavioral metatheory was meant to be an alternative to behaviorism; he told us that, for all the importance the brain had for behavior, it might as well be the big toe. There were other faculty members whose views also clashed, but they all got along and were cordial in their disagreements. It may have been a tradition there, for when I talked to graduate students at Indiana University 25 years later, they said the faculty still got along well.

My mentor at Indiana was by default William K. Estes. The psychology faculty was still at roughly its prewar level, and the small clinical faculty was reserved as mentors to students in the Veteran's Administration program. The rest of us clinical students had to find mentors elsewhere, so I stumbled onto this assistant professor who studied learning in rats. My research had nothing to do with his work, but he was a skilled research supervisor who started me on the long road towards being a decent writer. He was also a model scientist. Later, when he developed his first mathematical model of learning, he gave a talk at which he cited seven results supporting his theory and seven that did not. He and the other faculty inculcated scientific values, which I later tried to pass on to my own graduate students.

While I was at Indiana University, Alfred Kinsey (on the biology faculty) was interviewing people about their sex lives. He gave a talk to the psychology department, telling us about some of his findings—for example, the incidence of homosexuality—which for that era were shocking.

I married at the end of my first year of graduate school, and we moved into a 25-foot trailer in a trailer camp full of veterans and their families. It seemed that half the women were pregnant, and rumor had it that there was something in the water. We did not boil the water, so my wife became pregnant! The fellow in the next trailer and I tapped into the water supply for the laundry house, and then we had running water to replace the five-gallon crock we had used (no, I did not walk through the snow to school, uphill both ways). At the start of my third year, we had a son. Having a family and having spent three years in the army spurred me to finish graduate school quickly and start earning a living. The GI bill helped and so did a teaching assistantship, but our life was Spartan.

INTERNSHIP

In my fourth year (1950) I was on my internship at Worcester State Hospital in Massachusetts. As part of orientation we visited the Worcester Foundation for Experimental Biology, where one project was the study of female hormones. That research led to the birth control pill.

The hospital was an ancient pile of stones, dating back to the nineteenth century. The calculating machines—this was long before computers—were located in a basement room. I noticed an iron ring in the stone wall and was told that it held the chains that had once restrained patients. There were back wards: The farther away the ward was from central administration, the more disturbed the patients were. This was before the advent of antipsychotic drugs, and some of the back ward patients had been there for decades during that era.

I still remember two male manic patients at the state hospital during my internship. I tried to give one the Rorschach as he bounced a ball. Each time he bounced the ball, he offered a new response. After 22 responses on the first card, I snatched it away; same thing on the second card. I stopped after the third card, for my writing hand was tired and he had given more responses than most people do for all 10 inkblots. The other manic patient was given leave every year just before the Jewish holidays. Being the fastest chicken plucker in town, he was in demand by local butchers.

The orientation of the psychology staff was psychoanalytic; many of the guest speakers were traditional Freudians, and we attended a couple of meetings of the Boston Psychoanalytic Society. One speaker there complained about the excessive use of jargon, saying, "I cavil at the use of fancy words." One of my tasks was to master the enormous book by Otto Fenichel (*The*

Psychoanalytic Theory of Neurosis, 1945), who wrote in English, but it was almost like reading German. As with Skinner, so with Fenichel: I learned to use his vocabulary and understood the concepts but never became a true believer.

Through the kindness of Al Goss and the faculty at the University of Massachusetts, I was able to run experiments with subjects there for my dissertation research. I stayed with Al and Mary Goss for several weeks, repaying them by doing the dishes.

THE UNIVERSITY OF IOWA

I had my final oral examination in the fall of my fifth year while I was an instructor at the University of Iowa. I was there for only a year. The psychology department was uniformly behavioristic—specifically, the Hull-Spence version in which drive reduction was reinforcing—and strongly into logical positivism (the philosopher Gustav Bergman was an adjunct on the psychology faculty). Their approach, although well grounded in laboratory research, seemed as doctrinaire as the psychoanalytic orientation of my internship. Whenever I was exposed to doctrines—the behaviorism of graduate school and Iowa or the dynamic psychology of my internship—I simply could not buy them whole hog. Indeed, skepticism may be a general tendency of mine, strengthened by scientific training, for I also have been loath to accept the various "isms" of religion and politics.

At the end of the academic year, I was offered a job as a research psychologist working for the air force, and a job as chief psychologist in a psychiatric hospital in Indianapolis. I talked to the head of the department at Iowa, Kenneth Spence. (A head of a department has more authority than an elected chairman, and Spence's personality fit that dominant role.) He strongly recommended the research position as being closer to academia, but I was never one to quake in my boots at the voice of authority. I was trained as a clinician and was ready for clinical work, so I took the clinical fork in the road. As I left Iowa, I was told that it would be impossible to return to academia.

INDIANAPOLIS

I arrived as Carter Memorial Hospital opened, and we had considerable freedom to start its library. I ordered a large number of books in many areas of psychology and every journal I could think of, back ordering issues from the previous 10 years. We were also allotted money to bring in speakers. So despite being away from academia, we did have intellectual stimulation. I resumed doing research, encouraged the staff to do so, and we eventually published several joint papers.

I asked for an internship training program and was allowed to set one up, and later the APA approved it. Since our caseload was not overwhelming, we offered the interns a good deal of supervision. One intern, Jerry Wiggins, was later recognized for his important work in personality (Wiggins, 1979). Two staff psychologists also earned well-deserved fame. Morton Wiener went on to head up the clinical training program at Clark University. Marvin Zuckerman, who eventually went to the University of Delaware, initiated important research on sensation seeking and has theorized about it; his book (Zuckerman, 1979) is a major source on the topic.

I was determined to continue doing research, but now would move toward clinically relevant topics. One question was intriguing: When we call a patient hostile, what do we mean? The answer led first to my interview study and later to a self-report questionnaire called the Hostility Inventory (Buss & Durkee, 1957) which examined these specific aspects of aggressiveness: assault, indirect, irritability, negativism, resentment, suspicion, and verbal. This questionnaire is still in use today, although a revision 25 years later is much improved psychometrically (Buss & Perry, 1992). Constructing a questionnaire was valuable in teaching me that items need to be clear, specific, and, if possible, include idioms, for that is often the way information is encoded (e.g., "If someone hits me first, I let him have it").

My interest in aggression broadened as I systematically examined the research literature, and I decided to write a book on the topic. This was the mid-1950s, the peak of the Cold War, when this country and the USSR had the hydrogen bomb, some people were building bomb shelters, and Secretary of State John Foster Dulles espoused the doctrine of brinksmanship, meaning confrontation (up to a point) with Russia. I recall musing about the irony of a psychologist working on a book on aggression at a time when the world might blow itself up. (Also, ironically, as I write this, we are waging a war in Iraq and on worldwide terrorism.) It was also a time when very few psychologists wrote books, and I wondered, "Who am I to write a book?" There was only one way to find out, so I rushed forward to meet my fate.

Meanwhile, to give you an idea of what it was like to be a clinical psychologist in the fifties, consider what happened when a disturbed 9-year-old girl was sent to our hospital and placed on an adult women's ward (children's wards came later). She had been sent to us by the nearby child guidance clinic, which had given up on her as untreatable. After a psychiatric resident tried to work with her and could not, he asked me to try, so I reluctantly agreed. To this day I don't know why she improved, but she did, and was able to leave the hospital eventually and return to school. When I left the hospital two years later, she was still okay. But the psychiatrist who headed the child guidance clinic—the man who had given up on the child—tried to have me fired for practicing psychotherapy without medical supervision. He might have succeeded, for that was the prevailing opinion of the medical profession, and they ran the psychiatric facilities. If I had been fired, my professional life would have taken a markedly different path. But my superintendent stood up for me, wryly noting that after all, the girl had improved. In these days of psychologists prescribing drugs, the 1950s must seem like the Dark Ages.

By 1957, I was a diplomate in clinical psychology, and the internship program was going well. But after working in a mental hospital for almost five years, I realized that my interests were more academic. A job opened up for an associate professor at the University of Pittsburgh. A sticking point during negotiations for the job was the issue of tenure. The head of the department asked if I would come as an untenured assistant professor. I had more publications than several of his senior faculty, and the job was advertised at the associate professor level, so I held out for the latter position. He finally agreed, but if he had not, that would have been another road not taken.

THE UNIVERSITY OF PITTSBURGH

Aggression

While reviewing the literature on aggression, I was especially concerned with the practical and ethical difficulties of studying it in the laboratory. Aggression, from one perspective, is a subclass of the broader category of punishment. I realized that aggression could be studied by inverting the usual punishment paradigm: have the subject deliver electric shock to another ostensible subject (really an experimental confederate). There followed two years of pilot research, which resulted in the procedure called the *aggression machine* (an apparatus used to measure physical aggression in a laboratory). I subsequently used it to investigate the role of frustration on aggression, cognitive dissonance and aggression, and two experiments which I regard as especially enlightening: the effect of (seemingly) harming someone on aggression (Buss, 1966) and the effect of firing a weapon on aggression (Buss, Booker, & Buss, 1972).

The aggression machine paradigm first appeared in my book *The Psychology of Aggression* (Buss, 1961). When it was published, I received a call from a surprised (perhaps shocked) Stanley Milgram, who said he was using a similar experimental set up. His paradigm involved obedience to authority, research for which he became justly famous when he published it some time later (Milgram, 1963). The aggression machine evidently did answer a need for aggression researchers, for it was used extensively for the next decade or so, and modifications of it are in use today.

Another challenge to come from writing my book was the status of anger. I suggested that aggression accompanied by anger was different from aggression without anger. *Angry aggression* is rewarded by harming the other person (a child is teased so strikes the teaser), whereas *instrumental aggression* typically is rewarded by a nonsocial reinforcer (a child wants another's toy, so pushes him away and takes the toy). If there is a cathartic effect of aggression, it would be only when angry aggression occurs and if the anger is drained. I suggested that when anger cools, it often leaves behind the negative cognitive residue of resentment or suspicion, the two components of hostility. And there was research literature from the 1950s and earlier which demonstrated the negative impact of anger on the cardiovascular system. This topic would presently fall under the heading of health psychology.

Psychopathology

I was teaching a graduate course in abnormal psychology and decided to write an advanced abnormal psychology textbook (Buss, 1966). One of the chapters, on psychological deficit in schizophrenia, proved to be a historical bridge between several journals. The topic was reviewed jointly with a colleague, Peter Lang, then a recent PhD who would soon publish the first laboratory study on behavior modification. We sent our article to the *Journal of Abnormal and Social Psychology,* which was about to cleave into two journals: the *Journal of Personality and Social Psychology* and the *Journal of Abnormal Psychology.* The process took some time, during which the literature kept piling up, and our article grew too large for one issue. So the first part was published as the first article in the premier issue of the *Journal of Abnormal Psychology* (Buss & Lang, 1965), and the second part was published in the next issue (Lang & Buss, 1965). Our review demonstrated that the deficits in schizophrenia involved basic cognitive processes and that the deficits were likely to involve biological etiology. Other chapters in the book also documented research that demonstrated, contrary to the prevailing environmentalism of the 1960s, the importance of biological factors in psychoses.

I had wanted to teach introductory psychology. For reasons never offered (and it was not for lack of competence, because I had received good student evaluations), the head of the department would not allow it. That, and the defections to other universities of several faculty members, made me susceptible to a job offer. A new path opened up with a position at Rutgers University, and I went there in 1965.

RUTGERS UNIVERSITY
Introductory Psychology
There I gladly taught a year-long course in introductory psychology and decided to write a text for it. It had been 15 years since I had left graduate school, and psychology was expanding, especially the areas of behavior genetics, psycholinguistics, developmental, social, and neuroscience. Perhaps writing such a text might be an intellectual watershed for me.

In the 1960s, biologists and anthropologists were applying evolutionary theory to behavior, which piqued the interest of psychologists, including some of my colleagues. That intellectual path was exciting, and I decided to use evolution as the overarching theme of the book. Actually, there were three subthemes: How we are like other animals, how we are a unique species, and where we are in the evolutionary line that led to our species. Mine was one of the first introductory texts to describe the evolution of the nervous system, which today is found in virtually all such texts. Looking back, I am amazed at the amount of work it was, a feeling that may be common among older academics. But I have been repaid many times over for the years I spent on that book (Buss, 1973).

In early 1969, I negotiated a year's research leave and arranged to spend it in London with Hans Eysenck, but suddenly a job opened up at the University of Texas, to head the graduate program in personality. If I went to London, I would have been obligated to return to Rutgers and forget about Texas. Intrigued with leading a graduate program in personality, I chose Texas. What would my subsequent career have been if I had gone to London? Would I have become an Eysenckian? Would I have been influenced by the British brand of psychology and of a year immersed in that culture?

THE UNIVERSITY OF TEXAS
Research on Temperament
As part of a personality course, I taught the temperament theory of Solomon Diamond (1957), who took a comparative approach and insisted that other animals had personality traits. I agreed with him but had my own set of temperaments and a different definition of *temperament:* Personality traits with an

inherited component and first seen in infancy and continue on to adulthood in one form or another. Robert Plomin entered the personality program in 1970 and was attracted to the topic. We delineated four temperaments: emotionality, activity, sociability, and impulsiveness, which enabled us to call our questionnaire the EASI. Later, Plomin and I wrote a book (Buss & Plomin, 1975) which included our research on these temperaments, that of others, and our theoretical approach. The book was ignored for five years, but in 1980 it started to be cited and became part of the groundswell of research on temperament.

Plomin went on to a prolific career in personality and behavior genetics, and is now in the forefront of research linking molecular genetics to behavior. In 2000, our psychology department decided each year to honor a former graduate student; Plomin was the initial recipient. He might well be an example of the pupil outdoing the master.

Studies of Self-Consciousness

At about the same time two graduate students, Allen Fenigstein and Michael Scheier, told me about local research on self-awareness, using a small mirror. If the use of a small mirror is truly an effective manipulation, it should affect physical aggression. So we used the aggression machine paradigm and verified the impact of a small mirror. Fenigstein was about to start on his dissertation, and we needed a measure of the trait of self-consciousness. We wrote items for every aspect of self-consciousness, administered the questionnaire to large samples of students, and factor analyzed it. The three factors were private self-consciousness, public self-consciousness, and social anxiety (Fenigstein, Scheier, & Buss, 1975).

There followed a variety of experiments by graduate students, including Charles Carver, in both personality psychology and social psychology at the University of Texas and elsewhere. Much of this early research is reviewed in *Self-Consciousness and Social Anxiety* (Buss, 1980) in which I present theories of private and public self-consciousness, and discuss shyness. Fenigstein has since continued research on self-consciousness. Carver and Scheier (1981) have published many experiments on self-awareness and developed a theoretical approach different from my own, validating both their graduate training, which encouraged independence, and my belief in their talent.

Notice that I became involved in the topics of temperament and self-consciousness through the stimulation of graduate students. If not for their initiative, I might never have trod those paths. Also, my theory and research on shyness took me off the hook, for I am not shy. Previously, colleagues had teased me about my interest in aggression: "Is the book your autobiography?" they would ask, the implicit assumption being that our research mirrors our personality. (What would people have said if I had studied child molesters?)

Book on Evolution and Personality

One year I wrote a paper on evolution and personality and, on reviewing it, decided that it was not appropriate for a journal. It would have remained in a file drawer gathering dust, but several months later I was invited to give a talk at the Henry Murray lectures at Michigan State University, and evolution and personality was an appropriate topic. The written version appeared in a chapter in the edited book of that year's lectures.

The chapter was expanded into my book *Personality: Evolutionary Heritage and Human Distinctiveness* (Buss, 1988). It included seven personality dispositions observed in humans, other primates, and perhaps in some mammals. Each of them has human elaborations that have evolved because of our advanced cognitions and socialization practices. Thus, the self-esteem we see in our species may be regarded as a cognitive derivative of the dominance tendency we see in primates. Nonetheless, the origin of this book was a path that opened up when I was invited to the Henry Murray lectures.

Writing Personality Textbooks

The path metaphor may also apply to my teaching. I teach courses differently than most psychologists. For example, I highlight evolution as the overarching theme in introductory psychology. My teaching methods often did not fit standard textbooks, so my solution was to write textbooks. Personality texts were once like those in other areas of psychology, that is, organized by various topics in the field of personality. Now, most texts are organized around theories of personality, which I regard as a historical accident, namely, the success of the first theories-of-personality text many decades ago. I prefer the older organization of topics. By omitting ancient theories which do not drive research, I was able to include the research actually being done in the area of personality (Buss, 1995).

Until about half a century ago, many of the texts were by scholars who presented their view of the field. As I reflect about the various textbooks I have written, I realize that I have adopted that older view. And I am surprised to discover that in one sense at least, I am a traditionalist.

Teaching about the Self

I taught a course in the self for many years. There was no textbook for it—another open path—although by the time I completed one (Buss, 2001), two others had appeared. One problem with the self is that it spills over into other areas of psychology. But I use two defining characteristics to limit its scope. One is self-focus: self evaluation not evaluation of others. The other is the concept of a psychological boundary around the self, which involves whether one is an individualist (typical of our culture) or a collectivist (typical of Japanese culture). The book is organized around several dimensions, the end points of which are dichotomies. The most salient dichotomies are personal–social, central–peripheral, continuous–discontinuous, and aware–unaware.

A topic central to the self is identity, the answer to the question "Who am I?" The course and the book forced me to focus on my own identity and so did writing this essay. So I'll diverge from the pathways theme here to write about my identity. In the interest of brevity I'll limit it to family (husband and father) and profession (scholar and teacher).

FAMILY

Edith and Our Children

During World War II, I was stationed for a while at Michigan State College (now MSU). Several years later I visited East Lansing and was writing post cards in the Student Union where I met Edith Nolte, who was cutting a German class. We talked at length and agreed to correspond. The relationship deepened, and largely through the mails we discussed our different backgrounds. We married in 1948. She was a warm and lively woman, beloved by family and friends. She efficiently ran my laboratory at Pittsburgh, at Rutgers, and for several years at Texas. She mothered the research assistants, which substantially boosted their morale. She contributed enough to my research program to be a co-author on several of my papers and a book. In January 1989, Edith died of ovarian cancer. Being her husband for 40 years was an important part of my identity.

So was being the father of our children. They came out of the womb so different in personality that early in my career I recognized the role of heredity in determining personality. As a result, I was fully prepared to study temperament.

All three majored in psychology at college. My son, Arnold, Jr., went on to a get a PhD in operations research and is an academic. My other son,

David, and my daughter, Laura, both went to Berkeley and obtained PhDs in personality psychology. Having three children with PhDs is not uncommon, but more than one person has wondered how it was that two of my children studied the same field of psychology as mine, namely, personality. There must have been something going on in our home while they were growing up, but I had no idea what, so my standard reply became "because I beat them so much!" In any event, Laura is not a psychologist now and, instead, writes novels. David, after several years of research on personality, shifted to the new field of evolutionary psychology, where he has achieved considerable eminence (see Buss, D. M., 1994, 1999). Indeed, his prominence in psychology exceeds my own, which is all a father might hope for. But all three children have matured and lead satisfactory and fulfilling lives. And I have five grandchildren from them—another source of my identity.

Ruth and "Our" Children

In April 1989, I met Ruth Bennett on a blind date and experienced romantic love again. We married in 1990. Ruth has strongly supported my professional activities. To cite just one instance, her editing has firmed up this essay. She is a favorite in our community of friends and family, and it has been a pleasure to resume the identity of husband. A relative asked how I was able to marry two such wonderful women. That reminded me of the comment of a colleague who said my introductory psychology text was "surprisingly good!" Some compliments have a stinger nestled within them.

When I married Ruth, she had two college-age daughters. I have treated them as my own daughters, and they have regarded me as a second father. I went through the paternal role at their weddings, and as of this writing I'm a grandfather again, courtesy of Ruth's older daughter.

PROFESSION

I'm something of a people watcher, which may be why I became a psychologist. I like to observe the way people walk and talk, and in general, movements and posture; in one of my books (not cited) there is a chapter on personal style. But most of my scholarly work has been more formal research and theory, published in 76 journal articles and book chapters, along with a dozen books of my own. I've focused mainly on personality and social behavior. On the basis of citations in the literature, my principal contributions appear to be in the areas of aggression, temperament, self-consciousness, and shyness.

I've been a teacher for much of my adult life. My introductory psychology classes are large, the upper limit determined mainly by the size of the auditorium. At Rutgers it was 400 students and at Texas, 500. By a rough estimate, I've lectured to 20,000 introductory psychology students, usually in their first semester of college. It's a great opportunity to be the first psychologist to teach them, but teaching senior psychology majors is a pleasant complement.

Teaching graduate students of course means small classes, tutorials, and a lot of out-of-class contact. My training of graduate students is in small part a repayment of the training once offered to me, and I take vicarious pride in their subsequent success.

I still teach, and it's still an important part of my identity. Some of my students are the children of students I once taught, a testament to longevity in academia. But I have no plans to retire, for it's no longer mandatory. We do have post-tenure review, but I passed muster this year, and I'm too old for the moral depravity that might terminate tenure. I intend to die with my boots on, which in academia means keeling over while in front of a class of students, some of whom will surely notice.

REFERENCES

Buss, A. H. (1961). *The psychology of aggression.* New York: John Wiley.

Buss, A. H. (1966). The effect of harm on subsequent aggression. *Journal of Experimental Research in Personality, 1,* 249–255.

Buss, A. H. (1973). *Psychology: Man in perspective.* New York: John Wiley.

Buss, A. H. (1980). *Self-consciousness and social anxiety.* San Francisco: Freeman.

Buss, A. H. (1988). *Personality: Evolutionary heritage and human distinctiveness.* Hillsdale, NJ: Lawrence Erlbaum.

Buss, A. H. (1995). *Personality: Temperament, social behavior, and the self.* Needham Heights, MA: Allyn & Bacon.

Buss, A. H. (2001). *Psychological dimensions of the self.* Thousand Oaks, CA: Sage.

Buss, A. H., Booker, A., & Buss, E. H. (1972). Firing a weapon and aggression. *Journal of Personality and Social Psychology, 22,* 296–302.

Buss, A. H., & Durkee, A. (1957). An inventory for assessing different kinds of hostility. *Journal of Consulting Psychology, 21,* 343–349.

Buss, A. H., & Lang, P. J. (1965). Psychological deficit in schizophrenia. I. Affect, reinforcement, and concept attainment. *Journal of Abnormal Psychology, 70,* 2–24.

Buss, A. H., & Perry, M. (1992). The Aggression Questionnaire. *Journal of Personality and Social Psychology, 63,* 452–459.

Buss, A. H., & Plomin, R. (1975). *A temperament theory of personality development.* New York: Wiley Interscience.

Buss, D. M. (1994). *The evolution of desire.* New York: Basic.

Buss, D. M. (1999). *Evolutionary psychology.* Needham Heights, MA: Allyn & Bacon.

Carver, C. S., & Scheier, M. F. (1981). *Attention and self-regulation: A control theory approach to human behavior.* New York: Springer-Verlag.

Diamond, S. (1957). *Personality and temperament.* New York: Harper.

Fenichel, O. (1945). *The psychoanalytic theory of neurosis.* New York: Norton.

Fenigstein, A., Scheier, M. F., & Buss, A. H. (1975). Public and private self-consciousness: Assessment and theory. *Journal of Consulting and Clinical Psychology,* 43, 522–527.

Gardner, R. A., & Gardner, B. T. (1969). Teaching sign language to a chimpanzee. *Science,* 165, 664–672.

Lang, P. J., & Buss, A. H. (1965). Psychological deficit in schizophrenia. II. Interference and activation. *Journal of Abnormal Psychology,* 70, 77–106.

Milgram, S. (1963). Behavioral study of obedience. *Journal of Abnormal and Social Psychology,* 67, 371–378.

Wiggins, J. S. (1979). A psychological taxonomy of trait-descriptive terms: The interpersonal domain. *Journal of Personality and Social Psychology,* 37, 395–412.

Zuckerman, M. (1979). *Sensation seeking: Beyond the optimal level of arousal.* Hillsdale, NJ: Lawrence Erlbaum.

SELECTED BIBLIOGRAPHY

Buss, A. H. (1980). *Self-consciousness and social anxiety.* San Francisco: Freeman.

Buss, A. H. (1980). Social rewards and personality. *Journal of Personality and Social Psychology,* 44, 553–563.

Buss, A. H. (1988). *Personality: Evolutionary heritage and human distinctiveness.* Hillsdale, NJ: Lawrence Erlbaum.

Buss, A. H. (1989). Personality as traits. *American Psychologist,* 44, 1378–1387.

Buss, A. H. (1995). *Personality: Temperament, social behavior, and the self.* Needham Heights, MA: Allyn & Bacon.

Buss, A. H. (1997). A dual conception of shyness. In J. Daly, J. C. McCrosky, J. Ayres, T. Hopf, & D. M Ayres (Eds.), *Avoiding communication: Shyness, reticence, and communication apprehension* (pp. 109–127). Cresskill, NJ: Hampton.

Buss, A. H. (2001). *Psychological dimensions of the self.* Thousand Oaks, CA: Sage.

Buss, A. H., & Perry, M. (1992). The Aggression Questionnaire. *Journal of Personality and Social Psychology,* 63, 452–459.

Buss, A. H., & Plomin, R. (1975). *A temperament theory of personality development.* New York: Wiley Interscience.

Buss, A. H., & Plomin, R. (1984). *Temperament: Early developing personality traits.* Hillsdale, NJ: Lawrence Erlbaum.

Psychology staff and interns at Carter Hospital, 1955. Marvin Zuckerman is third from the left. Jerry Wiggins is fifth from the left, and Arnold Buss is next to Wiggins

The highly-educated Busses (four PhDs). Left to right: Arnold Buss, Jr., Arnold Buss, Sr., David, and Laura, 1995

Edith and Arnold in Heidelberg, 1983

Ruth and Arnold, 1996

CHAPTER 3

Discontinuities, Side Steps, and Finding a Proper Place

An Autobiographical Account

James N. Butcher
University of Minnesota

A West Virginia coal mining town in the 1930s was a rather harsh and austere point of entry to life. But I was born in one called Bergoo, West Virginia, in 1933. My father was a coal miner who had relatively few employment options or resources to deal with the harsh circumstances of day-to-day living in the Great Depression. With only a second grade education, there was no such thing as upward mobility for him—only downward into the coal mines—an occupation that took his life at the age of 35. Coal mining was very danger-ous work. The violent coal mining strikes of the 1930s made life even harsher than the already bleak existence of coal mining families. Some of my earliest childhood memories are of rough and rowdy miners on the picket lines with their pick axes and shovels, walking and rousting about, and the meager food parcels that were doled out by the miners union once a month to tide miners and their families over during a strike. When I was a small child, my father told me that I should never become a coal miner: "When you grow up, don't go into the mines. This is a bad life!"

Not long after the Second World War had begun, when I was return-ing from school one day in January 1942, our town of Winifrede Junction was alerted by the loud blaring of the mining company's siren that there was trouble at the coal mine. As I ran down the dusty road from my school, I encountered my Uncle Delbert, who also worked in the mine. He told me to go home because there had been a terrible accident and that my father was badly hurt and was being taken to the hospital. Later I learned that my dad had died while he was lying in the hallway of Charleston General Hospital awaiting admission (miners were often refused treatment because of their inability to pay). I was slightly more than eight years old at the time.

Shortly afterward, we left the mining town and moved to Charleston, West Virginia, because my mother could get work in a war production plant. This job enabled her to supplement the miner's compensation payments she received as a death benefit. There were five of us children living at the time. My family moved into a three-room house on the west side of Charleston. The house was quite old and in a general state of disrepair and we always worried about it catching fire. But even with its problems, this house was actually more comfortable than those belonging to the coal company—and we actually had an indoor bathroom. The little house had one bedroom, where my mother and older sister Gloria slept, and a living room where my sister Joan slept. There was a small glassed-in sun porch on the side that served as a bedroom for the three of us boys. The room was at first unheated; later we were able to get a small natural gas stove that provided some heat in the winter. It became even warmer when the broken pane of glass that allowed cold air to creep into the room was replaced by cardboard.

I was in the third grade when we moved to Charleston. I liked living in town better and enjoyed the grade school (Littlepage) I was attending near my home. I liked the teachers and the school had several rooms, unlike the two-room school that I attended at Winifrede where one room held grades one through three and the other held grades four through six. When I was in the fifth grade, in December 1944, my mother became quite ill with a lung infection. Her doctor began a treatment for pleurisy that involved putting a very tight binding around her chest, which caused her a great deal of pain. After a few days of this misery, she went to see the doctor to have the binding removed. Shortly after he removed the binding, while she was still in the doctor's waiting room, she had a coronary or an embolism and died there at the young age of 32, leaving five minor children to fend for themselves. At this time, Gloria was about 17, Joan was almost 16, I was not quite 12, my younger brother Jerry was almost 10, and my baby brother Dickie was then 7.

MANAGING ON OUR OWN

These were very troubling times for us, with no adult supervision, and the recurring fear that we would be discovered living alone and put in an orphanage. Although we were under age, we were determined to continue to live as we had been. Eventually our older sister Gloria married and moved out of our house and began a family of her own.

The fact that we were without adult supervision did not mean that we lived as feral children—not by any means. I began working as a newspaper boy before I turned 12, which became a primary source of income for the family along with the money we received from the miner's compensation payments, which was a total of $36.00 per month for the family plus $18.00 per month for each minor child. We tried to maintain a home life of sorts: we prepared our own meals, went to school, stayed at home most nights, maintained reasonable hours (everyone of our friends had to go in at night, so we didn't have any one to play with), and did everything we could to avoid being separated as a family. Joan was a very determined person and provided the glue to make this arrangement work. We were well aware that if we failed at these tasks or called attention to our unusual living situation, we might wind up living in an orphanage. That was unacceptable to us. We formed a very close-knit unit; it was us against the rest of the world.

Our family was able to stay together over the next years until Jerry and I graduated from high school and left for our respective venues in life—I went into the army and Jerry to the seminary. Joan got married. She and her husband Corky provided a home for Dickie, then had two daughters of their own.

Growing up without parents or any adults in our home was, at times, characterized by a lot of uncertainties and voids. There were many times when we felt isolated from society and very much alone. It would have been valuable to have some adult advice and perspective at times. It would have been comforting to have a parent's touch or advice in times of troubles or uncertainty, not to mention having help with creature comforts. There were many nights that we went to bed with empty stomachs and more nights when we went to bed without a sense of direction toward the future. Although children living alone can do plenty to support each other, there are many things that they cannot do. In some respects, however, we fared pretty well without adult supervision and without adult role models during our adolescent years. The closest thing to adult supervision that my brothers and I ever had was from Joan who tried to provide some guidance, but she asserted little in the way of control over our activities, especially as we grew older and were less receptive.

We had an official guardian, my Uncle Mark, who was a bachelor and had his own life to lead and a mother to care for. His duties as "guardian" were few and we seldom bothered him because we wanted to be left alone. At first we needed Mark to sign papers, but when we learned to reproduce his signature (e.g., to sign our report cards) we didn't need to call on him at all. (I can still do a pretty good job of endorsing his name even after all these years.) Mark lived a few miles away and we rarely saw him, although he was handy once when we needed to thaw our frozen water pipes. In a pinch we could get a bit of advice from our maternal grandmother who lived a few miles away (with Mark). She was in poor health (diabetes) and could not provide much help except occasionally taking my baby brother Dickie in for a meal and a bit of company for a while.

LEARNING TO BE RESOURCEFUL

Our circumstances clearly imbued us all with a strong sense of independence. The absence of adult role models was not something that we were particularly concerned about. We thought we were getting along pretty well without adults. An interested outsider, if there had been one, would likely have disputed this conclusion. Our deportment suffered somewhat; we didn't always have clean clothes to wear or particularly good table manners, but we pretty much stayed out of major problems. Much of our "adult" influence came from the movies. Movie characters were the people from whom we learned adult roles and adult behavior. There were times that we spent the entire day on Saturday and Sunday in the movies watching and re-watching whatever was playing; these were most often westerns with Gene Autry and Roy Rogers. We especially liked the war movies that were plentiful at the time. I think that when we "imitated" movie characters, such as the Three Stooges, our behavior problems might have been more evident.

The movies were essentially free for us. Every week Jerry and I would take an extra job of distributing fliers, "show bills" as they were called, in return for free passes. If we had one free pass, one person would go inside and then let the others in through the back door. On Saturdays, we often watched movies and ate popcorn and candy for lunch and supper. It never bothered us that sometimes when we left the theater we had splitting headaches. Movies were a great escape for us, and besides we had little else to do with our time. One time we stayed all night in the theater after the last show played and hung out in there until the next morning when we went home.

Some Sundays we had a way of getting a little change to spend. The three of us would go to Sunday school at a small church near home. At the end of the lesson the teacher would draw names from a hat and the winner would get a quarter. Since there was only one other boy in the class and there were three of us, we had pretty good odds of winning the quarter (my introduction to probability theory). We would take our quarter and go to a local drug store where there was a pinball machine. Getting five nickels change we would use one nickel in the pinball game and spend the rest on treats. One nickel usually sufficed for pinball because we were pretty adept (my brother Jerry being most facile) at putting our toes under the front legs of the pin ball machine to slow down the ball so that we had better control over it. We were able to run up a lot of games. When we tired of playing the pinball machine, we would sell the remaining games at a discount to anyone who was interested, so we had a few extra quarters to spend. We managed to have fun and earn a little extra cash at times.

We learned another way to have some extra coins to play the pinball games. One day we found a few broken records in a garbage can at a store. The records were made of a plastic-like substance (wax) that was quite malleable. We broke the records into smaller pieces and sat on the pavement rubbing them to the size and shape of various coins—not realizing that what we were doing was counterfeiting coins or breaking the law by making slugs. These slugs worked well for a while in the pinball machines. But our little project ended when the reality changed—the owners fixed the machines so that they would not accept slugs.

It was necessary for me, and later my brother, to obtain paper routes to provide money for the family—usually we needed all the money we could earn delivering papers in order to buy food. When I was 11 years old, I went to talk with the station manager of the *Charleston Gazette* about the possibility of taking over a paper route that I had heard from one of the other boys was vacant. The manager seemed very sympathetic to my home situation and my need to earn money but had some genuine concerns as to whether I was strong enough to carry a heavy load of newspapers and whether or not I could learn the route. So he gave me a test. He put a load of newspapers in a sack and told me to pick it up and carry it up the hill (Charleston is a very hilly city). Then he showed me the houses on several streets that subscribed to the newspaper as we went along the route. After a while we stopped and he backtracked to see if I could remember the correct houses, which I could. When we were through, he told me that I had the job and could start the next day. Thus I carried papers for the remainder of my school years, and for the last few years I had the job (along with my friend Bob Baker) of assistant manager for the substation. We opened up early in the morning, counted out the papers for each of the routes, and supervised the other boys. If anyone failed to show up, we delivered his papers. Bob and I split the salary for this job.

CELEBRATING CHRISTMAS OUR OWN WAY

For most of these times, my sister discouraged accepting any assistance from other family members such as aunts and uncles; that is, we refused what we perceived to be "charity" and wouldn't have anything to do with it. Christmas of 1945 stands out as a good example of the closed and resistant attitude we developed toward receiving help from other family members. Two of my distant aunts visited our house a day or so before Christmas one year and brought with them some food for us. My brother Dickie, being too young to be as defiantly proud as Joan was becoming, was quite excited, especially about the pies they brought. Joan and I refused to have anything to do with them, and after our relatives left we refused to eat the pies! As much as I try to figure why Joan took this strong stance with respect to gifts from the rest of the family, I can only say that it likely had something to do with my sister's refusal to accept anything because our relatives did not initially offer to help us in our plight. It was a matter of defiant pride. I was really too young at the time to understand much about the source of Joan's negative attitudes toward some of our aunts and uncles. I only knew that it was imperative for me to back her up to maintain the integrity of our foursome. I knew that I could not accept those pies, although I remember to this day how delicious they looked!

My brother Jerry and I wanted to make Christmas of 1946 a good experience for our little brother Dickie because he still believed in Santa Claus. We bought him a couple of presents although money was always scarce. After we had the little tree up in the living room (my sister was now sleeping in our mother's room and we had the front room as a sitting room), Dickie was very excited about Santa coming and wanted to stay up and wait for him. We did not think this would be a good idea, so we talked him into watching Santa from a hole we drilled through our porch room door looking into the front room. On seeing this peephole, Dickie wasn't totally convinced that it was adequate because he realized that Jerry and I would not be able to see Santa. So, he insisted that we drill two more holes in the door, Although it seems a bit silly now as I look back, we did so just to keep up the ruse. Had we had an adult living in the home, I am sure that we couldn't have gotten by with such property defacement. These three holes in the door, each at a different height, stayed there until we all eventually moved from the house. That Christmas Jerry and I also realized that we had to have a present to open ourselves to complete the "Santa" deception, so we purchased a very cheap paper airplane model so that every one would have something to open on Christmas morning after Santa finally came. Even today when my brother

Jerry and I have our annual holiday conversation, we still ask each other if we have our "Christmas holes" drilled yet.

Despite our difficult early life circumstances, or perhaps because of them, my brothers and I found some escape from our cares by retreating often to the woods north of our house. We went there whenever we could, and sometimes we would actually skip school to build our hideout in the woods. On some occasions, when rumor had it that we were going to be placed in an orphanage (Witherow's Home for Youth), we hid out in the woods until the threat blew over. No one could ever find us if we did not want to be found! The truth of the matter is that no social agency was ever involved or interested in our case. We basically went through our adolescent years without much pressure from outside.

It was very difficult for us to know what to do when one of us became sick, however. Even a minor cold or the flu, without a parent to guide us through the miseries, could produce great anxiety, so our imaginations might run wild as to what the illness meant. We had a group fear of illness, largely induced by the fact that we had been conditioned to expect the worst—death—because both of our parents as well as an older brother and sister had died earlier. Death was a close acquaintance to our family; we never knew when it would visit again, though we anticipated its presence. One day when I was about 13 another terrible thing happened. My sister Joan became quite ill with stomach cramps and had to go to the hospital. Appendicitis! My brothers and I were quite upset because the health care system did not have a very good track record with our family so far. Joan was in the hospital for several days recovering from surgery and we were on our own, but we took pride in being able to handle the situation without help from others. In addition to carrying my paper route in the morning, I took on Joan's usual task of preparing meals for my younger brothers. I took this responsibility very seriously and made sure that we all ate three meals every day. I developed a plan for providing the meals that we needed, which also included *saving* some money at the same time. So, I cooked the same thing for lunch and dinner, macaroni and cheese, even though my brothers complained a lot over the monotony of the meals.

When my sister got out of the hospital, she was concerned about how well we had taken care of ourselves. She was excellent in home economics at school and won awards in high school for food preparation and sewing. I proudly told her that we had eaten well and that I had actually saved some money as well. (I had spent about $1.00 of our food money for the week.) She was shocked that I had fed the family so well on so little. She asked what we had for meals. When I told her that we had macaroni and cheese every day, she almost laughed and cried herself back into the hospital. I didn't realize what was so funny to her at the time; I only felt proud that I had gotten by with such a savings.

Even without adults to provide guidance to our daily living, we walked a pretty narrow path and usually avoided major problems. Joan's influence on us was powerful and all she had to say was, "Don't get into trouble," and we knew to steer clear of mischief. For the most part, we heeded her words and stayed away from the darker side of the street. We did not take up habits such as swearing or smoking cigarettes or drinking alcohol that seemed to be practiced by others our age. We made a great effort not to call attention to ourselves and tried to do what "the good kids" in the community did—we went to school and did what odd jobs we could. Our rule was "no problems, no orphanage!" On the few occasions when we did get into a bit of trouble or thought that the authorities were getting too interested in us, we hid out in the woods until the trouble blew over.

COPING WITH THE SCHOOL SYSTEM

By agreement among ourselves—mostly to keep the authorities from getting interested in us—we usually went to school regularly. However, the school that I attended in the sixth grade (Tiskelwah) was not a very pleasant or supportive place, nor were the teachers at all understanding of our living circumstances. Admittedly, I did not functioning very well academically. I was also usually pretty tired, having to get up at 5 A.M. every day to deliver papers. Evidence of the insensitive school environment can be seen in a couple of things that happened to us, one to me and one to my brother. The most appalling lack of sensitivity that I experienced at this time was during a Parent-Teachers Association membership drive when I was in the sixth grade. The teachers were very interested in having 100% membership in the PTA chapter for their classrooms so began to pressure the children to register *both* parents by bringing in 50 cents in dues for each. Because I did not have any parents at the time, I thought I was exempt from the PTA, so I did not bring any money to school for this purpose. How wrong I was! Not only did they expect 100% registration, but the teacher actually put the names of the students on the blackboard who had *not* made their parents' contribution. Every time I saw my name on the list I got embarrassed. So, in order to remove my name from the list I took some of my paper route money and went to the teacher and paid for one parent registration. She accepted the money and erased my name from the blackboard.

Years after we grew up and made our way in life, my brother Jerry showed me one of his report cards that I think depicts the insensitivity of our school system very well. Jerry—who managed to do pretty well in life, having obtained a PhD and had a successful career as a minister—obviously had some talent that went unrecognized by any of his teachers. His grades in school were pretty abysmal and his report card showed it, but what was most pathetic about his report card was a hostile note that one of his teachers had scribbled on it: "Do not release this report card until this student's shop fees have been paid!"

Although there was pretty much of a black cloud over my school experiences during these middle years, not every day in this school was bad. One day our school was engaging in a scrap metal and paper drive in order to help the war effort. We were very enthusiastic about this project and we really enjoyed doing this—not just to get out of school for a bit—but because we felt as though we were doing something worthwhile by going out and picking up junk and old papers that could be used in the war production. One of the brightest moments of my early school days was when I took some of the papers that I had gathered up down to the basement of Tiskelwah School where the papers were collected and started to read some of the pages of the old newspapers that were stored there.

I found one bundle of papers that had been published in 1887 and started reading them. I found the topics fascinating and the old pictures intriguing. I found myself reading several of the papers and forgot about the time, returning quite late to the classroom. All through the scolding that I received, I kept thinking of how much more interesting those old papers were compared with the usual school routine. That was not my last trip to the storage basement. Shortly afterward, I went to school, but instead of going to the classroom, I decided to read newspapers instead—all the way through the lunch hour (I had brought a sandwich to eat) and into the afternoon. Unfortunately, before long though all the papers were taken away and I had to return to the regular school program. Incidentally, my interest in old documents continued into my adult years as manifested by my long-term avocation of collecting antique books and pamphlets.

MY GROWING INTEREST IN AVIATION AND THE ARMY

A second bright diversion during this time occurred when I found an intriguing object in a junkyard that I passed on the way home from school. It was an old army airplane that was just sitting there beckoning to be explored. This was shortly after the war ended when a lot of military hardware had begun to be dismantled and sold as scrap metal. I was fascinated with this old plane. I had heard a lot about these army planes on the radio—now here was one right up close! A friend and I planned an adventure and discovered a way inside the fence and climbed up on the wing (it was an Army Air Corps trainer) and into the cockpit. Even though it was incomplete and damaged—the left aileron was missing and the instrument panel had been mostly cannibalized—to us it was still a warplane! We went back a few more times before the honorable bird disappeared from the junk pile. Luckily, we were never caught at our nefarious game by the junkyard owner, who had the reputation of being aggressive in keeping people away from his junk. My interest in aviation continued into adulthood when I learned to fly, and aviation has also been a major professional interest—aviation psychology (airline pilot selection; Butcher, 2002a) and airline disaster response management (Butcher & Dunn, 1989).

I began to develop an interest in the military during those school years. World War II was a time of total mobilization, and many Americans were fully immersed in the war effort. Everything that happened seemed to relate to the war and to a devotion to the objectives of the military. Most families had loved ones in the service and proudly displayed the "stars" in their windows, signifying how many men and women from the family were serving in the military. This was a critical period in my development, from age 8 through 14, and I think I was "imprinted" by this national obsession and goal of winning the war. It was not simply that I was an impressionable youngster but rather that the whole social order was abuzz with the war effort: the radio, and of course the newspapers that I delivered, which constantly presented stories about the war and updates on the progress of the war. Many of the headlines that I yelled out as a newsboy on the streets of Charleston while selling papers related to the war.

During the war years, even some of our school lessons heavily emphasized the war. Geography lessons included the names of such exotic places such Tarawa, Guadalcanal, Anzio Beach, and many other places where our troops were fighting. In those days we were taught by society to respect and value the military—through the schools and the media. I have discussed my impressions of these early wartime attitudes with other people my age and have found similar feelings; the social context at that time seemed to be permeated with interest in things military. How could we not value such things? They were of the utmost importance. President Roosevelt frequently encouraged us to devote ourselves to the military effort!

What a person is or what they become is often set in motion in their early years. I was perhaps more extreme in my identification because I had few adult role models to learn from. To me a military career was a direct route to being accepted in life, even to being important. Throughout my school years my academic interests and experiences ran from lukewarm to cold. There was little incentive for us to do well, as our goal was to pass our classes and get promoted just to get through them and not call attention to ourselves.

FINDING A POSITIVE ROLE MODEL

Although school was generally pretty bleak for us, there was an occasional discovery that learning could be fun. There was one bright spot for me in high school—a teacher who made a difference in the way that I thought about something. In the ninth grade I performed pretty miserably with mostly D's and a sprinkling of C's until I encountered a particularly effective teacher, Mr. Thomas Hill, who happened to get my attention. Mr. Hill was a math teacher at Stonewall Jackson High School who also taught a course in aviation navigation that I took. Being interested in flying at the time, I took his class and earned an A. Mr. Hill told me that the stuff that I had learned about navigating an airplane was actually a branch of math called geometry and demonstrated that the procedures we had been using to plot an airplane's course were simply plane geometry. He encouraged me to take geometry and told me that he thought that I could do well in it. The next semester I took the course in geometry from him and was surprised at how much I enjoyed it; there must have been some spill over to other courses because I actually got all A's that term.

Mr. Hill was also involved in the high school branch of the Civil Air Patrol and invited me to join. This was a valuable experience in several respects. Being a cadet was somewhat like being in the army in that we wore uniforms and learned a lot about aviation. I actually had the opportunity to get a couple of flying lessons and spend some time flying an old Link trainer. Mr. Hill's classes were certainly the highlight of my high school days. He also showed a personal interest in me and invited me on a few family outings; he had a son who was somewhat younger than I. The problem with the public schools at that time was that there just were not enough Mr. Hills to go around.

Another positive learning experience I had during this time had nothing to do with formal education but was a clear harbinger of my interest in psychology. One of the women on my paper route (who had taken some college courses) and I were talking one day when I mentioned that I was interested in the work of a man named Freud who wrote about why people forget things. She gave me a copy of one of her books, a psychology textbook by Tiffin that contained many interesting ideas. But the military beckoned.

I couldn't wait until I could join the army and be part of things that I considered important in life. Then in 1950, a new war started in Korea, and American soldiers were being sent there to stop the aggression of the North Koreans toward the South Koreans. I was not quite 17, the minimum age for enlistment (I was actually several months short of it), but I thought that it was important that Americans stand up for the South Koreans in their troubles. I also saw my opportunity at last to enter the military, so I mentally increased my age a bit and went to the recruiting office in Charleston to enlist. My enthusiasm and exuberance must have been showing too much since I had taken along a packed bag—I was ready to go! After a brief and somewhat un-satisfying discussion with the recruiter, he informed me that I did not qualify because of my age and that I would have to wait until I was 17 to volunteer when I could enlist with parental permission. I was pretty disappointed by that turn of events. So I waited. By the time I reached 17, my last year of high school had begun and I had gained a bit of perspective on life, thanks to Mr. Steadman, the dean of students at Stonewall Jackson High School, and Mr. Hill who had encouraged me to stick it out a bit longer, until May, when I would get my high school diploma. I compromised my burning ambition to go into active duty military with an alternative that I thought could tide me over until May. I joined the 100th Division of the U. S. Army Reserves on my seventeenth birthday. I enjoyed playing the part of being a soldier for the six months that I had to wait to go on active duty. I finally graduated from high school on May 23rd, 1951, and departed for the army the next day. This time I waited until I had my ticket before I packed my bag to start a new life.

MILITARY SERVICE AND SEARCH FOR IDENTITY

I said goodbye to my sister and brothers, and my uncle drove me to the Charleston railway station. My train was scheduled to leave the station at 7 p.m. on May 24th. It was an uneventful sendoff; I waited on the station platform looking across the Kanawa River at the bright lights of the city until my train came. I felt very excited but not particularly sad about leaving; I was anxious to get my life under way. As Charleston disappeared, and the train began its long journey through the winding mountain trail on the way to Maryland, I anticipated what the next phase in my life held for me. I sat in my cabin on the train for a while savoring the novel experience of being on my own and taking a night train to what I considered to be such an important destination, the beginning of my military career. It felt good to be someone at last—finally to be part of something worthwhile and heading for the army.

An Infantryman's Life

When I went into basic training in the summer of 1951, I was exactly where I wanted to be even though I, like some of my buddies, had definite rough spots in adapting to the military way. We did not always see eye to eye with our non-commissioned cadre. The one ingredient that was not lacking from my thinking at the time, however, was the motivation to do well. Even more, I wanted to excel in basic training and go on to more challenging assignments—particularly airborne (parachute) training. As we settled into our routine, I quickly learned that it was unwise to inform my fellow trainees that I had enlisted in the army. Being *enlisted* was an invitation to ridicule, and my somewhat frail self-image could not handle too much joshing at the time. Most of the men in basic training had actually been drafted into the service and were very unhappy and unmotivated in the army. Most of the recruits were older, in their twenties, and many had college degrees. Several draftees in the training company even had PhD degrees and would have rather been elsewhere than in army basic training learning such things as how to use an M1 rifle and take night compass readings.

After the 12-week basic training course at Indiantown Gap, Pennsylvania, and a hard-won introduction to army life, I volunteered for the airborne infantry in the fall of 1951. Following army jump school training at Fort Benning, Georgia, I was assigned to the 82nd Airborne Division. This historic army division was an interesting assignment, and it was a lot of fun being a paratrooper in it. I enjoyed the duties of a rifleman in an airborne infantry line company. However, after a while I became somewhat restless with the routine of stateside duty and wanted to serve overseas, preferably in a combat unit. I decided that I wanted to go overseas, but obviously it would not be with the 82nd Airborne, America's stateside-bound honor guard. I then began to submit a flurry of transfer requests. Each week I went into the First Sergeant's office and requested that I be transferred to a combat unit in Korea. And each week the First Sergeant told me that our company was under strength and, because I was parachute qualified, I would remain with the unit.

One evening I took a dramatic step and wrote a letter to my senator from West Virginia, the Honorable Harley M. Kilgore, indicating that I was from West Virginia and that I had volunteered a number of times to serve in Korea but that my request had always been turned down. I pointed out to him that I was 18 years old and single. "Why not send me to Korea instead of someone who is married or has family responsibilities?" Within a week a response came from Washington—a very nice letter from the Senator indicating that he was proud that a fellow West Virginian had volunteered for

Korea the way I had and that he would see if he could do anything about my request. He indicated that he might not have much influence in such matters as army personnel movements but that he would inquire about my request. Senator Kilgore was a member of the Senate Arms Appropriations Committee and, among other duties, they voted on the promotions of general officers. His letter to me clearly understated his influence with the military and what he might do in terms of my request! Within hours after he made his inquiry with the 82nd Airborne Commanding General, I was called into the company headquarters. The First Sergeant was in a bit of a rage and told me that he did not like soldiers going over his head to get their way! He indicated that my request to go to Korea was being granted and that I was to be processed for immediate reassignment to Korea. But, in the meantime he had a number of jobs to keep me busy. Obviously he thought that I had too much time on my hands, so he provided some additional tasks for me to do to limit my letter writing! I was given a permanent KP assignment (kitchen detail) for the remainder of my time in the company.

Since scarcely a day goes by—even more than 50 years later—that I don't remember an occurrence of my tour of duty in Korea, or remember my buddies who died there, I wish to share my experience of that year in this autobiography. My arrival on the front lines in Korea in the fall of 1952 occurred just as a major offensive was being launched by the Chinese Communist Forces against the U.N. army. The Central front of the main lines had been a boiling caldron of activity from mid September through October of 1952. Several slopes became embroiled in what was referred to as the "Battle of the Hills" with Sniper Ridge, Whitehorse, and Triangle Ridge. My unit, F Company of the 17th Infantry of the 7th Army Division, was assigned to counterattack the Chinese positions on Jane Russell Hill, a part of Triangle Ridge. The unit to which I was assigned, first as a rifleman and later as a squad leader and platoon sergeant was involved in several engagements before the war ended in 1953, the most well known of which was Pork Chop Hill in April, 1953 (Marshall, 1956). Neither space nor the scope of this article allows for a fuller discussion of this period of my life at the front, although some of the most powerful influences in my life occurred then. Some of these experiences of the 17th Infantry have been described elsewhere (Butcher, 1999, 2000a, 2001; see also, Gonsalves, 2001).

One situation that occurred on Jane Russell Hill that October, shortly after my arrival, left an indelible mark on my thinking and clearly influenced my later choice of college courses and my later career as a psychologist with an international research interest. After our assault on the hill, we prepared our positions for the inevitable counterattack by the Chinese. My platoon sergeant assigned me the task of defending an approach to the hill along with a young South Korean soldier (about one-fourth of our company was made up of South Koreans at the time). He spoke no English and I spoke no Korean; and both of us being new to the front were somewhat unsure of what to expect. Throughout the long night—which seemed almost like daylight because of the constant flares bursting overhead—we developed a way of communicating and teaching each other about matters that counted at the moment. In addition to dealing with the military tasks at hand, we also learned a lot about each other's culture. During my time in Korea I had the opportunity to learn a great deal about other people from different cultures given the fact that the army was an international force (United Nations sponsored)—we had soldiers attached or serving in our unit from other countries including Colombia, Ethiopia, and Turkey.

After Jane Russell Hill, my company was in line for a rest and went in reserve for three weeks guarding POWs on Koje-Do Island—then back to the front in January 1953. The winter of 1952–53 was an especially cold one and much of our action involved running patrols into no-man's-land, either to reconnoiter or set up an ambush. In April 1953, the Chinese began a spring offensive that changed the make-up of our unit substantially and many of my close friends became casualties on Pork Chop Hill (Butcher, 1999; Gonsalves, 2001; Marshall, 1956). The remainder of my time in Korea, until I left in July 1953, I spent as a platoon sergeant. Upon my return to stateside, I was assigned as a platoon sergeant in an infantry company in the 82nd Airborne. This time around in the 82nd Airborne was different, however, as the new rank that I brought back from Korea involved more challenging responsibilities than during my first stint with the airborne infantry.

FINDING MY WAY IN CIVILIAN LIFE

I was discharged from the army in 1954, got married to Nancy Oakley from Greensboro, North Carolina, and returned to Charleston to begin life anew. This was not a particularly good time to begin a civilian occupation because few jobs were available. My home state was in an economic recession and employment prospects were few, particularly for someone only trained in military skills. I tried a couple of sales jobs for a few months but was rather unsuccessful. I enjoyed talking to people, but I did not find that selling adding machines or life insurance fit my personality style because it seemed too much like asking favors of my potential customer—which had been discouraged during my childhood.

Then I tried working as a private investigator for the American Detective Agency for a couple of years. The owner of the agency thought he would give me an opportunity because of my military combat experience, in spite of the fact that I had no police or investigative background. I enjoyed this line of work at first because it was an exciting way to work with people, provided some interesting problems to solve, and it seemed as though I was helping others while earning a living. It was interesting following people around, conducting surveillances, and even catching a few bad guys in crooked activities. However, this line of work had some unsavory aspects as well as erratic compensation. I recall one case that was particularly provoking. My supervisor assigned me to conduct a surveillance of a street in front of a client's home. I was to hide out in a large hedge and write down the license numbers of cars that came by during the night. This was pretty boring work except when a neighborhood dog spotted me and tried to protect the neighborhood from me. After a few days of this activity I happened to see the woman on her porch looking for something. I asked if she was looking for any thing in particular and if I might be helpful. She responded, "I am afraid of the little pygmy people who come to my window and shoot poison darts into my room." Even though I had no psychological training at the time, I had no trouble diagnosing the problem and recognizing that all of the notes that I was making had no bearing on her fears. When I raised this problem with my chief, he only said, "Keep watching and recording, they pay well!" It was not long after this that I decided to expand my occupational horizons.

In everyone's life there are human encounters that stand out as truly life-changing events. One such interaction occurred for me during this period. In fact, this situation was so instrumental in changing my life that I have wished many times since that I had recorded the name of the man who helped me so that I could thank him personally. I decided that my private detective job had a number of downsides, so I applied for a position as an insurance adjustor, an occupation that I thought would be more stable if not more respectable than my work as a private eye (invading people's privacy through surveillance and phone tapping were always a bit disconcerting to me). When I went to the interview with the company's representative (along with many others), I was given a psychological test dealing with mathematics and reasoning as well as an interview. Afterward, the job interviewer spoke frankly to me: "Mr. Butcher, it is clear from your background and ability scores that you could do this job. However, I am not going to hire you. I would be doing no service to you by doing so. Instead, I would encourage you to go to college using your GI Bill and get an education." At first, I felt discouraged about this rejection because I wanted to get a good job. But, as the message began to settle in, I felt buoyed about his confidence that I could do college work and his encouragement of me to take action, so I decided to explore this avenue further. Within a week, I was sitting in the admissions office at West Virginia State College at Institute (an all-Black University). I registered for two classes, basic English and math, which were remedial courses—better known as "bonehead basics," for students with a poor academic background. But it was a start! In retrospect, enrolling in an all-Black college in the segregated South was somewhat avant-garde in 1956, and I might add that this was an action that some of my friends questioned at the time. After all, it was the South in the 1950s. I was not attending this college as part of any social change movement. I was simply taking advantage of an educational opportunity. I was one of only a handful of Caucasians who enrolled in the college that year, and I was the only White person in both of my classes. My learning experiences in these courses clearly provided me with some confidence—I realized that I enjoyed the learning process and benefited from the discovery that I could learn at the college level.

GUILFORD: A COLLEGE THAT MADE A DIFFERENCE

Over the summer, I moved my family to Greensboro, North Carolina, and took a job as a "slubber tender" (a type of spinning machine) in a textile mill to support them (we had a one-year-old daughter, Sherry[1] at the time) and registered for evening school classes at the Greensboro Evening Division of Guilford College. In a short time I was a full-time student on the Guilford campus in a very accepting and academically stimulating college in addition to maintaining my full-time employment at Cone Mills. After my first psychology course with Patrick Comer in the evening school, I was hooked on the field and decided to actively pursue psychology as a major.

One of the most influential factors in my development as a psychologist was the Wednesday evening seminar for psychology majors held in the home of Guilford College President Clyde Milner and his wife Ernestine, who was chair of the psychology department. The social-academic climate of these seminars not only challenged my thinking but also provided me with a feeling of acceptance that I had rarely experienced before—as well as a

---

[1]Sherry became a successful museum curator, writer, and politician, serving two terms in the Eden Prairie (Minnesota) City Council, and ran for the Minnesota State Senate in 2002.

socialization experience as to how to behave in an academic environment. My experiences as an orphan, an infantryman, and private eye had in no way prepared me for the reflective life in an intellectual setting. The Quaker tradition at Guilford and the highly supportive faculty showed great tolerance for my lack of preparation for the academic life.

The learning environment at Guilford was exceptional. I was particularly influenced by the outstanding lectures and dedication to students shown by Professor Carroll Feagins in the philosophy department. The Quaker tradition taught me the value of individual thinking in a context of liberal social concern. The small class sizes allowed for a great deal of individual attention and placed great demands on performance—there were no large classes that enable students to withdraw into anonymity. The educational climate at Guilford more than adequately prepared me for the next step, graduate school. (My attachment to Guilford College was strengthened in 2002 when my youngest daughter, Holly, enrolled there as a freshman.

GRADUATE SCHOOL AT NORTH CAROLINA

In 1960, I entered a new phase of my career acquisition; I began graduate studies with Richard A. King in the Experimental Psychology Program at the University of North Carolina—in animal learning. I also worked for Dick King taking care of the animal lab as part of my assistantship. I have a number of rat bite scars as souvenirs from this period; however, that is not why I chose to go into the clinical program after finishing my MA thesis on *Resistance to Extinction as a Function of Reinforcement*—a study I did with my not-so-friendly rat colony. During my first year of graduate school I also took the basic clinical psychology curriculum and was assigned to a clinical practicum in the Durham VA Hospital over the summer of 1961. This intensive experience in clinical assessment (along with strong encouragement from Bob Carson and Charlie Spielberger, both Duke University faculty) solidified my career choice—I was going to become an assessment psychologist. At that time, I had also become interested in clinical research and during that summer began a study of personality similarities and differences between Black and Caucasian Americans with two of my co-students, Brenda Ball and Eva Ray, the latter an African American. This article (Butcher, Ball, & Ray, 1964) was my first professional publication, and I think it was the event that engaged me in Minnesota Multiphasic Personality Inventory (MMPI) research, an activity that I have been unable to avoid throughout the remainder of my professional career. My son, Janus Dale, was born during my first year of graduate school; he is named after my two army buddies who were killed in the Korean War, Janus Krumins and Dale Moss (who is pictured with me on Outpost Yoke in early 1953). Jay went on to become both a sports medicine physician and a colonel in the U.S. Air Force.

I completed my PhD in clinical psychology, having worked with both George Welsh and my academic advisor W. Grant Dahlstrom, both of whom were instrumental in reinforcing my budding interest in the Minnesota Multiphasic Personality Inventory. Not only did these two MMPI icons provide me with substantial encouragement during the remainder of my graduate school days, but they also influenced my job choice—teaching and researching at the University of Minnesota from which they both came.

During my last year in graduate school I had the opportunity to pay back a major gift that had been given to me by the folks at West Virginia State College, who had allowed me to start college in the first place with such a weak high school record. I accepted a part-time teaching job as a visiting faculty member at North Carolina College, an African American school in Durham. I taught two classes during the year (filling in for a professor who was on disability), on one occasion having to make my way past a KKK rally that was going on near campus. The 1960s were racially troubled times, but my experience while teaching at NCC was a rewarding one.

UNIVERSITY OF MINNESOTA

Upon completion of my doctorate, I had several job offers. One very tempting offer came from Harvard University where I was recruited to teach experimental psychology to clinical psychology students. However, the Clinical Psychology Program at the University of Minnesota appealed to me more because of the more "clinical nature" of the program, and I thought it might provide me with a good home to follow up on personality assessment research. Most of the faculty I met during the job visit were engaged in clinical work as well as research. My duties at Minnesota involved serving as assistant director of clinical training in a program that had over 120 active graduate students and teaching the two-quarter course on the Rorschach. It usually comes as a surprise to people to learn of this first teaching assignment, which I did for a year. I was, however, able to make the switch to the MMPI course the next year—an activity that I felt more attuned to do.

I became friends with many leaders in psychology at the time, such as Kenneth McCorquodale, Robert Wirt, and Starke Hathaway, and had the opportunity to work closely with new, fellow faculty members, Auke Tellegen, Irving Gottesman, and Tom Bouchard (each with different views and research interests than my own), who had a great deal of influence on my thinking at the time. Some colleagues who joined the department after my arrival, such as Phil Kendall, with whom I collaborated on several projects, were also influential in my assessment work. After a few years at Minnesota, I developed a graduate seminar in cross-cultural study of personality that I taught for the remainder of my career. On several occasions, I had two co-teachers in the course, June Tapp from the Institute of Child Development and Joe Westermeyer from psychiatry, both of whom brought unique and differing perspectives to the course. Our youngest son, Neal, was born shortly after my arrival in Minnesota.

Doctoral Advising at Minnesota

One of the greatest assets of the University of Minnesota Psychology Department has been its abundant supply of outstanding doctoral students that I have had the privilege to advise (48 PhDs in all). My own research program has been both stimulated and broadened substantially by the contributions of the many graduate students that I have worked with as academic advisor—to mention only a few, Yossef Ben Porath, Lee Anna Clark, Paul Clavelle, Kyunghee Han, Mary Koss, Jeeyoung Lim, Nathan Weed, and Steve Rouse. There were other Minnesota students who were interested in the MMPI, such as Paul Arbisi, Moshe Almagor, Steve Finn, and Alan Harkness, that I also had the privilege of working with, though not in the capacity of academic advising (see photo for the Minnesota contingent at the 37th Annual MMPI Symposium held in 2002). In many cases, these collaborative relationships continued well beyond their graduate school days.

In 1979, after having been divorced for five years, I married Carolyn Williams, a clinical psychologist trained at the University of Georgia, who was introduced to me by my colleague Bob Carson and his wife Tracey. Our daughter, Holly, was born in 1983. Early in life Holly became a seasoned traveler—accompanying us to the MMPI workshops Carolyn and I were doing around the globe. (See Figure 4.)

MMPI and Workshops

When I moved to the University of Minnesota from the hotbed of MMPI research in the sixties at North Carolina, I was all set to participate in further MMPI work with the two historical figures in this area, namely Starke Hathaway and Paul Meehl. I arrived only to find the MMPI research at Minnesota to be somewhat sparse. I was disappointed to learn that Hathaway had moved on to psychotherapy research and typically denied having any expertise on the MMPI test. Hathaway categorically refused to become involved in teaching people about the test. Meehl had likewise moved on to other venues. Shortly after I entered the department, I received several boxes of MMPI-related reprints—a gift from Paul, who thought that I needed the basic library more than he did at the time. Since both Hathaway and Meehl had taken up other research, who was I going to talk to about the MMPI?

During my first year at Minnesota, I decided that an open forum on the MMPI was needed, a national conference that was devoted to new research and development on the instrument. With the support of Fred Berger from the Department of Conferences, we conducted the first symposium on Recent Developments in the Use of the MMPI in 1966. Following this meeting, I received a great deal of encouragement from others to make the symposium an annual event. It brought in a plethora of MMPI researchers from all over the United States, including Jack Graham, Raymond Fowler, Ned Megargee, Roger Greene, and Dave Nichols. It was apparent from the beginning of the symposium that there was both a great need and a great interest in MMPI research. It also soon became apparent that there was an even greater need for practical training in interpretation of the instrument—so the next time around we began to offer practical workshops for practitioners to get basic or continuing training in interpreting the test. The foundation of these workshops included a commitment to presenting up-to-date research and clinical interpretive strategies to a broad audience of psychologists. This need for information about the MMPI was so strong that the workshops grew substantially. Following the revision of the MMPI in 1989 (Butcher, 2000b), training was provided to over 1200 people a year—thanks to the great contributions of Jack Graham, Yossi Ben-Porath and Carolyn Williams.

The MMPI workshops gave me a great opportunity to collaborate with many outstanding scholars from other areas of expertise and from other parts of the world. It was interesting to explore MMPI and MMPI-2 usage with other assessment techniques such as the Rorschach with John Exner, Irving Weiner, and Phil Erdberg, through lively workshops aimed at combining the use of the two instruments, and with Jay Ziskin and Ken Pope on using the MMPI/MMPI-2 in forensic evaluations.

The MMPI symposium and workshops went international in 1970 with a meeting in Mexico that brought together psychologists and psychiatrists from many other countries, who were interested in the test. One of the keynote speakers at this meeting was Starke Hathaway who gave much of his talk in Spanish. Hathaway had made annual treks to Mexico and promoted strong Latin American relationships during his career. (For an overview of

Hathaway's career and contributions to the field of personality assessment, see the biographical account published in the Pioneers of Psychology Series [Butcher, 2000c].

After this first meeting, it seemed that there was a steady flow of interested MMPI researchers from other countries who wanted to advance clinical practice and research in their country by co-developing MMPI meetings (e.g., Hedwig Sloore in Belgium, Haruyo Hama in Japan, Fanny Cheung in China, Moshe Almagor in Israel, Ellen Berah in Australia, Jan Derksen in Holland, and Saulo Sirigatti in Italy, to mention only a few). In 1972, during the second International MMPI meeting in Mexico City, I met Italian psychiatrist-psychologist Paolo Pancheri from the University of Rome, who was an inexhaustible researcher with strong clinical interests. Paolo was very active in conducting MMPI research in Rome. We developed a working relationship centered on exploring the cross-cultural application of the MMPI that culminated in the publication of our international MMPI handbook (Butcher & Pancheri, 1972). Paolo's approach to clinical problems and data-oriented practice were highly influential in my international work for the remainder of my career.

In most cases, interested international professionals initiated these meetings, and our conference series provided the training. The International Conference on Personality Assessment was founded to provide personality assessment training and a venue for the discussion of relevant research in other countries roughly every two years—17 international symposia have now been offered, the last of which was in The Netherlands in June 2002 under the co-sponsorship of the University of Nijmegen and the Free University of Brussels.[2] The MMPI workshops have been exported broadly and have been held in over 25 countries.

It is not too difficult for me to determine the initial motivation for my international research and teaching over the past 30 years—the night I spent on Jane Russell Hill in 1952 with the Korean lad, trying to understand the meaning of culture and life were clearly at the base of it.

Revision of the MMPI

One of the most challenging professional tasks that I encountered in my career was the revision of the MMPI, in large part because the test was so widely used and valued in the field of psychology. The first person with

---

[2]The Free University of Brussels, Belgium, awarded me an honorary doctorate in 1990 for my international contributions to the field of personality assessment.

whom I discussed the need for a revision of the MMPI was George Welsh in 1968 when he visited Minnesota to present at the annual MMPI. In Welsh's view, the MMPI was cumbersome and could be streamlined by using factor analytically derived scales in lieu of the original MMPI empirical scales. Although this approach was not ultimately an integral part of the revision strategy, Welch's encouragement to pursue a revision of the test was clearly instrumental in the next steps toward revision.

In 1969, I began a more active effort to bring attention to the need for revising the MMPI. At the next annual MMPI Symposium we devoted the entire program to the single topic, "Should the MMPI be revised, and if so, how should this proceed?" In a paper he presented at this symposium, Hathaway (in one of his last professional contributions on the MMPI) sounded an affirmative note about revising the test while lamenting the lack of progress in objective personality scale development: "Where have we gone wrong? The mystery of missing progress" (Hathaway, 1972). Hence, Grant Dahlstrom and I discussed the need for revision and made suggestions for how this might come about; Warren Norman and Jane Loevinger (both solid methodologists in the personality assessment field) discussed methodological issues and problems with the MMPI; Paul Meehl provided personal reflections about the MMPI and suggested problems that a revision would face; and finally, David Campbell presented cautions about test revision based on his experiences with revising the Strong Vocational Interest Blank. At this symposium, the methodological problems with the MMPI were duly noted, but the potential problems with revising a major psychological test weighed heavily on the conclusions. The presentations included in this symposium were later published in a book (Butcher, 1972). Although the problems with the original MMPI were clearly noted in this symposium and the follow-up book, the time was still not ripe for mounting a revision of the instrument. The MMPI test publisher at the time, the Psychological Corporation, and the copyright holder, the University of Minnesota Press, were not open to supporting a test revision, maintaining the general view of "Why change something that is so widely used and works so well?"

Several years later, we published a follow-up article (Butcher & Owen, 1978) calling more explicitly for a revision of the test and laying out a suggestion for a revision that would retain the essential ingredients of the original instrument yet allow for modernizing it and removing some of the idiosyncrasies that hampered test use.

The passage of time often provides a needed impetus for change. The MMPI leadership at the University Press changed hands in the 1980s, and the new editorial staff was more amenable to modernizing the test. Beverly

Kaemmer, the new MMPI editor, was very open to the need for a test revision and appointed the MMPI Revision Committee in the early 1980s (including myself, Grant Dahlstrom, and Jack Graham) to undertake the task. National Computer Systems willingly provided the necessary test scoring and processing needed for the analyses. Toward the end of the project, Auke Tellegen came on board to provide his substantial expertise in the mammoth task of analyzing the extensive normative and clinical data that had accumulated for several years (Butcher, 2000b).

Because of the need to preserve the strengths of the original instrument along with modernizing it, the early revision phase involved considerable consultation with experts in the field. When the revision got underway, I met with Starke Hathaway (then retired) on several occasions to keep him apprised of the project (often during the times that my son, Jay, worked for him cutting grass and trimming his many trees). Extensive data collection, both normative and clinical, was required to substantiate the ultimate changes made in the revision. The MMPI-2 was not completed until 1989, and the adolescent version of the test (MMPI-A) in 1992—more than 20 years after the 1969 symposium had explored the need for a revision!

Editing

Throughout my professional career, I have enjoyed the opportunity of working in an editorial capacity with numerous scholars in the personality assessment area, developing collaborative works on personality assessment. The first of these edited volumes, *Recent Developments in the Use of the MMPI* (Butcher, 1969), involved the publication of several papers from the annual MMPI symposium that had brought attention to numerous research developments and extensive applications of the test. While many of these edited volumes were devoted to MMPI topics, several were aimed at the broader assessment field, such as the 10-volume series *Advances in Personality Assessment* with co-editor Charles Spielberger (and Lawrence Erlbaum Press) and the comprehensive volume *Clinical Personality Assessment* with Oxford University Press (Butcher, 1995, 2002).

When I was invited by APA to edit the newly minted *Journal of Psychological Assessment*, I welcomed the opportunity. The six years that I served in this capacity were some of the most interesting times of my career. I took on the weighty task of editing a major psychology journal, in part, because I had been well indoctrinated into what is required in this role by Sol Garfield and Alan Kazdin, under whom I had served as consulting editor and associate editor. My editorial work was made easier with the appointment of three associate editors (Steve Haynes, Jack Graham, and Linda Nelson) who assumed responsibility for a number of the manuscripts.

COMPUTER-BASED PERSONALITY ASSESSMENT

My interest in computer modeling of psychological processes and the use of computers in interpreting psychological tests emerged when I was in graduate school in the 1960s when I took a basic course in computer programming. Main frame computers were all that were available at the time. However, computer data processing and computer-based test interpretation were beginning to develop even with the cumbersome hardware of the time. During that time, I explored an idea for a doctoral dissertation—to simulate schizophrenic thinking via computer. Fortunately, I discarded this topic as somewhat impractical in favor of a more doable project involving the study of manifest aggression using the MMPI. In the early 1960s, I also followed with interest the pioneering work of John Pearson and Wendell Swenson at Mayo Clinic in their efforts to develop a workable MMPI interpretation program by computer (Rome et al., 1961). I also learned a great deal from Ray Fowler who developed the first narrative-based MMPI computer interpretation program for Roche Laboratories (Fowler, 1985).

My interest in computer interpretations was reawakened in the early 1980s by my colleagues David Weiss and David Vale, who encouraged me to develop an MMPI-based interpretation program. This program was developed over several years and was published as the Minnesota Report. Work in the computer assessment field has been a major component of my professional life over the past two decades (Butcher, Perry, & Atlis, 2000).

CLOSING

I have often been asked, "How did you wind up as an academic psychologist with such a difficult beginning and with considerable discontinuity in your life?" I have to acknowledge that it took several years at Minnesota for me to gain a feeling of belonging and acceptance as an academic. However, after I became a psychologist and had the opportunity to work on a professional level for a few years, I began to accept the idea that academia was where I belonged. As I have reflected on this transition, I have come to the view that there were two main driving forces in this homecoming for me: The first involved the emergence of a strong, occupying professional interest—for me this was a long-term commitment to the field of personality assessment. The second source of strength that allowed me to attain my goals in the field was the fact that I was befriended by so many outstanding people who helped me along the way. Even though my pathway to the field of personality assessment was neither direct nor trouble free, the final destination has been an enormously rewarding one.

ACKNOWLEDGMENTS

I would like to express my great appreciation to Dr. Carolyn Williams, Holly Butcher, Dr. Jay Butcher, and Sherry Butcher for all their support and encouragement. I would also like to express my appreciation to my brother, the Rev. Jerry Butcher, PhD, for commenting on an earlier version of this article.

Comments and requests for reprints should be addressed to James N. Butcher, PhD, Department of Psychology, University of Minnesota, 75 East River Road, Minneapolis, MN 55455. e-mail: butch001@tc.umn.edu

REFERENCES

Butcher, J. N. (1999). From softball field to the gates of Hell. *The Buffalo Bugle, 9*, 24.

Butcher, J. N. (2000a). Return of morning calm. *Stars & Stripes, 59*, 44–45.

Butcher, J. N. (2000b). Revising psychological tests: Lessons learned from the revision of the MMPI. *Psychological Assessment, 12*(3), 263–271.

Butcher, J. N. (2000c). Starke Rosecrans Hathaway: Biography of an empiricist. In G. Kimble & M. Wertheimer (Eds.), *Portraits of pioneers in psychology,* Vol.4. Washington, DC: American Psychological Association.

Butcher, J. N. (2001). A fateful ambush patrol. *The Buffalo Bugle, 10*, 20–21.

Butcher, J. N. (2002). Assessing pilots with "the wrong stuff:" A call for research on emotional health factors in commercial aviators. *International Journal of Selection and Assessment.*

Butcher, J. N., Ball, B., & Ray, E. (1964). Effects of socio-economic level of MMPI difference in Negro-White college students. *Journal of Counseling Psychology, 11*, 83–87.

Butcher, J. N., & Dunn, L. (1989). Human responses and treatment needs in airline disasters. In R. Gist & B. Lubin (Eds.), *Psychosocial aspects of disaster* (pp. 86–119). New York: John Wiley.

Butcher, J. N., & Owen, P. (1978). Survey of personality inventories: Recent research developments and contemporary issues. In B. Wolman (Ed.), *Handbook of clinical diagnosis* (pp. 475–546). New York: Plenum.

Butcher, J. N., & Pancheri, P. (1976). *Handbook of cross-national MMPI research.* Minneapolis: University of Minnesota Press.

Butcher, J. N., Perry, J. N., & Atlis, M. (2000). Validity and utility of computer-based test interpretation. *Psychological Assessment, 12*, 6–18.

Fowler, R. D. (1985). Landmarks in computer-assisted psychological assessment. *Journal of Consulting and Clinical Psychology, 53,* 748–759.

Gonsalves, J. E. (2001). *Battle at the 38th parallel.* Central Point, OR: Hellgate.

Hathaway, S. R. (1972). Where have we gone wrong? The mystery of missing progress. In J. N. Butcher (Ed.), *Objective personality assessment: Changing perspectives* (pp. 21–44). New York: Academic.

Marshall, S. L. A. (1956). *Pork Chop Hill.* Nashville, TN: Battery.

SELECTED BIBLIOGRAPHY

Books

Butcher, J. N. (1990). *The MMPI-2 in psychological treatment.* New York: Oxford University Press.

Butcher, J. N. (1996). *International adaptations of the MMPI-2: Research and clinical applications.* Minneapolis: University of Minnesota Press.

Butcher, J. N. (Ed.). (1997). *Personality assessment in managed care: Using the MMPI-2 in treatment planning.* New York: Oxford University Press.

Butcher, J. N. (1998). *The Butcher Treatment Planning Inventory: Manual.* Toronto: MultiHealth Systems.

Butcher, J. N. (Ed). (2000). *Basic sources for the MMPI-2.* Minneapolis: University of Minnesota Press.

Butcher, J. N. (Ed.). (2002). *Clinical personality assessment* (2nd ed.). New York: Oxford University Press.

Butcher, J. N. (2004). *MMPI-2: A beginner's guide* (2nd ed.). Washington, DC: The American Psychological Association.

Butcher, J. N., Mineka, S., & Hooley, J. (2004). *Abnormal psychology and modern life* (12th ed.). New York: Allyn & Bacon.

Butcher, J. N., & Williams, C. L. (2000). *Essentials of the MMPI-2 and MMPI-A clinical interpretation.* (2nd ed.). Minneapolis: University of Minnesota Press.

Keller, L. S., & Butcher, J. N. (1991). *Assessment of chronic pain patients with the MMPI-2.* Minneapolis: University of Minnesota Press.

Kendall, P., Butcher, J. N., & Holmbeck, G. (Eds). (1999). *Handbook of research methods in clinical psychology* (2nd ed.). New York: John Wiley.

Pope, K. S., Butcher, J. N., & Seelen, J. (2000). *The MMPI/MMPI-2/MMPI-A in Court* (2nd ed.). Washington, DC: American Psychological Association.

Book Chapters

Butcher, J. N. (1991). Screening for psychopathology: Industrial applications of the Minnesota Multiphasic Personality Inventory (MMPI-2). In J. Jones, B. D. Steffey, & D. Bray (Eds.), *Applying psychology in business: The manager's handbook.* Boston: Lexington.

Butcher, J. N. (1995). Personality patterns of personal injury litigants: The role of computer-based MMPI-2 evaluations. In Y. S. Ben-Porath, J. R. Graham, G. C. N. Hall, R. D. Hirschman, & M. S. Zaragoza (Eds.), *Forensic applications of the MMPI-2*. Thousand Oaks, CA: Sage.

Butcher, J. N. (1996). Understanding abnormal behavior across cultures: The use of objective personality methods. In J. N. Butcher (Ed.), *International adaptations of the MMPI-2* (pp. 3–25). Minneapolis: University of Minnesota Press.

Butcher, J. N. (1999). Research design in objective personality assessment. In P. Kendall, J. N. Butcher, & G. Holmbeck (Eds.), *Handbook of research methods in clinical psychology* (2nd ed., pp. 155–182). New York: John Wiley.

Butcher, J. N. (2002). Assessment in forensic practice: An objective approach. In B. Van Dorsten (Ed.), *Forensic psychology: From classroom to courtroom* (pp. 65–82). New York: Kluwer Academic /Plenum.

Butcher, J. N. (2002). Computer-based psychological assessment. In J. R. Graham & J. Naglieri (Eds.), *Comprehensive handbook of psychology: Assessment psychology* (Vol. 10, pp. 141–164). New York: John Wiley.

Butcher, J. N., & Dunn, L. (1989). Human responses and treatment needs in airline disasters. In R. Gist & B. Lubin (Eds.), *Psychosocial aspects of disaster*. New York: John Wiley.

Butcher, J. N., & Han, K. (1995). Development of an MMPI-2 scale to assess the presentation of self in a superlative manner: The S Scale. In J. N. Butcher & C. D. Spielberger (Eds.), *Advances in personality assessment* (Vol. 10, pp. 25–50). Hillsdale, NJ: Lawrence Erlbaum Associates.

Butcher, J. N., & Miller, K. (1999). Personality assessment in personal injury litigation. In A. Hess & I. B. Weiner (Eds.), *Handbook of forensic psychology* (2nd ed., pp. 104–126). New York: John Wiley.

Butcher, J. N., Rouse, S. V., & Perry, J. N. (2000). Empirical description of psychopathology in therapy clients: Correlates of MMPI-2 scales. In J. N. Butcher (Ed.), *Basic sources of MMPI-2* (pp. 487–500). Minneapolis: University of Minnesota Press.

Hjemboe, S., Butcher, J. N., & Almagor, M. (1992). Empirical assessment of marital distress: The Marital Distress Scale (MDS) for the MMPI-2. In C. D. Spielberger & J. N. Butcher (Eds.), (1995). *Advances in personality assessment: Vol. 9* (pp. 141–152). Hillsdale, NJ: Lawrence Erlbaum Associates.

Journal Articles

Butcher, J. N. (1994). Psychological assessment of airline pilot applicants with the MMPI-2. *Journal of Personality Assessment, 62,* 31–44.

Butcher, J. N. (2000). Dynamics of personality test responses: The empiricist's manifesto revisited. *Journal of Clinical Psychology, 56*(3), 375–386.

Butcher, J. N. (2000). Revising psychological tests: Lessons learned from the revision of the MMPI. *Psychological Assessment, 12*(3), 263–271.

Butcher, J. N. (2002). Assessing pilots with "the wrong stuff:" A call for research on emotional health factors in commercial aviators. *International Journal of Selection and Assessment, 10*(1), 1–17.

Butcher, J. N., Arbisi, P. A., Atlis, M., & McNulty, J. (2003). The construct validity of the Lees-Haley Fake Bad Scale (FBS): Does this scale measure malingering and feigned emotional distress? *Archives of Clinical Neuropsychiatry, 473–485.*

Butcher, J. N., Ball, B., & Ray, E. (1964). Effects of socio-economic level of MMPI difference in Negro-White college students. *Journal of Counseling Psychology, 11*, 83–87.

Butcher, J. N., Cheung, F. M., & Lim, J. (2003). Use of the MMPI-2 with Asian populations. *Psychological Assessment, 15*, 248–256.

Butcher, J. N., Rouse, S. V., & Perry, J. (1998). Assessing resistance to psychological treatment. *Measurement and Evaluation in Counseling and Development, 31*, 95–108.

Butcher, J. N., & Ryan, M. (1974). Personality stability and adjustment to an extreme environment. *Journal of Applied Psychology, 59*, 107–109.

Jim Butcher (in highchair) and sister Joan Butcher (in rain barrel), c. 1934

Dale Moss (left) and Jim Butcher (right) on Outpost Yoke in South Korea, April 1953

Minnesota Contingent at the 37th Annual MMPI-2 Symposium. Front row, from left: Steve Finn, Kyunghee Han, James Butcher, and Carolyn Williams. Back row, from left: Al Harkness, Nathan Weed, Paul Arbisi, and Yossi Ben-Porath

Jim Butcher and Holly at an MMPI meeting in Seattle 1987

Lecturing on the MMPI in Tehran, Iran (with Reza Zamani), in 1975

CHAPTER 4

A Report on Myself

The Science and/or Art of Assessment

Richard H. Dana
Portland State University

> We create ourselves out of the stories we tell about our lives, stories that
> impose purpose and meaning on experiences that often seem random
> and discontinuous. As we scrutinize our own past in the effort to explain
> ourselves to ourselves, we discover—or invent—consistent motivations,
> characteristics patterns, fundamental values, a sense of self. Fashioned out
> of memories, our stories become our identities.
>
> —D. G. Faust (2003)

I acknowledge with gratitude this opportunity to provide a public memoir in
the form of a professional autobiography. To have a perspective on one's own
acts at the moment they occur is seldom feasible and their reconstruction
afterwards is ordinarily infeasible as well. Professionals, such as artists, poets,
or biographers, are typically employed to provide an external assessment
of one's life. However, as psychologists we are external observers without a
chronoscope to augment the accuracy of our observations, and so we inadvertently contribute some eisegesis, or "interpretation of a text . . . by reading
into it one's own ideas" (Merriam-Webster, 2003). Generations of my own
students learned to discover and understand statements betraying their own
eisegesis in their psychological reports.

Although this self-assessment inevitably contains my own eisegesis, it also
employs a method designed to augment reliability in high inference clinical
assessment described elsewhere (Dana, 1966a, b; Dana, 1982, pp. 59–66;
Dana, Bolton, & West, 1983). Four levels serve to reduce the magnitude

of the gap between descriptive data and the interpretive inferences contained in reports. Level I data bits are found in events, persons/relationships, and products in the sections relevant to my childhood and education, professional beginnings (1953–1969), years in Arkansas (1969–1988), and my retirement (1989–2005). In Level II, my traits (adjectives/concepts) are abstracted and summarized from these data. Level III provides a report on myself as a professional psychologist interrelating the Level II contents in a version of understanding that is an idiosyncratic embodiment of the human "science" method. Although a Level IV diagnostic statement is omitted, a peroration completes the structured format of this autobiographical report.

I begin with the premise that what we do by way of vocation is inseparable from who we are. Our extrusion into vocations and avocations are predicated on private and often unacknowledged values and motives impacted by events, encounters, or relationships with other persons as intimates, mentors, colleagues, students, and friends who share the fabric of our lives. In retrospect, for example, I recall acting unwisely in public discourse by caricaturing and oversimplifying the personal origins of research and clinical enterprises conducted by anonymous faculty colleagues and myself (Dana, 1960). While requiring no less audacity, the present venue is a vehicle more suited for an exercise in personality reconstruction and the presentation of an assessment report.

LEVEL I: MY CHILDHOOD/EDUCATION

My father, Richard Henry Dana (1875–1954), was a scion of an Episcopalian Mayflower family whose namesake uncle authored *Two Years Before the Mast* (1840). Raised to be a country gentleman, my father eschewed a Harvard education in favor of managing the Toronto branch of the family import-export business for 16 years and became the best amateur athlete of his generation. He introduced tackle football in Canada, played ice hockey with the original Maple Leafs before they became a professional team, held the national cricket championship for numbers of runs for many years, and played golf and tennis with Don Budge and other professionals. He was also an accomplished naturalist/woodsman who recognized every bird by flight pattern or song, every animal by its tracks, and identified every plant and tree. While we had little time together, he taught me to fly fish for trout, to identify snipe and ducks from a blind with decoys, and to love nature and be comfortable in the outdoors. He was also a connoisseur of good living with extraverted social skills and professional-level aptitudes in identifying Oriental rugs, French wine, and creating detailed drawings of sailing ships from memory. World War I obliterated the family business and during the Depression he struggled without success, away from home, as a social worker, dahlia grower, and manufacturer of steel screening. He was a profoundly gentle, sensitive, loving, and honorable man who entered the twentieth century ill equipped to thrive economically.

Meeting on the boat crossing the Atlantic as adolescents prior to 1900, my mother's parents were of nominally Jewish origins from Eastern European countries. English was the only language spoken in their home. Educated in Newburg, New York Catholic schools, my mother went from the *Newburg Daily News* to her own column in *The Herald Tribune*, actively participated as a founder of the New York Newspaper Women's Society, and after my birth, turned to publicity and college fund-raising. Her avowed atheism and passage into a gentile world of facile accomplishment distanced her from her two brothers and their families. Her admonition to me was to deny her family origins, a burden that was onerous for me, increasingly infeasible over time, and leading to a feeling of loss for that part of my heritage she withheld from me. Immediately after moving from New Jersey to Arkansas in her eighties due to failing eyesight, she went with me to a birthday party for Dr. Benjamin Spock, the noted pediatrician, where I discovered they were old friends who had shared participation in peace marches for many years. She quickly became a leader in the local Unitarian Fellowship, penned literally scores of letters to the editor that were published in Arkansas newspapers presenting political and social views that were controversial and responded to with vigor. She finally moved into a retirement home where her awesome social talent, visible and rampant with increasing years, precluded censure and maximized enthusiastic and joyous responses from others to her needs, wishes, and whims. She moved through life assertively for 95 years, breaking gender role boundaries, flouting social conventions in youth, and participating in social activism with SANE, a national peace organization dedicated to a sane nuclear policy. I always respected the immensity of her strength, the intensity and single-mindedness of her actions, convictions, passion, and autonomy. We did not know each other when she was a distracted and unavailable mother who firmly believed the teachings of John B. Watson. Nonetheless, during her final years in Arkansas, it was my privilege to get to know her and to realize that she had always struggled to be a responsible, loving, and competent mother.

I was named after my father's uncle, Richard Henry Dana, III, and over time I dispensed with the "III" and ultimately with the "Henry." As an only child, I was raised and nourished from infancy by three loving and diverse women from Jamaica, Poland, and Ohio, who presented me with different faces of devotion, strength, and integrity. At six, I lied about my age in order to sell 100 newspapers daily, ostensibly to help support my mother, but actually to gain her attention. I worked at every opportunity as a baby sitter and yard boy, and caught "special order" fish for St. Armand's Key housewives and cooks during a winter in Florida while I was avoiding surgery for a sinus condition. In Florida, my mother divorced my father for "desertion" while he and I sat in the car outside the courthouse waiting to return home where we remained for several months. I remember this winter because of the memorable times I shared with my father who never interfered with my prosaic use of bait for bottom feeders like grouper while he caught pompano and weakfish for our table, using artificial lures. I also remember doing so well on a standardized reading test that I was taken out of my regular fifth grade class and "punished" by having to fight each day at noon all fifth and sixth grade boys. No one was physically hurt by this diurnal activity, although the following summer at the junior naval academy in New London, Connecticut—among other traumas—I was put in the ring with a 16-year-old who managed to knock me out after two hours of pummeling, thereby terminating any interest I might have in boxing.

I recapitulated these family dynamics in TAT (Thematic Apperception Test) stories I wrote prior to beginning graduate assessment courses as an undergraduate. These stories were included with those of other college students from my undergraduate thesis as interpretive examples in my 1982 book *A Human Science Model for Personality Assessment with Projective Techniques*. Incidentally, my undergraduate thesis resulted in my election as an associate member of the society of Sigma XI. During the summer following my graduation in 1949 from Princeton University, I interpreted these TAT stories as part of a research assistantship (Dana, 1949). For example, the story for Card 19 reads:

> The great bat, symbol of the night wind, is winging along in the oncoming dusk. Inside the house, floating on a sea of foam, are three people. The youngster, a child of three, is reciting Swinburne to an old man sitting with his head in his hands near a curtained window. Across the room is a woman, much younger than the man, who is making faces in a long, green-framed mirror hanging from the ceiling. She walks back and forth. The child croons, "Here where the world is quiet. . . ." The old man looks up furtively and groans. The woman walks faster now. The child is shouting, "Nor sleep of things diurnal. . . ." Suddenly the great bat compresses, swoops through the window, knocking the woman into the mirror, shattering it, picks up the child by his left leg, and drags him across the floor. The old man jumps up shouting, "For thine is the Kingdom," a maniacal glare in his eye. The woman has a glass halo, and the boy, as he is carried through the window, intones the last line, "In an eternal sleep. . . ." (Dana, 1982, pp. 403–404)

My Early Education

A couple of early events had implications for my later education. First, as soon as I was able to read and until I entered Princeton at 15, I faithfully consumed a book each day and wrote poetry that I submitted for occasional publication. Following military service when I was 18, these poems received a book publication offer, which I summarily rejected, with naïve virtue, because I already knew I was to become a psychologist. Second, because I was a behavior problem in a Bronxville (New York) kindergarten, I was not promoted to first grade. We had moved to the Bronx for an impoverished year when my mother was unemployed, and then to Orange and West Orange. So I entered first grade when I was eight and skipped from second to fifth grade and had two years of high school, first at Westtown, a Pennsylvania Quaker school, and then at Scott High School when we lived in Bloomfield and East Orange, New Jersey. While I was in high school, my mother remarried a widowed, gentile who was a suburban health officer. Unable to accept the fact that one of my closest friends was Black, his tirades alleged I was destroying his professional reputation! Therefore, I welcomed the pressure from my high school teachers to strive for early graduation, a fortuitous expediency because I probably would not have gone to college otherwise, although I certainly would have left home as I did once (with permission) to hitchhike to a fanciful destination—Mexico City—returning after discovering Iowa!

My Undergraduate Years

As a self-supporting Princeton scholarship student, I immediately chose courses in the humanities, including literature and languages, with majors in French and Spanish (excluding the mandatory thesis) prior to entering military service during my sophomore year. Although my earlier educational experiences had neither prepared me for serious academics nor fostered any sense that I might be reasonably intelligent, I believed I had a bona fide creative flair. I wrote poetry and took notes simultaneously during college lectures, a habit I continued in graduate school, though substituting research designs for poems! To this day, even a stimulating lecture finds me receptive both to the external input and to my own scribbling.

My college was interrupted for 13 months of service at the end of World War II, working in New Jersey army reception centers as a clerk (Ft. Hancock, Ft. Monmouth, Ft. Dix). Having stewardship for a paper company while at Ft. Dix, I had a jeep and was able to travel back and forth to Princeton regularly. Upon my return to college in 1947, I saw a notice on a bulletin board describing a summer student group being sponsored in Washington, D.C., by the Congress of Racial Equality (CORE) and sponsored the Quaker Fellowship of Reconciliation (FOR). During that summer, under the charismatic tutelage of Bayard Rustin, our nonviolent sit-downs in segregated restaurants led to violent consequences coupled with limited successes. But I learned something of what it meant to live with oppression in a Black community. As student leader in this summer group, I relished the activism and as a public speaker became less of a reticent, unresponsive, knowledge-absorbing sponge. The most salient outcome of this experience, however, was my determination, on returning to college, to find safe haven for my political/social ideals by becoming a psychologist. Unfortunately, another outcome that my own immaturity precluded was any real confrontation with my own White privilege and the subsequent failure of my choice of profession to provide a milieu for exploring the substantive lessons of this opportunity for responsible identity development. Although I have not viewed my becoming a psychologist as a "mistake" in the sense of regret, I believe it did foreclose on a unique early opportunity to become more aware of my own human obligations.

Subsequently, during the 1970s, a number of my White undergraduate students from Arkansas also participated in a Washington demonstration accompanied by sufficient police brutality to necessitate their seeking sanctuary within the Black community. On my 60-acre mountain top in Arkansas, I gave shelter to those few students who returned to heal from trauma, an outcome contrasting to my own earlier experience with the police in DC, and similar in acceptance by the local Black community.

Discovering psychology in my junior year at Princeton permitted me to write one of the required papers for that year entitled "The Use of 'Race' as a Psychological Bulwark for Anti-Semitism." I did not receive the usual rave review perhaps due to the unresolved identity schism portrayed in the following Card 16 TAT story:

> This is a child standing in a ray of sunshine in front of a house. The child has long blond hair, red cheeks, and a twisted smile, In his hands he holds a vase of flowers. He has come from over the hill in the background, down the path into the shaft of sunlight by the open door. The child remembers with the mind of an old man. He is playing the game called "Conformity" and he is very old inside. He is alone with the wisdom that loneliness has incorporated into his life, the beauty of the flower, and the form of the vase. These are his own and he holds them gently in his hands. The flower came from a field where many were growing, open to the sun. He will also grow but not as the flower, straight and tall, budded and blossoming. He

will grow in his mind and devour the beauty that is his for creating, exact-ing the precious essence of the flower and the vase. He holds them gently, tenaciously: they are his only for a minute, he must return them. Nothing remains but the scent in his nostrils, the picture in his mind. They will always be his, and on every breeze the odor of a rose will come to him, and in every object of man he will see beauty. This is the lonely way, the child's way. It will also be the way of the man. (Dana, 1949)

Undergraduate psychology at that time was not memorable except for courses in social psychology. However, I was permitted to take graduate courses in the Rorschach and the Thematic Apperception Test (TAT). Silvan Tomkins was my thesis advisor, mentor, model, advocate, progenitor, and lifetime intellectual companion. His course consisted of one four-hour meet-ing a week during which he employed his interpretive method to describe 12 of 20 single-paragraph TAT stories, a feat beyond my wildest delusions of a competence then and now. Our assignment was to complete the analysis, and I produced a report of more than 70 pages; his comment was that no other student had faithfully applied his interpretive approach (Tomkins, 1947). Twenty-six years later, on behalf of the Social Psychology Association, having had no contact with Tomkins during this interval, I presented him with the Bruno Klopfer Distinguished Contribution Award. His first words were that the most significant part of that ceremony was the fact of my presence to bestow the award on him. There can be no comparable professional moment for me.

My experience in Joseph Zubin's Rorschach course exemplified an equivalent sensitization to the potential descriptive contents of Rorschach re-sponses measured by over 100 scales, although this information was indeed difficult for me to organize into a personality description! Fortunately, a grad-uate student assistant named Phelan taught Beck scoring and interpretation and after graduate school I learned Klopfer scoring and eventually integrated both systems (Dana, 1982).

Graduate School: University of Illinois
These assessment courses served me well in graduate school at the University of Illinois, especially during my 39 hours per week of VA internship training because Leon Pennington deferred supervising my diagnostic efforts in order to share with me his therapy with psychopaths. Since these patients were able to con me immediately, he used his power and expertise to break down their defenses, release anxiety, and then remanded them to me for treatment

as neurotics. My on-campus clinical training consisted of two courses during three semesters. The course in intelligence testing required 150 reports without benefit of feedback. Following this course, while participating in a WAIS subtest standardization effort, I was the solitary team member sufficiently comfortable with Blacks in their homes. This example suggests widespread administration bias or, at least, sampling irregularities. Rex Collier taught two semesters of psychotherapy, using careful and informed work of his own interventions with war veterans suffering from "battle fatigue." Otherwise, although ostensibly in a clinical program, I was exposed primarily to learning theory by Bob Grice and Art Irion and experimental psychology by Charles Osgood. Although approximately 250 students were admitted to the program, only John Stern and I received degrees in four years, not because we were necessarily the best students but because we were fortunate enough to eschew faculty prima donnas engaged in internecine warfare, with disastrous consequences for their students in preliminary examinations. My graduate academic training resulted in sufficient respect for methodology and statistics, and a fascination with research design so that I attended graduate statistics courses each decade thereafter and worked collaboratively with bona fide statisticians, particularly Art Thomas, Dennis Bonge and Brian Bolton.

My VA clinical internship training, except for Pennington's protective aegis, consisted of psychotherapy practice based on Dollard and Miller (1950). In a five-minute weekly psychiatric supervision session I was asked the same question, "Have you done anything pre-oedipal this week with your psychotherapy patients?" Bewildered, my reiterated, ignorant, and unrepentant response was uniformly negative. Ultimately, I completed my internship in Fresno where I received genuine supervision of assessment reports and group therapy.

As a largely self-taught clinician, believing equally in practice using behavioral and humanistic interventions, I received the Diplomate in Clinical Psychology (ABPP) in 1960. Ed Shneidman observed my assessment proceedings and examined the written report—a delightful and supportive experience. Later, as an unorthodox, and unconventional private practitioner in Nevada, I employed out-of-office physical interventions to prevent suicides. Still later, during a Portland State University reception, Walt Klopfer and I were the only therapists willing to acknowledge such unorthodox suicide prevention behaviors. Walt and I shared many rewarding professional experiences over the years, including a number of symposia. As editor of the *Journal of Personality Assessment* (*JPA*) he tolerated some fatuous and inadvertent nonsense and wrote a genuinely appreciative review of my projective assessment book (Klopfer, 1982), omitting the on-target critique provided by Al Rabin (1983). As Walt's onetime doctoral student, my wife Joan Dayger Behn, describes him as a teacher and mentor similar to myself—high praise indeed to be compared with someone we both admired and sorely miss.

An education is preparation for life, for doing something worthy to pass on to others, and has a symbolic and literal meaning as well as a palpable cohesion that can be identified and understood. In this instance, I was venturing into the professional world having analyzed my own TAT stories, not once but twice (Dana, 1949, 1982). Since predictive validity is a credible TAT research finding, relevant data to support this notion appear in the following Card 17BM TAT story:

> The man is an ex GI who remained in Gigulippithia, India, to work with a fakir. Together they are holding a large crowd spellbound with their chicanery. The young man supplies the brains, the old fakir provides the atmosphere of magic. Theirs is a trick older than custom or civilized dream. It is the trick of mind over mind, the mass hypnosis that the young man and the wizened fakir playing his reed have perfected. The young man will climb on up the rope, never realizing that it is he who has been duped by a law far older than that of suggestion. He will climb until he is a black speck, retreating up the slim rope into the blinding sunlight, and then disappear into the solitary clouds drifting over the unhappy land. (Dana, 1982)

PROFESSIONAL BEGINNINGS (1953–1969)

It is important to begin my depiction of this era with my first post-graduate summer preoccupation—writing science fiction short stories and an incomplete sci-fi novel about the first space station. I soon realized that even if I sold every word I wrote I could not survive on considerably less than either of the two initial academic offers I spurned to accept a VA position in Denver. However, this position was terminated almost immediately by a reduction in force (RIF) because funding for the position was only temporary to support staff promotions. This fortuitous slight-of-hand permitted me to meet Lewis Bernstein, an embodiment of the scientist-professional functioning with equal probity and competence as both a researcher and clinician. We formed a close relationship that immediately yielded careful assessment research and ultimately led me to a psychology departmental chairmanship at Marquette University and medical school teaching appointment. A book on interviewing, in several editions, was an outcome of our collaborative training of these medical students (Bernstein & Dana, 1970).

Between the brief month with the VA in Denver in 1953 and teaching at the medical school at Marquette (1967–1969) were years of mobility and turbulence initiated by two brief research positions, one spurious (in Winona, Minnesota) and one genuinely productive (at St. Louis State Hospital). In Minnesota, eager to initiate a research-oriented community service for chronic clients, I soon learned that the "research" had already been completed remotely without benefit or contamination by local data. In St. Louis, where I was responsible for Abel Ossorio's grant-funded research program and supervision of master's level psychologists, I experienced some of the virtues and difficulties of conducting research in a community setting and began working with the MMPI (Dana, 1956).

From 1956 to 1969, five universities (University of Wisconsin-Milwaukee, University of Nevada, West Virginia University, University of South Florida, and the University of Wyoming) provided students who did awesome and socially responsible professional activities and filled my publication larder with the essential ingredients for a bifurcated professional self—as researcher and teacher.

These remarkable students were Buell Goocher, Phil Comer, John Condry, Rodger Hornby, and Rod Cocking. After acceptance to law school, Buell took my undergraduate abnormal psychology course and remained to share research with me before attending graduate school. As lifetime Director of Edgefield Lodge in Portland, Goocher enacted a successful behavioral intervention model with very disturbed children. During one sabbatical, we tried unsuccessfully to write a book about his well functioning, socially responsible agency, predicated on a behavioral model incorporating individual differences and funded on the basis of positive intervention outcomes. Phil Comer's West Virginia MMPI feedback dissertation provided the model for what is now called therapeutic assessment. His course-in-oneself provided an additional assessment model for generations of his own students. With my students, I subsequently created a dozen similar manuals for a variety of courses-in-oneself which were helpful, I believe, to the students and participating community persons, although criticized by colleagues as a waste of time. John Condry was not a clinical student, but he occasionally sat in on my clinical course and outperformed all students on the final exam, an act of effortless competence. He and I planned a series of careful research studies and theoretical presentations that catapulted him from West Virginia to UCLA and ultimately to Cornell where he mentored Rod Cocking who experienced a similar leap from Wyoming to Cornell. Rod worked with me on the methodologically sophisticated Lens Model, construct validation, and assessment studies while doing a thesis documenting an Arapaho cultural ritual. Ultimately, his cross-cultural interests impacted NIMH and Smithsonian research priorities.

Rodger Hornby came to my attention as an undergraduate leader of mentally handicapped boy scouts in Laramie. He worked with these boys all of his life, keeping them out of institutions, and helping them lead responsible and productive lives. Rodger impacted my life as my student, friend, and colleague. From 1965 to 1993 he guided the multicultural professional and personal experiences that shaped my eventual retirement commitment to research and practice with cultural issues as proximal variables. I have acknowledged Rodger's professional contributions in detail elsewhere (Dana, 1987, p. 13). I have written poems describing Buell, John, and Rodger; all of these former students enriched my personal life as friends, and have shared and informed my research as colleagues.

The published products of these years were not only numerous but cluster neatly into diverse research studies and a more covert humanistic-existential literature in obscure journals, presaging what was to become a human science assessment model in 1982. In addition to assessment studies and review of instruments, my additional publication topics included psychological report contents as predictors of counseling outcomes with juvenile delinquents, egregious abuses of power in residential treatment, evaluation of community agencies, and training in clinical psychology. The "covert" side during these years described clinical psychology training, anxiety, psychopathology, and psychotherapy, leading ultimately to a description of personal growth (Dana, 1978a).

Another apparently adventitious constellation of events, from 1962 to 1965 concerned the Seven Squares Test, developed in South Africa as a new "projective intelligence" measure. As a prelude to marketing in the United States, after many local publications, this instrument was sent to a test publisher and forwarded to me for commentary. Subjects were asked to arrange these squares on a sheet of white paper; White subjects created representative patterns while Black subjects, coerced into compliance, did as little as possible. Reviewing this research with Walt Voigt, using Underwood's five description-explanation levels, we concluded that substitution of causal naming for phenomenon naming was not only sheer fantasy serving apartheid but poor science as well. I have regretted other published professional debates, but the measure was not published in the United States and the major researchers subsequently lost their positions at the University of Witwaterstrand!

Each extreme of my then false dichotomy was recognized and rewarded in personally meaningful and memorable ways independently by Rollo May and David McClelland. Rollo May provided momentum as a personal reaction for making his 1959 APA symposium participants wait while my Clinical Skills Revisited symposium with Paul Meehl and other notables concluded. The following paragraph from my graduate education paper appeared in May's book *Existential Psychology* (1961):

> I suspect that the common, salient outcome of our previous four or five (or six) graduate years was caution—not breadth or depth of scholarship or ability to generalize—but mere caution. A kind of trained adherence to limited inferences from data collected under rigorous conditions of control. Caution is indeed necessary in diagnostic testing or treating other persons but caution alone is stifling for either individuals or professions. . . . We possess the methodological sophistication; we lack the grand concepts and may be diminishing our professional potential for generation of theory by exclusive preoccupation with science. To be sure, we must be scientists but we also must be *sapient* humans, first. (p. 37)

Many years later at a party, Rollo May admitted gleefully that he had inserted this quote in his book to brand me with a deserved identity that I did not recognize at the time.

David McClelland's generous presence in my life began as the Van Nostrand Series editor responsible for my first book (Dana, 1966a). This book chronicled the emergence of a low inference science of clinical psychology, and the Spanish edition was used in Argentina until the 1990s. Dr. McClelland later invited me to consider a Harvard position. With eisegesis research in hand, I jousted with Harvard faculty and students concerning my methodology and have never I experienced a more stimulating reaction to a presentation! Lacking the social skills for their position and knowing that a five-year appointment precluded permanency at Harvard, I returned happily to Morgantown, West Virginia. My first generations as a psychologist heralded a clear margin of victory for the conventional clinical scientist, although behind my professional persona was a poet and an advocate of an alternative human science.

I recall with delight the West Virginia graduate student refrain, "If you can't publish in an American journal, try Darshana!" Indeed, my first Darshana paper, "Psychology: Art or Science?" (Dana, 1961) presaged a continuing extrusion of this theme into my professional acts and publications. This student refrain was coupled with a prominently displayed percentage chart of citations of my own papers in my published articles. Their creative labels for increasing percentages were prominently displayed for my benefit. These labels were more accurate than I acknowledged at the time.

MY YEARS IN ARKANSAS (1969–1988)

Leaving Marquette while activists occupied the Student Union Building, I was recruited to the University of Arkansas, thanks to Jack Marr, on the basis of my research contents rather than on numbers of publications. Fayetteville was then a sleepy town awakening to student activism. I immediately marched with my Arkansas students through jeering crowds, and afterwards, the campus bristled with guns while students, like hunters after a frightened squirrel, circled a high tree containing a lone student peace advocate.

There were four distinct strands to my Arkansas sojourn: (a) my association with Ted May, health psychology, and professional training; (b) Society for Personality Assessment (SPA); (c) human science; and (d) cross-cultural research and practice: with Aaron Antonovsky and Rodger Hornby. Ted May was colleague, mentor, and my closest friend. From 1969 to 1994, we shared internship training and research that resulted in my excursion into health psychology assessment (Dana, 1984a; Dana, & Hoffmann, 1987), and our joint appraisal (Dana & May, 1986). Examining internship training permitted us, as authors (Dana & May, 1987) to review the history of professional psychology and, as editors, to reprint relevant articles. We surveyed the adequacy of academic training as preparation for internship (Dana, Gilliam, & Dana, 1976) which led to case studies, using time logs and Barker's stream of behavior methodology, to evaluate academic programs producing outstanding interns (Dana, 1978b) as well as internship programs (Dana & Brookings, 1987). For many years, working together to establish a professional psychology school in Memphis, Ted May and I developed program, secured a tentative site, and collaborated with local groups, but ultimately were unable to foster a viable outcome. My time as Arkansas clinical training director was part of this relationship; Ted's Memphis internship program became the model for my expectations and evaluations of other internship sites for my Arkansas students.

The SPA has always been the primary anchor for my professional activity while the JPA has been the home for the largest numbers of my assessment papers and reviews, including the Bruno Klopfer Award presentation (Dana, 1984b). During this time, Phil Erdberg's trips to Tulsa, bearing gifts of San Francisco sourdough bread, and his experience with the joint feedback technique (Dana, Erdberg, & Walsh, 1978) were instrumental in the development of my own assessment service delivery model for feedback of psychological assessment findings (Dana, 1982, 1985a). One memorable assessment symposium (Dana, 1996) included as a discussant, former Arkansas student Gary Grant, whose trifurcated identity embodies multicultural competence as therapist and high inference assessor using the Kahn Test of Symbol Arrangement. Following the symposium and throughout the remainder of the meeting, practitioners and students clustered around Gary, resonating to his manifest humanity and avidly consuming his wisdom.

These strands evidence a narrowing of the earlier schism represented by my diverse publications and provided the first genuine support from students and colleagues for the human science approach in my initial assessment book (Dana, 1982), which after a 17-year delay in completion was published too late for a high-inference approach to be credible for training in most programs. Jeff Brookings, an experimental student, who did a construct validity dissertation on alienation (Brookings, Dana, & Bolton, 1981), was the only student to my knowledge ever to read all of my covert publications. Shirley Leech, who understood existential psychology much better than I, was persuaded over time that existential assessment was not simply a misnomer (Dana & Leech, 1974). Later, an undergraduate, Kathy Ronan, taught a course in the human science model (Ronan & Dana, 1981). These students acknowledged that my advocacy of a human science had merit and thereby nurtured my professional identity aspirations in ways I continue to appreciate.

The beginnings of my cross-cultural/multicultural interests were a by-product of a trip to Israel for other purposes (Dana, 1985b). I journeyed to Beersheba to visit Aaron Antonovsky, the sociologist responsible for emphasizing health status, who was employing a salutogenesis model to contrast with pathogenesis. This model was depicted using generalized resistance psychosocial resources, including cultural stability that provided meaningful and coherent life experiences shaping the sense of coherence measured by his derivative instrument. Dr. Antonovsky examined our paper (Dana, Hoffmann, Armstrong, & Wilson, 1985) and provided a careful lesson in cross-cultural assessment. Years later, a former student as editor of *Contemporary Psychology* graciously permitted me to review Antonovsky's final book (Dana, 1989, p. 40).

During these Arkansas years, I regularly drove 738 miles to the Rosebud Reservation and Sinte Gleska College in South Dakota to learn research and assessment practice with Native Americans from Rodger Hornby (1993). Tom Hoffmann, an Arkansas student, shared this research with us (Dana, Hornby, & Hoffmann, 1984; Hoffmann, Dana, & Bolton, 1985). Rick Whatley followed Tom and also completed MMPI research with African Americans that still retains critical relevance (Dana & Whatley, 1991; Whatley, Allen, & Dana, 2003).

I came to Arkansas following a diagnosis of pancreatic cancer, later proven by surgery to be inaccurate, but which was responsible for these lines in my poem "An Arkansas Traveller," which I wrote on the flight south:

> . . . I look down on the endless surface of my days:
> short hops from sand mountains to green cities,
> from idiot child to changeling man.
> Bottle-fed, uptight, semi-student scanning
> the ignorant earth for his own spoor
> while circumstance erodes the dry ravines.
> Impersonal tracker, comparing signs,
> processing the past for human relics
> of presence and belief, for caring and tomorrow.
> I have not made this trip before. . . .

I may have stayed too long in Arkansas because of a house. As a freshman undergrad, I spent a summer in Madison doing an apprenticeship with poet Karl Shapiro and sojourning at Taliesen East (the summer counterpart to Frank Lloyd Wright's winter studio in Scottsdale, Arizona) while examining the architect's lifework to crystallize a poetic portrait of his accomplishment in "The Magic Violin of Frank Lloyd Wright." Disparate lines from my poem ("as etch intent upon a hill" and "stone foundation for the living dream") foreshadowed the features of my own Arkansas house. This home on 60 isolated mountainside acres was vintage, rural, quintessential Wright and was largely responsible for my 19-year tenure at the University of Arkansas. Written when I was leaving Arkansas in 1988, my poem "Moving Day" contains lines reminiscent of the Card 17BM 1949 TAT story: "A fakir put into the sky a rope climbed by a fictive boy. And people with their feet on earth saw him retreat beyond the clouds."

RETIREMENT (1989–2003)

The transition from Fayetteville, Arkansas, to Portland, Oregon, is a complex story. Disappointment concerning the anticipated Memphis professional school was followed by my inability to recruit space for a psychology department health assessment lab. After applying for six jobs, I discovered ageism but managed a short tenure as professional school dean before writing part of the 1991 grant at the Regional Research Institute for Human Services (RRI), in Portland State University that formalized and supported my retirement preoccupation with cultural issues.

These years introduced me to new students, new courses, new colleagues, and new friends. These years also served to blend and consolidate the disparate strands of my professional history and identity. With an abiding focus on culture, my perception of the meaning, responsibility, and obligation for assessment as human science and intervention has clarified and deepened. This section forgoes detailed descriptions of my products in favor of exposing and acknowledging the human associations I have had following my "retirement."

Teaching has always been the impetus for my professional growth in the form of shared learning, relationships, research, and practice. Formal and informal teaching as retiree, adjunct, guest, volunteer, consultant, and dissertation committee member/chair is now less structured, more personal, and more focused than earlier in life. These different forms of teaching in diverse settings have encouraged me to develop a global focus, thanks to invitations from Argentina, Brazil, Portugal, and Spain, and have also led to contacts with multicultural students and faculty at the Fielding Institute, CSPP-San Diego, the University of Alaska, Fairbanks and Anchorage, the University of La Verne, and numerous workshops nationally and internationally.

At the University of Lisbon, Teresa Fagulha and Danilo Silva encouraged my teaching, sponsored and invited me to address a conference, permitted me to serve ex-officio on dissertation committees, and fostered my understanding of socially responsible assessment in Portugal (Fagulha & Dana, 1997). Eliana Herzberg, University of Sao Paulo, shared research processes with me, sponsored my teaching, invited presentations, and enabled me to talk with many of her colleagues concerning their socially relevant research.

Since 1992, Jim Allen has been responsible for my many workshop, conference, and teaching endeavors in South Dakota and Alaska, including a course in psychological assessment for consumers, as well as for sharing publications, symposia, and above all, his friendship. Stan Sue perceived inadequacies in my Multicultural Assessment-Intervention Process (MAIP) model (Dana, 1993), which led to revision, with assistance from Nancy Hansen, Jim Allen, and Mike Conner (Dana, 2000a), and eventual application in a public agency (Dana, Aragon, & Kramer, 2002). Giuseppe Costantino invited my participation in symposia on several continents, and we are preparing, with Bob Malgady, The Tell-Me-A-Story (TEMAS) assessment of children in multicultural societies book is in press with Lawrence Erlbaum. Giuseppe has contributed as colleague and friend to my empirical and clinical understanding of limitations in standard assessment instruments for cross-cultural applications.

The University of La Verne (ULV) enabled me to teach multicultural students standard and multicultural assessment in the same courses (Dana, Aguilar-Kitibutr, Diaz-Vivar, & Vetter, 2002). During these years I administered standard tests and moderators and provided feedback to dozens of multicultural students and cross-cultural student sojourners in the United States. I have immense gratitude for their forbearance and patience with these standard emic instruments, used as imposed etics, as well as with the limited plausibility of my interpretations.

CSPP-San Diego permitted me to offer a research methodology course to American Indian tribal leaders and healers. Following criticism of the imposed European-American research model, these students articulated their cultural-specific assumptions and ground rules for method. Although still an incomplete product, sharing and consensus resulted in an atmosphere of mutual understanding and respect not ordinarily apparent in a mainstream classroom. As a byproduct, Nancy Moon, of the Tlingit, completed a qualitative dissertation with me,, exploring the manifold strengths of Native students that enabled their survival in graduate school.

As an outcome of my ULV teaching, one of their faculty, Glenn Gamst, an erstwhile Arkansas experimental student, and I are collaborating on research using the MAIP model to embed culture in a community mental health center. Products of this research (e.g., an abbreviated multicultural counseling competence measure, the California Brief Multicultural Competence Scale (CBMCS) (Gamst et al., 2004) and a training manual (Dana, 2002b, 2003a), constructed to represent the CBMCS items, have been supported and endorsed by the California Department of Mental Health. In addition, associated published studies, current studies, and dissertation products will be incorporated into a planned issue of the *Journal of Community Psychology*. We have also been invited to submit a proposal for a text bridging research and mental health applications of this model in a multicultural society.

Finally, the opportunity for continuing my professional activities during retirement was afforded by Barbara Friesen, director of the research and training center at ULV, who fostered my Minority Cultural Initiative Project. This facilitation has been continued by RRI directors—Nancy Koroloff, William Feyerherm, and Arthur Emlen—across the years since 1991. I am no less indebted to Ron Talarico, assistant to the director, and to Denise Schmit and many others, for a thousand acts of facilitation and kindness. These RRI years have resulted in several books (Dana, 1993, 1998, 2000a) and a host of chapters and articles in which culture is treated as a proximal variable within a human science model (e.g., Dana, 2003b).

LEVEL II: TRAITS/CONCEPTS

Level II data presented in Table 1 come from the contents of the previous sections entitled childhood/education, professional beginnings, years in Arkansas, and retirement in this chapter. These data lack any reliability check and thus provide a token demonstration rather than a replicable product.

TABLE 1
Level II Data: Events, Persons, Relationships, and Products

Childhood/Education	Professional Beginnings	Years in Arkansas	Retirement
Mother: Jewish origin denied: ambitious, successful, dominant. Raised by other women to 12. Father: gentile, gentle, loving. Step-father: biog. Reading as childhood focus. College: Languages/ poetry. Military service then DC activism. Undergrad assessment training: Rorschach + TAT: Stories: family drama, identity conflict with achievement and competence not relevant to immediate conflict resolution.Graduate school: Research and clinical training separated. Survival lessons for academia. Mentors: Tomkins, Pennington. Cross-cultural interest: Native Americans/Chinese. Dichotomies: poet vs. psychologist gentile vs. Jew scientist vs. clinician.	Years of mobility after poor start. Student influences. Mentor impact as scientist-clinician. Equal roles as teacher, clinician, researcher. David McClelland/ Rollo May. Dichotomy: human science writings vs research products. 1966 book 7 Squares Test	After surgery: relocation/retreat. Ted May: focus on internship (1987 book), training (1987 paper), community. Assessment service delivery model. Self-assessment workshops. Rodger Hornby Books (1981, 1984). Personal growth paper (1978).	Portland: RRI International perspective: teaching, research, consultation. Learning/ cross-cultural psychology. Books (1993, 1998, 2000). MAIP model Human Science research with practical applications. Social responsibility. Personal and professional identity. Resolution of false dichotomies.

Note. RRI = Regional Research Institute for Human Services; MAIP = Multicultural Assessment-Intervention Process model.

LEVEL III: REPORT ON MYSELF

My major professional endeavor across the years has been as an assessor to understand other persons. My primary personal motivation for this vocation has been to understand myself, perhaps to come to terms with the three major dichotomies (gentile vs. Jew; poet vs. psychologist; clinician vs. scientist) structuring my childhood, and educational and professional years, symbolized by my TAT stories and many poems, and affecting my choice of mentors, and retrospectively visible in research products as well as in many obscure papers.

A secondary motivation has been a sense of responsibility, initially for myself, my mother, and other individuals, and later expressed as social obligation in teaching, program development and evaluation, concern for persons-in-community, and persons-in-distress served by health and mental health systems. My many covert existential-humanistic publications have described the human capacity for sharing the communication of social feeling and exercising foresight in professional contexts. Because responsibility is a byproduct of any relationship in which one person tells another about him/ herself, professional acts that embody these qualities are necessary to foster trust and facilitate accountability. Psychologists extrapolate these behaviors from the personal origins of their own lives for their professional transactions. Successful applications are dependent upon self-awareness, understanding, learning from experience, and a capacity for one's own growth.

Understanding persons requires an assessment science that acknowledges the inherent unsteadiness of human data as well as the selectivity of human observers, particularly in conventional scientific postures requiring detachment and manipulation as methodological imperatives. As a Boulder Model progeny, I was influenced too much and too little by Edwin Boring's histories lionizing Wundt, deprecating Brentano and Vico, and crystallizing the self-image of psychology as science, but not necessarily as a human science.

A human science is responsible to human beings, and coherent ethical practice requires parameters acknowledging respect, caring, compassion, and mutual obligations in the conduct of research, assessment, intervention, and professional training. Since one locus of our professional power lies in methodology and the exercise of power proceeds stepwise toward human consciousness, a human science focuses on appreciation of applications of power that are nutrient (concern for others) and integrative (abet others' power) (R. May, 1972). A human science permits combining the experimentalist and clinician resources of my person (see Dana, 1982, Chapter 2) representing "hard" and "soft" science (Kimble, 1984) and elucidated by John Conway (1992) as follows:

Though scientists and humanists may ignore one another and still each
contribute valuable knowledge about humans, it is foolhardy for one to
hack away at the roots of the other. The roots are too deep and too extensive to be severed. We will always have among us those who . . . know
something about the sciences and the humanities, who can trim the excesses
in the metaphysical values of both, and who can graft one root structure on
to the other. For such hybrid souls, we should be thankful. Our fundamental values are grounded, in part, in pre-reflective cognitive and personality
characteristics. (p. 18)

My human science ideology embraces existential-humanistic and be-
havioral-cognitive endeavors simultaneously, a not surprising outcome of my
training, and encourages utilization of low and high-inference personality
interpretation to make sense of professional assessment activities. Exclusive
reoccupation with either endeavor is a false dichotomy that is incomplete
and inadequate to provide description as well as explanation in the form of
understanding human personality. Either extreme is incapable of satisfactory
incorporation of the personal equation within a scientific focus. Nor can
either extreme contain the scientist/assessor /therapist and the participant/
client/consumer within an interactive relationship as mutually responsible
and respectful equals.

A human science of assessment is mandatory for cross-cultural understanding because European-American scientific values and methods cannot
be imposed on dissimilar cultures, although this conceit is still the hallmark
of exported tests/methods and interventions. Applications of our instruments
and interventions internationally need to be tailored by culture-specific normative data and research designed to demonstrate cultural equivalence not
only in translations but in constructs and methods as well (Dana, 2000b).
These applications should be accompanied by explicit recognition that ethical issues may transcend our European-American expectations for responsible assessment practices (Dana, 1994).

As a human science advocate, I am primarily a "local clinical scientist"
(Stricker & Trierweiler, 1995) applying a nomothetically based idiographically applicable configural model that employs an empirical data base implemented by conceptual configurative thinking, or immediate use of crystallized
intelligence followed by fluid intelligence. This process requires "movement
between and reflection on the normative and idiographic, the past and the
present, and the public and the private" (Stricker & Gold, 1999, p. 247), or
low and high-inference interpretation recommended for multicultural assessment (Dana, 2005).

A second prerequisite for a human science is that assessment must be coextensive with intervention, as in therapeutic assessment. In other words, assessment is a professional activity designed to implement individual and social responsibility for alleviation of human distress. Our science of personality assessment has to be connected empirically to processes and outcomes of subsequent interventions. The MAIP model attempts to combine awareness of the continuous impact of cultural issues upon how we use information/data to make decisions that facilitate understanding and moderation of human distress and to ultimately demonstrate socially relevant professional acts. This model includes but is not limited to medical model diagnostic utilities but encompasses problems-in-living, including the immediate and transgenerational consequences of oppression as well as the imbroglios of acculturation processes and outcomes. Public sector managed mental health care utilization of the MAIP model provides an increasingly responsible awareness that applications of empirical knowledge concerning individual and cultural differences can facilitate intervention outcomes (Dana, 2002a; Dana, Aragon, & Kramer, 2002).

I am outliving and circumnavigating my own personal TAT prophecy but have not succeeded in disappearing in any sense. In fact, I have remained faithful to my original bifurcated identities, although I now recognize that these onetime extremes are now interrelated, inseparable, and fused in my values as person and scientist. Although I have not succeeded in fusing the disparate familial origins of my cultural identity, described in the conflicted and unresolved story of Card 16, I have endeavored to reconcile the unresolved consequences of my poignant experiences of racism in Washington, D.C., the summer of 1947 by recognizing my White privilege, attempting to understand my identity development within the Helms (1990) model (Dana, 2005, chapter 5), and conspicuously incorporating awareness of oppression and White privilege into a multicultural training process (Dana, 2002b, 2003a). I have been fortunate to mold the convoluted clay of my early beginnings with some subjective artistry to shape a professional life history by including the persons and events relevant to the process of my teaching and learning with students and colleagues as well as through the tangible products described herein.

PERORATION

Whatever possessed me to write so many books, manuals, papers, assessments, and book reviews with generations of students and colleagues, along with a continuous outpouring of poems trying to understand poets (e.g., W. S. Merwin, John Berryman, Alan Dugan, T. S. Eliot), notables such as Frank Lloyd Wright and John Kennedy, as well as my students, friends, family members, and those I loved? What motivated me to interpret and reinterpret my own TAT stories, teach assessment to several hundred students, and create myriad psychological reports and receive feedback from so many recipients? This report on myself, although focused on professional contributions, has incorporated my sense of the personal historic landscape in which I have quested for identity embodied in a human science model and applied in multicultural training, research, and practice.

REFERENCES

Bernstein, L., & Dana, R. H. (1970). *Interviewing and the health professions.* New York: Appleton-Century-Crofts.

Brookings, J. B., Dana, R. H., & Bolton, B. (1981). Alienation: A multitrait-multimethod analysis. *Journal of Psychology, 109,* 59–64.

Conway, J. B. (1992). Presidential address. A world of differences among psychologists. *Canadian Psychology, 33*(3), 1–24.

Dana, R. H. (1949). *The case of A: A study in TAT analysis.* Princeton, NJ: Study of Education.

Dana, R. H. (1956). *An MMPI compendium.* St. Louis State Hospital Research Project.

Dana, R. H. (1959). American culture and Chinese personality. *Psychological Newsletter, 10,* 314–321.

Dana, R. H. (1960). *Psychologists' power, problems, and responsibility.* Psi Chi Annual Dinner address, University of Nevada.

Dana, R. H. (1961). Psychology: Art or science. *Darshana, 1*(4), 91–96.

Dana, R. H. (1966a). *Foundations of clinical psychology: Problems in personality and adjustment.* Princeton, NJ: Van Nostrand.

Dana, R. H. (1966b). Eisegesis and assessment. *Journal of Projective Techniques and Personality Assessment, 30,* 215–222.

Dana, R. H. (1978a). Personal growth and societal function. *Journal of Thought, 13*(2),117–124.

Dana, R. H. (1978b). Comparisons of competence training in two successful clinical programs. *Psychological Reports, 42,* 919–926.

Dana, R. H. (1982). *A human science model for personality assessment with projective techniques.* Springfield, IL: C. C. Thomas.

Dana, R. H. (1984a). Assessment for health psychology. *Clinical Psychology Review, 4,* 459–476.

Dana, R. H. (1984b). Megatrends in personality assessment: Toward a human science psychology. *Journal of Personality Assessment, 48,* 562–590.

Dana, R. H. (1985a). A service-delivery paradigm for personality assessment. *Journal of Personality Assessment, 49,* 598–604.

Dana, R. H. (1985b). Israel: A culture in conflict. *Grapevine, 17*(1), 1, 15.

Dana, R. H. (1987). Training for professional psychology: Science, practice, and identity. *Professional Psychology: Research and Practice, 18,* 9–16.

Dana, R. H. (1989). Coping with the poetry of social existence. (Review.) A. Antonovsky, Unraveling the mystery of health: How people manage stress and stay well. *Contemporary Psychology, 34,* 39–41.

Dana, R. H. (1993). *Multicultural assessment perspectives for professional psychology.* Boston: Allyn & Bacon.

Dana, R. H. (1994). Testing and assessment ethics for all persons: Beginning and agenda. *Professional Psychology: Research and Practice, 25,* 349–354.

Dana, R. H. (1996, March). *Culturally competent assessment of visible racial/ethnic groups in the United States: 1996.* Symposium conducted at the midwinter meeting of the Society for Personality Assessment, Denver, CO.

Dana, R. H. (1998). *Understanding cultural identity in intervention and assessment.* Thousand Oaks, CA: Sage.

Dana, R. H. (2000a). *Handbook of cross-cultural and multicultural personality assessment.* Mahwah, NJ: Lawrence Erlbaum.

Dana, R. H. (2000b). Culture and methodology in personality assessment. In I. Cuellar & F. Paniagua (Eds.), *Handbook of multicultural mental health: Assessment and treatment of diverse groups* (pp. 97–120). San Diego, CA: Academic.

Dana, R. H. (2002a, July). The development of cultural competence in California public sector mental health services. In S. Lurie (Chair), *International innovations in community mental health I.* Symposium conducted at the 14th International Congress of Law and Mental Health, Amsterdam, The Netherlands.

Dana, R. H. (2002b). *Manual for multicultural competence training: Preliminary version.* Unpublished manuscript.

Dana, R. H. (2003a). *Manual for multicultural competence training: Revised version.* Unpublished manuscript.

Dana, R. H. (2003b). Assessment training, practice, and research in the new millennium: Challenges and opportunities for professional psychology. *Ethical Human Sciences and Services, 5*(2).

Dana, R. H. (2005). *Multicultural assessment: Principles, applications, and examples.* Mahwah, NJ: Lawrence Erlbaum.

Dana, R. H., Jr. (1840). *Two years before the mast. A personal narrative of life at sea.* New York: Harper's.

Dana, R. H., Aguilar-Kitibutr, A., Diaz-Vivar, N., & Vetter, H. (2002). A teaching method for multicultural assessment: Psychological report contents and cultural competence. *Journal of Personality Assessment, 79,* 207–215.

Dana, R. H., Aragon, M., & Kramer, T. (2002). Public sector mental health services for multicultural populations: Bridging the gap from research to clinical practice.

In M. N. Smyth (Ed.), *Health Care in Transition* (Vol. 1, pp. 1–13). Hauppauge, NY: Nova Science.

Dana, R. H., Bolton, B., & West, V. (1983). Validation of eisegesis concepts in assessment reports using the 16PF: A training method with examples. *Third International 16PF Conference Proceedings* (pp. 20–29). Champaign, IL: Institute for Personality and Ability Testing.

Dana, R. H., & Brookings, J. B. (1987). Program evaluation: An evolving methodology. In R. H. Dana & W. T. May (Eds.), *Internship training in professional psychology* (pp. 436–442). New York: Hemisphere.

Dana, R. H., Erdberg, W. P., & Walsh, P. J. (1978). *The joint-feedback technique: A new model for the integration of assessment findings into the treatment process.* Workshop conducted at the midwinter meeting of the Society for Personality Assessment, Tampa, FL.

Dana, R. H., Gilliam, M., & Dana, J. (1976). Adequacy of academic-clinical preparation for internship. *Professional Psychology, 7,* 112–116.

Dana, R. H., & Hoffmann, T. A. (1987). Health assessment domains: Credibility and legitimization. *Clinical Psychology Review, 7,* 539–555.

Dana, R. H., Hoffmann, T., Armstrong, & Wilson, J. (1985, April). *Sense of Coherence: examination of the construct.* Paper presented at the meeting of the Southwestern Psychological Association.

Dana, R. H., & Leech, S. (1974). Existential assessment. *Journal of Personality Assessment, 38,* 428–435.

Dana, R. H., & May, W. T. (1986). Health care megatrends and health psychology. *Professional Psychology: Research and Practice, 17,* 251–256.

Dana, R. H., & May, W. T. (Eds.). (1987). *Internship training in professional psychology.* New York: Hemisphere.

Dana, R. H., & Whatley, P. R. (1991). When does a difference make a difference? MMPI scores and African Americans. *Journal of Clinical Psychology, 47,* 400–406.

Dollard, J., & Miller, N. E. (1950). *Personality and psychotherapy.* New York: McGraw-Hill.

Faghula, T., & Dana, R. H. (1997). Professional psychology in Portugal. *Psychological Reports, 81,* 1211–1222.

Faust, D. G. (2003). Living history: A schoolgirl's letter to "Mr. Eisenhower" illuminates a childhood in the segregated South. *Harvard Magazine, 105* (5), 39–46, 82–83.

Gamst, G., Dana, R. H., Der-Karebetian, A., Aragon, M., Arellano, L., Morrow, G., & Martensen, L. (2004). Cultural competence revised: The California Brief Multicultural Competence Scale. *Measurement and Evaluation in Counseling and Development, 37,* 165–188.

Helms, J. E. (1990). *Black and White racial identity: Theory, research, and practice.* Westport, CT: Praeger.

Hoffman, T., Dana, R. H., & Bolton, B. (1985). Measured acculturation and MMPI-168 performance of Native Americans. *Journal of Cross-Cultural Psychology, 16,* 243–256.

Hornby, R. (1993). Competency training for human service providers. Rosebud, SD: Sinte Gleska University Press.

Kimble, G. A. (1984). Psychology's two cultures. *American Psychologist, 39,* 833–839.

Klopfer, W. (1982). (Review.) A human science model for personality assessment with projective techniques. *Journal of Personality Assessment, 46,* 658–659.

May, R. (1961). *Existential psychology.* New York: Random House.

May, R. (1972). *Power and innocence.* New York: Norton.

Merriam-Webster's Collegiate Dictionary (11th ed.) (2003). Springfield, MA: Merriam-Webster.

Rabin, A. I. (1983). Humanistic assessment. (Review.) *A human science model for personality assessment with projective techniques. Contemporary Psychology, 28,* 629–630.

Ronan, K. A., & Dana, R. H. (1981, April). *A college course in the human science approach to psychology.* Paper presented at the meeting of the Southeastern Psychological Association, Houston, TX.

Stricker, G., & Gold, J. R. (1999). The Rorschach: Toward a nomothetically based, idiographically applicable configural model. *Psychological Assessment, 11,* 240–250.

Stricker, G., & Trierweiler, S. J. (1995). The local clinical scientist: A bridge between science and practice. *American Psychologist, 50,* 995–1002.

Tomkins, S. S. (1947). *The Thematic Apperception Test.* New York: Grune & Stratton.

Whatley, P. R., Allen, J., & Dana, R. H. (2003). Ethnic differences on the MMPI: Relation of African American racial identity to MMPI scores. *Cultural Diversity and Ethnic Minority Psychology, 9,* 344–352.

SELECTED BIBLIOGRAPHY

Dana, R. H. (1966). *Foundations of clinical psychology: Problems in personality and adjustment.* Princeton, NJ: Van Nostrand.

Dana, R. H. (1968). Six constructs to define Rorschach M. *Journal of Projective Techniques and Personality Assessment, 32,* 204–214.

Dana, R. H. (1982). *A human science model for personality assessment with projective techniques.* Springfield, IL: C. C. Thomas.

Dana, R. H. (1984). Megatrends in personality assessment: Toward a human science model. *Journal of Personality Assessment, 48,* 562–590.

Dana, R. H. (1987). Training for professional psychology: Science, practice, and identity. *Professional Psychology: Research and Practice, 18,* 9–16.

Dana, R. H. (1993). *Multicultural assessment perspectives for professional psychology.* Boston: Allyn & Bacon.

Dana, R. H. (1997). Multicultural assessment and cultural identity: An assessment-intervention model. *World Psychology, 3*(1–2), 121–142.

Dana, R. H. (1998). *Understanding cultural identity in intervention and assessment.* Thousand Oaks, CA: Sage.

Dana, R. H. (1998). Projective assessment of Latinos in the United States: Current realities, problems, and prospects. *Cultural Diversity and Mental Health, 4*(3), 165–184.

Dana, R. H. (1999). Cross-cultural and multicultural use of the Thematic Apperception Test. In M. L. Geiser & M. I. Stein (Eds.), *Evocative images: The Thematic Apperception Test and the art of projection* (pp. 177–190). Washington, DC: American Psychological Association.

Dana, R. H. (2000). Culture and methodology in personality assessment. In I. Cuellar & F. Paniagua (Eds)., *Handbook of multicultural mental health: Assessment and treatment of diverse groups* (pp. 97–120). San Diego, CA: Academic.

Dana, R. H. (2000). The cultural self as locus for assessment and intervention in American Indians/Alaska Natives. *Journal of Multicultural Counseling and Development, 28,* 66–82.

Dana, R. H. (2000). Multicultural assessment of child and adolescent personality and psychopathology. In A. J. Comunian & U. P. Gielen (Eds.), *Human development in international perspective* (pp. 233–258). Lengerich, Germany: Pabst Science.

Dana, R. H. (2002). Examining the usefulness of DSM-IV. In K. Kurasaki, S. Okazaki, & S. Sue (Eds.), *Asian American mental health: Assessment, theories, and methods* (pp. 29–46). New York: Kluwer Academic/Plenum.

Dana, R. H. (2002). Mental health services for African Americans: A cultural/racial perspective. *Cultural Diversity and Ethnic Minority Psychology, 9,* 3–18.

Dana, R. H. (2005). Assessment training, practice, and research in the new millennium: Challenges and opportunities for professional psychology. *Ethical Human Sciences and Services, 5*(2), 127–140.

Dana, R. H. (in press). *Multicultural assessment: Principles, applications, and examples.* Mahwah, NJ: Lawrence Erlbaum.

Gamst, G., Dana, R. H., Der-Karabetian, A., Aragon, M., Arellano, L., Morrow, G., & Martensen,L. (2004). Cultural competency revised: The California Brief Multicultural Competence Scale. *Measurement and Evaluation in Counseling and Development, 37,* 165–188.

Richard Dana, 3 years and 4 months old, with father

Mother, 1936

Richard Dana, left, with Nelson Jones and Molly Harrower, 1980

At the Society for Personality Assessment's 1984 midwinter meeting. Top row, from left: Charlie Spielberger, Richard Dana, Sid Blatt, and Tom Patterson. Bottom row, from left: Carl Zimet, George Stricker, Walter Klopfer, and Mary Cerney

CHAPTER 5

A Psychologist Grows in Brooklyn

Reflections from the Past

Leonard Handler
University of Tennessee

> Let down your tap root
> to the center of your soul
> suck up the sap
> from the infinite source
> of your unconscious
> and
> Be evergreen
> —D. W. Winnicott[1]

It is a well-known and frequently experienced phenomenon that time seems to pass more quickly as we get older. I must say that this observation is true for me since it seems like only yesterday that I graduated from Michigan State University (1964) with a PhD in clinical psychology. Suddenly, I find myself writing an autobiography. But as I continue in this process, thinking and feeling about important details in my life, I find that time also seems to be lengthening as I re-experience the events about which I write. I recently talked to Paul Lerner in Maine, who was also writing his autobiography for the *Journal of Personality Assessment*. He described the experience as a "second analysis," and I share his characterization of the experience as transformative.

---

[1]Schacht, L. (2001). Between the Capacity and the Necessity of Being Alone. In M. Bertolini, A.Giannakoulas, & M. Hernandez (Eds.), *Squiggles and spaces: Revisiting the work of D.W. Winnicott, Vol.1* (p.112). London: Whurr.

One thing I have learned from this exercise in introspection is that in many ways my life has not been consciously planned. I had little or no overall plan for my future and my life's work, even in college. Rather, I seem to have been guided by a less conscious, at least unverbalized and seemingly unreflective decision-making process. One reader of an earlier draft of this chapter said it "meanders (wonderfully) like the Tennessee river." Although I revised it to meander much less, I am pleased by the comment because it means I have been successful in describing my life as I have experienced it. I take great delight in that aspect of my life because I am quite happy about the path I've taken and the personal and professional choices I've "made" over these many years. As you will see, I made some major decisions about my life in a seemingly rapid and impulsive manner, with little conscious forethought. Therefore, I've had many rewarding experiences and wonderful surprises, such as the invitation to write about my life for *JPA*. Had anyone ever suggested to me that such an honor would befall me, I would certainly have thought they were insane, or at least completely wrong.

THE BEGINNING

I was born on September 6, 1936, to Fanie and Nathan Handler, both immigrants from Eastern Europe, arriving sometime in 1919 or 1920. My mother came from a small town that was originally part of the Austro-Hungarian Empire. A current map, however, shows the town as part of the Ukraine. Her large family came over in small groups, the older children first. They got jobs and earned enough money to bring the others over. My mother came when she was about 12 or 13, with her mother. The ship was very crowded and unsanitary; my mother contracted typhoid and temporarily lost all her hair.

My father came from a small town on the border between Poland and Russia. This border changed frequently, depending upon the outcome of battles that often took place. At the time he came to the United States, the Russians and the Poles were fighting again. They used young Jewish boys and men as cannon fodder, by putting them in the front line, to be shot at first. My father's older brother had been chosen to go to the front line, but his mother substituted my father for the older brother. Realizing it would mean certain death, my resourceful father, then only 15 or 16 years old, somehow obtained a false passport and slowly made his way to the coast, to board a ship for passage to America. He hid in dark, wet, and dirty basements during the day, traveling only under cover of darkness. He was frightened that he would be caught with the false passport he had and would have to return to his home town and face certain death.

Both my mother and father settled, separately, with other family members on the Lower East Side of Manhattan, in small, crowded ghetto-like apartments called "cold water flats" because they had no hot water. My mother had a fourth grade education and my father had no formal education at all. He knew how to speak a number of languages, but never did learn to read or write English. He also spoke with a very heavy accent, often hilariously fracturing the English language. My mother soon went to work in a factory in which girls and young women sewed beads on women's garments. My father became a restaurant worker, first a waiter and then a salad and sandwich man in various restaurants and cafeterias. They met by introduction and married about a year later. I have a sister, six years older than myself, who lives in New Jersey.

When I was growing up, we lived in a rather small three-room walk-up (no elevator) apartment in the Brownsville section of Brooklyn. In its day the apartment house, pretentiously called the Bernice Laura Court, was quite attractive, but by the time we moved in, Bernice Laura had long since become a faded beauty. Gone was the impressive canopy at the building's entrance, and there were only remnants of the very ornate carriage lamps that lit the entranceway of her huge lobby. Despite its decline and the lack of privacy we had, it was the only home I knew until I left for graduate school at Michigan State University (MSU).

In 1976 on our way to the airport for a trip to Europe, 16 years after I left New York, we took a detour to visit the old neighborhood. I was shocked by what I saw. The old neighborhood was gone; the streets were filled with rubble from houses that were torn down further down the block, and it looked as if the neighborhood had been bombed. A policeman with a large German shepherd guard dog in tow patrolled the street. The Bernice Laura Court was still standing, but no one lived there any longer. The windows were boarded up and much of the building had been burned out.

MY CHILDHOOD

Very shortly after I was born, my mother developed blood clots throughout her body and became quite ill. She had to remain in bed, with little active movement, for about six months. My aunt Clara, who later became "Claire," in order to become Americanized, moved in with us and took excellent care of me. I have some very early memories from about age two or earlier, when I made a special effort to climb out of my crib to join the adults, who sounded as if they were having fun. Another very early memory from about the same time was of my mother putting me next to my ailing grandmother, in her bed, so she could hug and kiss me. Many years later I learned that she died soon thereafter, so that memory is a very important one for me because it is the only one I have of her.

I remember my grandfather, who had a long white beard and walked very erectly, with a keen sense of pride. He spoke almost no English, and communicated mostly with my mother, who was then to give me instructions on how I should conduct myself and what I should study. In some old European cultures, the head of the household did not speak directly to the children until they were much older, but his wishes were communicated directly to the children by the mother. I became quite proficient in Yiddish, because that was the language with which my parents communicated when they did not want me to know what they were saying. Looking back, it is amusing for me to see the powerful effects of motivation; if my parents had spoken Hebrew so that I would not have understood what they were saying I might have done much better in Hebrew school!

We played many street games in the neighborhood, such as iron tag (you were safe if you were touching something made of metal), stickball, and Johnnie on a Pony, in which a boy would take a running jump and land on the back of another boy, who was bent over, his body parallel with the ground. Then another boy ran and jumped on *him*, and then another and another, until there were no boys left to run and jump, or the first boy collapsed under the weight of the pile of boys.

I remember many events, such as the day we entered the Second World War after the bombing of Pearl Harbor; war bond rallies, ration coupons, saving tin cans, paper and animal fat (used to make ammunition), and the huge celebrations on VE Day (Victory in Europe) and VJ Day (Victory over Japan). There was more confetti showering down than I have ever seen, before or since; music blaring in the streets; people shouting, hugging and kissing; and huge block parties in many neighborhoods. Lights were strung and tables were placed in one continuous line on the streets, and everyone brought out mounds of food and drink. I also remember five-cent subway rides; watching the New York Rangers play hockey in Madison Square Garden (for 50 cents); Saturday matinees at Radio City Music Hall, complete with the Rockettes (also 50 cents); and the local movie theater, the People's Cinema, where for 10 cents you could see three films, the news, two short features, a bunch of cartoons, and the coming attractions.

I was very active, and looking back, it seems that I was probably an AD/HD child. I was always doing two or three things at once and losing track of assignments, papers, keys, and such. My parents were often told by friends and family members to leave me at home when they came for a visit because I would touch and sometimes break household objects. I feel fortunate that there was no Ritalin available back then because I was forced to struggle in order to deal with the problem, with good albeit hard-won results. Becoming reflective and introspective was part of the personal work I did to deal with the hyperactivity, although the process was slow and unconsciously driven. Although I read quite early, my fine motor skills were poor, and I always got D's and F's in penmanship. My handwriting is still awful, as is my fine motor coordination.

EARLY INFLUENCES

My father's experience in escaping to America left him rather anxious and sometimes even frightened. He was always concerned with his health and was obsessed with cleanliness, a holdover from living in wet, dirty basements. Since he could not read or write and because he had come to America on a false passport, he did not become a citizen for many years. It was my frightening job each year to register him as an alien at the post office, as required by law. We were even more frightened during the McCarthy era, when being from Russia was a distinct disadvantage, socially and politically. I feared that he might get deported, and he worried as well. Eventually the federal government declared an amnesty for people who came to America in questionable ways; he memorized the necessary information to become a citizen, and we all rested more easily. My father was a very intelligent man, who had a keen interest in politics and history. Although I understood his demons because of his rather traumatic early life, I was always sad to see him struggle to support us when he was capable of so much more.

After some consideration many years ago, I came to the conclusion that I began my career choice of psychology by becoming a caretaker to my parents. I have already described how I registered my father as an alien. I tried to help him with his anxiety, but I was not successful. I also "took care" of my mother, whose health was sometimes fragile. I did many chores to lighten her burden; I was quite sensitive to her need for assistance and I felt it was my responsibility to do some of the hard work.

MY EARLY SCHOOL YEARS

I was an average to poor student in elementary school; my hyperactivity and inattention caused some minor discipline problems and I was frequently an indifferent student. I loved to read, however, and I spent much of my free time with my nose in a book. The first novel I ever read, in the third or fourth grade, was *A Tree Grows in Brooklyn* by Betty Smith (1943), from which this autobiography gets its title. As I now understand, reading about other people's lives was part of the development of the reflective process; I found myself reading biographies of famous people who struggled in their lives, such as George Washington Carver and Thomas Edison. Nevertheless, I did not like formal education. If anyone had ever suggested that I would become a teacher, I would never have believed their prophecy. But I remember clearly how my future began to change, and the story goes like this: I attended a new school in the seventh grade, a junior high school. The teacher, an irritable and quite stern older woman, seated me in the very back of the room, where I entertained myself by doing almost anything except listen to what she was saying. Fortunately for me, she did not return after the Christmas break. In her place there appeared a new, young and attractive blond teacher who found me in the back of the room and moved me to the very front. I could tell that Miss Weinstein liked me and I certainly liked her! Recognizing that I had a high energy level, she asked if I, along with several others, would be willing to put on plays to illuminate some of the events we were studying in social studies. Naturally, I jumped at the chance, and we produced a number of very interesting and funny plays. I became more and more involved in my schoolwork, and my grades went up and up and up. I remember feeling so very competent and so much more sure of myself. I began to enjoy learning and made even more effort to write more clearly, to do better in math, and finally, to find ways to become a much better speller, all areas that were problematic for me earlier.

EARLY WORK EXPERIENCE

I began working on weekends and in the summers when I was 13, mostly in the grocery store adjacent to our apartment house. I worked after school every weekday and on Saturday, beginning when I was 16. These jobs were very important to me because they supplied much needed money for recreation and helped balance the family budget. But they were important for another reason. I gained a sense of competence in the "real world" and I was very proud of being able to handle many hours of outside work along with my studies.

My early work experience did not go as smoothly as my later work. I began as a busboy in the cafeteria in which my father worked. On the first day I accidentally dropped a bottle of ketchup. It smashed and stained the light tan suit of a customer who was sitting at the table. The manager was naturally unhappy, but he paid to have the man's suit cleaned and didn't fire me, probably because of my father. I learned to master many jobs in that cafeteria, eventually working behind the counter and in the kitchen.

HIGH SCHOOL

I became much more social in high school and pledged for a unique high school fraternity called the Longfellows, boys who were six feet tall or taller. Anybody who knows me knows that I am not six feet tall, but the fraternity members "surreptitiously" allowed me to put paper in my shoes, for the extra three inches I needed. Pledging was difficult because there was so much hazing, but I stayed with it and became a member. The club was, in part, a service organization and we volunteered at a local chronic disease hospital, where, weekly, we worked with patients who had multiple sclerosis.

It was through a member of the Longfellows that I got my next job, in a local dry cleaning store and factory, set in a "melting pot neighborhood," owned and run by a hot-headed Romanian immigrant. He argued with customers and regularly ordered several of them out of the store, shouting as they exited, "Don't you *ever* come back!" After I had mastered the various jobs involved in cleaning clothes, the owner would leave after I arrived. I learned more there about how to take care of people and soon became quite friendly with many of the customers. Many would come back when they knew I was there and the owner had gone. I would repair the insult they had endured and would give them better service, paying much attention to their individual needs.

Looking back, I believe that this formative experience, coupled with the pattern of caring for my parents' needs, were powerful forces in guiding me towards psychology, and towards clinical psychology in particular. I got a great deal of pleasure from solving the comparatively simple problem of removing an unsightly stain from a valuable suit or dress, or in making certain that the clothes had been satisfactorily pressed. Although today I am still a local "expert" in stain removal, there was a significant learning curve to this process. Once I treated a woman's dress that was covered with rust stains, using a chemical that removed rust. As I poured the liquid onto her dress, there was a puff of smoke and large sections of the dress actually disappeared. Had I read the label on the dress, I would have learned that it was made of a fiberglass-like material and that the chemical that removed the rust, hydrofluoric acid, also etched and dissolved glass.

COLLEGE YEARS

I worked at the dry cleaning store for six years, all the way through college; my employer was flexible enough to allow me to design my work schedule around my school hours. In this manner I was able to work about 30 hours a week while attending school. During the summers and my school vacations I worked 12 hours a day, including Saturdays. I learned a great deal about people and got a broad practical education about various cultures in this melting pot neighborhood. This practical experience was a very important part of my "real-world" education, and it also taught me how to work hard to do the best job possible. I also had money for college textbooks, but thankfully my college education was free because I earned a high enough test score to be admitted.

I began attending Brooklyn College in the fall of 1954 as a biology major. I chose biology because of a teacher in high school, Mr. Berman, who taught an advanced biology course in which we designed and carried out our own long-range experiments. I thought biology research might be an interesting career. However, the professor who taught the required biology courses was a grouchy person who focused primarily on the identification of various minute plants and animals we saw under the microscope. We were required to render drawings of each specimen, which were graded, and after weeks of tedious drawing, we would have a lab practical, in which we had to identify the plants and animals we had seen previously. I was fascinated by the things I saw in the microscope and wanted to share my amazement with the other students and discuss what I saw. Unfortunately, the teacher wanted no part of such discussion and insisted that each one of us do our work, quietly and independently. I felt like the proverbial "fish out of water," especially because my ability to render the microscopic specimens on paper was very poor. The course had become unbearably boring, and I finally decided to change my major. When I faced the registrar, who asked me to what major I was changing, I realized I had not considered an alternative. Nevertheless, I found myself saying psychology. I changed from biology to psychology rather impulsively, without ever having taken a psychology course. Somehow I trusted these instincts and allowed myself to make sudden twists and turns in my life, just like the Tennessee River.

I was delighted by the class interaction in the psychology courses; the professors were very open, dynamic, and available. I knew very quickly that psychology was the right place for me. I can still recall many of my teachers, such as Edward Girden, who taught introductory psychology in a very dramatic and compelling manner. His obituary in the *American Psychologist* said, "His presence was daunting both because of his incredible energy and because of a confrontational style of questioning that demanded nothing less than total commitment to clear perception, thinking, and communication" (Pollio, 1999, p. 777). Harold Proshansky, the co-founder of environmental psychology, taught an outstanding personality theory course. In Evelyn Raskin's testing course, we learned to administer, score, and interpret the

Stanford Binet (Terman & Merrill, 1937) and the Wechsler (Weschler, 1949). Herbert Freudenberger, who taught abnormal psychology, was a psychoanalyst who later coined the term "burnout." Another outstanding teacher was Pearl Meissner, who was one of the authors of a book by Herman Witkin, *Personality Through Perception* (Witkin et al., 1954), in which the terms "field dependent" and "field independent," which Witkin coined, were summarized for the first time. Meissner taught child psychology. A gentle, soft-spoken woman, she invited a friend and me to observe and do research at the Early Childhood Center, which was filled with very active four and five-year-olds. We did a study entitled "The Concept of Mother Among Four and Five Year Old Children," in which we used interviews and doll play to examine the child's conceptualization of his or her mother.

WORK AND GRADUATE SCHOOL

Just before I graduated from college, with no plans for the future, I impulsively decided to take an exam to become a "welfare investigator" and began my training a week after graduation. My job was to visit single-parent families to determine whether they were still eligible for welfare payments. These payments were rather small and did not go far in the typically large families. I found a way to provide extra money, legally, to the families by authorizing extra funds for clothing each season, for each child. Contrary to popular public opinion, I did not find many families who were given money undeservedly. I learned a great deal about myself and the world around me at the welfare department, but mostly I learned humility and respect for the families I visited, who were locked in a fight to fulfill their basic human needs, and were struggling for respect and recognition. I also learned that it is difficult to have self-respect when you cannot care for yourself, and when the attitude of the helping agency is contentious at best.

Before graduation from Brooklyn College, I made an application to the City University (known then as City College, New York) M.A. program, and to my surprise, I was accepted. The courses during the first year were taught in the evenings, so I continued working for the welfare department during the day. I had some very impressive teachers, such as Daniel Lehrman, a superb researcher and teacher of comparative psychology, and Erwin Singer, a training analyst at the William Alanson White Psychoanalytic Institute, a Sullivanian training institute. Singer was one of the founders of the New York University Postdoctoral Program in Psychotherapy and Psychoanalysis and was the author of the classic text, *Key Concepts in Psychotherapy* (Singer, 1965). I also took a two-semester Rorschach course taught by Camilla Kemple, who was, for a short time, the editor of *JPA*, and Florence Miale, the co-author of a well-known sentence completion test and the translator for Bruno Klopfer when he first came to this country. Lloyd Silverman taught the Rorschach lab. He later became quite well known for his subliminal perception research with schizophrenics.

The second year courses were taught in the daytime, so I had to give up my job at the welfare department. I applied for a fellowship with the Board of Higher Education, the administrative group that ran the New York City public colleges, and I got the award. My job, for about 20 hours a week, was to teach student teachers, mostly females, how to operate audio-visual equipment, as part of their coursework.

In the second year we did a great deal of testing in the "600 Schools," institutions whose students could not be managed in a regular school. Policemen patrolled the corridors, an unusual event back then, and the atmosphere was quite prison-like. Sometimes there was very little room to test; I once gave a WISC using a pool table in a recreation room as a desk. We had to be at the school, ready to test, by 8 A.M., which meant that I had to be on the subway train by 6:30 A.M. I worked out a way to get a seat for the long ride to the school, and a way to get an end seat on the way home so that I could read *Rapaport* (Rapaport, Gill, & Shafer, 1945–46) and have room to fold out the double pages without hitting the passenger sitting next to me. My "seat-procuring technique" was quite simple. Trains came along every two or three minutes, but people still piled up on the platform, sometimes 10 deep, all trying to squeeze into the train that just pulled into the station. I stayed back and let them all squeeze in, which left me first on the platform, closest to the door, in the next pileup. When the doors opened, the crowd behind me literally propelled me into the train car, and I sat in the seat of my choice.

MICHIGAN AND BATTLE CREEK VA HOSPITAL

When I suddenly announced to my family that I had decided to apply to doctoral programs away from New York, they were confused and unhappy. Their idea was that I would become a high school teacher and live nearby. Nevertheless, I decided to begin seeing the rest of the country and applied to schools in several states. I was especially interested in MSU because the very first assessment book I read, *An Introduction to Projective Techniques*, was written by Harold and Gladys Anderson (Anderson & Anderson, 1951), a husband and wife team who taught there. Recently I described that book as an intellectual transitional object (Handler, 2001b).

One day I received a telegram from MSU, offering me entrance to graduate school and an assistantship, working at the Battle Creek VA Hospital. Battle Creek was and still is the home of Kellogg's. As a 22-year-old New Yorker who had never been out of the New York metropolitan area, the only thing I knew about Battle Creek was that I had sent many cereal box tops to Kellogg for various prizes. Nevertheless, with a sense of breathless adventure, I quickly wrote back my acceptance. Despite my initial expectations, I never did work with the Andersons, because they spent most of their time collecting research data in several different countries.

Upon leaving New York on my pilgrimage to Michigan, I felt like an adventurer, ready and able to see the world. It was a heady experience, one that was so much more harmonious and stress free, I mused, compared to the way my parents felt on *their* first travel experience. It was on that voyage to Michigan, and during my very first time on an airplane, that I decided to travel as much as I could in the future and see as much of the world as possible. One day in 1975, when my parents were visiting, I told them that Barbara, my wife, and I were going to Europe. In a puzzled and somewhat anxious voice, my father responded, "Why do you want to go? I ran away from there?"

I arrived in Michigan early in June of 1960, to begin work at the VA hospital so that I could earn enough money for tuition for the first quarter. The hospital was located some distance from the city of Battle Creek, on an air force base that was no longer in operation. It was a huge installation, comprising several hundred buildings with large screened-in verandas spread out among mighty oaks. I lived in the nurses' quarters for a dollar a day, in a sparsely decorated room with a dim light and several pieces of metal furniture. It was quite Spartan, but very reasonably priced. It was difficult to sleep for the first week, because of the deafening sound of the crickets. I found this situation rather humorous since I had managed to sleep quite well in New York, even though the apartment house we lived in was quite close to the elevated subway line that ran across the street. Although the noise of the trains was deafening, I never heard that noise, nor did I hear the crickets from the second week on.

One substantial drawback that summer was that no one else I worked with lived on the base, and so when 4:30 came, all of my work associates went home and I was left alone with little to do. For this reason and because I was lonely, I decided to go up on the hospital wards and spend time with the patients. I did that on many late summer afternoons and was surprised to find that most patients were quite lucid and easy to talk to, despite the fact that they were on locked wards. This, then, was the beginning of my adaptation to people with severe emotional problems. Realizing that they were, in part, quite like me, I remembered something I had read in one of Harry Stack Sullivan's books, *Conceptions of Modern Psychiatry,* concerning the one genus hypothesis, "We are all more simply human than otherwise" (Sullivan, 1953, p. 16). I was quite anxious, however, when I met my first schizophrenic patient, a week after I had arrived. I protested to my supervisor that I had never had a therapy case before, let alone a severely regressed schizophrenic. "Don't worry," he said, "you can't hurt him any more than he's already been hurt." With that "reassurance," he sent me to see the patient, who was not at all interested in communicating with me. He paced around the room, holding a lighted cigarette, which was burning his fingers, but he did not seem to notice. He told me his mother was dead, which confused me because his records showed that she was indeed alive. It was only when he referred to her as "a refrigerator" that I finally got the message: he felt she was a cold person who gave him no comfort. I continued to do therapy with psychotic patients, and by the end of the summer I felt much more at ease and felt I could possibly be of help.

I had a great deal of assessment experience in my first year placement at "Battle Creek," where I learned about testing seriously disturbed patients. In my second-year placement, at the Dearborn VA Hospital outpatient clinic, I assessed and did psychotherapy with less severely disturbed patients. I earned the title of the slowest assessor in the entire group, because I spent a great deal of extra time in collaborative assessment with patients and in facilitating their performance using a variety of Testing of the Limits techniques, borrowed from Bruno Klopfer's approach to Rorschach testing. At that time the VA policy was for the social worker to obtain the patient's history, the psychologist to do the testing, and the psychiatrist to make the final decision concerning ward placement. I never liked that arrangement, because I could not get to know the patient without discussing aspects of his family life and work life. I believed the assessment would be worthless unless I understood his background, thoughts, and feelings. Therefore, I began with a lengthy interview and integrated the personal history with test results in my reports, and tied them together. By the time we were through with the assessment, I felt we had established a fairly good relationship. More and more I felt that the division between assessment and therapy was a foolish and arbitrary one. Nevertheless, it was not considered good form to take as your psychotherapy patient someone you had assessed, because it was felt that the transference relationship would be unduly affected and thereby impair the treatment. My opinion was exactly opposite, and I managed to get permission to see some of the patients I had assessed. The therapy went quite well *because* of the relationship we had established and because I really knew and understood the patient from the assessment and could be more sensitive to his feelings. Although the approach I used in the assessments was a far cry from being therapeutic assessment, as I look back I believe that was the beginning of my focus on the integration of assessment and therapy.

COURTSHIP, MARRIAGE, AND FAMILY

I met my wife, Barbara, on campus at MSU at the beginning of the first quarter of my first year. We courted for less than five months when I proposed, and were married four months later, in June 1961, after my first year in graduate school. Our son, Charles Andrew, was born in 1967, and our daughter, Amy Elisabeth, was born in 1971. Charlie graduated from Louisiana State University with a PhD in industrial-organizational psychology. He has been a pioneer in the area of selection of employees by use of the Internet. Amy graduated from the University of Texas, at Austin, with a master of fine arts in children's theater. She worked for the Cartoon Network for over five years in cartoon development. Beginning in the fall of 2003 she began working at a charter school in Atlanta, teaching and developing creative programs for children. Being creative and entertaining, Amy has been the best example to me of what Winnicott (1971a) described when he wrote about play and playfulness. She is "in the room with me" often when I do therapy. I consult with her about gardening as I do with Charlie about buying a new car. Both children are married, Charlie to Ann Ballard churchill, and Amy to Phil Oppenheim, so we have already expanded our family. Barbara and I have a grandson, Oliver William Oppenheim.

As our children grew up, Barbara and I traveled much more, often to places quite far away. The children also traveled to international camps, sponsored by Children's International Summer Village (CISV), where four 11-year-old children and an adult leader from a number of countries go to a camp somewhere in the world for an entire month. Charlie went to a camp near Lake Como, in Italy, and Amy went to the Philippines. The following two years of the program are devoted to an exchange, in which a child spends a month with a family in a country different from his or her own, and the next year the process is reversed. Charlie went to Helsinki, Finland, were he stayed with the Valle family. The next year Jussi Valle came to our home for a month. He was a remarkable child, wise beyond his age, and we all bonded quite nicely. Jussi continued to write to us after he returned to Finland and we wrote often as well. When Jussi was 17, he came to Knoxville to live with us for a year and to complete his senior year at a local high school. Thus began a wonderful relationship that has continued to this day, some 20 years later. Jussi visited us often in the ensuing years and continues to visit, now with his family, and we visit them and his parents quite often. He and his children have become an adopted member of our family, as have his wife, Marianna, and their two children.

Barbara earned her doctorate in math education in 1982. Her dissertation demonstrated a novel way to resolve math anxiety, involving instruction and group therapy. She taught computer programming and math courses at the University of Tennessee and at several other local colleges, before her 11-year stint as a systems analyst and a research associate at a department of Energy facility, where the fuel for the first atomic bomb was manufactured. About a year ago she started her own business, combining mathematics with her interest in art; she teaches quilting by machine. As "The Quilt Handler" she travels around the country, giving workshops and selling quilting supplies.

GRADUATE SCHOOL AND ENDURING FRIENDSHIPS

I found the first year at MSU very stressful; there was more work to do than anyone had time for, and I was not used to the 10-week quarter system. We (fellow graduate students) traveled to Battle Creek very early each Tuesday morning (6 A.M.) and worked there for two days, returning to East Lansing quite late on Wednesdays. We were also responsible for the proseminar readings, in which all areas of psychology were covered, in rapid succession, over three academic quarters and for two statistics courses. At the end of the year we took the dreaded comprehensive exams, called "qualifiers," three-day exams covering all we were supposed to have learned during the first year. If a student didn't pass the first time, he or she was allowed to take the exams a second time; if the unfortunate student failed again, he or she could not continue in the program. The pressure was intense and there was a great deal of competition among the students. For example, sometimes students cut the required reading journal articles out of the volume so that no other students could access them.

The stress of the first year was often intense and my friends began to joke about how pale I got before exams. At that time the psychology department was housed in a huge and very long quonset hut, called, in typical Midwest picturesgue language, "B-3." Everyone joked that there must be an exam coming because Len had "B-3 pallor." Several of us established a cooperative study group, in which we each outlined portions of the reading material and distributed carbon copies among ourselves for exam preparation.

In June, a week before my wedding, we took qualifiers. Each student was assigned a number so that the results could be posted without names. I remember writing my number on the inside of a matchbook cover. When Barbara and I returned to campus after a two-week honeymoon, we went directly to B-3, even before going to our married housing apartment so that I could learn the results of the exam. I looked at the list, my heart pounding. Number 6 got second place honors and number 9 failed. I couldn't tell if my number was a 6 or a 9, and I had to wait until the next day to find out. Happily, my number was 6, and my B-3 pallor became part of history. Three of us in the study group, and no others, got honors scores, so we proved that collaboration was more effective than competition in learning.

My next placement was at the MSU Psychological Clinic, where I saw mostly children and their parents. In my last year I was an assistant instructor at the Counseling Center, where we did in-depth psychotherapy with the college students. I was really impressed with the MSU faculty, especially Bert Karon. His book, *Psychotherapy of Schizophrenia: The Treatment of Choice* (Karon & VandenBos, 1981), has become a classic. I learned a great deal from him about doing effective psychotherapy with schizophrenics, *without using medication*. I admired his courage in this approach to patients and was—and still am—impressed with the effectiveness of his treatment. We became good friends and he has come to UT several times to lecture.

The most colorful and best-known faculty member of the clinical program was Albert I. Rabin, a seasoned clinician and researcher, who had worked with Samuel Beck and was the author or coauthor of several widely-used assessment books. Rabin was an imposing and somewhat formal man, with an impressive Viennese accent. The nickname that his graduate students gave him, "Card IV," reveals how they felt about him. He loved that role, knew about the Rorschach nickname, and would often laugh about it. Several years ago I put together a symposium about the Rorschach at SPA, which included Rabin and John Exner. When I introduced Al to the audience and told them that in graduate school he was often referred to as Card IV, everyone laughed, including Al. They laughed even more when John Exner said, "They used to call *me* Card IV too."

I made several very good friends in graduate school, especially Herb and Jan Potash. It was from Herb that I first got the idea of how to teach assessment, which he taught in the master's program at Fairleigh Dickinson University for many years. We became very close friends and have shared each other's lives for over 44 years. We have always been there for each other, sharing both the good and bad times. I also respect Herb and Jan a great deal for their honesty, their frankness, and their clear-thinking ability.

Ira Weinstein, who began the MSU doctoral program a year or two after I did, taught at UT for several years, became director of the counseling center at the University of California, Santa Barbara, and then began a private practice there. He and his wife, Lotte, are very close friends. We always show up for each other's surprise birthday celebrations; we laugh a great deal and always have fun together. As with Herb and Jan Potash, the Weinsteins have cheered our successes and commiserated with us when bad things have happened. There are no better friends in the world than Herb and Jan Potash and Ira and Lotte Weinstein.

About five or six years ago I ran into Phil Caracena at an Annual Meeting of SPA, where he was selling RorScan, which he had created as a more user-friendly alternative to the Rorschach Interpretation Assistance Program (RIAP). Phil and I were at MSU at about the same time and worked in the same settings, though not at the same times. We had not seen each other for over 30 years. I am delighted that he is now a member of the SPA Board and in charge of our website. That reminds me of an old folksong, "May the Circle be Unbroken."

EARLY RESEARCH INTERESTS AND JOB HUNTING

My interest in the Draw-A-Person Test (DAP; Machover, 1949) began at City University of New York, and continued at MSU. I decided that I wanted to determine whether a variety of so-called DAP anxiety indices were related to physiological anxiety. This could be accomplished, I proposed, by hooking subjects up to a polygraph to record their galanic skin response (GSRs) as they drew the male and the female figures and an automobile control figure. While collecting pilot data I noted that the drawings all seemed to reflect a great deal of pathology. So intent was I on collecting the data that I had not realized that I had set up an extreme anxiety-producing situation for my subjects. We were in a very small soundproofed room, with double doors and no windows. The only sound was the whining of the exhaust fan, and the clicking of the marker pen on the huge six-channel polygraph, replete with glowing lights, to which I hooked up the subject. The wires ran from the amplifiers to the fingers of the subject's non-preferred hand. Eventually it dawned on me that the pathological drawings were due to the subjects' anxiety because they believed they would be shocked while drawing. This experience led me to conduct another experiment concerning the effects of stress on the Draw-A-Person Test (Handler & Reyher, 1964). Before graduation I sent an article based on my dissertation to the *Journal of Consulting Psychology* and it was accepted (Handler & Reyher, 1966), except that the editor wanted me to omit much of the lengthy literature review. While I was elated at its acceptance, I was disappointed that the literature review would not be published, because it summarized 51 DAP studies concerning anxiety indices, examining validity findings on each of about 20 drawing indices. The results were surprising because, despite the very bad press researchers had given the DAP, there were a number of very significant findings for about 10 of the drawing variables. I sent an abbreviated review to the *Journal of Personality Assessment*. To my surprise, I got a letter from Walter Klopfer, Bruno's son, then editor of *JPA*, accepting my submission, if I would make the paper *longer*, to amplify the contents of the table, which I did (Handler & Reyher, 1965). This was the first and only time an editor has ever asked me to make a paper longer rather than shorter! By the time I graduated from MSU I was surprised to note that I had four papers in press. I had not viewed myself as a researcher, but was more self-identified as an applied clinician.

During my last year at MSU, as I worked on my dissertation and passed my French language exam, I found myself wondering, "What next?" To my surprise, I began thinking about a university position. I had no teaching experience, so I had no real basis for my choice, but along with a friend who had also discovered that he had similar interests, I sent letters to the chairpersons of almost every APA approved program we could find. One day, Lee Winder, the chairman of the MSU psychology department, talked to me into interviewing at UT. He had just returned from Knoxville, where he had been a consultant to the new department head, Bill Verplanck (who had been a colleague and a friend of B.F. Skinner) in an effort to revamp the clinical program. "Tennessee?" I said incredulously, "That's the South; I don't think I could live in the South." Winder replied, in a much more patient tone than mine, "Well, Len, there's going to be a renaissance there and I believe it would be an excellent place for you." Reluctantly, I agreed to look at the position and several weeks later left for Knoxville to interview. My attitude about Tennessee and the South was based on no real direct experience; I had only lived in two states by this time and had traveled very briefly to only one other nearby state.

TENNESSEE

When I left East Lansing in mid-March, it was snowing heavily and my feet sank into the deep wet snow. But when I arrived in Knoxville the sun was shining, it was delightfully warm, and the spring flowers were in bloom. There was a very friendly atmosphere in the psychology department, and I got along quite well with the faculty during the interviews. I had known one of the faculty, Howard Pollio, very slightly in New York, when we were both at Brooklyn College. I felt we were destined to become good friends, and I was right. Howard and I spent a great deal of time together and he was an excellent mentor. He also enhanced my knowledge of phenomenology and demonstrated that it was possible to do sound research using phenomenological approaches. Eventually, I chaired several such dissertations. Howard and I, and our wives, have shared many personal and professional issues. I am consistently impressed with his teaching ability, the breadth and depth of his thinking, his honesty, and his sound advice whenever I seek him out for consultation.

Returning from my UT interview, I said to myself, "Well, Lee Winder was right, this place has everything I could ask for. I hated the cold and the snow; I loved to garden (even as a boy I grew flowers and vegetables on the fire escape outside my window); the people were wonderful; and I felt there would be a place for me to do the work I wanted to do. Another convincing point was that although the department head was an experimental psychologist and a Skinnerian to boot, he had gathered a group of excellent psychodynamically-oriented clinicians into the clinical program, despite the fact that he said he disliked the approach.

When I got back to East Lansing and the airplane door opened, I saw it was still snowing. Hugging my wife, I remember saying, "If they make me an offer, I'd like to take the job." "Well," she replied, "how about trying it for a year?" When Verplanck called and offered me the job, paying $7,000 a year, I readily accepted. I turned down a salary of almost twice that at a Midwestern medical school because the atmosphere at Tennessee felt so good and the work, I felt, would be much more interesting and challenging. That was a mere 41 years ago and we are still in Knoxville, despite some very tempting offers over the years.

FINDING A FOCUS AND DEVELOPING A CAREER

I was younger than a number of graduate students I taught and it took me several years to feel less like a student and more like a faculty member. I wanted to relate to my students in quite a different manner than was typical at MSU. Although the MSU faculty were not harsh or disinterested, they did not provide much feedback to students concerning their performance. When several of us got honors on the qualifiers, none of the faculty ever mentioned it to us. I recall the day Al Rabin returned from a sabbatical and called a meeting of the clinical faculty. I was walking down the corridor of our newly refurbished psychology building and Rabin was walking towards me. I said,

"Welcome back, Dr. Rabin." He replied in his dulcet Viennese accent, "Oh, Handler," and he paused, "we were just talking about you." And then he was gone, with no further explanation. I puzzled over his terse response for several weeks, wondering what the substance of the discussion had been about me, not knowing if I should feel good or bad about the comment. Because of the lack of feedback and the lack of encouragement at MSU, I vowed to be a better mentor and to provide feedback and to praise my students at UT when they made effort and when they were successful. Although it is painful to give negative feedback, such discussions go far in helping students repair personal and professional problems. In addition, it is a genuine pleasure to recognize skill and excellence. Graduate students may be able to prosper without such feedback, but they blossom and flourish with enthusiastic feedback. While I related to the graduate students as friends because they were about my age, as I got older, the relationship between myself and my students became more fatherly. Lately, I find I am about the same age as some of the students' grandfathers, and so I have slipped a generation. Recently, however, a graduate student who was leaving for an internship told me that my nickname with many of the students is "Papa Len." While "Card IV" has some clout, I prefer the "papa" moniker.

The first two years of teaching were quite hectic; I taught three courses a quarter, including introduction to assessment and an assessment lab. I also supervised six graduate students in assessment and psychotherapy, did research, and served on university and community committees. Although I managed to accomplish this without having had any previous teaching or supervisory experience and got promoted to associate professor four years later, in 1968, my anxiety level as a new assistant professor kept me from fulfilling my teaching mission at first. Initially, I found it difficult to communicate my enthusiasm for assessment and psychotherapy. I was lucky enough to require very little sleep, because I worked on my research very late at night, when everyone at home was sleeping and there was comfortable silence.

My initial anxiety led me to read *Psychological Abstracts* (the forerunner of PsychINFO and PsychLIT, in journal form) every month and to write authors for reprints. I did this for more than a year, amassing a huge collection of reprints, most of which turned out to be irrelevant to my developing interests in assessment, psychotherapy, neuropsychology and hypnosis. Since I had no previous teaching experience but had plenty of anxiety, I wrote all of my lectures and "presented" them, primarily by reading them. It was most certainly a very boring experience for students and for me. Some time in the second quarter of this ridiculous exercise, I forgot my written lecture and was faced with the frightening task of being spontaneous. After class one very kind student came up and said, "Dr. Handler, that was a great class we had today." I was quite surprised and spent a great deal of time between that experience and the next class contemplating a new approach to teaching. That's how I discovered how I could teach best, with just a few notes, and with lots of class discussion. Since that time, my students have enjoyed the classes and I find I also learn a great deal. The discussions generate many important ideas, some of which we test as research projects. I discovered that to be an effective teacher in the area of personality assessment (and in other areas as well), it is important to be supportive and facilitating, in a holding environment that allows students to feel safe and hopefully more sure of themselves. I gradually began to recognize that my most important role and contribution in psychology would be as both a teacher and as a student. I have spent many years studying and reflecting on the teaching-learning process in personality assessment and psychotherapy, which eventually led to a co-edited book with Mark Hilsenroth, *Teaching and Learning Personality Assessment* (Handler & Hilsenroth, 1998). I have always felt the need to continue learning, both intellectually and experientially, and I enjoy sharing what I have learned with students, who often then teach me much as well.

I focus my teaching of the interpretation and integration of assessment data on the use of several approaches taken from creativity research, divergent thinking (e.g., In how many different ways can a piece of data be interpreted?), and convergent thinking, the integration of diverse pieces of information to form an interpretation that is unique (Handler, 1998). In addition, I also teach the use of symbolism in the interpretive process.

Despite my heavy schedule, I found time for other activities, including working in the Johnson-Humphrey presidential election campaign in 1964, beginning a private practice in assessment and psychotherapy, consulting a day a week at a rehabilitation center for emotionally disturbed and brain damaged children, and consulting to a regional stroke program. As I began to be more experienced in psychotherapy with children, I incorporated graduate students into my work. This approach—two therapists working simultaneously with one child—was an excellent training experience and allowed us to do better treatment with the children. I continued in this position for 14 years, eventually passing it on to one of my former graduate students, Jeff Slavin, who had worked with me there when he was a student. Many years later Jeff and I still continue to learn from each other, about psychology and about life; he is also my photography teacher and critic. About 20 years ago several of my former graduate students and I established a group practice, and six years ago we built a new office building on the same street where Barbara and I lived for our first three years in Knoxville.

It was in my private practice that I began to try out new ways to use tests and develop a much more collaborative and therapeutic approach to assessment with children and adults. Many of my papers were based on assessment experiences I had with patients in this setting (e.g., Handler, 1996a, 1996b, 1996c, 1997; 1999a, 1999b; Handler & Hilsenroth, 1994). I also brought this material into the classroom where students often saw many more meanings in the data than I had originally seen. This experience even more emphatically illustrated the importance of being both a student and a teacher, in reciprocal fashion.

An example of this process comes from my interest in neuropsychology, an area in which I am still active, stemming from my experiences at the Battle Creek VA. We often got referrals from psychiatry that read, "Differential diagnosis, brain damage or schizophrenia." I struggled with these referral issues, trying out a host of long-since abandoned tests I found that had once been used to assess brain damage, but to no avail. I felt frustrated because I often could not answer the referral question with any degree of assurance. Then one day, one of Ralph Reitan's associates came to do a brief seminar about the Halstead-Reitan Neuropsychological Screening Battery (Reitan & Wolfson, 1986). I knew then that I would eventually get training in the administration and interpretation of the battery. At Tennessee I obtained funds to attend a one-week training session with Reitan and his associates. I also purchased the equipment necessary to give the long test battery, attended three advanced Reitan training seminars over the next few years, and brought three graduate students with me. Their insights and enthusiasm sparked my own continued interest in the area. Eventually I taught a course in the assessment of brain dysfunction, using the Reitan battery and other material I had gathered from attending other workshops. Together with a student (Frisch & Handler, 1974), I also published a paper and gave a number of convention papers in the area (Handler, 1991; Handler, Wesch, Byrne & Brody, 1969).

I also maintained an interest in hypnosis, stimulated originally by my major professor, Joe Reyher, and I taught a graduate seminar in hypnosis for many years. I still maintain an interest in hypnosis and especially in the amazing writings of Milton Erickson, the person who heavily influenced Jay Haley's theoretical approach. One day, impulsively, I picked up the telephone and called Erickson about the possibility of visiting him. All he said was "Come on." When I asked for clarification, he told me to come when I wanted to, and when I asked about fees he said, "Whatever you decide it's worth to you." Barbara and I arrived in Phoenix later that spring. I was ushered into Erickson's office by his wife. At that time he was working on his first coauthored book with Ernest Rossi (Erickson, Rossi, & Rossi, 1976). Erickson was in the process of hypnotizing Rossi's wife, Sheila, and demonstrating various hypnotic phenomena to be included in the book. He was in a wheelchair because of two bouts with polio and severe crippling arthritis. Nevertheless, his gaze and the way he made eye contact seemed quite riveting. Several times during the session he leaned forward and gazed at me, holding that position. When he did so I felt my body could not move at all. Then he would lean back and break his gaze and I felt free to move again. This occurred several times during the two-hour demonstration. To this day I cannot tell whether this was something I created because of the "master's" gaze or something he did on purpose. I stayed in Phoenix for five days, talking with Erickson, observing his work and being a subject. He demonstrated a technique of induction, whereby he facilitated my hands lifting off my legs, into the air. To demonstrate how to bind a person in a deepening process, he created a contest between my two hands, wondering aloud which hand would beat the other in touching my chin, after which I would go into a deeper trance. It was an amazing experience for me, and I learned to apply some of Erickson's principles in my psychotherapy work. For example, I told a new patient, a young lady who had terminated prematurely in several other psychotherapy attempts, and who always tried to prove me wrong in our interactions, that she would probably be an early terminator in her therapy. Several years later, when she completed her work, she said, "See, I wasn't an early terminator after all." Even more important, Erickson's instruction helped me to reaffirm the importance of unconscious or unverbalized processes in guiding behavior and seemed to me to reaffirm my consciously unplanned personal and professional life.

Gradually, over the years, as I became more productive in research, my course load was lightened, so that by the time I was promoted to professor, four years later, in 1972, I was teaching one course a quarter, plus supervision. I was also then actively working with many graduate students on their dissertation research. Although I do not have an exact count, I know for certain that I have chaired at least 100 doctoral dissertations and a bunch of master's theses.

I am also very proud of the psycho-social cancer program I started at the University of Tennessee Hospital in 1974, which I ran for five years. Several graduate students worked with me in this setting, with patients and their families, as well as with nurses and physicians. I experienced the constant loss of people with whom I had formed a meaningful bond, and it eventually became harder and harder to go up on the cancer ward. The burnout I was beginning to experience made me turn the program over to a colleague.

I continued doing research with the DAP because it is the only test for which there is no standard stimulus. The person creating the figure has to produce it from his or her conceptualization of self or other. Because of this lack of structure, it becomes quite easy to see pathology if the person being tested is disturbed. I also developed and published a DAP anxiety indices scale (Handler, 1967); validated the use of a control figure, the drawing of an automobile, to deal with the issue of artistic ability; and demonstrated the skills necessary for accurate interpretation of the DAP. Good undergraduate and graduate interpreters were more empathic, more intuitive, and more cognitively flexible. Of all the studies I have done, I like this one best because it has implications for the interpretive processes involved in all implicit (projective) tests and for training in psychotherapy. For me, these findings emphasize the importance, as Winnicott (1971b) says in the poem at the beginning of this paper, of "being evergreen," of being open to the material. I stress this approach to the interpretation of a drawing by asking the student to "be" the person drawn and then to examine his or her thoughts, feelings, and attitudes. The paper was rejected by several journals, but it was finally published in Emanual Hammer's newest book, *Advances in Projective Drawing Interpretation* (1997) as an entire chapter (Burley & Handler, 1997). Hammer, the guru of the DAP, wrote an introduction to the chapter, lauding the study.

In recent DAP workshops and in several book chapters, I have described and illustrated the significant changes that occur in the drawings of patients who have improved during therapy. One might never know that the same person drew both the "before" and the "after" figures (Handler, 1996a; Handler & Riethmiller, 1998). This result led me to isolate several DAP variables (head and body simplification, distortion of body parts, omission of major body parts, vertical imbalance, and marked transparencies) whose presence indicates marked pathology, independent of the patient's skill in drawing; these indices provide evidence of psychopathology and are not affected by the artistic ability of the patient.

In my continued attempt to integrate assessment and psychotherapy, I began experimenting with the use of various kinds of drawings as a way to combine assessment and psychotherapy with children. This led me to Winnicott's Squiggle Game (Winnicott, 1971), and eventually to the use of fantasy animal drawings with the children. I began asking children to draw "a make believe animal" and then to tell a story about it. I was startled by how much I was able to understand about the child in a short time by using this approach. For this reason, I began crafting stories that had therapeutic value to the children in response to their stories, stories that symbolically expressed messages concerning the problems they illustrated in their drawings and stories (Handler & Hilsenroth, 1994; Handler, 2002; Mutchnick & Handler, 2002). I am almost finished writing a book entitled *Therapeutic Assessment with Children and Adolescents* that describes this approach and many others that can be used to combine assessment and therapy, on an ongoing basis. Using these approaches, it is very easy to track changes in the child as treatment proceeds.

As I reflect upon my research and teaching over the past 41 years, I have come to see a second important focus related to the issue of the reciprocity between teaching and learning, a tenacious focus on finding new and better ways to do assessment and psychotherapy. Influenced by the work of Ernest Schachtel and Harry Stack Sullivan, I began to focus more actively on the patient's experience of each assessment instrument and of the entire assessment process. I continued to devise various methods of exploring the personal meaning of the responses and to devise interventions with various IQ measures, self-report measures, and implicit measures that would help me understand what they were thinking or feeling when they gave certain responses (e.g., Handler, 1988, 1996c, 1998a, 1998b, 1999a, 2002). For example, after the Rorschach is given in the standardized manner, I ask patients to sort the cards into a pile they like and a pile they dislike, ask them why they either like or dislike each card, and tell how a disliked card could be improved. These efforts usually identify problem issues much more clearly than the patient's original responses. I sometimes ask patients to give me "playful responses," which often allows for amplification of underlying issues; to tell me stories about selected percepts; or to give the percept a voice. For example, a rather schizoid patient saw "a mushroom" in a tiny Dd area of Card I. When I asked, "If that mushroom could talk, what would it say?" the patient answered, "Don't step on me; everybody tries to step on me and crush me." He also saw a "wolf's face" as a whole response to Card I. When I asked him to give the wolf a voice, he said, "You don't bother me, I won't bother you; you go your way and I'll go mine." His responses helped me see that I was being too intrusive and that he experienced me as aggressive. I immediately altered my approach, sat a bit further from him, and became more playful. I bring these examples to class as illustrations of how one can approach patients to mutually explore and understand their world.

LONDON AND THE TAVISTOCK CLINIC

In 1977 I became interested in learning more about British Object Relations Theory and was given a sabbatical for part of the year to visit the Tavistock Clinic in London, where this theory was a central focus. I sat in on David Malan's brief psychotherapy seminar and attended a family therapy seminar, in which I was introduced to the work of Salvatore Minuchin. I also met an Adlerian psychiatrist, Joshua Bierer, the founder and editor of the *International Journal of Social Psychiatry*, and the founder of the first-day hospital program. Trained in Vienna by Alfred Adler, he had known both Melanie Klein and Anna Freud. He told me about their antagonism toward each other. He said that once at a conference he found himself sitting between them. When he turned his attention to "Anna," he recounted, Melanie Klein kicked him under the table, and when he paid attention to "Melanie," Anna Freud poked him with her elbow. Bierer invited me to sit in on his twice-weekly group therapy sessions, as an observer or co-therapist, and I did so for the time I was in London. In addition I was very fortunate to become reacquainted with Sid Blatt, who was also on sabbatical. We had a great deal of time to talk about psychotherapy and assessment as well as to socialize. Sid is an impressive fountain of knowledge and it was a privilege to listen to and learn from his discourses.

THE RESEARCH LAB

Some time in the early 1980s I organized a formal research lab, the goal of which was to conduct research in personality assessment as it relates to psychotherapy. The theoretical focus of the group was object relations, with a healthy dose of phenomenology, so that experiential issues could be explored. The lab was organized as a collaborative or networking group; students worked on several different projects at any one time, doing tasks they especially enjoyed or tasks they wanted to master. One or two students would collect data or organize archival data, another student or two might do the statistical analysis, and various students and/or I would write portions of each study for presentation or publication.

Our productivity was, and remains, quite high; lab students present many papers at SPA and at other annual meetings, and we publish a number of them as well. The active involvement of the lab members facilitates close working relationships and allows time for enjoyment and celebration as well. One or two weeks before the annual meeting we all gather at my home for paper presentation rehearsal. We critique each paper, suggest possible revisions, and time the presentations. On Saturday evening after the SPA Annual Meeting is over, Barbara and I take the students out for a celebration dinner. Some of these students have not made research their central interest, although they enjoy the collaboration and get ample assistance from me or from other lab members to make research and presentation rather painless.

Our lab has recently focused on a wide assortment of projects, many generated by the members themselves. They include the validation of various Rorschach aggression indices; an in depth assessment of Rorschachs from Alzheimer patients; a comparison of multimethod test data before and after treatment from adolescents in a residential treatment program; the ability of Klopfer's Rorschach Prognostic Rating Scale (Klopfer, Kirkner, Wisham, & Baker, 1951) to predict progress in psychotherapy; the meaning of the use of white space on the Rorschach; the continued validation of the Tennessee Object Relations Inventory (Eskra & Handler, 1995), among many others. We are also focusing our attention on a new test, the Adult Attachment Projective (George & West, 2001), as an alternative to the lengthy and laborious Adult Attachment Interview (Hesse, 1999). I spent two weeks in a workshop last summer, learning to administer, score and interpret the test, using attachment theory. I was fortunate this summer to obtain scholarships for two lab students to attend the workshop. We are preparing to investigate the relationship between this attachment theory-based test and object relations data derived from the Rorschach and the Thematic Apperception Test (TAT; Murray, 1943).

A third important focus, writing interesting nondata papers to explore personal aspects of psychology, stem from my early adolescent fantasies of writing novels or short stories. Although I never pursued such a career, I have expressed this fantasy by being a personality assessment biographer. I am especially proud of the articles I wrote in which old assessment texts were reviewed in retrospect to reassess their contribution to assessment. Learning more about an author and understanding how the book got written helps to put it in a personal, social, political, and economic perspective. Each article also included some oral history of assessment, obtained informally from people who made or helped to make assessment history. We have lost and will continue to lose a great deal of assessment information as those who created the tools and techniques we use and study and those who wrote about them pass into history. That is one of the reasons for this autobiographical series for which I am now writing, as indicated by its editors, Bill Kinder and Steve Strack.

For my review of the three Klopfer "grey books" (Handler, 1994), I was fortunate to speak with Mary Ainsworth, who was a coauthor of the first volume. For *Rorschach Psychology* by Maria Rickers-Ovsiankina (Handler, 1995),

I spoke with Maurice Farber, Jerome Frank, Leslie Phillips (he wrote a classic Rorschach text), Eliot Rodnick (a key figure in schizophrenia research), Saul Rosenzweig (author of the Picture Frustration Test, 1994), and Marianne Simmel, among others. In a review of John Exner's first book, *The Rorschach Systems* (1969), in which he reviewed each Rorschach scoring system and compared them, I got John to recall the times, as a graduate student at Cornell, he spent with Bruno Klopfer and Samuel Beck (Handler, 1996b). It was for the review of the book *Assessment of Men* (Handler, 2001a), about the Office of Strategic Services (OSS) program to select American spies during the Second World War, that I was really able to reconstruct an entire era in the history of assessment. I was fortunate enough to have spoken with Henry Murray's wife, Caroline "Nina" Murray, as well as Urie Bronfenbrenner (a distinguished developmental psychologist), Bertram Forer (author of a sentence completion test), Jacob Getzels (an important figure in creativity research), Morris Stein (a contributor to creativity research and author of a TAT book), John W. Gardner (president of the Carnegie Foundation; Secretary of Health, Education and Welfare in the Johnson administration, and founder of Common Cause), Eugenia Hanfmann (a central figure in the development of Gestalt psychology), and Donald Fiske (who made important contributions in the area of personality measurement).

I have been blessed with many excellent graduate students, many of whom have become innovators in the areas of assessment, psychotherapy, forensics, and administration. Among them is Alan Sugarman, who is a psychoanalyst in San Diego, who has written extensively about assessment and psychoanalysis; and Elgan Baker, an associate clinical professor, Indiana School of Medicine, who is on the editorial board of the *International Journal of Clinical and Experimental Hypnosis* and has done groundbreaking work in hypnosis and psychotherapy. Todd Burley, an unusually talented teacher and clinician, trains practitioners in Gestalt therapy, all over the world. Lance Laurence has been a leader in health care legislative efforts, nationally and in Tennessee. He is an impressive visionary concerning clinical and legislative issues and runs the legislative directorate of the Tennessee Psychological Association, where he interfaces with our lobbyist, often also writing bills for the legislature. He also teaches in our doctoral training program and is the director of the UT Psychological Clinic. His famous saying, "Don't let the issue get in front of the object relations." has become a mantra for us. He is a close personal friend whose relationship I have treasured for the past 25 years.

Two other quite memorable graduate students were Mark Hilsenroth, now an associate professor at Adelphi University, and Chris Fowler, now at the Austen-Riggs Center. Mark, Chris and I began our very productive collaboration when they were graduate students. Mark is the most affiliative and productive psychologist I have ever met. He collaborates very effectively and he builds strong bonds with many people. We share a special affection and respect for each other and for each other's talents and have learned much from each other. Chris is an unusually talented psychotherapist and with Mark, has become a creative and quite productive assessment and psychotherapy researcher. Their energy and dedication is impressive and infectious. We have a very close bond and a great deal of affection for one-another. It was Chris who first became interested in early memories as a projective test, and as an instrument to predict the kind of relationship the patient would establish with his or her therapist. This resulted in several papers (Fowler, Hilsenroth & Handler, 1995, 1996, 1998) that demonstrated a link between assessment and psychotherapy process. We use Fowler's early memories procedure in the UT Psychological Clinic, and I teach new graduate students how to use it in my assessment course. Here again, the student learns from the teacher and the teacher learns from the student, allowing us all to continue in the creative learning process. Another very talented and productive student was Amanda Jill Clemence, with whom I have collaborated on a number of papers and book chapters (e.g., Handler & Clemence, 2003; Clemence & Handler, 2001). Her clinical and research sophistication are very impressive. Many of my former students hold positions as mental health center directors, faculty members in medical schools, department of mental health directors, as well as college and university teachers.

SPA

I joined SPA in 1965, soon after graduation, and became a fellow in 1969, thanks to the efforts of Earl Taulbee, who was an associate editor of *JPA*. I remember how awestruck I was when I attended my fist SPA Annual Meeting. But I found the movers and shakers in the world of assessment to be very approachable and quite helpful. I never expected, at that time, to be elected to the SPA Executive Board for two successive terms. Two years ago I had the very special honor of becoming president-elect of SPA, which was another delightful surprise. By the time this is published, I will be proudly serving as past president.

I wish there were space to mention all the graduate students with whom I have worked as well as the many colleagues in SPA that I have come to know and admire over these many years. I mention as many people as space allows. I met Connie Fischer and Steve Finn some years ago and was fascinated by their unique contributions to assessment—Connie, with her very creative collaborative assessment approach, and Steve, who created one of the most revolutionary approaches to assessment, a major paradigm shift, known as therapeutic assessment. It was Steve and Connie who first labeled what I had been doing for some time as therapeutic assessment. I treasure their friendship and creative ability.

One very special colleague and friend is Paul Lerner, whose wise counsel I respect very much. We often share "growing up" stories and reminisce about the old days. It was Paul who first pointed the way for me to become more active in SPA. Irv Weiner has been a respected friend and colleague who has been very supportive of my work over the years. He and Shira Tibon, from Tel Aviv University, served as my examining committee for diplomate status on the American Board of Assessment Psychology (ABAP). I met Shira about four years ago and she sponsored my visit to Israel, where I lectured in several cities, including Tel Aviv University. Shira and her colleagues, Lily Rothschild and Ruth Sitton, have become my special friends. They were our constant guides and caretakers in our three-week visit. I have also had the pleasure of knowing our new board member, Anna Maria Carlsson from Stockholm, and Carl-Erik Mattlar from Helsinki, who is an extraordinary host and friend. Of course, the other members of the past and present board, Judy Armstrong, Anita Boss, Virginia Brabender, Phil Caracena, Barton Evans, Chris Fowler, Radhika Krishnamurthy, Marty Leichtman, Joni Mihura, Dave Nichols, Sandra Russ, Bruce Smith, Irv Weiner, Jed Yalof, and Paula Garber, Adminstrative Director of SPA. have all played important roles in my professional life; I am proud to know them and I value their friendship.

Another person who has been a good friend and colleague is Bill Kinder, the former editor of JPA. It was Bill Kinder and Steve Strack who conceived the idea of including autobiographies in JPA so that psychologists who come after us will understand the context from which our work was developed. I feel especially fortunate to know Larry Erlbaum, our publisher, and to call him a friend. He is truly "a man for all seasons," warm and caring, a true scholar, bright, creative and urbane—a "mensch."

I first met Greg Meyer, our new JPA editor, in 1994. We had both responded to the SPA board's request for proposals to demonstrate the validity of personality assessment instruments and the board asked us to work together. It was quickly obvious to me that Greg had a much better research idea than mine, so we used his plan, which proved to be a much larger job than we both expected. I continue to marvel over his careful, thorough, and inspired approach to research. While I am proud of the article we published together, the meta-analysis of the Rorschach Prognostic Rating Scale (Meyer & Handler, 1997), the honor mostly belongs to Greg.

THE FUTURE

The idea of retirement is not a welcome one for me, because I still believe I have ample tread left on my tires. In 2007, I will retire from the SPA board after serving as president and past president. I am still deeply engrossed in the teaching-learning process and try to communicate my new learning to students as I process the material. Their input is often helpful in taking the material several steps further. Early in my career I thought I would retire at 55 and travel around the world. Well, instead we managed to travel a great deal well before I was 55. Next year I will be 70 and I will retire from full-time work at UT, but I will continue on teaching two courses a year as an emeritus professor. I am still teaching and learning, learning and teaching. I love my work and am happy that I allowed myself the freedom to choose my life path in the unverbalized or unconscious manner I described earlier. But if I have not yet demonstrated the power of the unconscious, or at least the unverbalized approach in guiding me along this rambling path of life, expressing itself in helpful ways, I close with a story about me that should make the point with more poignancy.

For several years after my mother died, I experienced an anniversary re-action near the date of her death; I would get rather irritable and depressed for a week or two. One year there was no sign of an anniversary reaction, so I thought I had worked through the issue. However, one day, near the date of my mother's death, I noticed that my left wrist was itching underneath my watchband, one that I had worn for several years. I took the watch off and found the area beneath it red and swollen. Puzzled, I shifted the watchband to my right wrist and a few days later my left wrist had healed, so I returned the watch to my left wrist. Within a day the swelling, redness and itching returned. I was puzzled; after all, I asked myself, my right wrist and my left wrist are the same, so why does this appear only on the left one? Suddenly, I recovered an old memory. When I was four or five, I fell from a high place in the courtyard of our apartment house and broke my left wrist. The memory I recovered was of my mother and me, sitting at the hospital, waiting for the doctor. I saw myself crying, while my mother held me and comforted me. Amazed at the way my body had spoken to me, I smiled with some satisfaction. That was the end of my anniversary reactions.

Winnicott was indeed correct: suck up the sap

> from the infinite source
> of your unconscious
> and
> Be evergreen.

ACKNOWLEDGMENTS

I thank Howard Pollio, Barbara Handler, Lotte Weinstein, Bill Kinder, and Steve Strack for reading previous drafts and for their editorial comments, and Barton Evans for providing the citation for the Sullivan quote. I also thank my family, friends, colleagues and students, who have enriched my life, far more than I ever dreamed was possible.

REFERENCES

Anderson, H, & Anderson, G. (1951). *An introduction to projective techniques.* Oxford, England: Prentice Hall.

Burley, T., & Handler, L. (1997). Personality factors in the accurate interpretation of projective tests: The Draw-A-Person Test. In E. Hammer (Ed.), *Advances in projective drawing interpretation* (pp. 359–380). Springfield, IL: Charles Thomas.

Clemence, A., & Handler, L. (2001). Psychological assessment on internship: A survey of training directors and their expectations for students. *Journal of Personality Assessment, 76,* 28–47.

Erickson, M., Rossi, E., & Rossi, S. (1976). *Hypnotic realities: The induction of clinical hypnosis and forms of indirect suggestion.* Oxford, UK: Irvington.

Eskva, D., & Handler, L. (1995, February) *The Tennessee object Relations Inventory.* Paper presented at the Annual Meeting of the Society for Personality Assessment, Atlanta, G. A.

Exner,. (1969) The Rorschach System New York: Grune & Stratton.

Frisch, G., & Handler, L. (1974). A neuropsychological investigation of "functional" disorders of speech articulation. *Journal of Speech and Hearing Research, 17,* 432–445.

Fowler, C., Hilsenroth, M., & Handler, L. (1995). Early memories: An exploration of theoretically derived queries and their clinical utility. *Bulletin of the Menninger Clinic, 59,* 79–98.

Fowler, C., Hilsenroth, M., & Handler, L. (1996). A multimethod approach to assessing dependency: The early memory dependency probe. *Journal of Personality Assessment, 67,* 399–413.

Fowler, C., Hilsenroth, M., & Handler, L. (1998). Assessing subject relatedness with the transitional object early memory probe. *Bulletin of the Menninger Clinic, 62,* 455–474.

George, C., & West, M. (2001). The development and preliminary validation of a new measure of adult attachment: The adult attachment projective. *Attachment and Human Development, 3,* 30–61.

Handler, L. (1967). Anxiety indexes in projective drawings: A scoring manual. *Journal of Projective Techniques and Personality Assessment, 31,* 46–57.

Handler, L. (1988, March 13). *The use of inquiry and testing of the limits in WISC and WAIS interpretation.* Paper presented at the Annual Meeting of the Society for Personality Assessment, New York.

Handler, L. (1991, March). *Psychotherapy with brain injured patients.* Paper presented at the Sixth National Traumatic Brain Injury Symposium, University of Maryland, Baltimore.

Handler, L, (1994). Bruno Klopfer, a measure of the man and his work: A review of *Developments in the Rorschach Technique: Vols. I, II, and III. Journal of Personality Assessment, 62,* 562–577.

Handler, L. (1995). Maria Rickers-Ovsiankina: A Russian expatriate in America. A review of *Rorschach Psychology. Journal of Personality Assessment, 65,* 169–185.

Handler, L. (1996a). The clinical use of the Draw-A-Person Test, the House-Tree-Person Test and the Kinetic Family Drawing Test. In C. Newmark (Ed.), *Major psychological assessment techniques* (2nd ed., pp. 206–293). Englewood Cliffs, NJ: Allyn & Bacon.

Handler, L. (1996b). John Exner and the book that started it all: A review of *The Rorschach Systems. Journal of Personality Assessment, 66,* 650–658.

Handler, L., Wesch, J., Byrne, J., & Brody, Z. (1969, April). *Assessment of brain damage in severe closed head injury: A case study.* Paper presented at the Southeastern Psychological Association Convention, New Orleans, L.A.

Handler, L. (1996c, March 15). *Single projective test responses that illuminate therapeutic issues.* Paper presented at the Annual Meeting of the Society for Personality Assessment, Denver, CO.

Handler, L. (1997). He says, she says, they say: The Consensus Rorschach in marital therapy. In J. Meloy, C. Peterson, M. Acklin, C. Gacano, & J. Murray (Eds.), *Contemporary Rorschach interpretation,* Hillsdale, NJ: Lawrence Erlbaum.

Handler, L. (1998a). Schachtel and teaching: What color is the couch? *Journal of Personality Assessment, 71,* 172–181.

Handler, L. (1998b). Generating hypotheses in psychological assessment. Invited symposium paper, Annual Meeting of the Society for Personality Assessment, Boston, MA.

Handler, L. (1999a). The assessment of playfulness: Hermann Rorschach meets D. W. Winnicott. *Journal of Personality Assessment, 72,* 208–217.

Handler, L. (1999b, March 18). Playfulness and a life otherwise in despair. Symposium paper, Annual Meeting of the Society for Personality Assessment, New Orleans, LA.

Handler, L. (2001a). Assessment of men: Personality assessment goes to war. *Journal of Personality Assessment, 76,* 558–578.

Handler, L. (2001b). Introduction to A. I. Rabin, Projective Techniques in Midcentury: *An Introduction to projective techniques* by Harold and Gladys Anderson. *Journal of Personality Assessment, 76,* 352.

Handler, L. (2002, March 14). *Therapeutic assessment with children: The case of Walter.* Paper presented at the Annual Meeting of the Society for Personality Assessment, San Antonio, TX.

Handler, L., & Clemence, A. (2003). Education and training in clinical psychology. In J. Graham & J. Naglieri (Eds.), *Handbook of assessment psychology* (pp. 181–212). New York: John Wiley.

Handler, L., & Hilsenroth, M. (1994, April 10). *The use of a fantasy animal drawing and storytelling technique in assessment and psychotherapy.* Paper presented at the Annual Meeting of the Society for Personality Assessment, Chicago, IL.

Handler, L., & Hilsenroth, M. (Eds.). (1998). *Teaching and learning personality assessment.* Mahwah, NJ: Lawrence Erlbaum.

Handler, L., & Reyher, J. (1964). The effects of stress on the Draw-A-Person Test. *Journal of Consulting Psychology, 28,* 259–264.

Handler, L., & Reyher, J. (1965). Anxiety indexes in the Draw-A-Person Test: A review of the literature. *Journal of Projective Techniques, 29,* 303–313.

Handler, L., & Reyher, J. (1966). Relationship between GSR and anxiety indexes in projective drawings. *Journal of Consulting Psychology, 30,* 60–67.

Handler, L., & Riethmiller, R. (1998). Teaching and learning the interpretation of figure drawings. In L. Handler & M. Hilsenroth (Eds.), *Teaching and learning personality assessment.* Mahwah, NJ: Lawrence Erlbaum.

Hesse, E. (1999). The adult attachment interview: Historical and currrent perspectives. In P. Shaver & J Cassidy (Eds.), *Handbook of attachment: The ory, research and clinical application* (pp. 395–433). New York: Guilford.

Karon, B., & VandenBos, G. (1981). *Psychotherapy of schizophrenia: The treatment of choice.* Northville, NJ: Jason Aronson.

Klopfer, B., Kirkner, F., Wisham, W., & Baker, G. (1951). Rorschach Prognostic Rating Scale, *Journal of Projective Techniques, 15,* 425–428.

Machover, K. (1949). *Personality projection in the drawing of the human figure.* Springfield, IL: Thomas.

Meyer, G., & Handler, L. (1997). The ability of the Rorschach to predict subsequent outcome: A meta-analysis of the Rorschach Prognostic Rating Scale. *Journal of Personality Assessment, 69,* 1–39.

Murray, H. (1943). *The Thematic Apperception Test manual.* Cambridge, MA: Harvard University Press.

Mutchnick, M., & Handler, L. (2002). Once upon a time . . . : Therapeutic interactive stories. *Humanistic Psychologist, 30,* 75–84.

Pollio, H. (1999). Obituary: Edward Girden. *American Psychologist, 54,* 777.

Rapaport, D., Gill, M., & Schafer, R. (1945–1946). *Diagnostic psychological testing.* Chicago: Year Book.

Reitan, R., & Wolfson, D. (1986). The Halstead–Reitan Neuropsychological Test Battery. In A. Horton & D. Wedding (Eds.), *The neuropsychological handbook: Behavioral and clinical perspectives* (pp. 134–160). New York: Springer.

Rosenzweig. S. (1944). *Rosenweig P–F Study.* Oxford, England: Author.

Singer, E. (1965) *Key concpts in psychotherapy:* New York: Random House.

Smith (1943). *A tree grows in Brooklyn.* New York: Harpers.

Sullivan, H. (1953). *Conceptions of modern psychiatry* (2nd ed.). New York: W. W. Norton.

Terman, L., & Merrill, M. (1937). *Measuring intelligence: A guide to the administration of the new Stanford–Binet Tests of Intelligence.* Oxford, England: Houghton Mifflin.

146   PIONEERS OF PERSONALITY SCIENCE

Wechsler, D. (1949). *Wechsler Intelligence Scale for Children: Manual.* Oxford, England: The Psychological Corporation.
Winnicott, D. (1971b). *Therapeutic consultations in child psychiatry.* New York: Basic Books.
Winnicott, D. (1971a). *Playing and realry.* Oxford, England: Penguin.
Witkin, H., Lewis, H., Hertzman, M., Machover, K., Meissner, P., & Wapner, S. (1954). *Personality through perception.* New York: Harper.

SELECTED BIBLIOGRAPHY

Burley, T., & Handler, L. (1997). Personality factors in the accurate interpretation of projective tests: The Draw-A-Person Test. In E. Hammer (Ed.), *Advances in projective test interpretation* (pp. 359–380). Springfield, IL: Charles Thomas.
Fowler, C., Hilsenroth, M., & Handler, L. (1995). Early memories: An exploration of theoretically derived queries and their clinical utility. *Bulletin of the Menninger Clinic, 59,* 79–98.
Fowler, C., Hilsenroth, M., & Handler, L. (1998). Assessing subject relatedness with the transitional object early memory probe. *Bulletin of the Menninger Clinic, 62*(4), 455–474.
Handler, L. (1972). Amelioration of nightmares in children. *Psychotherapy: Theory, Research, and Practice, 9,* 54–56. (Reprinted in Schaefer & Millman, *Therapies for Children,* Jossey Bass, 1977.)
Handler, L. (1988). Utilization approaches in a case of hospital phobia: An integrated approach. *American Journal of Clinical Hypnosis, 31,* 257–263.
Handler, L. (1994). *Bruno Klopfer, A measure of a man and his work: Developments in the Rorschach Technique,* Vols. I, II, and III. Rorschach Classics in Contemporary Perspective. *Journal of Personality Assessment, 62*(3), 562–577.
Handler, L. (1995). Maria Rickers-Ovsiankina: A Russian expatriate in America. Rorschach Classics in Contemporary Perspective. *Journal of Personality Assessment, 65*(1), 169–185.
Handler, L. (1997). He says, she says, they say: The Consensus Rorschach in marital therapy. In J. Meloy et al. (Eds.), *Contemporary Rorschach Interpretation.* Hillsdale, NJ: Lawrence Erlbaum.
Handler, L. (1998). Schachtel and teaching: What color is the couch? Rorschach contributions of Ernest Schachtel. *Journal of Personality Assessment, 71,* 172–181.
Handler, L. (1999). The assessment of playfulness: Hermann Rorschach meets D. W. Winnicott. Invited Special Series. The Assessment of Psychological Health. *Journal of Personality Assessment, 72,* 208–217.
Handler, L. (2001). Assessment of men: Personality assessment goes to war. *Journal of Personality Assessment, 76,* 558–578.
Handler, L. (2003). Education and training in clinical psychology. In J. R. Graham & J. A. Naglieri (Eds.), *Handbook of assessment psychology.* New York: John Wiley.
Handler, L., & Habenicht, D. (1994). The Kinetic Family Drawing Test: A review of the literature. *Journal of Personality Assessment, 62*(3), 440–464.

Handler, L., & Reyher, J. (1965). Anxiety indexes in the Draw-A-Person Test: A review of the literature. *Journal of Projective Techniques and Personality Assessment,* 29, 305–313.

Hilsenroth, M., Handler, L., Toman, K., & Padawer, J. (1995). Rorschach and MMPI-2 indices of early psychotherapy termination. *Journal of Consulting and Clinical Psychology,* 63(6), 956–965.

Hilsenroth, M., Handler, L., & Blais, M. (1996). Assessment of narcissistic personality disorder: A multimethod review. *Clinical Psychology Review,* 16(7), 655–683.

Handler, L., Fowler, C., & Hilsenroth, M. (1998). Teaching an advanced course in personality assessment. In L. Handler & M. Hilsenroth (Eds.), *Teaching and learning personality assessment* (pp. 431–452). Mahwah, NJ: Lawrence Erlbaum.

Handler, L., & Hilsenroth, M. (1998). *Teaching and learning personality assessment.* Mahwah, NJ: Lawrence Erlbaum.

Handler, L., & Hilsenroth, M. (in press). The use of the Rorschach in the diagnosis of narcissistic personality disorder. In S. Huprich (Ed.), *The Rorschach in the diagnosis of personality disorders.* Mahwah, NJ: Lawrence Erlbaum.

Handler, L., & Meyer, G. (1998). The importance of teaching and learning personality assessment. In L. Handler & M. Hilsenroth, (Eds.), *Teaching and learning personality assessment* (pp. 3–30). Mahwah, NJ: Lawrence Erlbaum.

Handler, L., & Potash, H. (1999). The assessment of psychological health: Introduction. Invited Special Series, The Assessment of Psychological Health. *Journal of Personality Assessment,* 72, 181–184.

Meyer, G., & Handler, L. (1997). The ability of the Rorschach to predict subsequent outcome: A meta-analysis of the Rorschach Prognostic Rating Scale. Invited paper. *Journal of Personality Assessment,* 69(1), 1–38.

Mutchnick, M., & Handler, L. (2002). Once upon a time . . . : Therapeutic interactive stories. *Humanistic Psychologist,* 30, 75–84.

Naglieri, J., Drasgow, F., Schmidt, M., Handler, L., et al. (2004). Psychological assessment on the Internet. *American Psychologist,* 59(3), 150–162.

Riethmiller, R., & Handler, L. (1997). Problematic methods and unwarranted conclusions in DAP research: Suggestions for improved procedures. *Journal of Personality Assessment.* 69(3), 459–475.

Schacht, L. (2001). Between the Capacity and the Necessity of Being Alone. In M. Bertolini, A. Giannakoulas, & M. Hernandez (Eds.), *Squiggles and spaces: Revisiting the work of D.W. Winnicott, Vol. I* (p.112). London: Whur.

Sprohge, E., Handler, L., Plant, D., & Wicker, D. (2002). A Rorschach study of oral dependence in alcoholics and depressives. *Journal of Personality Assessment,* 79, 142–160.

Len Handler at 6, sister behind, mother to his right

As a college sophomore, 1956

Our wedding day, June 25, 1961

University of Tennessee faculty and some graduate students, 1964 (I'm at the bottom)

Our family, Mother's Day 1987

Barbara's doctoral graduation, 1982

At the Clinton-Gore Inauguration Ball,
1992

CHAPTER 6

A Lifelong Attempt to Understand and Assess Personality

Robert R. Holt
New York University

I was born both earlier and later than expected, according to two different family stories. Mother had hoped I would be a Christmas baby, but I showed up two days later (in 1917). The story continues, however, that my grandmother shouted down to her husband, "Tom, call the baby—the doctor is here already!" Mother told me a number of times that her milk was "too rich for me," so I had to be put on a bottle. I seem to have survived anyway.

My maternal grandfather, Thomas Hilditch, was a Liverpuddlian who had come to this country a decade or so earlier. He met and married a New Jersey girl, Elizabeth (Lizzie) Hall, and together they made their way to Jacksonville, Florida. There he founded a successful laundry business and they had my mother, followed by two more girls and one son. Papa (as my grandfather was known even to my sister and me) was a tall, handsome man who had a fine singing voice. He supposedly started as a first tenor and ended up as a second bass as he aged. He seems to have bestowed good musical genes on his descendants, for my mother became a professional singer, one of my sons is a professional musician, and I have spent many of my most enjoyable leisure hours as an adult singing. Once, I got paid (as a member of the Harvard chapel choir), so I can say that I have been a professional too. Tom Hilditch sang in churches as well as in a reformed synagogue, where years later my mother became a mainstay in the choir. I often attended choir rehearsal with her, so I had the distinction of having spent many more hours at *shul* than anyone in my present wife's whole family of irreligious Jews. When my tenor voice developed, Mother even arranged for me to sing a solo at a service to have three generations represented.

Mother's first marriage (to Walter Watson) ended in divorce after two children and a stillbirth. The first child, my sister Dorothy, and I went to live with our grandparents in a two-story house on the northern edge of Jacksonville. There were open fields and woods not far away as well as a vacant lot next door and many others nearby, for me to wander in and acquire a lifelong love of nature.

I was a skinny kid, always tall for my age, and used to being taken for older than I was. That helped me a bit when I was "skipped" ahead half a grade in grammar school and made it a full-year promotion by going to summer school once. The fact that I was always poor at sports hurt my success on the playground, however. Papa Hilditch, who died before I started kindergarten, had always been a mark for itinerant book salesmen, so he left an impressive library. I soon discovered that many of these handsome books in sets with identical bindings had uncut pages, but attractive illustrations. One set, of sacred books of Asian religions with pictures of bizarre deities, particularly appealed to me. I recall as an adolescent reading the *Egyptian Book of the Dead*, when I would have done better to have learned to play baseball or to sail a boat, two skills I never acquired.

When (in 1922) Mother told me that she was planning to marry that nice Mr. Holt she had been dating, I followed the oedipal script and tried to talk her out of it. But the "loss" of my "real" father had left a lasting longing in me, which Frank Holt came to satisfy pretty well. He tried hard to be a good father to me, adopted me and had my name changed, and we came to love each other. But he was distressed by my puny muscles and engaged me in regular morning sit-ups at first. Later, we got up early every morning and drove to the yacht club to which he belonged, to swim in an open-air pool, even in winter. Though it never snowed in our part of northern Florida in my childhood, the temperature occasionally got down to freezing, but the artesian water was warm enough. That was after we had moved, in 1927, from his parents' house in an old, nondescript part of town to a higher-toned neighborhood. There he had a whitewashed brick house built, in which I lived the rest of my Florida years.

By that time Dad, as I came to call my stepfather, had become pretty successful. The son of a poor-but-honest railway clerk, he dropped out of high school to get a job and help support the family. He decided to become a lawyer, which was possible then for men (not yet women) who "read law" on their own and passed the bar exam. He did so, joined a law firm with two friends, and gradually became a prominent citizen, president of the Children's Aid Society, the Kiwanis Club, even commodore of the yacht club (though our family never owned a boat). My mother had gone to college before her marriage but dropped out after a year at about the time she developed occasional grand mal and more frequent petit mal seizures. Although these were mostly controlled by heavy doses of Phenobarbital—which may have accounted for some of her cognitive shortcomings that used to annoy my sister and me—she had idiopathic epilepsy the rest of her life.

My sister Dorothy and I remained very good and affectionate friends long after we were separated at about the time Mother remarried. My father had custody of her, so she grew up in his second family when he remarried and had two more boys. They lived some distance away from us on the other side of the city, so visits had to be carefully arranged and were infrequent enough that we never developed any sibling rivalry so we always found our time together special. We loved each other dearly up until Dorothy's premature death from cancer when she was barely 60.

When Dorothy, who was a year and a half my elder, reached high school age, mother decided that she had to have her little girl and prevailed on Daddy to let her come live with us. My cynical hunch was that Mother was mainly concerned that my sister should move to more of an upper-class neighborhood, meet "nice boys," and marry one of them after having become a debutante. Neither Dorothy nor I felt much depth or warmth in Mother's lavish praise and declarations of adoration.

Today, I can look back on my mother with some affection and understanding because of her emotionally crippling upbringing by my prissy, moralistic grandmother, and with sympathy for her psychosomatic disorders. Her mother (Lizzie) was always greatly preoccupied by the goal of having regular bowel movements, with the result that by the time my mother was an adult, she was completely dependent on laxatives. In another instance, Mother and her sisters realized after their engagements that they had made a mistake and wanted to back out, but Lizzie would hear none of it: "The invitations have been sent out, the silver is engraved, and you will go through with it!" Not having had much mother-love herself, Gracie (as my mother was known) couldn't give much. Fortunately, however, a series of Black maids and cooks who worked in our household throughout my childhood filled the gap, with their loving devotion.

My mother was such a complicated and paradoxical person that I have long thought that I became a psychologist in an unconscious attempt to understand her. Our relationship was ambiguous and difficult up to the last year or so of her life, when her cortex began to atrophy. The nasty part of her died first, leaving a sweet and loving, if progressively incapacitated, frail person whom at last I could love unambivalently.

A half century earlier, Dad managed to hang on to our new house despite the onset of the Great Depression after the stock market crash of 1929, but I remember it as a time when he was haggard with anxiety and overwork. The yard man was dismissed and his duties were turned over to me at five cents an hour. I came out of it thoroughly indoctrinated in penny-pinching and conservation of all resources.

There was another significant female in my early life. Frank Holt had an older sister, my Aunt Fannie, who took a liking to me. Unmarried, she devoted her life to running Camp Keystone for girls, in Brevard, North Carolina. We spent at least part of every summer escaping from the Florida heat to the cool, beautiful Blue Ridge mountains. Sometimes Dad would help open the camp, sometimes close it; one year I joined another boy who was the son of a counselor to participate in everything as if we were (freeloading) campers. I had a good deal of freedom to roam the woods and deepened my love for nature. I learned enough so that when I was in my mid-teens, Aunt Fannie had me take over the role of what she called "male protector," as nature counselor. Another summer, she and the director of a nearby boys' camp arranged a trade: his daughter came to Keystone, and I had a great summer at Mondamin, where I learned such skills as wood carving, tennis, and horseback riding.

Dorothy and I were in the same grade when we entered Robert E. Lee Senior High School, from which we graduated in 1934. Pretty, charming, and socially skillful, she was chosen most beautiful in the graduating class; I was named most studious. She had many close girl friends, which helped me get over my enormous shyness and start tentatively dating. I was extremely inhibited, however, and never had the courage to kiss a girl before going to college.

I began to do well academically in high school, got deeply interested in science, and became head of the Science Club. I reported to that group my discovery in the public library of a book by Binet and Simon on intelligence testing. It gave a new focus to my interest in psychology, which had been stirred by reading Karl Menninger's (1930) *The Human Mind*. So I decided to take a course in psychology as soon as I got to college.

My parents decided, however, that at 16 I was too young (and socially immature) for college, and sent me for a year to the Hill School, a college preparatory school in Pottstown, Pennsylvania. There I learned that the guys I hung out with were going to either Yale or Princeton, so I sent a letter of application to Princeton University, but addressed to New Haven, Connecticut. (That was how much I knew about either place.) If the post office had not sent my letter to New Jersey, I might well have gone to Yale.

COLLEGE

Herbert Langfeld, the department chairman, taught Psychology 101 at Princeton. As one of those academics who used the same notes year after year, he made the subject so boring that I almost decided to major in English and become a literary critic. The course in social psychology taught by a new, young man looked interesting, however, so I gave the subject one more try. Almost at once, Hadley Cantril stepped into the open position of mentor and surrogate father for me. I still get a warm feeling when I think about that gangly, near-sighted, humorous fellow who had a great passion for his subject. In his course, for the first time, I got a glimpse of a new and transformative way of looking at the world and that perhaps I could help influence it for the better. I was hooked on psychology.

I majored in psychology and got good grades, but felt that outside of Cantril's courses the only really good one in the field at Princeton was Philosophy of the Mind, in which we read the entire two volumes of William James's *Principles*. Hadley responded to my excitement by taking me under his wing, but made me feel as if I were a colleague, not an overgrown kid. It was at his house in the country outside of Princeton that I first heard Bach's monumental *Passacaglia in C Minor* on Cantril's phonograph after an afternoon of doing yard work together. He was the only faculty member who had anything but contempt for Freud and even assigned some bits. He also introduced me to Gestalt psychology, G. W. Allport, and H. A. Murray, and got me out of some onerous departmental requirements. At his suggestion, I decided to go to Harvard for graduate work with Gordon Allport, who had been Cantril's own mentor and close friend.

Under Cantrils' sponsorship, I spent most of my senior year writing my honors thesis, on the psychology of personal names. The topic obviously grew out of my personal experience of having had my name changed. Having gotten Phi Beta Kappa in my junior year, I was allowed into the "no course plan" to work on a thesis undistracted by other requirements, though I might attend any classes that interested me. What a great experience! The main thing I learned was that I loved doing research on meaningful topics in psychology, and decided to make that my career. Since I happened to pick a topic on which there was virtually no previous psychological research, I roamed through various literatures, thought up and conducted a variety of little studies—some more clinical and some more experimental—and wrote a small book about it. Hadley gave it the highest grade he could and I graduated in 1939 with highest honors, immediately heading with my parents for the World's Fair in Flushing, NY.

GRADUATE SCHOOL: HARVARD

In those simple days, you just decided where you wanted to go for graduate study, applied, and were accepted. I had had some scholarship help at Princeton and got teaching assistantships at Harvard after the first year, with Dad making up the difference. After the third year, my assistantship with Murray paid well enough ($500!) so that I was self-supporting and paid for my analysis. Of course, I could buy a dinner for 35 cents in those days, and splurge on steak for half a dollar.

Psychology at Harvard was a new world, intellectually, orders of magnitude above Princeton. The faculty included E. G. Boring, Gordon Allport, Smith Stevens, Kurt Lashley, Robert W. White, and a series of visiting professors such as Kurt Lewin, Kurt Goldstein, and W. H. Sheldon (from whom I learned somatotyping). Perhaps even more impressively, the graduate students just ahead of me included Jerry Bruner, Doc Cartwright, Mason Haire, John Harding, Jack French, and Al Baldwin. They knew so much; they were so intellectually sophisticated; they could toss ideas around so brilliantly! I felt like a poor cousin from the sticks the first year, but I learned a huge amount from daily lunches in the lab with them and with young faculty members like Leo Hurvich and Irv Child.

My first-year peers were no slouches, either. We suffered through a punishing "pro-seminar" in basic psychology and then studied together for prelims. Harvard had the custom of giving them after one year of courses; if you passed, you could continue and get an MA just by applying for it (and paying a nominal fee). Then you were expected to start work on a dissertation while taking some more course work.

One night in the spring of that year (1940), I had a grand mal seizure—my first, though I had had petit mal disturbances without loss of consciousness every now and then since early adolescence. After a thorough workup at Massachusetts General Hospital, Stanley Cobb gave me the diagnosis of idiopathic epilepsy, put me on a nightly small dose of phenobarbital, and recommended psychoanalysis! A fateful event: the diagnosis automatically excluded me from the draft, and the treatment started me down a road that I am still following.

In the fall, I started biking every morning down Memorial Drive, across the Charles River, and to the Boston Psychoanalytic Institute, where I entered treatment with Nils Antonisen, a recent graduate. He played it safe, mostly keeping silent except when he offered a standard-issue interpretation. Nothing happened.

Happily, Antonisen left Boston at the end of one year, referring me to Felix Deutsch. Right away, I felt engaged in a real process, and things started to move. It was still pretty classical: no major life decisions, no reading of Freud; but it seemed to work.

During my second year at Harvard, with Allport's guidance, I started looking into the literature on level of aspiration and found myself a thesis topic. The other notable event of that year was his seminar on personality, not for its academic content but because I had to write a research paper for it. One of my roommates, Freed Bales (who later became a distinguished professor of sociology) and I decided to revise and extend Dollard's (1935) list of criteria for life histories and illustrate their usefulness by writing an exemplary case study. We found an interested volunteer, a recent Harvard graduate, who loved taking tests. We gave him all the personality tests we knew of, had him write his life's story, interviewed him at length, even putting him on the couch for a couple of hours of free associations. A couple of friends helped out with tests we knew nothing about, the Rorschach and the Wechsler-Bellevue. (I had decided not to take the only course in the department's offerings that was called Clinical Psychology when I found out that it covered only intelligence testing.) We did our best to integrate it all into a personality study that owed more to Allport than to Freud, but we learned something about assessment from that first plunge. Over two decades later, I got my "subject" to undergo a second assessment and built a little book on the topic around the results (Holt, 1969).

Gordon and I had never hit it off as well as Hadley and I had hoped we might, and now at the beginning of my third year he crushed me by suggesting that I try another topic. But the legendary Harry Murray had just returned after an absence of some years, with a new grant to do another big cooperative research at the Harvard Psychological Clinic. I timorously took my proposal, on level of aspiration, down to see what he thought of it. With his characteristic ebullience, he declared it splendid and welcomed me, not only as his advisee but as a staff member, to join in the exciting new enterprise! Thus began the first great intellectual adventure of my life.

Murray was at its center, of course. Tall, athletic, charismatic, brimming with enthusiasm and excitement over ideas and the study of human lives, he attracted an extraordinary group of people. There was also the enigmatic, patrician beauty who shared in the invention of the Thematic Apperception Test, Christiana Morgan, who was rumored to be Murray's mistress. Harry's second in command, Bob White, made up with steadiness and depth what he lacked in his chief's color and bounce, but equaled Murray in warmth and intellect. I had come to know and respect him the previous year when I had joined his informal, no-credit seminar on the interpretation of the TAT, using stories told by intensively studied Harvard students. After reading them, all of us offered interpretive hypotheses, which White then tactfully evaluated in relation to his extensive life history materials on the subject.

The staff included two recent immigrants, Jurgen Ruesch and Fred Wyatt, who later acquired reputations they lacked at the time; so did Elliot Jaques, who just recently died after a distinguished career in his native Britain. Silvan Tomkins' PhD was in philosophy, but after a Kleinian analysis he was deep into psychoanalysis and had a surprising talent for research. Other graduate student members included James Grier Miller and Leopold Bellak.

Every day, many of us shared a lunch where the conversation was as nourishing as the hot food. Harry did things in style, often inviting visiting luminaries like Gregory Bateson, Paul Robeson, or David Rapaport to join us. Later, Christiana would serve tea, which was followed by a staff meeting. Sometimes these were devoted to theoretical matters, like the presentation and discussion of the latest edition of Harry's personological taxonomy, a list of needs that had grown to a Mendeleeviam 92 by the inclusion of traits, sentiments, structural and other variables. Each participant in the joint study presented a proposed research problem and design at staff meetings. I was scared when my turn came, but the discussion—led as usual by Harry—was supportive and helpful. I proposed to treat the setting of goals in experimental tasks as a challenge to one's self-esteem, part of a larger process of self-evaluation.

I now had an office at 64 Plympton St. near Silvan's. He and I both spent more than eight hours a day there and became best friends. A man of enormous warmth, humor, and spontaneity, he also had deep intellectual interests and an introspective, intuitive sensitivity. To see him at a party, you knew he was an extrovert; to be with him in his study, you became aware of his true introversion. He generously shared with me his extensive notes on his vast readings in psychiatry and psychoanalysis, only one of many ways in which I learned from my co-workers.

The general shape of the research owed a lot to the thesis research of my friend Dan Horn, an ambitious attempt to study and analyze the process of cooperative multiform personality assessment of the 10 undergraduates who were our focus. They had been certified normal by the Grant Study, which turned over to us their mostly anthropological and medical data. The participating assessors numbered about 30, each contributing a different test, interview, or experimental procedure to the pool of data on each man. The central group of 10 staff (including two graduate students Dan and Leo Bellak) besides me, was split into two diagnostic councils, each member becoming the "biographer" for one subject (or S, as we always called research participants in those days). The biographer undertook to assemble and digest all of the available data gathered by the other four members of his (or in the case of Christiana, her) council, plus selected other materials such as the autobiography and some standard inventories. Harry and Bob White, the two council leaders, gave the TAT to their council's five Ss; each other member was paired with a corresponding person. I, for example, ran my experiment on levels of aspiration and other self-evaluations on our five Ss and also gave them Dan Horn's Repeated Questionnaire, while he collected data for my dissertation on his council's five.

Dan knew statistics thoroughly and informally taught me more than I had learned in two courses. Actually, he later achieved fame as the statistician who designed the research that first established the link between smoking and lung cancer. He had the original idea of treating the fluctuations in the ratings people gave themselves on questionnaires as meaningful. His questionnaire, several dozen statements based on definitions of Murray's principal needs, required ratings on "how you feel today" on a 20-point (!) scale administered weekly 10 times. For each S individually, items were intercorrelated over time and were subjected to an ingeniously simple form of cluster analysis Dan devised. It was a subtle method of assessment since the level of each rating was subject to conscious control but their covariation was not, and the focus was on finding what fluctuated weekly with what. For several of my Ss, items measuring overt need, Aggression for example, had high negative correlations with *covert* n Agg (e.g., in fantasy).

That taught me two valuable lessons: that many assertions from clinical lore could be independently and statistically verified, but that they were true of only some people, not universally. A few years later, I used the same technique to show that the unreliable changes in reactions to pictured faces in the Szondi test were meaningfully related to changes in self-ratings on a form of the same Repeated Questionnaire in one subject (Holt, 1950). A good many years after that, when I got a student to try it again on four more people, wholly different patterns appeared, this time none of them vindicating either Susan Deri or David Rapaport. That proved a valuable lesson in the limitations of single-case research, no matter how statistically sophisticated.

Dan's thesis project attempted to study the validity of assessments of many aspects of personality based on systematically varied kinds and amounts of data. Thus, each member of each diagnostic council had to study the same battery of procedures for each *S*, but in a different order, rating him (using a short Likert-type scale) on all of Murray's 92 variables at each stage. It was done blind; not only were all identifying data removed, but each council worked on persons they had never tested or interviewed. Everyone started with a "face sheet" of basic demographic facts. An assessor might get the autobiography first on one subject, but the TAT first on another, and so forth, while each other member of his team rated that same *S* on the same data in a different order. It was possible to study the effect of the sheer number of procedures unconfounded by their nature, and to compare the validity of ratings based on the TAT not only alone but in terms of its increment of validity when combined with other tests.

The validity criterion was the ratings made by the other council on the men they had assessed using *all* available data after intensive discussion of each case in a series of meetings led by the biographers. Finally, after Horn's thesis was completed, the reunited staff had a meeting devoted to each *S*, at which all ratings based on multiple data were reviewed and discussed, and then reviewed again comparatively.[1] The final criterion ratings were available to over two dozen researchers who had supplied observations, contributing to several other dissertations besides mine and Dan Horn's. His design greatly influenced two of my main subsequent researches (Holt & Luborsky, 1958; Barr, Langs, Holt, Goldberger, & Klein, 1972).

That rich research experience influenced me in many other ways. I learned by bitter experience how easily one can be misled by too much identification with one's subject; how a persuasive or dominant person can bias a group's consensus; how easily a brilliantly convincing hypothesis about a person can be proved wrong if enough independent data are available to test it. I was both sold on the power of clinical inferential judgment and made aware of its many pitfalls and vulnerabilities—all this before I had first tested a patient!

After Dec. 7, 1941—a day that was supposed to "live in infamy"—Murray, Allport, and a few other faculty members organized a "morale seminar," in which most other graduate students and I participated, on the hypothesis that the best way psychologists could contribute to the war effort was to study

---

[1] The procedure is described more fully in Holt (1993), a much more extended and inclusive recounting of my career.

how to maximize its attitudinal and motivational underpinnings. Soon, however, Murray left Harvard and his unfinished project to engage in secret work (at the Office of Strategic Studies). Since I had a medical deferment from the draft, I was able to finish my dissertation with Allport's generous help.

Meanwhile, I had become emotionally involved with a brilliant graduate student of sociology, Louisa Pinkham, after meeting her in an invigorating seminar on culture and personality given by Murray and Clyde Kluckhohn. Under her influence, I took a course on social theory with her sponsor, Talcott Parsons, and through her was able to join an informal evening seminar on psychoanalysis and social science, which met at his house. Clyde and his wife Florence, and the senior analysts Ives Hendrick and Edward Bibring, were among the others. Louisa and I and my friend Freed Bales—the only graduate students—felt enormously privileged to share these high-level conversations.

My analysis came to an amazing climax in a day of almost continuous petit mals after which they ceased forever.[2] The last session took place in one culminating week when I also passed my doctoral oral and got married to Louisa. At about that time, Murray called from an undisclosed location offering me a job. The work was so secret that he could only tell me that it was war-related, based on what we had done together at the Plympton Street clinic, and that I would have to spend all my time at it, able to spend only occasional weekends with my bride. Much as I was tempted, that last stipulation dissuaded me, plus the fact that I had another offer of a job that would contribute to winning the war.

SURVEY RESEARCH

It just happened that during the previous few years I had had opportunities to learn sample-surveying of public opinion. First, I was trained as an interviewer in a couple of commercial Roper surveys in Boston—a good way to earn extra money and follow up an interest that had led me to take the first course in public opinion research given at Princeton. My first-year office mate and then (with Bales) roommate for a year, Bob Knapp, had decided to study rumor for his dissertation, before the war began, and so had soon been employed by the city as its rumor expert. He learned that the United War Fund needed to know whether adding Russian War Relief to its collection of good causes would drive away potential donors. He proposed to do a

[2]I did however have a grand mal seizure shortly after stopping medication. I resumed taking it for awhile, again tried quitting with the same result, and kept up for a decade. After that, I stopped permanently with no bad results. An EEG in 1954 was normal.

public opinion survey to find out, counting on me to direct it. So I had, for once, the experience of being a sort of businessman, recruiting and training interviewers, and "meeting a payroll." I also put my academic knowledge to work using US Census data to draw a stratified random sample, punching the results on Hollerith cards and statistically analyzing the data.

On the strength of those experiences, Rensis Likert hired me to join his staff at the Division of Program Surveys in Washington. It happened to be in the Department of Agriculture, but most of the work I did was on contract to Treasury, helping them find out how best to sell war bonds. Two very eventful years will have to be condensed here into a few words, since they seemed to be a diversion from my assessment-related work. Yet I have always felt, since then, that the experience had been invaluable and directly contributory to my subsequent research. I learned about the technical niceties of drawing samples, but (more to the point) about the importance of sampling as a logical basis for making generalizations. Nothing could have more convincingly shown me how flimsy a foundation most psychological research has on which to draw conclusions about people in general. When, a little later, I read Egon Brunswik (1956) on sampling objects, its importance immediately struck me as another widely ignored limitation of our work.

At Program Surveys, opinions were not assessed by "polling," i.e., asking questions with precut standard answers. The work had been more clinical from the beginning, in that interviewers trained in nondirective, open-ended methods had conversations with farmers about their experiences with New Deal farm programs. They sent their transcripts of verbatim Q & A back to Washington, where another highly trained group used content analysis on them. First, using a set of pretest results to "build code," they would prepare outlines listing all the significant topics/issues people spoke about in relation to each question, and then applied that to the final interviews as they came in, making changes and additions as needed. Each protocol was coded independently by two persons until they could agree at a predetermined, high standard. Years later, when I encountered exponents of hermeneutics and similar doctrines who claimed that qualitative, verbal meanings could not be treated by the scientific manner, I knew that they were speaking from theory-based supposition unsupported by relevant experience. With enough care and effort, it is not only possible but routine practice for workers without extensive academic education to achieve high reliability in content analysis, yielding data that can be subjected to rigorous statistical processing. Here was another reason I was predisposed to trust open-ended methods of personality assessment, like projective techniques, over self-administered paper-

and-pencil inventories, but I also knew that such data were tricky and had to be handled with care—and ingenuity.

Again, I was blessed by finding myself surrounded by talented, stimulating, charming coworkers, like Dorwin (Doc) Cartwright, Angus Campbell, Eleanor Maccoby, Jim Bayton, and George Katona. Not only did they teach me a lot, but most of them also became good personal friends.

Maintaining our interests in psychoanalysis and related ideas, Louisa and I took night courses at the Washington School of Psychiatry. Taught by Harry Stack Sullivan, Clara Thompson, David Rioch, and Erich Fromm, they were my first exposure to the interpersonal branch of analytic theory. I also had a course with Ernst Schachtel on the Rorschach, which if nothing else convinced me that it had a great deal more to offer than Ruesch had suggested in a mini-course he had given fellow-workers at the Harvard Clinic so that we could make something of the test as part of our multiform assessment. Amusingly, the atmosphere there had been so defensively pro-TAT as to be somewhat hostile to the Rorschach, which we knew only as interpreted by cookbook rules based on intuitively meaningless ratios.

When the war drew to a close, I became restless to get back into the clinical psychology I had known at Harvard. I let Harry Murray know this, and he gave David Rapaport my name when he came East recruiting staff for the Winter VA Hospital. It was a fit on both sides; soon Louisa and I, with our baby daughter Dorothy, arrived in Topeka, Kansas, in February 1946. I was 28 years old.

WORKING AT THE VA AND THE MENNINGER CLINIC

Unknown to me, it was a fateful moment in history. The many psychiatric casualties of World War II had caught the services unprepared. Young physicians with no prior interest or training in psychiatry, assigned to work with such patients often became fascinated as well as frustrated by it, and in unprecedented numbers sought residency training in psychiatry afterwards. Karl Menninger rose to the challenge and undertook to found the world's largest school of psychiatry at Topeka's backwater VA hospital, of which he became manager. It was to be revolutionized, converted into an active treatment center. That meant a greatly increased staff of all relevant disciplines, attracted by a unique opportunity: to be part of a historic turnaround of psychiatry under the influence of psychoanalysis and the integrated clinical team approach that the Menninger Clinic had developed. The goal was for every new patient to be tested by psychologists, interviewed by psychiatrists and social workers, cared for (and observed) by psychiatric nurses and ward attendants, and given individual and group psychotherapy as well as any indicated treatment by drugs, shock, etc., plus occupational and recreational therapy by specialists.

Any institution being built or fundamentally reorganized, especially by a competent and charismatic leader like Harry Murray or Karl Menninger, is an exciting, even thrilling place to work. A can-do atmosphere of optimism and determination arises by the interaction of individually inspired people. So it was at the Menninger School of Psychiatry, where we felt part of a great, exhilarating adventure. Being able to work with people of the stature of Margaret Brenman, Sybille Escalona, Merton Gill, Robert Knight, the Menninger brothers, David Rapaport, and Roy Schafer provided endless stimulation and challenge, even though I had not previously heard of more than a couple of them.

Though my job was with the VA, my training began at the Menninger Clinic along with other members of the new department of psychology, chaired by Robert Challman and later by Helen Sargent: Maryline Bernard, John Chotlos, Michael Dunn, and Milton Wexler.[3] We observed the Menninger staff psychologists give the standard battery, read the newly published monograph (Rapaport, Gill, & Schafer, 1945–46), and then administered "the battery" to patients at the nearby Topeka State Hospital: first the Wechsler-Bellevue, a story recall test, the Sorting Test, Word Association and Szondi tests, occasionally the TAT, and finally, the Rorschach. Soon George Klein joined the group of learners, though he was never on the VA payroll.

We spent a good part of each day in an intensive seminar on interpretation and diagnosis with Rapaport, going over data on patients we had tested and offering interpretive hypotheses, which we had to back up theoretically if possible. He would then give his interpretation with a full theoretical rationale and sometimes cite relevant research. He taught us how to use cognitive and psychoanalytic psychology to understand the processes by which responses to tests came about, and how to read the resulting rationales backward to form interpretative hypotheses. Those, however, always had to be tested on new, independent data, verified or discarded if they could not be reshaped to fit the data and the emerging picture. We were taught also to write brief, focused reports as free as possible from psychological jargon.

Six months after my arrival in Topeka, Rapaport drafted that initial group of learners to supervise the diagnostic testing of students in the newly created

---

[3]Later, Martin Mayman, and (for a short time) Roy Schafer joined the VA department.

Menninger School of Clinical Psychology (affiliated with Kansas University). It was learning by doing, on the VA job, capped with learning by teaching—happily, with Rapaport always around to back us up. I also gave these students and the psychiatric residents a course on theories of personality.

Largely because of the revered (and feared) Rapaport, diagnostic testing had enormous clout in Topeka at the time. At the VA hospital we copied the Menninger Clinic's routine of diagnostic conferences, with independent evaluations presented by the hapless resident followed by two professionals, the social worker and—most dreaded—the psychologist. It was a comical inversion of the usual prestige hierarchy in hospitals. But the blind evaluations served all participants as useful checks on one another, offering an excellent learning opportunity. Living and working in the hospital, psychologists could follow the clinical course of many patients, also.

It is difficult to express adequately what a huge role Rapaport played in my professional development, both generally and with particular reference to assessment. Like Murray, he always had a holistic, implicitly systems-theoretical approach to understanding and conceptualizing personality as well as to assessing it, despite the fact that we were tightly focused on diagnostic testing. Psychopathology could be meaningfully and effectively evaluated only in terms of a whole person with interacting biological, social/cultural, unconscious and conscious psychological subsystems. Thus, even independent and blind testing had to be as multiform as possible, using a carefully chosen array of tests. Deeply read in both psychoanalytic and academic psychology, Rapaport developed an eclectic synthesis to provide rationales undergirding the use and interpretation of each source of data.

A test was not just its pattern of scores; it was an opportunity to observe a person under a certain kind of standard interpersonal stress and to attend closely to the many channels through which he was communicating to the tester. Hence, the stress on verbatim recording of all that was said, gestured, conveyed by facial expression and other revelations of emotion. Thus, even though we did not have access to interview data about personal history and symptoms, we had the obligation to make maximum use of a rich clinical encounter. Some tests of course were intended to measure intellectual functioning, others to reveal thought disorder or ideational content, etc. But Rapaport taught us to look at each as a possible source of clues to unconscious fantasies, cognitive competence, the working of personal styles and defenses. He had poorly-concealed contempt for colleagues who plunged into "deep dynamic" speculation on the basis of single tests, and urged us to restrain our fantasies about childhood traumas and the like until we had converging evidence with which to evaluate them.

In those days, of course, none of us had heard of systems theory, which was barely aborning. Rapaport thought of his work as ego psychology and stressed the structural point of view (from metapsychology). In diagnostically similar patients, he had found recurrent patterns of test scores, which he called types of ego structure. They could be seen functioning adaptively in nonclinical ("premorbid") personalities, and existed in exaggerated ("decompensated") form in psychopathology. Diagnosis thus was not classification, but an attempt to conceptualize how someone with a given defensive structure, which we later called style, used it in an attempt to cope with a stressful life situation. He did not of course neglect what most clinicians call "dynamics," the pattern of motives and fantasies growing out of traumas and other significant events, but insisted that they be seen as only part of a total picture of a person in a crisis. His approach complemented what I had learned at Harvard, adding dimensions of assessment hardly mentioned there.

In the fall of 1946, I attended my first big professional conference, the first APA convention since the beginning of the war. From that heady experience I have space to mention only one afternoon's off-program meeting: an assemblage of workers with the TAT. Everyone found it so stimulating to learn what others were up to that someone suggested a newsletter so we could all keep in touch. I was the only volunteer. Thus began the *TAT Newsletter*, an informal mimeographed quarterly, my first major editorial experience. In 1949, the *Journal of Projective Techniques* asked to incorporate it, and it reached a wider audience there. Three years later I turned it over to Ed Shneidman who kept it going for awhile, primarily as a cumulative bibliography.

Important events in my personal life during these Topeka years include the birth of our second daughter, Catherine, my return to psychoanalytic treatment after the failure of my marriage and the exacerbation of the duodenal ulcer that had begun on Felix Deutsch's couch (my complaints of which he simply interpreted as oral cravings) and which was now medically treated. My new analyst, William Pious, made it possible to cope with these problems and helped me discover a lot about myself.

The other major experience of those years that shaped my work in personality assessment goes under the name the Selection Project. At the time the School of Psychiatry was first planned, David Rapaport and Karl Menninger decided to study the process of selecting young physicians for training in psychiatry. At first, the design was simple: they had each applicant interviewed by three staff psychiatrists and tested by a staff psychologist. All four rated the young doctor on a 10-point scale of his suitability for the residency, and recommended acceptance or not. The researchers planned to follow up all those accepted (on the basis of these ratings) while they were residents by collecting ratings from supervisors.

In mid-1947, Rapaport hired me to work with him on the project and recruited Lester Luborsky, who joined us a little later. A year afterward, Rapaport went to the newly rejuvenated Austen Riggs Center, leaving us to carry on without him. We set about planning a new design, after hiring another psychologist, Bill Morrow, fresh from the Berkeley Authoritarian Personality Project. He convinced us of the value of creating careful scoring manuals to systematize and discipline the evaluation of our principal instruments. We chose some new tests and developed original ones, then decided to study small samples of the current residents who were judged most and least competent, using all our instruments plus a redesigned interview.

After we had pored over the data obtained by using our enlarged assessment battery on that small sample, we created manuals for the four most promising procedures, listing the signs or cues that differentiated the known extremes and, for each item, the underlying psychological variable presumably being assessed. We then planned a cross-validation, a predictive study using a couple of sequential classes of new residents, who continued to be evaluated and chosen in the old familiar way. Meanwhile, we were developing methods by which the residents evaluated one another (at first, peers' nominations for best and worst resident) and were rated by their supervisors on their several functions (e.g., diagnosis, ward administration, psychotherapy) plus overall competence.

Loosely following Dan Horn's design, each member of our little staff evaluated each new subject's dossier, beginning with the basic demographic data and letters of recommendation, adding the interview or one of four tests (including the Rorschach and TAT), then each remaining source of data, stage by stage. At each stage of analysis, the predictive judge applied the relevant manual but then also made clinical ratings of personality variables, taking into account all data available at that point. We tried to predict the same aspects of psychiatric work on which criterion ratings were to be based.

Briefly, we found that the quasi-objective scores from the manuals had no more validity than the predictive ratings from the old, seat-of-the-pants method. By and large, validity (against both peers' and supervisors' evaluations after at least two years of residency) of all judgments based on one or two procedures were little better, but there was a perceptible cumulative effect, and some of us were able to make predictions at the final integrative stage that were a significant improvement. (For the full story and all of the complex body of results, see Holt & Luborsky, 1958).

This relative success of a kind of clinical prediction, coming just as the controversy started by Meehl (1954) was getting under way got me into a complicated brouhaha, the story of which is too long to recount here. In a series of papers (collected in Holt, 1978) I kept trying to clarify the issues—how to discipline and improve the indispensable function of clinical judgment—while many persisted in casting me as the champion of naïve clinicians vainly attempting to compete in races stacked against them.

THE NEW YORK YEARS

Before the analysis of the data was complete, I left for New York to accept Stuart Cook's offer of an associate professorship at New York University and the job of director of the newly created Research Center for Mental Health. I took it on condition that he would make a similar offer to George S. Klein, who also arrived for the fall semester of 1953. He and I had become such good friends in Topeka that we decided to work together as soon as we could find a suitable place to create our own new research institution. George took the title of research director at first; a few years later we called ourselves co-directors. On the whole, it was a fruitful and agreeable arrangement, only slightly marred by my competitiveness and (to a smaller extent) his.

A second reason for my move to New York was that I wanted a larger pool of prospects for a remarriage. Before long, I found one, a graduate student of clinical psychology in another program, Crusa Adelman. After a successful reanalysis, I overcame my inner blockage, and we were happily married on my 40th birthday. A year and a half later, on our second delightful vacation in Europe together, she misjudged a curve and our little car turned over. I had one scratch; she was killed. It was devastating. I resumed treatment with my analyst, Charlotte Feibel, who helped a lot. So did my dear friend, David Rapaport, who was taking a sabbatical from Riggs at NYU that year. Since George was away on leave also, David had the office next to mine and we saw each other every day.

To finish this interpolated brief summary of my personal life in New York, I became much more active politically on my return from a year in California (see below), and fell in love with another lovely graduate student whom I met in the peace movement. Joan became my wife in August 1963 (just 40 years before these words are being written). We spent our honeymoon on Cape Cod, and luckily were able to buy a house in Truro where we have spent every summer vacation since. Our happiness together was only intensified by the two sons who arrived in 1965 (Danny, now a lawyer) and 1968 (Michael, a musician, poet and creative cook).

George's and my appointments allowed us to devote most of our time to developing and working at our new Center, teaching only one course per semester. We soon got a grant from NIMH for our initial project, a study of the influence of subliminal inputs on various perceptual and cognitive tasks, following up some work George had begun at Harvard (where he had been for the previous few years). Throughout, he took major responsibility for the experimental projects, for which he was much better trained and experienced than I. In addition to the administrative work, I concentrated on the other of Cronbach's (1957) "two disciplines of scientific psychology," the psychometric. We were in full agreement that the Center's work was to be devoted to a scientific evaluation of the psychoanalytic theory of thinking.

A year before leaving Topeka, I had met Bruno Klopfer at an APA meeting and accepted his invitation to join a team (Klopfer, Ainsworth, Klopfer, & Holt, 1954) that was drastically revising and enlarging his book on the Rorschach (Klopfer & Kelley, 1942). My task was to write the theoretical chapter, examining the Rorschach from the perspective of the principal theories of personality. The main upshot of that endeavor was my realization that the dual instinct theory and Hartmann's concept of neutralization were directly applicable to Rorschach responses. I therefore set up a simple scoring system, creating a variable for each of the so-called partial drives and aggression, distinguishing neutralized and nonneutralized forms of each. That soon grew into a scoring manual. I applied it tentatively to known cases, extended and enlarged it, realizing that it was better conceptualized as a way of assessing the concept of the primary and secondary processes.

As our center grew and prospered, grants were so easy to get in those days that George and I thought we had the golden touch. We attracted a talented staff and, as research assistants, the best of the graduate students in the NYU training program in clinical psychology.

Three staff members made especially valuable contributions to developing the Rorschach manual: Joan Havel helped me to turn Rapaport's *verbalization* scores into formal signs of the primary process and to turn into Controls and Defenses the perceptible differences between the ways the same sexual and aggressive Content or Formal deviations of thinking showed up in the Rorschachs of healthy, creative people, and in psychopathological cases, especially schizophrenics. One way was that the former group tended to enjoy seeing motivationally "hot stuff" and offering loose, nonrational notions, while the latter produced similar material with anxiety and displeasure. Fred Pine suggested that we simply add to the inquiry brief questioning about "how you felt when you saw that"—the Affect Inquiry, which proved highly valuable clinically as well as in the scoring. Finally, in a dissertation which I supervised, Leo Goldberger (1961) developed a way of combining the scores to rank order small groups of subjects on Kris's (1954) regression in the service of the ego. I later converted that into the Adaptive Regression Index, probably the most widely and successfully used variable measured by what came to be known as the "pripro" scoring method.

During the first decade or so of such developmental work, our whole staff participated in an intensive seminar on psychoanalytic theory, led by Benjamin Rubinstein and to some extent, Rapaport (by long distance from Stockbridge). That made an important contribution to the development of the pripro scoring system. So did my private practice of diagnostic testing during the years 1953–60, which was largely concentrated on evaluating more or less neurotic business executives.

Shortly before his tragic early death in 1960, David had asked me if I would take over a job for him. His classic monograph on diagnostic psychological testing (Rapaport, Gill, & Schafer, 1945–46) was out of print and there was a lot of demand for it. Would I take out the much-criticized parts of it that attempted to be a statistical study and produce a single, clinically focused volume? Of course, I agreed, and after a few years got it done (Holt, 1968).

I omit here an account of the experimental work at the Center, except for the cooperative study of the effects of LSD, in which our entire staff and corps of graduate students took part (see Barr, Langs, Holt, Goldberger, & Klein, 1972). An important part of our ambitious attempt to study a psychedelic drug that reportedly produced a temporary psychosis was the multiform personality assessment of our 30 subjects, all male unemployed actors. We developed dossiers on them as fat as those at the Harvard Clinic, and used the procedure of assigning biographers and having various stages of assessment using a common descriptive language, which also bore traces of its lineage. The final consensual ratings again made a face-valid criterion of which we made good use in analyzing the data from many an experiment.

The participants in the LSD study who actually took 100 micrograms of the drug in our double-blind design (20 more got a similarly flavored placebo) took Rorschachs which were duly scored on the semifinal (10th) edition of the pripro manual. As predicted, the drug significantly increased the amount of scorable primary process. I could also study the construct validity of my principal indices, using the group's ratings plus many scores from inventories and other tests.

The assessments also helped us flesh out the study's most notable contribution: delineating the numerous types of response to identical doses (e.g., elated and creative, purely somatic, cognitively impaired, delayed frightening breakdown) and the pre-existing personality configuration associated with each. Different trips for different folks—not so much of a generalized "drug effect."

Meanwhile, however, I was developing a new and absorbing interest in Jane Loevinger's sentence completion test of "ego development." I never liked the concept and often argued with her about it, but I thought highly of her instrument. We had met at an APA meeting, discovered our many mutual interests as well as the shared task of making a reliable scoring system for a projective test, and remained in close touch. When her manual (Loevinger, Wessler, & Redmore, 1970) appeared, I began teaching a course in personality development in the adult years and training students in her method. Several of them did dissertations using it, and I did some research with it too, including a project with Daniel Yankelovich, integrating my work in sample surveys and in assessment (Holt, 1980).

At about that time, I conceived a grand scheme, and deferred publication of the pripro manual and supporting data until one more cooperative project could be completed. I had been distributing copies of the scoring manual to many people who had asked for them after reading early publications about the method, and I was aware that a good deal of successful research was accumulating. I wrote to them, asking for the loan of their raw data—the scored Rorschachs plus independent criteria—and so many complied that I soon had a data base of over a thousand cases.

The full story of what happened next is too long to be retold here (see Holt, 2005). I will simply say that the grandiose project failed, in considerable part because I did not supervise closely enough the assistants who had the tedious jobs of collating and encoding this huge mass of data, resulting in such serious confounding that I could not trust the findings. The project also suffered from being begun just a few years too early in the computer era, when good programmers and people experienced in working with large data bases were hard to find.

A further reason for my negligence is that after my stimulating California year at the Center for Advanced Study in the Behavioral Sciences, I got much more deeply involved with theoretical work. First, I read the *Standard Edition* of Freud as each volume came out, focusing on mastering ego psychology and penetrating the obscurities of metapsychology, and then I gradually developed a series of critiques (Holt, 1989).

But beginning in 1982, I became so concerned about the looming threat of nuclear war that I devoted most of my time to organizing first a faculty seminar on Nuclear War and its Prevention, then to a collaborative undergraduate course with the same title, and finally an undergraduate minor and a master's program. All of that was known as the Program on Peace and Global Policy Studies, which I directed until my retirement in 1989. Much of the research my students and I were doing in those last years at NYU was also related to peace.

RETIREMENT

When I turned 70 near the end of 1987, the Research Career Award that had underwritten most of my salary and supported me in other ways terminated, and NYU then had mandatory retirement at the end of the year. I arranged for one final year's adjunct appointment so that I could try to find a replacement to direct the peace studies program, but failed. After several months of celebratory travel (in Italy, Turkey, Alaska, and the Canadian Rockies), Joan and I completed the move to our former summer cottage, enlarged and winterized, and have lived in Truro, Massachusetts, ever since.

Here I have been able to discover the joys of living in a small, rural town which depends heavily on retirees to volunteer many of the services that are provided by paid civil servants in larger cities, and where I see friends every day at the post office picking up the mail. Joan and I have served on various town committees, including unofficial ones aimed at solving various civic problems, and for the first time feel integrated into a real community. We are within walking distance of a beach, I can happily grow a vegetable garden once again, and there remains time for some writing.

After I finished editing the papers of my dear friend from early Topeka days, Ben Rubinstein (Holt, 1997), I was able to devote all of my work time to my long-delayed book on the primary process. As I write this, the proofs for the first volume have been finished, and the work is slated for publication soon (Holt, 2005). The first volume focuses on the theory of the primary process, ending with an attempt to sketch a testable neuropsychoanalytic theory of thinking as well as some ways the pripro research has begun to validate parts of it. In the second volume, to appear on a CD, are the final revision of the complete manual for the pripro scoring of the Rorschach and an attempt at an integrative summary of the research on it done by many hands. It also comprises my adaptations of Marty Mayman's (1970) form-level scoring system, and of Carol Eagle's (1964) extension of the pripro scoring to TAT stories, dreams, and free verbal texts, as well as many suggestions for further research on and for using these combined methods. I only hope to live long enough to see a fresh wave of interest and research to continue and expand what I see as my main contribution to the assessment of personality.

I was asked to add some comments about the recent progress of the field as a whole and its future direction. The narrowness of my concentration on an attempt to provide more of a future for judgment-based rather than primarily statistical/actuarial methods of assessment makes it hard to give an informed critique of what others have been doing. It is encouraging that, despite unrelenting harsh criticism, projective techniques still have valiant defenders who are teaching them to new generations. The future of diagnostic testing in the United States seems doubtful, however, because of its indirect dependence on the nature of the whole health care system. Yet I strongly believe that even in this politically regressive nation, a tax-supported, single-payer system will eventually become inevitable. Then there may be the economic base for a regrowth of multiform assessment of individual persons, ideally coordinated by research with a spectrum of treatment methods. As long as the present market-based scheme of managed care persists, economic pressures will make clinically sophisticated assessment increasingly available only to the most affluent patients.

Although I spent a good many years in research on how to improve the selection of the most qualified persons for limited educational opportunities, the underlying undemocratic nature of the work increasingly troubled me. Ideally, assessment for educational and vocational purposes should focus on finding the best ways for *all* individuals to maximize their potentialities and become as mature, socially useful, and constructive persons as their unique natures permit. Adjustment and happiness would emerge as byproducts, and probably health as well. If I figure out how to attain those goals, I won't keep the answers to myself; meanwhile, breathe normally.

REFERENCES

Barr, H. B., Langs, R. J., Holt, R. R., Goldberger, L., & Klein, G. S. (1972). *LSD: Personality and experience.* New York: John Wiley.

Brunswik, E. (1956). *Perception and the representative design of psychological experiments.* Berkeley: University of California Press.

Cronbach, L. J. (1957). The two disciplines of scientific psychology. *American Psychologist, 7,* 173–196.

Dollard, J. (1935). *Criteria for the life history.* New Haven: Yale University Press.

Eagle, C. J. (1964). An investigation of individual consistencies in the manifestations of primary process. Unpublished doctoral dissertation, New York University. *Dissertation Abstracts International,* 1965, 25(3), 2045.

Goldberger, L. (1961). Reactions to perceptual isolation and Rorschach manifestations of the primary process. *Journal of Projective Techniques, 25,* 287–302.

Holt, R. R. (1950). An approach to the validation of the Szondi test through a systematic study of unreliability. *Journal of Projective Techniques, 14*, 435–444. (Abstract in *American Psychologist*, 1949, 4, 269.)

Holt, R. R. (1969). Assessing personality. Part 4. In I. L. Janis, G. H. Mahl, J. Kagan, & R. R. Holt, *Personality: Dynamics, development, and assessment.* New York: Harcourt, Brace, & World.

Holt, R. R. (1978). *Methods in clinical psychology: Vol. 2: Prediction and research.* New York: Plenum.

Holt, R. R. (1980). Loevinger's measure of ego development: Reliability and national norms for short male and female forms. *Journal of Personality and Social Psychology, 39*(5), 909–920.

Holt, R. R. (1986). Clinical and statistical prediction: A retrospective and would-be integrative perspective. *Journal of Personality Assessment, 50*(3), 376–386.

Holt, R. R. (1988). Judgment, inference, and reasoning in clinical perspective. In D. C. Turk & P. Salovey (Eds.), *Reasoning, inference, and judgment in clinical psychology* (pp. 233–250). New York: Free Press.

Holt, R. R. (1989). *Freud reappraised: A fresh look at psychoanalytic theory.* New York: Guilford.

Holt, R. R. (1993). An exploratory study of life: Progress report. In C. E. Walker (Ed.), *A history of clinical psychology in autobiography: Vol. 2* (pp. 159–229). Pacific Grove, CA: Brooks/Cole.

Holt, R. R. (Ed.). (1997). *Psychoanalysis and the philosophy of science: The collected papers of Benjamin B. Rubinstein.* Madison, CT: International Universities Press. Also in *Psychological Issues*, Monograph No. 62/63.

Holt, R. R. (2005). *Primary process thinking: Theory, measurement, and research* (2 vols.) Madison, CT: International Universities Press. Also, *Psychological Issues,* Monograph No. 63, 65–66.

Holt, R. R., & Luborsky, L. (1958). *Personality patterns of psychiatrists* (2 vols.). New York: Basic Books.

Klopfer, B., Ainsworth, M. D., Klopfer, W. G., & Holt, R. R. (1954). *Developments in the Rorschach technique: Vol. 1. Technique and theory.* New York: World.

Klopfer, B., & Kelley, D. M. (1942). *The Rorschach technique.* New York: World.

Kris, E. (1952). *Psychoanalytic explorations in art.* New York: International University Press.

Loevinger, J., Wessler, R., & Redmore, C. (1970). *Measuring ego development: Vols. 1–2.* San Francisco: Jossey-Bass.

Mayman, M. (1970). Reality contact, defense effectiveness, and psychopathology in Rorschach Form-Level scores. In B. Klopfer, M. M. Meyer, F. B. Brawer, & W. G. Klopfer (Eds.), *Developments in the Rorschach technique: Vol. 3. Aspects of personality structure* (pp. 11–46). New York: Harcourt Brace Jovanovich.

Meehl, P. E. (1954). *Clinical vs. statistical prediction.* Minneapolis: University of Minnesota Press.

Menninger, K. A. (1930). *The human mind.* New York: Knopf.

Rapaport, D., Gill, M. M., & Schafer, R. (1945–46). *Diagnostic psychological testing:* Vols. 1–2. Chicago: Yearbook Publishers.

Rapaport, D., Gill, M. M., & Schafer, R. (1968). *Diagnostic psychological testing* (rev. ed. by R. R. Holt). New York: International Universities Press.

SELECTED BIBLIOGRAPHY

Holt, R. R. (1954). Implications of some contemporary personality theories for Rorschach rationale. In B. Klopfer, M. D. Ainsworth, W. G. Klopfer, & R. R. Holt, *Developments in the Rorschach technique: Vol. I. Technique and theory* (pp. 501–560). New York: World.

Holt, R. R. (1958). Formal aspects of the TAT—A neglected resource. *Journal of Projective Techniques, 22,* 163–172.

Holt, R. R. (1966). Measuring libidinal and aggressive motives and their controls by means of the Rorschach test. In D. Levine (Ed.), *Nebraska symposium on motivation, 1966* (pp. 1–47). Lincoln: University of Nebraska Press. Reprinted in P. M. Lerner (Ed.), *Handbook of Rorschach scales.* New York: International Universities Press, 1975.

Holt, R. R. (1961). The nature of TAT stories as cognitive products: A psychoanalytic approach. In J. Kagan & G. Lesser (Eds.), *Contemporary issues in thematic apperceptive methods* (pp. 3–43). Springfield, IL: C.C. Thomas.

Holt, R. R. (1969). Assessing personality. Part 4 in I. L. Janis, G. H. Mahl, J. Kagan, & R. R. Holt, *Personality: Dynamics, development, and assessment.* New York: Harcourt, Brace, & World.

Holt, R. R. (1977). A method for assessing primary and secondary process in the Rorschach, Chapt. 11. In M. A. Rickers-Ovsiankina (Ed.), *Rorschach Psychology* (rev. ed., pp. 375–420). Melbourne, FL: Krieger.

Holt, R. R. (1978). *Methods in clinical psychology: Assessment, prediction and research* (2 vols.). New York: Plenum.

Holt, R. R. (1999). Empiricism and the Thematic Apperception Test: Validity is the payoff. In L. Geiser & M. I. Stein (Eds.), *Evocative images; The Thematic Apperception Test and the art of projection* (pp. 99–105). Washington, DC: American Psychological Association.

Holt, R. R. (2005). The Pripro scoring system. In R. Bornstein & J. Masling (Eds.), *Scoring the Rorschach: Eight validated systems.* Mahwah, NJ: Lawrence Erlbaum.

Holt, R. R. (in press). Primary process scoring for the TAT. In S. L. Jenkins (Ed.), *Handbook of clinical scoring systems for thematic apperception techniques.* Mahwah, NJ: Lawrence Erlbaum.

Holt, R. R. (2005). *Primary process thinking: Theory, measurement, and research.* (2 vols.) Madison, CT: International Universities Press. Also, *Psychological Issues,* Monograph No. 63.

Holt, R. R., Barrengos, A., Vitalino, A., & Webb, K. (1984). Measuring systems thinking and belief in systems philosophy. In A. W. Smith (Ed.), *Proceedings, Society for General Systems Research, Vol. I. Systems methodologies and isomorphies* (pp. 5–11). Seaside, CA: Intersystems Publications.

Rapaport, D., Gill, M. M., & Schafer, R. (1968). *Diagnostic psychological testing* (rev. ed. by R. R. Holt). New York: International Universities Press.

(1939, age 21). The Oxford Four, first year graduate school at Harvard. From left, Daniel Mungall, William Moore, Kent Cooper, RRH

(1948, age 30). Going-away party for the Rapaports, Topeka. Back row: Maryline Barnard, RRH, Elvira Rapaport, Louisa Holt; front row: Lee Wexler, David Rapaport, Martin Mayman, Milton Wexler

(1958, age 40). RRH, at left, with Lester Luborsky

(1970, age 52). With sons Danny and Michael

(2000, age 82). With great-grandson Joshua Vaclav

(2003, age 85). With my wife Joan

CHAPTER 7

Over Half a Century of Playing with Inkblots and Other Wondrous Pursuits

Wayne H. Holtzman
The University of Texas at Austin

Born January 16, 1923, in Chicago, I lived across the street from my elementary school in a middle-class neighborhood close to Evanston and Lake Michigan. My father was educated at the University of Illinois as an agricultural engineer. He started out managing an experimental farm but had to leave for the city when my mother grew seriously ill during the great flu pandemic that swept the country around 1920. His father was a botanist and school principal in Chicago and offered my father the lot next door to his homestead in Rogers Park. Although my family suffered during the Great Depression, I had what I considered to be an idyllic childhood. A graduate of Northwestern University, my mother had been a schoolteacher who made sure that I kept ahead of my class. My grandfather next door taught me a great deal about plants, butterflies (which I collected), and carpentry. My younger sister and I had over a dozen playmates on our city block. And the beach at Lake Michigan was easy to reach on my bicycle, as was a large gravel pit full of water with fish waiting to be caught. Our Methodist minister lived next door, encouraging us to attend West Ridge Community Church and Sunday school regularly.

Starting when I was only five, my father took me on short fishing trips to Wisconsin and Minnesota. I loved the North Woods and eagerly looked forward to each trip. It was also a great way to be close to my father. When I was eight, I lost Grandfather Holtzman who died suddenly of a heart attack. Several years later my grandmother moved in with us, helping to care for my ailing mother. From a very young age, I had regular household chores because my mother was limited physically in what she could do. I sold the weekly *Saturday Evening Post* door to door, making enough money finally to buy a bicycle. While in high school, I worked 20 hours a week for a local cleaner and tailor shop, sewing cuffs and buttons on clothes, and delivering dry cleaning on my bicycle. I saved enough to pay for my first year at Northwestern University where I received a scholarship in chemistry.

On the eve of my entry to Northwestern while I was on a canoe trip in the Quetico Park of northern Minnesota, my mother died of a heart attack. Although she had been in poor health for many years, mother's death was a severe blow to all of us. Fortunately, my grandmother was like a second mother to my younger sister and me. Soon we all closed ranks to move forward as a family. Mammam, as I called grandmother, had a strong sense of social responsibility, serving as a voluntary social worker for the juvenile courts. She taught me many things about public service and caring for others.

Scouting became one of my favorite activities as a young teenager. While a junior in high school, I joined other Sea Scouts on a long summer cruise across Lake Michigan and Lake Huron aboard an old three-masted schooner that had been rescued by Henry Ford from running rum during prohibition days. The schooner had no ship-to-shore radio or auxiliary engine, placing us at the mercy of the wind and waves. A fog becalmed us in the second week, and we fell behind our schedule, which created anxiety among the parents. The *Chicago Tribune* came out with a front-page headline, "Coast Guard Hunts Scout Ship," but fortunately coast guard patrols found us and reported that all was well.

As a result of many such scouting adventures, I knew I wanted to be a naval officer. My father had been a student ROTC leader and Second Lieutenant during World War I. Although I received a BS degree in chemistry from Northwestern University, my heart and mind were with the Naval ROTC from which I was commissioned an ensign in February 1944. My assignment as an anti-aircraft gunnery officer on the *USS Iowa* in the Third and Fifth Pacific Fleets gave me many hours of daily routine between battles to think about my future and what I really wanted to do with the rest of my life. I had taken only one elementary course in psychology at Northwestern, but the behavior of the men under stress on my ship was a subject of great interest to me.

BECOMING A PSYCHOLOGIST

After the war, while driving alone from Seattle to Long Beach to rejoin my ship, I wandered into the main quadrangle at Stanford University looking for someone who could give me advice. Christmas holidays had just begun and hardly anyone was there. By chance I ran into Professor E. R. (Jack) Hilgard working in his office. When I learned that he also had received a BS degree in chemistry before studying psychology at Yale, I really got interested.

After my discharge from active duty in June 1946, I returned to Northwestern seeking graduate work. The head of the psychology department, Robert Seashore, was looking for someone with engineering experience to be his laboratory assistant in building motor skills apparatus. To my surprise, he told me he had been a geologist before following his father, Carl Seashore, into psychology. In those days, many graduate students in psychology had majored in a different field as undergraduates. I enthusiastically accepted his offer, agreeing to take a heavy course load in order to receive a master's degree the following summer. My fiancee, Joan King, was a senior music student and we wanted to get married when she finished her undergraduate studies. That first year was a busy one. In addition to working for Seashore and doing my master's thesis on a motor skills problem, I served as an assistant to A. C. Van Dusen, head of the counseling center and did statistical work and typing for other students to make extra money. By January I knew I wanted to enroll at Stanford to continue working toward a PhD degree. Hilgard offered me a position as his teaching assistant, beginning in the fall of 1947. When Joan received a scholarship from Stanford in music education, that settled it.

We were married in her hometown of Aberdeen, South Dakota, on August 23rd and headed west with all our belongings in my 1935 Ford that had been newly acquired for the occasion.

Graduate work in psychology at Stanford was exciting during those postwar years. Such well-known figures as Lewis Terman, E. K. Strong, Calvin Stone, Maud Merrill James, Quinn McNemar, Paul Farnsworth, and Jack Hilgard were active at the time, along with a number of younger faculty members in emerging new areas of psychology such as clinical. In my second quarter at Stanford, I elected courses in clinical psychology, personality, and social psychology while minoring in mathematical statistics with George Polya, Meyer Girshick, and Albert Bowker, a combination that I continued until finishing my coursework in August 1949. After a two-quarter stint as an assistant in the student counseling center, I was awarded a half-time fellowship in neuropsychiatry at Stanford Lane Hospital in San Francisco, a major teaching hospital for Stanford Medical School, where I studied clinical psychology under the direction of Katharine P. Bradway.

In the spring of 1949, my key mentor, Hilgard, strongly urged me to apply for a new position on the psychology faculty at The University of Texas at Austin (UT). UT had a small department but big plans for the future. Karl Dallenbach and Glenn Ramsey had arrived at Texas from Cornell and Indiana University, respectively, the year before, each with very different ideas of how to build a new department. Psychology was looking for an experimental/research-design psychologist as well as a clinical psychologist but had only one new position. Since I had good credentials in statistics, experimental, and clinical psychology, both factions wined and dined me in the hope that I would join them. The small, friendly reception I got when visiting Austin and their ambitious plans for a new five-story, air-conditioned psychology building convinced me that Texas was the place for me, a decision I have never regretted.

BECOMING ESTABLISHED AS A RESEARCH SCIENTIST

As a young graduate student, my fascination with inkblots stemmed from an interest in the unconscious and in ways in which deeper aspects of one's personality might be expressed. Until World War II, the mainstream of academic psychology looked askance at the Rorschach movement, criticizing its cultist character and lack of scientific discipline. This schism between Rorschach workers and academic psychology grew out of the two completely different traditions that characterized scientific psychology and clinical practice in America and Europe. The academicians were chiefly concerned with the development of general laws to explain sensation, perception, learning, and motivation. Clinicians working with the Rorschach and other psychoanalytically based techniques were mainly interested in a deeper understanding of individual personality. World War II changed all this with the sudden urgent need for new devices for psychiatric screening and personality assessment in the armed services. By 1945, the Rorschach technique was firmly established as the leading clinical instrument for psychodiagnosis, a position it still holds in some circles in spite of mounting evidence concerning its flaws.

Studies With the Rorschach

While searching for a dissertation topic, I seized upon the Rorschach technique as a diagnostic instrument badly in need of scientific evaluation, employing the latest methods of experimentation and control. The outcome of this activity was a dissertation demonstrating that such personality traits as impulsivity and personal adjustment, based upon peer-group ratings of college students living together, could be predicted by the way in which a person responded to inkblots. Overreaction to the color of the inkblots was related to lack of control in special situations. A large number of "clinical signs" that had grown out of earlier experience with the Rorschach proved to be correlated with the degree of personal maladjustment, unhappiness and anxiety of the people in the study, resulting in three journal publications soon after I received my PhD degree (Holtzman, 1950a, 1950b, 1952).

Spurred on by these positive though modest findings that confirmed some of the earlier clinical hunches about the meaning of inkblot responses, I joined a host of other young investigators interested in experimental studies with inkblots. Countless studies soon piled up a wave of criticism from which the Rorschach movement has never fully recovered. While much of this research was either irrelevant or badly conceived, a growing number of carefully designed studies yielded negative results. Typical of these criticisms were the attacks leveled by Zubin (1954) at a symposium, sponsored by the Society for Projective Techniques, on the failures of the Rorschach. He charged seven major failures as follows: (1) failure to provide an objective scoring system free of arbitrary conventions and showing high interscorer agreement, (2) lack of satisfactory internal consistency or test-retest reliability, (3) failure to provide cogent evidence of clinical validity, (4) failure of the individual Rorschach scoring categories to be related to diagnosis, (5) lack of prognostic or predictive validity with respect to outcome of treatment or later behavior, (6) inability to differentiate between groups of normal subjects, and (7) failure to find any significant relationships between Rorschach scores and intelligence or creative ability.

During 1950–53, I was a primary research scientist on a large U.S. Air Force contract at the School of Aviation Medicine in San Antonio where I was teaching extension courses in statistics and test theory for The University of Texas. The purpose of the research was to develop new psychiatric screening instruments to improve the selection of air force pilots. Much of the research dealt with anxiety and reactions to stress (Holtzman & Bitterman, 1952, 1955; Holtzman, Calvin & Bitterman, 1952; Holtzman, 1956).

One of the air force studies we undertook was to employ 20 prominent Rorschach experts to predict personality maladjustment under stress in otherwise "normal" individuals, using only projective technique protocols including the Rorschach. The task proved too difficult in spite of the confidence generally expressed by the clinicians concerning their predictions. When reported in a major Rorschach symposium at the 1953 annual convention of the American Psychological Association (APA) (Holtzman & Sells, 1954), these negative findings were interpreted by most academicians as the ultimate in damning evidence of the "nonsense" sometimes published in the name of projective techniques and the Rorschach. My own enthusiasm was badly shaken by the utter failure of these prominent clinicians, using various projective techniques as well as the Rorschach, to predict which air force pilots would later become psychiatric casualties. Nevertheless, I continued to believe strongly that the fundamental ideas underlying the technique were still intuitively attractive and could not easily be set aside, especially since I had just completed a separate study of college women that revealed a significant relationship between anxiety and color responses to inkblots (Holtzman, Iscoe, & Calvin, 1954).

Visions of a New Inkblot Technique

A faculty research fellowship from the Social Science Research Council in 1953–55 made it possible for me to undertake experimental studies of personality and perception as a follow up to my dissertation. Correspondence with Gardner Murphy and visits to the Menninger Foundation in Topeka, Kansas, where similar work was underway, led to close collaboration with both Gardner and Lois Murphy until their retirement.

In September 1955, I moved my primary office at the university from Psychology to the Hogg Foundation for Mental Health as the Foundation's first associate director in charge of research. The Foundation's budget had doubled, and one half of it was my new responsibility to spend wisely. An integral component of UT, the Foundation is privately endowed and supports mental health projects throughout Texas. The appointment allowed me to continue my teaching in psychology and my research on personality and perception while taking on new responsibilities to develop a major mental health research program throughout the state. Encouraged by the promising results of my early experiments and by my colleagues in the Hogg Foundation and Psychology, I embarked upon the large-scale, national development of a new personality test modeled after the Rorschach.

A fundamental confusion in much of the controversy over the Rorschach that continues unabated even today arises from failure to distinguish between the Rorschach as a projective technique in the hands of a skilled clinician and the Rorschach as a psychometric device that yields scores having relevance for personality assessment. What few clinicians realize, however, is that as soon as one decides to classify and enumerate any characteristic of a subject's responses to the inkblots, however crude and elementary the system, one has shifted from a purely projective point of view to a psychometric frame of reference (Holtzman, 1959). To classify a given response to the whole inkblot as

W, for example, assigns meaning to the response that transcends the private, idiosyncratic world of the subject. A crude form of ordinal measurement is achieved which leads to inferences of intensity as well as kind once the number of Ws is counted.

Unlike acceptable psychometric instruments that have many independent stimuli or items to each of which the subject is expected to give a response, the Rorschach has only 10 inkblots as stimuli, to each of which the subject is encouraged to give as few or as many responses as he or she wishes. As Cronbach (1949) pointed out, the resulting wide range in number of responses with only 10 inkblots is a fatal psychometric flaw in the Rorschach that cannot be overcome adequately by any statistical manipulation. Even Hermann Rorschach really wanted more than 10 inkblots. He originally had 35 but had to settle for only 10 since he had no funds to reproduce all of them (Ellenberger, 1954).

While these serious weaknesses in the standard Rorschach discouraged most experimentally oriented psychologists from further work with the method, it was becoming increasingly clear to me that a fresh point of view was urgently needed. I was convinced that the major limitations in the Rorschach could best be overcome by developing a completely new technique using many more inkblots with simplified standard procedures for administration. How could one develop psychometrically sound scoring procedures for responses to inkblots while preserving the rich qualitative projective material of the Rorschach?

Several clues to the solution of this problem were provided by research completed in the period of intense research activity immediately following World War II. Blake and Wilson (1950) had demonstrated that the first response of a person to each inkblot had all the necessary ingredients for the standard Rorschach scoring systems. Why not limit the subject to one response per card and increase the number of inkblots? And while developing a new technique, why not construct two parallel forms that could be used inter-changeably for repeated assessment in the study of personality change? Still another innovation was suggested by Zubin's elaborate rating system for the Rorschach, which required a simple inquiry immediately after each response while it was still fresh in the mind of the subject (Zubin & Eron, 1953).

Seizing these ideas, we conducted some exploratory work on a small number of cases, asking for a single response and following it with a very simple twofold question. Where was the reported percept in the inkblot, and what about the blot suggested the percept? We estimated that a set of 45 inkblots, requiring only one response each, would take no longer to administer than a standard Rorschach. Special efforts would have to be made, however, to develop new inkblot materials which have high "pulling power" for responses involving small details, space, and color or shading attributes, to compensate for the tendency to give form-determined wholes as the first response to an inkblot. I realized that it would take a great deal of time, money, effort, and the cooperation of psychologists throughout the country to develop and standardize superior sets of inkblots for major populations of individuals. Greatly encouraged by Gardner Murphy and other friends, and with financial support from the Social Science Research Council, the Hogg Foundation, and the National Institute of Mental Health, I embarked on a research program that continued for over 20 years.

Publication of the Holtzman Inkblot Technique

Development of the inkblots and national standardization of the new technique lasted from 1955 to 1962 and involved over a dozen well-known collaborators throughout the country who collected data on well-defined clinical populations. Containing 45 inkblots in each of two parallel forms, the Holtzman Inkblot Technique (HIT) was published by the Psychological Corporation (Holtzman, 1961). The accompanying book, *Inkblot Perception and Personality*, authored jointly with three of my graduate research assistants, Joseph Thorpe, Jon Swartz, and Wayne Herron (Holtzman, Thorpe, Swartz, Thorpe, & Herron, 1961), was awarded the Helen D. Sargent Memorial Prize by the Menninger Foundation in 1962 (Holtzman, 1963).

Subsequently the HIT was translated into other languages and used as a research tool and for clinical assessment in many countries. Suitable versions for group administration using projected images of inkblots were also developed and published (Swartz & Holtzman, 1963; Holtzman, Moseley, Reinehr, & Abbott, 1963).

Donald Gorham, a long time colleague of mine in the Veterans Administration (VA) developed a computer-based scoring system that was used in cross-cultural studies of college students in 17 different countries who were given the group-administered version of the HIT (Gorham, 1967). The inkblots were displayed on a screen before a group of subjects who wrote their responses in spaces provided on the answer sheet, circling the area of the inkblot used on an outline of each blot. Computer-scored group HIT norms for these subjects as well as for high school students, U.S. Navy enlistees, schizophrenics, depressives, psychoneurotics, alcoholics, and chronic brain-syndrome patients—a total of over 5,000 subjects—were published by Gorham, Moseley, and Holtzman (1968). The computer-scored version compared favorably with subsets of hand-scored protocols on most of the ink-blot scores. Unfortunately, the computer system developed by the Veterans Administration Hospital at Perry Point, Maryland, was written in machine language and did not prove sufficiently popular to justify later conversion for use by modern desktop computers.

In 1988, I received the Bruno Klopfer Distinguished Contribution Award by the Society for Personality Assessment in recognition of this work on the HIT that is summarized in an address to the Society (Holtzman, 1988). An annotated bibliography and research guide containing summaries of over 800 articles, books, and reviews of the HIT through 1998 has been published by the Hogg Foundation for Mental Health (Swartz, Reinehr, & Holtzman, 1999).

My interest in cross-cultural studies of personality was sharpened by a year at the Center for Advanced Study in the Behavioral Sciences at Stanford in 1962–63. We were already underway with a longitudinal study of person-ality development among school children supported by the National Institute of Mental Health when Rogelio Diaz-Guerrero visited me at the Center and suggested that we include a similar sample in Mexico. We designed a major international project on child development in Mexico and the United States, with a team of psychologists working in Mexico City under Diaz-Guerrero and a similar group in Austin under my direction. Over 800 children were tested annually for six years in an overlapping, longitudinal, cross-cultural design, using a variety of personality, cognitive, and perceptual tests, includ-ing the HIT. Published simultaneously in both Spanish and English, *Personality Development in Two Cultures* (Holtzman, Diaz-Guerrero, & Swartz, 1975) contains a wealth of information concerning both similarities and differences in Mexican and North American sociocultural premises and culturally deter-mined personality characteristics. Several journal articles on various specific findings were also published (Holtzman, 1965; 1982; Holtzman, Diaz-Guer-rero, Swartz, & Lara-Tapia, 1968).

A BROADENING OF INTERNATIONAL INTERESTS

Throughout most of my professional career, I have been deeply involved in international psychology. My involvement began in the summer of 1955 when Werner Wolff, Secretary General of the Interamerican Society of Psychology, dropped by my office at the Hogg Foundation and asked me to consider hosting the Third Interamerican Congress of Psychology at UT. Werner was a persuasive individual who had established a good reputa-tion as a personologist in Germany before he fled from the Nazis to Spain and then to Bard College in the United States. I was familiar with his book, *Diagrams of the Unconscious* (Wolff, 1948), and fascinated by his intriguing ideas. I asked my colleagues in both the Foundation and the psychology department what they thought of the idea and got a strong vote of support.

Lifelong Ties to Mexico

The Third Interamerican Congress was held at UT in December 1955 and was pronounced a big success. Among the 30 Mexicans attending was Rogelio Diaz-Guerrero with whom I would later develop a lifelong friendship as well as many collaborations, both personal and professional. The next year, I led a delegation of psychologists to Mexico for a three-day planning conference with our new friends, resulting in a series of small international projects. In June 1957, I made a longer trip by auto with my family, spending a few days with Rogelio and his family and touring parts of Mexico. Thereafter, we made at least one trip a year to Mexico for many years, and Rogelio did the same to Texas.

Meanwhile Joe Neal, Director of the International Office at UT, took me on one of his trips to Monterrey where we worked out some agreements with another psychologist, Edgardo Reyes Salcido, at the Instituto Tecnologico y Escuela Superior de Monterrey. Soon the Hogg Foundation was supporting several research projects in Texas and northern Mexico dealing with mental health, juvenile delinquency, and culture. Books on these and other cross-cultural, mental health topics were subsequently published by the University of Texas Press in a series of research monographs that I edited or authored.

This international activity with Mexican psychologists and other social scientists grew rapidly over the next several decades. In addition to visiting professorships in psychology at UT and its counterpart in Mexico, the Universidad Nacional Autonoma de Mexico, I organized a series of exchanges for the psychology faculty and their students between UT and various Mexican universities. In January 1961, over 100 Mexican psychologists spent three weeks in Austin, attending short courses offered by our faculty, making new friends in the community, and learning about American culture. The success of this first exchange led to four more like it over the next 15 years as well as to many smaller exchanges in both directions, some of which are still continuing to this day. Over 400 psychologists from Mexico and 100 faculty and graduate students from Texas benefited from these exchanges (Holtzman, 1970). Many of the Mexicans are now in positions of leadership throughout their country. Many Austin families also enjoyed serving as hosts for the visitors.

Years later, Rogelio and I even exchanged sons when they were in college. The eldest of my four sons, Wayne Holtzman, Jr., spent a year with Rogelio's family while working on a master's degree in education. He was already thoroughly bilingual and shortly thereafter married a Mexican psychologist, Elsa Hernandez. Both of them completed their graduate studies in school psychology at UT before accepting faculty appointments at the National University in Mexico. Rogelio's son, Rolando Diaz-Loving, lived with us in Austin while enrolled as a psychology undergraduate at UT. He later completed his doctoral work at UT in personality and social psychology before returning to Mexico where he has been a leading psychologist on the faculty at the National University.

For many years, I continued to be deeply involved in the development of psychology in Mexico, elsewhere in Latin America, and throughout the world. I was elected President of the Interamerican Society of Psychology in 1966 and received the first Interamerican Psychology Award in 1979, the same year in which I was recognized as a *Profesor Honorario* by the Universidad San Martin de Porres in Peru. The ceremonies that evening in Lima, Peru, were held in spite of the fact that a minor revolution underway made travel across the city difficult. In 1987, my many friends and former students in Mexico organized a special ceremony to elect me as their first foreigner to be an Honorary Life Member of the Mexican Society of Psychology.

A Global Expansion of Interests

My activities became global in 1972 when I was elected Secretary General of the International Union of Psychological Science. Members of the Union are national psychological societies or national science academies, one per country. The Secretary General is the chief executive officer who must travel to distant lands and help organize international congresses for psychologists. My wife Joan and I would always travel together on these trips, frequently visiting former foreign students whom we had met at UT. When possible, our sons would also travel abroad with us. During several summers we traveled across Europe in our Volkswagen camper, mingling with local families and enjoying a few rounds of golf. These were great educational experiences for the whole family. In 1984 I was elected President of the Union and continued to serve on its Executive Committee until retirement in 1992, the same year in which I received the Centennial Award from the American Psychological Association for distinguished contributions to international psychology. In 1996 at the 104th Annual Convention of the American Psychological Association, I received the Award for Distinguished Contributions to the International Advancement of Psychology.

After stepping down as an officer of the Union, I continued to be involved in international psychology, most recently as a co-author with Mark Rosenzweig, David Belanger, and Michel Sabourin of *History of the International Union of Psychological Science* (2000). At the time of my retirement in 1993 from full-time employment as President of the Hogg Foundation and Hogg Professor of Psychology and Education at UT, I agreed to be the initial director of a new bicultural center between Mexico and Texas. With an ungainly but meaningful title, the World Health Organization Collaborating Center for Research and Training in Mental Health and Psychosocial Factors in Health has focused particularly on La Patria Chica, the 1,000-mile border region defined by the Rio Grande River between Mexico and Texas. The Center has grown to consist of over 70 scientific associates—psychologists, psychiatrists, sociologists, public health specialists, and other behavioral scientists from the major universities of Mexico and Texas who are actively involved in cross-cultural studies in mental health and behavioral medicine.

ADMINISTRATION, PUBLIC SERVICE, AND FAMILY LIFE

In addition to my professional activities as a psychologist, I have always had administrative and public service responsibilities, beginning with being assistant chairman of Psychology at UT under Dallenbach in 1951–54, and continuing with the Hogg Foundation thereafter. In 1964, I was appointed Dean of the College of Education at UT where I led a reorganization of the College, greatly strengthening the graduate research faculty with key joint appointments from many other departments. It was a wonderful time to develop new programs in education because of the major expansion of federal activities under the Great Society movement of the late 1960s. At Texas we were able to launch major new educational research laboratories, ranging from computer-assisted instruction to science and mathematics curriculum centers. The nationally recognized Research and Development Center for Teacher Education and the Southwest Educational Development Laboratory were also founded during this period. From 1970 until my retirement in 1993, I served as president of the Hogg Foundation for Mental Health while continuing as Hogg Professor of Psychology and Education.

Throughout my career as a research psychologist, professor, and administrator, I have been fortunate to enjoy a supportive, enthusiastic, highly talented wife and four sons, Wayne, Jamie, Scott, and Karl, who understood when it was time to work and when it was okay to relax, play, and have a good time together. From my childhood on, I have been blessed with good health, lots of energy, and a positive, can-do attitude toward life and its challenges. I have always enjoyed hard work, especially physical activity, and as a student I developed a knack for getting things done quickly and efficiently—personal traits that have served me well over the years. While moving from Stanford to Texas in the summer of 1949, we took advantage of the auto trip to see the national parks of the Southwest and to spend several days in Denver attending my first convention of the American Psychological Association. Our first born, Wayne, Jr., was then only 10 months old. I carried him on my back everywhere, much to the amusement of other conventioneers. Ever since, each year on the way to and from professional meetings, we vacationed together as a family, often camping in national parks or in my beloved North Woods.

There is nothing like a tent and campfire cooking to promote family togetherness! On one occasion, our tent was pitched on the sands of Cape Hatteras just as a hurricane blew in. Much of the night was spent with Joan and the three older boys holding down the tent's four corners while I held on to the center pole. The next morning, our gear was completely buried in the sand and a lake had formed outside. As we staggered out into the sunlight, I was surprised and pleased to see an old psychology friend, Nick Hobbs, flying a kite and welcoming us on the beach.

Like many other psychologists, during my career I served on countless committees and boards. While serving as chairman of the American Psychological Association (APA) Committee on Ethical Standards (1956–62), the committee revised the initial code and accompanying case book assembled by Nicholas Hobbs, resulting in a streamlined version of two dozen principles and corollaries that served as a basis for subsequent revisions. I also served as a member of the APA Education and Training Board (1958–61) during the period when the plan for clinical training programs established at the Boulder conference was being seriously questioned.

Among my favorites were committees dealing with international affairs—the APA Committee on International Training (1962–63), the Science Committee of the U.S. National Commission to UNESCO (1963–66), the APA Committee on International Relations in Psychology (1966–68), the NRC

Committee on International Relations in the Behavioral Sciences (1966–71), the Executive Committee of the International Union of Psychological Science (1972–92), and the International Social Science Council (1976–84). One of my international projects was full of adventure. In 1963 at the time the Peace Corps was just getting underway, Nick Hobbs persuaded me to take on a major study of the Peace Corps volunteers who were destined to work in 23 small, isolated communities scattered along the San Francisco River in northern Brazil. Shortly after we signed the contract and completed the initial assessment of the 125 volunteers while in training, a revolution occurred in Brazil and the counterpart Brazilian partners for each of the Peace Corp volunteers never materialized, nor did the infrastructure support promised by the Brazilian government.

Rather than abandon the study, we completely changed the design. Instead of studying the impact of the volunteers upon the 23 communities, we evaluated the stressful impact of village life upon the isolated volunteers. My partners who were collecting data in Brazil visited all the communities and gathered extensive information about each volunteer after 18 months in the field. Sadly, the Brazilian pilot of the small plane chartered for travel from one village to the next died in a jungle crash toward the end of the study, but fortunately my research associates were not hurt. Several of the assessment instruments, including the HIT and the Edwards Personal Preference Inventory, yielded personality measures that were significantly correlated with subsequent performance of the volunteers in the field. We wrote a book two years later, describing the project and its findings (Holtzman, Santos, Bouquet, & Barth, 1966).

During a long career in mental health, I also served the National Institutes of Health in various capacities starting with the Behavioral Sciences Study Section (1957–59) and continuing with the Mental Health Study Section (1959–60), the Psychology Training Committee (1959–62), the chairmanship of the Personality and Cognition Research Review Committee (1968–72), the chairmanship of Social and Behavioral Development for the President's Biomedical Research Panel (1975–76), and the National Advisory Mental Health Council (1978–81).

Other noteworthy appointments include my serving on the Board of Directors for the Social Science Research Council, 1957–63, serving three terms as a trustee of Educational Testing Service between 1972 and 1986, and serving on the boards of the Foundations' Fund for Research in Psychiatry (1973–77), the Board of Trustees for the Center for Applied Linguistics, and the IBM Latin American Advisory Board (1985–89). My old friends, Bob Glaser and Ralph Tyler, persuaded me to join the Board of Visitors for the Learning Research and Development Center at Pittsburgh where I kept a hand in educational research (1969–86). During that same period, I was president of the Southwest Educational Development Laboratory (1969–76) and chairman of the NRC/NAS Committee to Study the Selection and Placement of Students in Programs for the Mentally Retarded (1980–82). Within psychology I served as president of The Texas Psychological Association (1956–57), the Southwestern Psychological Association (1958–59), the Interamerican Society of Psychology (1966–67), the APA Division of Evaluation and Measurement (1969–70), and the International Union of Psychological Science (1988–92). In my role as a foundation head, I was elected president of the Conference of Southwest Foundations (1978–79), and of the Philosophical Society of Texas (1982–83).

In addition to my personal research and writing, I served as editorial advisor for psychology books published by Harper and Row from 1963 until 1975. I was editor of the *Journal of Educational Psychology* (1966–72) and associate editor of the *Journal of International Psychology* (1973–84), as well as consulting editor for a number of journals throughout the world.

Over the years, I have had more than my share of honors and awards. In addition to those mentioned earlier from the American Psychological Association and the Society for Personality Assessment, I was recognized in 1974 by the Texas Psychological Association that gave me their first Distinguished Psychologist Award. Again in 1990, the Texas Psychological Association gave me their first Distinguished Professor Award. I was also the first to receive the Interamerican Psychology Award from the Interamerican Society of Psychology. And in 1979, I received an award for outstanding contributions to the field of mental health by the Association of Psychiatric Outpatient Centers of America. One year later, I was awarded an honorary Doctor of Humanities degree from Southwestern University. At the time of my retirement in 1993, I was very pleased to learn that my friends had raised enough money to endow the Wayne H. Holtzman Chair in Psychology at UT in my honor.

Although retired from full-time teaching and administration, I continue to be active on a half-time basis with the Hogg Foundation, as a trustee of the Menninger Foundation, as a director of the Menninger Clinic, as Chairman of the Population Resource Center in Princeton, New Jersey, and as a member of the Development Board for the University of Texas Medical Branch in Galveston. Most of all, I enjoy life in Austin, Texas, with my wife Joan, and with our four sons, their wives and 10 grandchildren, while continuing to participate actively in many community affairs and writing occasional papers on psychology or mental health. It has been a great half-century in so many ways, and I continue to be optimistic about the future, especially for psychology, mental health, and the behavioral sciences in general.

REFERENCES

Bitterman, M. E., & Holtzman, W. H. (1952). Conditioning and extinction of the galvanic skin response as a function of anxiety. *Journal of Abnormal and Social Psychology, 47,* 615–623.

Blake, R. R., & Wilson, G. P., Jr. (1950). Perceptual selectivity in Rorschach determinants as a function of depressive tendencies. *Journal of Abnormal and Social Psychology, 45,* 459–472.

Cronbach, L. J. (1949) Statistical methods applied to Rorschach scores: A review. *Psychological Bulletin, 46,* 393–429.

Ellenberger, H. (1954). The life and work of Hermann Rorschach. *Bulletin of the Menninger Clinic, 18,* 173–219.

Gorham, D. R. (1967). Validity and reliability studies of a computer-based scoring system for inkblot responses. *Journal of Consulting Psychology, 31,* 65–70.

Gorham, D. R., Moseley, E. C., & Holtzman, W. H. (1968). Norms for the computer-scored Holtzman Inkblot Technique. *Perceptual and Motor Skills, 26,* 1270–1305 (Southern Universities Press, Monograph Supplement 5–V26).

Holtzman, W. H. (1950a). Validation studies of the Rorschach Test: Shyness and gregariousness in the normal superior adult. *Journal of Clinical Psychology, 6,* 343–347.

Holtzman, W. H. (1950b). Validation studies of the Rorschach test: Impulsiveness in the normal superior adult. *Journal of Clinical Psychology, 6,* 348–351.

Holtzman, W. H. (1952). Adjustment and leadership: A study of the Rorschach test. *Journal of Social Psychology, 36,* 170–189.

Holtzman, W. H. (1956). A factorial study of adjustment to stress. *Journal of Abnormal and Social Psychology, 52,* 179–185.

Holtzman, W. H. (1959). Objective scoring of projective tests. In I. A. Berg & B. M. Bass (Eds.), *Objective approaches to personality assessment* (pp. 119–145). Princeton, NJ: Van Nostrand.

Holtzman, W. H. (1961). *Holtzman Inkblot Technique* (Manual, Forms A & B, answer sheets, scoring sheets). New York: Psychological Corporation.

Holtzman, W. H. (1963). Inkblot perception and personality: The meaning of inkblot variables. *Bulletin of the Menninger Clinic, 27,* 84–95.

Holtzman, W. H. (1965). Cross-cultural research on personality development. *Human Development, 8,* 65–86.

Holtzman, W. H. (1970). Los seminarios internacionales de psicologia de Texas: Un experimento continuo de intercambio transcultural en psicologia. *Interamerican Review of Psychology, 4,* 279–282.

Holtzman, W. H. (1982). Cross-cultural comparisons of personality development in Mexico and the United States. In D. A. Wagner & H. W. Stevenson (Eds.), *Cultural perspectives on child development* (pp. 225–247). San Francisco: W. H. Freeman.

Holtzman, W. H. (1988). Beyond the Rorschach. *Journal of Personality Assessment, 52,* 578–609.

Holtzman, W. H., & Bitterman, M. E. (1952). *Psychiatric screening of flying personnel, VI: Anxiety and reactions to stress.* Project No. 21–37–002, Report No. 6. USAF School of Aviation Medicine, Randolph Field, Texas.

Holtzman, W. H., & Bitterman, M. E. (1955). *Psychiatric screening of flying personnel. Conditioning and extinction of the galvanic skin response as a function of adjustment to combat crew training.* Report No. 55–29. USAF School of Aviation Medicine, Randolph Field, Texas.

Holtzman, W. H., Calvin, A. D., & Bitterman, M. E. (1952). New evidence for the validity of Taylor's Manifest Anxiety Scale. *Journal of Abnormal and Social Psychology, 47,* 853–854.

Holtzman, W. H., Diaz-Guerrero, R., & Swartz, J. D. (1975). *Personality development in two cultures.* Austin: University of Texas Press. (Also published in Spanish as *Desarrollo de la personalidad en dos culturas: Mexico y los Estados Unidos.* Mexico City: Editorial Trillas, 1975.)

Holtzman, W. H., Diaz-Guerrero, R., Swartz, J. D., & Lara-Tapia, L. (1968). Crosscultural longitudinal research on child development: Studies of American and Mexican school children. In J. P. Hill (Ed.), *Minnesota symposia on child psychology, Vol. II* (pp. 125–159). Minneapolis: University of Minnesota Press.

Holtzman, W. H., Iscoe, I., & Calvin, A. D. (1954). Rorschach color responses and manifest anxiety in college women. *Journal of Consulting Psychology, 18,* 317–324.

Holtzman, W. H., Moseley, E. C., Reinehr, R. C., & Abbott, E. (1963). Comparison of the group method and the standard individual version of the Holtzman Inkblot Technique. *Journal of Clinical Psychology, 19,* 441–449.

Holtzman, W. H., Santos, J. F., Bouquet, S., & Barth, P. (1966). *The Peace Corps in Brazil: An evaluation of the San Francisco River Project.* Austin, Texas: The University of Texas.

Holtzman, W. H., & Sells, S. B. (1954). Prediction of flying success by clinical analysis of test protocols. *Journal of Abnormal and Social Psychology, 49,* 485–490.

Holtzman, W. H., Thorpe, J. S., Swartz, J. D., & Herron, E. W. (1961). *Inkblot perception and personality.* Austin: University of Texas Press. (Featured in N. J. Smelser (1987). (Ed.), *Contemporary classics in the social and behavioral sciences.* Philadelphia: ISI Press.)

Rosenzweig, M. R., Holtzman, W. H., Sabourin, M., & Belanger, D. (2000). *History of the International Union of Psychological Science.* Hove, UK: Psychology Press.

Swartz, J. D., & Holtzman, W. H. (1963). Group method of administration for the Holtzman Inkblot Technique. *Journal of Clinical Psychology, 19,* 433–453.

Swartz, J. D., Reinehr, R. C., & Holtzman, W. H. (1999). *Holtzman Inkblot Technique research guide: An annotated bibliography.* Austin, Texas: Hogg Foundation for Mental Health. (As long as they last, a free copy may be obtained by serious investigators who write Communications Division, Hogg Foundation, Box 7998, University of Texas, Austin, TX, 78712.)

Wolff, W. (1948). *Diagrams of the unconscious: Handwriting and personality in measurement, experiment, and analysis.* New York: Grune & Stratton.

Zubin, J. (1954). Failures of the Rorschach technique. *Journal of Projective Techniques, 18,* 303–315.

Zubin, J., & Eron, L. (1953). *Experimental abnormal psychology.* New York: New York State Psychiatric Institute.

SELECTED BIBLIOGRAPHY

Bitterman, M. E., & Holtzman, W. H. (1952). Conditioning and extinction of the galvanic skin response as a function of anxiety. *Journal of Abnormal and Social Psychology, 47,* 615–623.

Gorham, D. R., Moseley E. C., & Holtzman, W. H. (1968). Norms for the computer-scored Holtzman Inkblot Technique. *Perceptual and Motor Skills, 26,* 1270–1305 (Southern Universities Press, Monograph Supplement 5–V26).

Holtzman, W. H. (1950a). Validation studies of the Rorschach Test: Shyness and gregariousness in the normal superior adult. *Journal of Clinical Psychology, 6,* 343–347.

Holtzman, W. H. (1950b). Validation studies of the Rorschach Test: Impulsiveness in the normal superior adult. *Journal of Clinical Psychology, 6,* 348–351.

Holtzman, W. H. (1952). Adjustment and leadership: A study of the Rorschach Test. *Journal of Social Psychology, 36,* 170–189.

Holtzman, W. H. (1956). A factorial study of adjustment to stress. *Journal of Abnormal and Social Psychology, 52,* 179–185.

Holtzman, W. H. (1959). Objective scoring of projective tests. In I. A. Berg & B. M. Bass (Eds.), *Objective approaches to personality assessment* (pp. 119–145). Princeton, NJ: Van Nostrand.

Holtzman, W. H. (1961). *Holtzman Inkblot Technique.* (Manual, Forms A & B, answer sheets, scoring sheets). New York: Psychological Corporation.

Holtzman, W. H. (1963). Inkblot perception and personality: The meaning of inkblot variables.*Bulletin of the Menninger Clinic, 27,* 84–95.

Holtzman, W. H. (1965). Cross-cultural research on personality development. *Human Development, 8,* 65–86.

Holtzman, W. H. (1970). Los seminarios internacionales de psicologia de Texas: Un experimento continuo de intercambio transcultural en psicologia. *Interamerican Review of Psychology, 4,* 279–282.

Holtzman, W. H. (1982). Cross-cultural comparisons of personality development in Mexico and the United States. In D. A. Wagner & H. W. Stevenson (Eds.), *Cultural perspectives on child development* (pp. 225–247). San Francisco: W. H. Freeman.

Holtzman, W. H. (1988). Beyond the Rorschach. *Journal of Personality Assessment, 52,* 578–609.

Holtzman, W. H., & Bitterman, M. E. (1952). *Psychiatric screening of flying personnel, VI: Anxiety and reactions to stress.* Project No. 21–37–002, Report No. 6. USAF School of Aviation Medicine, Randolph Field, Texas.

Holtzman, W. H., & Bitterman, M. E. (1955). *Psychiatric screening of flying personnel. Conditioning and extinction of the galvanic skin response as a function of adjustment to combat crew training.* Report No. 55–29. USAF School of Aviation Medicine, Randolph Field, Texas.

Holtzman, W. H., Calvin, A. D., & Bitterman, M. E. (1952). New evidence for the validity of Taylor's Manifest Anxiety Scale. *Journal of Abnormal and Social Psychology, 47,* 853–854.

Holtzman, W. H., Diaz-Guerrero, R., Swartz J. D., & Lara-Tapia, L. (1968). Cross-cultural longitudinal research on child development: Studies of American and Mexican school children. In J. P. Hill (Ed.), *Minnesota symposia on child psychology: Vol. II* (pp. 125–159). Minneapolis: University of Minnesota Press.

Holtzman, W. H., Diaz-Guerrero, R., & Swartz, J. D. (1975). *Personality development in two cultures.* Austin: University of Texas Press. (Also published in Spanish as *Desarrollo de la personalidad en dos culturas: Mexico y los Estados Unidos.* Mexico City: Editorial Trillas, 1975.)

Holtzman, W. H., Iscoe, I., & Calvin, A. D. (1954). Rorschach color responses and manifest anxiety in college women. *Journal of Consulting Psychology, 18,* 317–324.

Holtzman, W. H., Moseley, E. C., Reinehr, R. C., & Abbott, E. (1963). Comparison of the group method and the standard individual version of the Holtzman Inkblot Technique. *Journal of Clinical Psychology, 19,* 441–449.

Holtzman, W. H., Santos, J. F., Bouquet, S., & Barth, P. (1966). *The Peace Corps in Brazil: An evaluation of the San Francisco River project.* Austin, Texas: The University of Texas.

Holtzman, W. H., & Sells, S. B. (1954). Prediction of flying success by clinical analysis of test protocols. *Journal of Abnormal and Social Psychology, 49,* 485–490.

Holtzman, W. H., & Swartz, J. D. (1963). Group method of administration for the Holtzman Inkblot Technique. *Journal of Clinical Psychology, 19,* 433–453.

Holtzman, W. H., Thorpe, J. S., Swartz, J. D., & Herron, E. W. (1961). *Inkblot perception and personality.* Austin: University of Texas Press. [Featured in N. J. Smelser (1987). (Ed.). *Contemporary classics in the social and behavioral sciences.* Philadelphia: ISI Press.]

Moore, B. M., & Holtzman, W. H. (1965). *Tomorrow's parents.* Austin: University of Texas Press.

Rosenzweig, M. R., Holtzman, W. H., Sabourin, M., & Belanger, D. (2000). *History of the International Union of Psychological Science.* Hove, UK: Psychology Press.

Swartz, J. D., Reinehr, R. C., & Holtzman, W. H. (1999). *Holtzman Inkblot Technique research guide: An annotated bibliography.* Austin, Texas: Hogg Foundation for Mental Health. (As long as they last, a free copy may be obtained by serious investigators who write Communications Division, Hogg Foundation, Box 7998, University of Texas, Austin, TX, 78712.)

Wayne with his mother, Lillian Manny Holtzman, after joining the safety patrol at his elementary school, c. 1934

Antiaircraft officer on the battleship *Iowa* in the Pacific Fleet, c. 1945

Heading for Stanford after marrying Joan King, c. 1946

Rogelio Diaz-Guerrero with Wayne (right) at a conference in Mexico, c. 1966

Wayne as president of the Hogg Foundation for Mental Health, c. 1982

CHAPTER 8

Have PhD, Will Travel[1]

Samuel Karson
Chevy Chase, Maryland

Until I was 18, I had traveled very little. My enlistment in the U.S. Army Air Corps in October 1942 changed all that. Up until then my life had been programmed for me. I was the last child of my mother, who was 40 when I was born in Baltimore in January 1924. My mother had previously had six children by her first husband, and I was the second son by her second husband whom she divorced a short time after my birth. I liked living in a family group since there were always plenty of interesting people around. My two older half brothers, now deceased, were about 20 years older than I. I also grew up with three older half sisters, who ranged from 10 to 15 years older than I. During World War II, my mother had four sons serving in the U.S. Army.

My mother worked in an open-air market when I was a preschooler, and I recall helping her load a bag of "soup 'n' greens" that sold for three cents a bag. Later she sold fish and this meant that the unsold ones were brought home to swim around in the bathtub for a day or so. My mother was everything to me. I would run home from school on the days she was home so I could be in her presence for as long as possible. She would usually be cooking, or cleaning and humming, or singing a quiet song from her native

[1]Michael Karson critiqued the original manuscript for this article, some of which was previously published as "A Psychologist's Odyssey (Have PhD Will Travel)" in *Psychotherapy in Private Practice*, 1992, 10, 53–78, and is used here with the kind permission of Haworth Press.

201

Russia. How I loved that woman. Because she started to lose her hearing before she was fully assimilated, she barely spoke any English. I wonder if my early appreciation for what lies beneath the words people use made me a better clinician. I know that she succeeded in putting a permanent smile on my face and in my heart.

Next to my mother, the most influential person in my childhood life was my only full sibling, Albert, who was two and a half years older than I. He was an avid reader, and he started taking me to the library at a young age. It wasn't until years later that I became aware that he had an amazing memory, and that he could essentially read a book and practically memorize it in about 30 minutes. During WWII, my mother sent me a long newspaper article detailing that Al had made the highest test scores of nearly one million soldiers processed at Camp Campbell, Kentucky. This did not particularly surprise me. Al, incidentally, retired as professor of American Thought and Language after nearly three decades at Michigan State University. He died in February 1999.

I never liked school, primarily because it was so confining. When I was in the third grade, attending a Catholic elementary school taught by nuns, I developed what was probably a school phobia and stayed home for a couple of months. To cover my absence, I wrote a postcard to the school that Samuel was having surgery and Al signed my mother's name. One day, while looking out the window, I saw a school bus pull up, and out came Sister Mary and all my classmates, bringing candy, flowers, and comic books. I jumped into bed, pulled the covers up to my chin, and pulled it off with just a twinge of guilt.

I tried to get school over with as soon as possible: I was in the rapid advance classes in junior high school and graduated from Morris High School in the Bronx, New York, when I was 16. My teenage years were probably the happiest of my life. I belonged to a clique of approximately a dozen kids, and half of them lived in the same apartment house on Clinton Avenue that I did. We essentially spent all our waking hours together from ages 13 to 18. There was George (the fastest runner), Sol, Izzy (the star pitcher), Itchy (the Rabbi's son), Goldie (the only one with American parents), Ruby, Fat Al, Alex (the best fighter) and Jack, who were brothers, Lester and Benny (who died young), and Fly and Tubby who were witnesses at my wedding. During my adolescence I had two nicknames, Muscles and Blacky, related to my body build and swarthy complexion. Perhaps it was also related to the fact that my favorite all-time baseball player was Muscles (Ducky) Medwick of the St. Louis Cardinals. Other than him, I had no real life heroes, only fictional ones like Bomba the Jungle Boy, and Tarzan. Years later, when I saw the Ingmar

Bergman film, *The Seventh Seal*, I realized that I had been preparing to arm wrestle the Devil if he ever came for me. And how I loved to arm wrestle.

In my prime I was built like a welterweight boxer. I stood all of 67½ inches tall with a 17½-inch neck and weighed 145 pounds. In early adolescence, over the summer, I had played dice with the big boys, who were mostly the older brothers of my friends, and wound up owing $5. In order to pay my huge gambling debt, I read about a job in the newspaper classifieds and appeared at the given address. There was a fairly large crowd of boys assembled in the back of Goldman's Yarn Shop in response to the ad. Out came the boss, who looked over the group, and then pointed at me and said, "You've got the job. The rest can go." The work turned out to be carrying heavy barrels of wool, shaped like beer kegs, up two flights of stairs. After a week, the boss came up to me and said, "Hey kid, you're fired." "But, Mr. Goldman," I demanded, "How come you hired me in the first place?" "You really want to know?" he replied. "You looked like the strongest and the dumbest." I learned from this episode that it is not always good to be selected or necessarily bad not to be chosen. I did pay off my debts, though.

My three years in the Army Air Corps proved to be a learning experience. I was sent to radio operators and mechanics school at Truax Field in Wisconsin, and graduated at the top of my 500-member class. Two years after serving in Oahu, Saipan, Guam, and Okinawa, I had risen to the rank of corporal. I recall being on kitchen duty one day, watching an officer flirt with a nurse I liked. I wondered why he was where he was and I was where I was. It was then and there that I decided to go to college after the war was over.

After being discharged from the army in November 1945, I intended to go to New York University, but that would have required waiting for a fall admission. So, instead, I registered as a freshman in February 1946 at Long Island University, and had courses from psychology professors like Drs. Robert D. Weitz and Arthur Weider. By taking 18 credit hours each semester, and attending summer school and intersessions, I received my BS degree in June 1948. During that time I married the beautiful and intellectually gifted Dorothy Libert, whom I have known since I was eight years old. Dorothy was also a WWII veteran, serving in the Navy as a hospital physical therapist (Pharmacist's Mate Second Class). I had planned to become another Walter Winchell, but one day Dorothy, who was also attending LIU, told me there was an advertisement from the Veterans Administration (VA) to the effect that the U.S. government would pay to train clinical psychologists. This resulted in my becoming one of the 10,000 applicants who applied for the 200 openings nationwide. I wound up being interviewed for admission at Washington

University in St. Louis by Dr. Robert I. Watson. Drs. Saul Rosenzwieg and
W. B. Webb were also on the faculty. I was admitted to the VA Training Program in September 1948, and had completed all requirements for the PhD
by January 1952, again getting it over with as quickly as possible (the power
differential between faculty and graduate students being as aversive to me as
that between officers and enlisted personnel in the service). Our daughter,
Linda, was born during a blizzard in St. Louis just before my doctoral orals.

MY FIRST JOB IN PSYCHOLOGY,
OR "CALIFORNIA, HERE I COME"

After graduation I had a choice of several jobs in the VA, which did not particularly interest me, since the clock there seemed to move very slowly. So it
came down to an offer as an assistant professor in Iowa, or a federal job with
the U.S. Navy in San Diego, and I chose the latter.

San Diego was a beautiful, clean, and uncrowded city in 1952. We drove
out on U.S. Highway 80 in my green, two-door, 1949 Hudson Super Six, our
first car and by far my favorite of all the cars I've ever driven. I had bought it
after successfully arm wrestling the salesman for a further $100 deduction.
The U.S. Naval Training Center was located at Point Loma where one could
see the whales coming by at appropriate times during the year. I reported
for work at Med 2, the psychiatric unit, which was charged with screening
all incoming naval recruits (which ran about 6,000 per month at the time).
My boss was Lt. Commander John Laudenslager, who had previously served
as skipper of a minesweeper in WWII. The back of his office was lined with
stacks of case folders containing the results of a battery of psychological tests
which included the Otis, MMPI, and Navy Medical Screening Form A. The
job of the psychology staff was to pick off some cases from the pile each
morning and dictate a brief report, including a recommendation to the Aptitude Board, which would make the final decision about whether the sailor
should be discharged from the navy. (It may come as a surprise to learn that
bedwetting, or symptomatic enuresis, for which no organic basis could be
found, was by far the largest single reason for discharge from the U.S. Navy
recruit training centers in the 1950s.) In the afternoon, we screened the
recruits in about a three-minute interview, which usually provided enough
time for a quick perusal of the file and one question. The recruit would be
naked, except for a bath towel wrapped around his waist as I asked, "What
would you do if someone gave you a pet elephant for a gift?" As the sailor
laughed or started to grin, I would usually say "Next!" One day I was testing
a navy chief's son and, as I presented the Porteus Mazes, he said, "Can I ask

you a question? Do they pay you to do this?" Apparently, this did not seem like adult work to him.

While working at the Naval Training Center in the early 1950s, I took two Rorschach courses with Dr. Bruno Klopfer. His ability to diagnose with the Rorschach was awesome. In class he would lift his spectacles onto his brow, and it looked like he was actually sniffing the responses. One evening he invited Commander Laudenslager and me to his house for drinks. I couldn't help chiding him by saying, "Professor, if you told the class to go to the window and fly away, half of them would break their necks trying." "But not you," he replied, pointing his finger at me with a smile. Later, I came to know his son, Walter, who called me in Melbourne, Florida, in September, 1983, soon after I arrived there, to inquire whether I would be interested in serving as editor of the *Journal of Personality Assessment* (JPA). After thinking it over carefully, I declined with regret for lack of time. It was to be the only chance I ever had to be the editor of a psychology journal (though I did serve as consulting editor for over 20 years for *JPA* and for *Multivariate Behavioral Research*.

Our son Michael was born in San Diego during our first year in the city. With two babies, I was content to stay at the psychiatric unit for over three years, which, for me, was tantamount to settling down. Eventually, though, my tendency to become easily bored and my achievement needs set in, so when the opportunity presented itself, I went on active duty in the U.S. Air Force. Luckily, I was assigned to the Department of Clinical Psychology at the School of Aviation Medicine at Randolph Air Force Base (AFB) in San Antonio.

This proved to be one of the most interesting jobs I ever had. The late Dr. Saul B. Sells was the department head, and the staff included John Barry (later a professor at the University of Georgia), Sam Fulkerson (later at the University of Louisville), David Trites, Bart Cobb, and eventually Capt. Sheldon L. Freud. I was also assigned an airman, Kenneth B. Pool, who assisted me materially in my research and clinical work, co-authoring numerous publications. At the time, this was the largest military pilot screening service in the country, and it was also responsible for developing and recommending the psychological screening battery for the U.S. Air Force. Dr. Sells had appointed Raymond B. Cattell from the University of Illinois as our consultant. On a visit one day, "Professor" Cattell (which he preferred to "Doctor") asked, "Where is this chap Pool you publish with?" Ken, who was sweeping out my cubicle at the time, replied, "Here I am!"

When Professor Cattell lectured to the staff in 1955, it was the first time I paid attention to the 16PF. I delivered an attack on his questionnaire method, questioning in particular the brevity of his measure of intelligence and the absence of facially pathological items in the inventory. Instead of getting angry and defensive, he invited me to do a study on the 16PF, displaying a scientific attitude that in my experience is all too rare in psychology. (Interestingly, the very same criticism of the 16PF, regarding item content, led my colleague Jim Butcher to exclude it from his 1995 compendium of practical clinical instruments [Butcher, 1995], even though it seems fairly well established that it is not item content but the ability of the scale to differentiate psychopathology that matters.) I was so taken with Cattell's ability to stand the gaff, and his apparent openness as well as his obvious intellectual brilliance, that I found myself admiring a real live person at last. At age 31, I had found a father figure, of sorts. Little did I suspect that his intellectual brilliance was masking a virulent, colonial attitude toward blacks and Jews; however, over decades of correspondence and personal interactions with him, I never saw this side of him. Perhaps this too was evidence of his ability to separate the personal from the scientific.

I mounted a clinical research program on the 16PF and MMPI that eventually validated many of Cattell's ideas about personality and extended them into the clinical arena. Cattell always responded positively to my efforts, cementing my interest in his test. Ken Pool and I (1958) identified the Self-Control (or Persistence) factor, which I originally labeled sociopathic deviance versus obsessive compulsivity, now considered one of the Big Five. Ken and I (1957) questioned and eventually supported much of the construct validity of the test. Paul Winder, Jerry O'Dell, and I (1975) improved motivational distortion scales for the 16PF. Jerry O'Dell and I tried to make Cattell's erudite theory and predilection for neologisms accessible to clinicians (Karson, 1959; Karson & O'Dell, 1976). *Contemporary Psychology* reviewed our book, *A Guide to the Clinical Use of the 16PF*, in February 1978. The first paragraph of this brief review by Dr. Keith Barton stated: "The authors of this book provide for the 16PF and Cattell what Flavell has done for Piaget; that is, a lucid and accurate translation of a system." Most reviews, in my experience, are not this accurate.

While at Randolph AFB, I contracted bilateral uveitis and was practically blind for a month. It was the first serious illness I had ever had, and it was quite anxiety provoking. Shortly thereafter I requested a transfer. So after 18 prolific months, which included acting in several plays for a small theatre group, I was transferred to the Bolling AFB hospital in Washington, DC. At the hospital I worked closely with the chief psychiatrist, Lt. Colonel Leonard J. Wiedershine, who encouraged me to develop a group psychotherapy program for the busy outpatient service (Karson & Wiedershine, 1961). Lenny, it developed, had many years before worked in a supermarket in St. Louis owned by the father of one of my classmates at Washington University.

One day I was asked to greet General Curtis LeMay, who was scheduled to arrive at the hospital. At the appointed hour, his plane rolled down the runway and stopped. The imposing general, with his ever-present cigar, stood at the gangway. "Is that the hospital?" he asked, pointing at the wooden structure. "Yes sir," I responded. "I'm not going into that dump!" he replied, and he reboarded his plane, which whirled around and took off. When I told Colonel Jennings what had happened, he produced an atomizer and sprayed me out of sight. I took the hint and ended my air force career by hand carrying my orders by ferryboat from Bolling to the Pentagon. After two and a half years my active duty military career was over, although I remained in the reserves for another two decades. Hooked on the identification, I still wear military belts.

MY FIRST UNIVERSITY APPOINTMENT

Dorothy and I were in New York in early September 1957, attending an annual meeting of the American Psychological Association (APA) where I was giving a paper. Afterwards, a member of the audience came up and introduced himself as Dr. Herbert Carroll, chair of psychology at the University of New Hampshire. He took us to lunch and seemed charmed when Dorothy mentioned the author Gladys Hastie Carroll, who was his wife. (Dorothy's vast store of general information eventually led to a career as a research librarian, and a winning performance on the game show, Jeopardy.) He then invited me to come for an interview to see about joining the psychology department in Durham. I did, and accepted the offer made to me as assistant professor. We rented a house on a farm, and Dorothy got us all moved in, and the kids, then four and five, registered in school. I recall Dr. Carroll handing me my 12-hour, four-different-course teaching assignment with no prior consultation, apparently routine practice at that time. As Dorothy was unpacking, I remember saying, "If I were you, I wouldn't unpack too carefully. I have the feeling we're not going to be here too long." She protested by throwing newspaper wrapping from the barrel at me. Nevertheless, nine months later, I was looking for a better, and warmer, job on a trip to Florida. I called her to tell her I had turned down an offer from Florida State. She told me I'd better find something soon, because the movers were coming in a couple of days.

THE SUN SHINES BEST ON MIAMI

Under these circumstances I wound up with one of the most satisfying jobs I've ever had. It was at the Dade County Child Guidance Clinic as chief psychologist, group supervisor, research director, and assistant director. Dr. Leonard Lesser, a psychiatrist who had trained with Dr. Leo Kanner, was the clinic director, and my two psychology colleagues were the late T. Douglas Haupt and the late David J. Markenson, a former classmate and friend from Washington University. Doug was the saintliest man I have ever met. Jeannette B. Schwartz was the active chief social worker. There was also a staff of some half dozen social work graduate students, and an assistant professor from Florida State University, who supervised them. I took on the training task of teaching the entire staff to become group therapists, teaching the psychiatric staff and third-year residents to do group play therapy. This was the most enjoyable training I have ever done, and I dedicated myself wholeheartedly to this task (Karson, 1965). I was especially pleased when Dr. Gabriel Casuso, a child analyst, told me that he would be including group play therapy in the children's treatment program at Jackson Memorial Hospital in Miami.

One day I was interviewed at the School of Nursing by Dr. Dora Blackmon, its chairperson, for what I thought was a consulting job, but it turned out to be a regular faculty appointment as a research assistant professor at the University of Miami, which had a federal grant to study attrition in nursing (described in Cattell, Eber, & Tatsuoka, 1970, p. 205). With this added income, and Dorothy's job as a junior high school teacher, we were finally able to buy a house and enjoy some of the luxuries that Miami had to offer.

During this busy time I served as a softball coach for a neighborhood Khoury league team on which Michael played second base and pitcher. I was also active in the U.S. Air Force Reserve, and served as chairperson of the Ethics Committee of the Southeastern Florida (later, Dade County) Psychological Association, and was president-elect when I left Miami in September 1962, after four years at the clinic.

During my time in Florida, I taught a college-level course in child psychology to the Black community, but was amazed to learn that the Black students would have to be taught in their neighborhood, and would not be allowed on campus. Separate Black and White water fountains were common all over the state at that time. Racial, religious, and sexual discrimination has always taken me by surprise, despite its ubiquity. This, perhaps as much as yet another change in administration at the clinic, meant the end of the apparent paradise, so we headed north.

BACK TO UNCLE SAM (1962–1966)

The only time in my life I ever quit a job without another offer in hand was when I resigned from the Dade County Clinic. Coming home that very day, I asked Dorothy if I had any mail. There was a letter from Shelly Freud saying that the Federal Aviation Agency (FAA) was setting up a psychiatry and psychology staff. He had been contacted by them and had recommended me as chief clinical and research psychologist at the FAA and their Georgetown Clinical Research Institute. I called the number immediately, and heard the voice of Dr. Herbert C. "Pat" Haynes, the chief psychiatrist, for the first time. Little did I suspect that this call would initiate a lifelong relationship with one of my closest friends and colleagues. So we sold our house (our first) at a big loss, and watched our children painfully separate from their neighborhood friends of the past four years. We were on our way back to Washington, and I was now a GS-14 at $12,210 per annum. On this salary in 1962 we could afford a large four-bedroom, two-and-a-half-bath home in Bethesda, Maryland, one of the wealthiest communities in the country.

My work consisted of half-time research on aging in airline pilots and the other half doing extensive evaluations on commercial airline pilots who had been turned down for a first class medical certificate for psychological reasons of one sort or another. Pat Haynes did a thorough psychiatric evaluation following my assessment and, based on our written reports, made a recommendation to the Federal Air Surgeon regarding the pilot's current status. My test battery for this work usually took a minimum of eight hours, and typically included a WAIS, MMPI, Rorschach, 16PF Forms A and B, Bender, Porteus Mazes, Color-Form, and Draw-A-Person.

Occasionally, Pat and I would be called on to serve as expert witnesses in an administrative hearing before a federal hearing examiner. The pilot requesting the hearing would have the benefit of its taking place in or near his hometown. Typically, he would have his expert witnesses in psychiatry and clinical psychology, as well as other specialists, and the hearing would usually last several days. A court reporter would transcribe all of the legal proceedings. This role suited me to a tee, and I was in my glory. Not only did it include a thorough diagnostic evaluation and review of the records, but it also entailed reading the research literature on each test, and on testing in general. This role also involved helping the attorney set up the case and materially assisting in the cross-examination of the other side's expert witnesses, who were frequently well-known university professors of clinical psychology and psychiatry. It sort of felt like a sporting contest; only the results were not known until weeks later when a written decision was rendered by the administrative judge based on the testimony.

The FAA was an exciting place to work under its regal administrator, Najeeb Halaby, whose daughter became Queen Noor of Jordan. Pat and I initiated a nationwide air traffic controller screening program during this tour, for which he was later given the prestigious Longacre Award by the Aerospace Medical Association; all I got was a warm handshake from Pat. I had proposed the 16PF and MMPI for screening, but a U.S. Senate committee, chaired by the late Senator Sam Ervin, eventually ruled out the MMPI for this purpose, seeing it as an invasion of privacy. I attended all of these meetings and observed Dr. Arthur Brayfield, executive officer of APA, valiantly but unsuccessfully attempt to explain to Senators Bob Dole and Robert Kennedy that items like "I believe in the second coming of Christ" were not actually religious in nature, and that the MMPI was an empirically based test.

I also recall that committees from both the APA and the American Psychiatric Association visited the Office of Aviation Medicine, which employed me. They were surprised to learn that the entire staff for this nationwide effort consisted of three people: Carol Cannon, the administrative assistant, Pat Haynes, the psychiatric consultant, and myself. It was abundantly clear that there was no featherbedding in this project. We had given a contract to Professor Cattell through the Institute of Personality and Ability Testing (IPAT) to sanitize the 16PF by getting rid of objectionable items, and we developed the necessary infrastructure to test all 21,000 of the controllers and applicants in the air traffic control centers, towers, and terminal facilities. My supervisor during this time was the late U.S. Air Force Colonel Hayden Withers, MD, who ran the entire air traffic controller health program, of which the psychological screening was a part. This program produced what was an unusual publication for psychologists (Karson & O'Dell, 1974), unusual because there was no sampling: we tested them all.

In 1966, my brother Al came to visit from East Lansing. He indicated that he much preferred university life to work in the government. After four years with the FAA, I felt a need to move on, possibly to academe. Things came to a head when I did not receive a promotion to a super grade (i.e., GS-16), which was hard to come by, especially for a clinical psychologist in an office primarily staffed by physicians. Just after resigning, I was invited to a farewell luncheon attended by Drs. Pete Siegel, the Federal Air Surgeon, his deputy Homer L. "Rick" Reighart, Pat Haynes, and Hayden Withers. Pete handed me an envelope at the end of lunch, and in it was my appointment as a consultant to the FAA Office of Aviation Medicine, effective the next day. It was a memorable surprise that kept me involved with aviation psychology for years to come.

LIFE AT EASTERN MICHIGAN UNIVERSITY (1966–1977)

In the summer of 1966, I was offered a job as a tenured professor and head of the Department of Psychology at Eastern Michigan University (EMU) in Ypsilanti, Michigan. Until then, at age 42, I had not remained in any position for over four years. It was an inescapable fact that I had a roving nature, especially once a job became routine. But I accepted and changed jobs yet again.

The late Dr. Donald F. Drummond, a historian, was our dean of the College of Arts and Sciences, meaning that our money, space, and supplies were at his discretion. He once described me as the irresistible force and himself as the immovable object. He asked me how I was so successful over the years at getting him to accede to so many of my major departmental requests. "Well, Don," I replied, "my mother was broke and deaf most of her life, and after her, you were easy." Dean Drummond was an extremely patient and fair-minded gentleman who seemed never to be in a hurry. I had a great many dealings with him over the next decade, not only as psychology head, but also as the elected chairperson of all the heads of the College of Arts and Sciences for about six years.

When I got to Ypsilanti, the Dean mentioned that one of the art professors, John Pappas, had won the Prix de Rome, and that his house would be for rent. That settled our housing problem for the moment. Fortunately, EMU ran a campus laboratory school called Roosevelt, which was highly regarded and we were able to get Linda and Michael enrolled in it.

The department did not then have a clinical doctoral program. The psychology staff included nine Phi Beta Kappas, among them Jerry O'Dell and Stuart Karabenick, who had been hired upon their graduation from the University of Michigan. Bill McKeachie, chair of psychology at Michigan at that time, was an EMU graduate, and I invariably found him to be cooperative and gracious when I needed help finding someone to teach a course. I would also run into him on more than one occasion at the Detroit Metropolitan Airport on our way to Washington, I headed for the FAA and he to APA, where he was president for a year and active in APA governance for many years.

Most of the early work at EMU consisted of structuring the department so we could meet our teaching responsibilities and still leave the faculty time to do research. At one point, our 24-person, full-time staff was teaching 9,000 students a year, and producing 25,000 credit hours year after year. The psychology faculty included Francis Canter, a brilliant classmate at Washington University; the late Judy Gallatin; Ferdinand Stern, now deceased; Zakhour Youssef, and the prolific Richard Lerner, who was our most outstanding faculty member with regard to teaching and research productivity. He joined our staff at age 23, prior to completing his doctorate. At the time, he already had five publications in the literature. I appreciated the fact that I was one of the three Sams to whom he dedicated his first book, *Concepts and Theories of Human Development* (Lerner, 1976). (Also dedicated to me was my son Michael's second book, *Patterns of Child Abuse* [Karson, M., 2001].

One of my outstanding memories is of the day Dr. Gallatin stood at my office door and sailed a telegram at me which she had shaped into an airplane. She and a University of Michigan faculty member had been awarded a research grant of $1 million to study the development of political thinking in adolescents. No one in the department matched that accomplishment in over a decade. Later, she published a textbook on abnormal psychology and included a picture of me testing a minority patient during my internship year (Gallatin, 1982).

One of the best things about my 11 years at EMU was the opportunity to work with Jerry W. O'Dell. Our relationship has endured through two books, four chapters, half a dozen papers, and a computer program. I have an abiding affection and a great respect for him. With people of Jerry's caliber in the profession, I am not surprised that clinical psychology has gained such wide acceptance in America in only five decades. Our approach to computerizing my 16PF interpretations was a bit unusual. Rather than merely mull over, write, and organize interpretive statements, Jerry undertook an objective analysis of hundreds of my actual clinical reports (Karson & O'Dell, 1975, 1987a). The resulting computer program then attempted to mirror what I do, not just what I think I do. Perhaps this objective approach contributed to the successful validity studies later conducted on the program (Dana, Bolton, & West, 1983; Endres, Guastello, & Rieke, 1992).

After 11 years in Ypsilanti, our children had moved east, and I was getting itchy to move on. Michael had graduated from the University of Michigan clinical psychology program, and was still living in Amherst, Massachusetts, where he had spent his internship year. Linda married Richard Lehfeldt in June 1977, and was living in Cambridge, Massachusetts, where she eventually received her MA in counseling psychology from Boston University and where Richard completed Harvard Law School and the Kennedy School of Government. Pat Haynes phoned one day and told me he had become chief psychiatrist for the U.S. Department of State, and that I was now officially a consultant to the Office of Medical Services. Later, a letter arrived from the

Department of State Medical Director to James Brickley, President of EMU, to the effect that there was a need for my services, and requested that I be given a three-year leave of absence to assist the U.S. Foreign Service. The upper echelon administrators apparently saw this as an opportunity to be rid of me, and I was offered a two-year leave of absence as a professor, with the possibility of a third year left open. A few years earlier I had appeared in federal court before Judge Damon Keith as a witness in a suit brought by three professors against the university for denial of tenure. Since the department had unanimously voted tenure for the psychologist involved in the case, and I had approved the recommendation, I appeared as a favorable witness for him. He also happened to be the president of the Students for a Democratic Society, which was actively protesting the Vietnam War. The case was settled with a cash award to the psychologist in question, but his dismissal stood.

Dorothy had earlier taken a master's degree in library science at the University of Michigan and was employed as a reference librarian in the Ypsilanti Area Public Library, but she was not averse to moving back to the Washington area. Fortunately, she also has an adventurous streak, which has lately proved more durable than mine.

LIFE AS A SENIOR FOREIGN SERVICE OFFICER (1977–1983)
At age 53, I embarked on a Foreign Service career, finally achieving the elusive super grade, and was issued a black diplomatic passport that went with the appointment. After three weeks, my rating officer, Pat Haynes, asked if I'd be interested in a trip to Vienna to assist the regional medical officer with his mental health program. I was asked to conduct Parent Effectiveness Training classes with embassy parents, and to run educational groups for children on drug and smoking prevention. I was happy to oblige. Upon advice from my daughter's father-in-law, Dr. Hans Lehfeldt, I was booked in the Palais Schwartzenburg, a five-star hotel within walking distance of the Kerntnerstrasse. I recall taking a taxi one day to the Freud museum. The cabdriver told me that Freud couldn't be very famous since he had no street named after him. (Recently, that oversight was corrected.) My memory of that visit centers around a letter written by Dr. Freud to the effect that he was not personally worried about the impending Nazi *anschluss* since, after all, he had served as an officer in the Imperial Austrian Army. It saddened me to realize that, coping with stress and advanced age, even the great Freud had a denial system not so different from that of more ordinary mortals.

Back at State, I would typically be the first person to meet with an employee with psychological problems being returned (med-evac'ed) from overseas. I would usually tell the employee to get some rest and come see me the next afternoon. The test battery I used included the MMPI, 16PF Forms A and B, Shipley, and the Bender. Most of the time I could get the job done with this basic battery, but occasionally I supplemented it with Porteus Mazes, the Color-Form Test, the Rorschach, and selected WAIS subtests. Diagnostic evaluations have been a lifetime fascination for me, and my interest in assessment has rarely wavered. I did my dissertation on the Rorschach, but over the years I tended to use it less frequently, except with pilots. With them, whether military or commercial, I considered the Rorschach to be indispensable. This is not to say that I ever enjoyed being cross-examined on its validity by attorneys whose rebuttal experts had read the long series of critical reviews in Mental Measurement Yearbooks.

One of my overseas trips was to Moscow and St. Petersburg, in 1980, at the request of the post medical officer, Dr. Carl Nydell. It gave me an opportunity to return to the land of my forebears for a few months. My mother had been raised near Nijninovgorad, and had been lucky enough to obtain a green card and emigrate to America around 1920. As a matter of fact, whenever I saw a queue at the visa offices at any post I ever visited, I never failed to conjure up a vision of my mother standing in a long line of people, waiting and hoping. As a former army private, I got an especially big kick out of being moved to first class on the flight to Moscow over a navy rear admiral. It forced me to recognize that I had come a long way.

Landing in Moscow was like landing in Detroit: cold, hard mud, and somehow barren. Being in a foreign culture, especially with no understanding of the spoken or written language, intensifies the feeling of strangeness and isolation. Luckily, I made friends with the school psychologist, Gill Reeve, whose husband was the British commerce secretary, and this helped considerably. I recall visiting a Soviet research facility and answering questions about my research on air traffic controllers. When I asked some questions in return, however, the visit was abruptly terminated.

The stress for embassy employees in Moscow was increased by the fact that there were armed Russian soldiers on many busy streets, as well as a contingent around the clock in the apartment compounds where many of the personnel lived. It was apparent that all comings and goings by car were checked. Many employees reported that they felt their phones were monitored, and that they believed their living quarters were also bugged. After a few weeks I started having these same feelings. During my weeks in Moscow I was kept quite busy, including most evenings. To become better acquainted with the stressful conditions, in the hopes that I would recommend an increase in the post's stress pay, I was assigned an apartment like a regular employee, and I quickly learned that the Russian cockroaches were larger and harder to discourage than any of the roaches I had encountered anywhere else.

The closest I came to getting hurt in the Foreign Service occurred on this trip, when an explosion occurred in the visa office while I was in the nearby embassy cafeteria having coffee. An armed man had gotten into the visa office, and one of the Russian guards shot him. He retaliated by exploding a bomb he was carrying under his coat, and it caused considerable damage. So when a call came shortly thereafter for my services in St. Petersburg, I was not at all reluctant to leave. As a guest of the consul general there, I was given a small apartment in what had been the Czar's summer palace. "If my mother could only see me now," I thought when I was saluted by the Russian soldiers posted as guards. As a lover of art museums, I also got to go on an all-day tour of the Hermitage, which thrilled me.

What a beautiful city! Wide streets, clean air, majestic trees, colorful plants and flowers, and lots of students eager to practice English with an American. But I found it quite mysterious since I couldn't understand the language and the signs were Greek to me. It made me realize how dependent most people are on external cues for feedback from a familiar environment, and how necessary this process is to maintain a sense of identity and personal security. It also made me understand more fully why so many psychiatric medical evacuees had reported how much better they felt as soon as they boarded an American airplane with its familiar signs, faces, and language, so that their own lagging identity felt reinforced. My visit to St. Petersburg, however, succeeded in quickly dissipating the mountain of paranoia my stressful weeks in Moscow had created in me.

It was apparent that the climate at the post in St. Petersburg was a lot less stressful than the one in the Soviet capital. It was at this point that I began thinking about developing an Embassy Characteristics Index, which was probably the best unfunded idea I had in the Foreign Service. I did conduct an unpublished study of stress ratings by physicians and nurses who had been assigned to various worldwide posts, and found good reliability for overall ratings in different cities and for the factors causing the stress.

As a senior Foreign Service officer I was met, according to protocol, by a car and driver whenever I traveled outside of the U.S. The black passport was also a big help in getting through customs quickly. Typically, when arriving at post, the protocol was to drop off a calling card at the deputy chief of mission's office so that your presence would be known. I was usually invited to the ambassador's country team meeting a day or two later, where all of the top aides or division chiefs were assembled. This gave them an opportunity to meet me, and to present any problems they were facing with employees. All families and children were also offered an opportunity to make office appointments. I was typically scheduled to have dinner with employee groups, such as secretaries and communicators, to discuss the problems they were coping with, and to make suggestions for ameliorating them. Early on, I would usually show a film made under the direction of Pat Haynes, called "Something of the Danger That Exists," starring Dr. Stanley Gitlow. It depicted Foreign Service officers discussing the stresses of living overseas and the prevalence of alcohol at all social events. It was an excellent vehicle for getting a lively discussion going, and for breaking the ice. I would also visit the American International School, and be available for both teacher and student consultations.

Stateside, I often thought that, if a successful measure of climate stress was ever developed, I would not be surprised if the stress level at headquarters, namely at 21st and C Streets, NW, Washington, DC, would be found to rank first place. I was therefore quite pleased with the many opportunities that presented themselves to provide services to overseas posts during my tour in the department, even though diagnostic work accumulated whenever I traveled. I also enjoyed working with some of the most skilled and knowledgeable psychiatric consultants I have ever met.

With the taking of the hostages at the American Embassy in Tehran in November 1979, our work in the Mental Health Services suddenly came into the spotlight, and we became the focus of national attention. Well-known television reporters like Diane Sawyer called me more than once. President Carter actually visited us at headquarters to learn about our plans for the hostages upon their release, and to inquire what we were doing for their families in the meantime. Pat Haynes came up with a brilliant plan for debriefing the hostages and getting them back into contact with what had transpired in the country and the world while they were held captive. During their week in Germany to decompress, which we insisted on from our knowledge of past experiences, they had access to free phone calls with family and a specially edited newsreel that covered what had happened, including sports, while they were away. We gave them a plethora of choices—menus, schedules, activities—to get them used to being free. Strangely enough, neither Pat nor Dr. Jerry Korcak, the medical task force commander, ever received any special awards for their planning and successful execution of what was clearly a tour de force. Instead, I was present at a ceremony with General Alexander Haig, then Secretary of State, when he presented one special medal to a Foreign Service officer who primarily handled the public relations aspects of the affair. The physicians, social workers, and nurses, who seemed to me to be at least equally worthy of such recognition based on their service contributions to the hostages' welfare and the morale of their families received, like me, only certificates of appreciation. Such is the politics of life in the age of mass media.

When I tried to retire in 1980, the new Director-General turned down my application on the grounds that I was avoiding overseas duty. Unfortunately, his office didn't bother to check the files, which contained not one, but several requests of mine for overseas assignments to such posts as Vienna, Bangkok, and Cairo. This dispute was settled—after I hired a lawyer—by my being assigned to the American Embassy in Bangkok in August 1981, for a two-year tour. When I once asked the medical director if he would assign a psychologist to the field as regional mental health officer, a position ordinarily filled only by psychiatrists, he replied, "No. But I'd send you." I succeeded in establishing a career path in regional medical offices, but not for psychologists, as was my goal, but only for myself: I was offered another overseas post in 1983 but declined, and my final Officer's Efficiency Report recommended me for Chief of the Mental Health Service, a position theretofore filled only by psychiatrists.

THE GREAT ADVENTURE (1981–1983)

When my orders to go to the American Embassy in Bangkok arrived, I was thrilled to be going overseas as a regional psychologist with responsibilities covering all of the major Foreign Service posts in Southeast Asia, including Hong Kong, Shanghai, Guangzhou, Beijing, Kuala Lumpur, Singapore, and Jakarta. Unfortunately, Dorothy, being a dutiful daughter, had recently permitted her elderly and ailing mother to move into an apartment in our Washington, DC, townhouse, so she could not easily share my great adventure. So I went alone, taking my record collection, my stereo set, and my basic library, including E. R. Guthrie's, *The Psychology of Human Conflict,* Stone and Stone's, *The Abnormal Personality Through Literature,* and some Maugham, Updike, Philip Roth, Malamud, and Hemingway. I stopped over in San Francisco to visit with Linda and Richard (he was clerking in a law office there) for a fun-filled and relaxing week.

My orders directed me to stop at Clark Air Force Base in Manila and become acquainted with the hospital facilities there. I stayed at the Hotel Manila, and since there was trouble brewing at the time, I was subjected to a body search by security police upon arrival at the hotel. In the evening, at the American Club, I had dinner with Dr. Jack Berry, an old friend, now deceased, who was stationed there as regional medical officer. He quickly brought me up to date on what was transpiring with the Ferdinand Marcos government.

When I finally arrived at the airport in Bangkok, I was greeted by the embassy nurse, Edna McGuire, and the medical unit driver, Tsieng (pronounced "Chen"), who was to play an important role in my life for the next two years. He was a personable man of about 30 who spoke English and had a great deal of street smarts, as well as being cooperative and loyal. I had known him from a previous visit to Bangkok, when I had found him to be thoroughly trustworthy.

The embassy physician and regional medical officer, Dr. Henry Wilde, had been posted in Bangkok for nearly a decade, and he was very much at home in Thailand, being fluent with the language, and completely at home in the culture. He is one of the most direct, responsible, and competent persons I have ever met, and I have no doubt that he is an extraordinarily effective physician. He was also gracious enough to divide his office overlooking the *klong* (canal) in half to make room for me. He would occasionally ask me to edit his medical journal articles before sending them off for publication. One in particular that I recall was published in the *American Journal of Surgery*. It recounted his adventures in retrieving and sewing back on the penises of 18 men who, because they were unfaithful, had been given the ultimate punishment by their respective Thai wives or mistresses. As I recall, over 80% of the operations were successful, and Dr. Wilde reported that a similar percentage returned to their former relationships, though it was not perfectly clear that the two groups were coextensive as it were.

BANGKOK

What a city! So unlike any other, even for an experienced traveler. Take the traffic, for example. Long lines of three-wheeled putt-putts, used as taxis, in the same stream of motion with water buffaloes, Mercedes Benzes and Toyotas, and an occasional elephant lumbering along in the ever so slowly moving traffic. There is so much pollution that it has been estimated that living in Bangkok is equivalent to smoking two packs of cigarettes daily. It typically took 20 minutes by car to cover the two miles from my residence to the Embassy.

Each morning, "Mickey" McGuire, the embassy nurse, would read the cable traffic and indicate the ones that required some action on my part. Those would include everything from requests for consultation from a regional medical officer, to assistance from the family liaison officer in establishing a mental health service, to giving a series of lectures at an international school on drug prevention education and how to handle questions from adolescents after a student's suicide.

Through Dr. Wilde's good graces, I received a letter from the Dean of the medical school at Mahidol University requesting that I teach a course on the Rorschach to their graduate psychology students, which I agreed to do. Wan Lop, a master's-level psychologist at the time, was assigned as my translator in the course, even though all of the students ostensibly spoke English. I had the only textbook available, which was Bruno Klopfer's second volume of *Recent Developments in the Rorschach Technique* (Klopfer B., Ainsworth, Klopfer, W. & Holt, 1956). Never have I encountered such eagerness to learn on the part of the students, or such good manners. One day the Dean invited me to lunch and told me he was very much interested in achievement motivation, since he was attempting to move the entire academic community toward greater productivity, which he hoped would spread throughout the country. This was not a person with small goals.

My biggest professional surprise came when I was invited to attend a meeting of the Thai Psychological Association, which well over 100 people attended. Shortly thereafter it was suggested that I give a 16PF workshop. With the help of the school psychologist, Joan Fedoruk, of the International School, our daylong workshop, with presentations by Joan, Dr. Chantima (a consulting psychiatrist to the Embassy that I appointed), and myself, to an audience of nearly 200 psychologists and counselors, was a huge success. At the end of it, the president of the Thai Psychological Association, La-iad Chooprayoon, presented me with an award and commemorative plaque. Because so many bridges were crossed, it was the highlight of my professional career.

"Vanity, vanity, all is vanity" hits right on the mark in my case. One day in Singapore I was visiting the government hospital chief psychologist. When he appeared, he asked me if I was the Sam Karson who had coauthored a 16PF book, and I simply nodded 'yes' in astonishment. He then went on to say that the government had just directed his department to start screening all air traffic controllers, and the first thing he had done was to have my book, *A Guide to the Clinical Use of the 16PF*, translated into Chinese.

While in Singapore I visited the university campus and noticed that the library did not contain a single book by Freud. Nor did the National University of Singapore have a separate department of psychology. In contrast, the University of Indonesia in Jakarta had a huge psychology department, and its dean told me he had written his doctoral dissertation on Cattell's 16PF in Germany. I wondered whether the difference between the two countries in their views of the importance of psychology was a related to their religious preferences, namely Islam versus Buddhism. The dean offered me a faculty appointment on the spot and when I suggested he hire a younger man, he replied, "In my culture, we have great respect for white hair." Would it were so in the good old USA.

I did something in Bangkok I had never previously done. I completely furnished a 2,500 square-foot apartment, including the furniture, rugs, silverware, dishes, art works, and tapestries. Admittedly I had a great deal of help from Joan and a couple of bachelor friends—Bruno, a German engineer, and Theera, a Thai attorney. Also, for the first time in my life, I employed a cook, driver, and a maid as household staff.

The women in Thailand are generally acknowledged to be among the most attractive in the world. I found the Thai men I encountered to be excellent workers, and among the most accomplished furniture makers anywhere. In fact, I bought a living room set of rosewood made without the use of a single nail. When the Thai craftsman delivered it, he said, "Sometimes, after a few years, the furniture may require tightening. No charge, of course." This attitude about work represents the kind of perfectionism I deeply admire.

One day I visited a residential drug addiction center, which housed hundreds of men and women, and was run by a Thai bishop. It fascinated me to see that the camp was run like a therapeutic community, with an emphasis on job training, group meetings, and the teaching of responsibility within a highly structured, drug-free, family milieu. My escort was the widow of a former ambassador who lived on the palace grounds. "You're not a farang. You're a Thai and you smile a lot like the Thais." These were sentiments I heard on more than one occasion during my two-year tour in Thailand (land of the free). No wonder I felt so very much at home there. Little did I suspect that residential drug treatment lay in my professional future.

MELBOURNE, FLORIDA (1983–1989)

Upon my return to the United States in August 1983, after completing my two-year tour in Southeast Asia, I received a thorough medical examination, which resulted in my undergoing an echocardiogram plus an examination called the "PTP plus Stress" (pre and post exercise radionuclideventriculography). It was suspected that I had a left bundle branch block, but a leading Georgetown University cardiologist reviewed my films and commented, "If you have any coronary artery problems, yours is the first heart I've seen that looks better under exercise than it does resting." My youthful athleticism turned out to be an investment in the future, rather than merely the exuberance it seemed at the time. Thereupon, I retired from the U.S. Foreign Service, becoming the first psychologist ever to do so.

I was pleased when the medical director offered me a six-figure contract to do the psychological assessments back at Florida State. Instead, I opted to go to the School of Psychology in the Florida Institute of Technology (FIT) as professor, and two years later became Director of Clinical Training of their Doctor of Psychology (PsyD) program. Some of the faculty were first-rate, especially Dr. Carol Philpot, who eventually wrote an exemplary chapter on the use of the 16PF (Philpot, 1997). It was an interesting six years in a school which, unlike my previous state university experience, depended heavily on its enrollment fees. Most of the students were women, and the PsyD program gave those who qualified an excellent opportunity to get into the burgeoning field of clinical psychology. It was quite a change for me in terms of how I had previously viewed clinical training during my own student days. In my clinical training, four students were admitted each year, compared to about 40 each year at FIT, which had a maximum of seven full-time clinical faculty on staff during the years I spent there. Student ability varied considerably at first, but as the program aged, a larger, more capable applicant pool appeared. My major complaint about such programs is that many of them do not require a doctoral dissertation for graduation. Other than this, it seems to me that the PsyD students are at least equal to, if not superior to, their PhD counterparts with regard to competence in diagnostic and therapy skills. The PsyD program was fully accredited by APA in 1985. Upon resigning in June 1989, I contributed the bulk of my personal library to FIT, which was sorely in need of books and journals in psychology. I returned to Melbourne in January 1990 to enjoy my house, and the mild Florida winter, for the last time. In April my lovely house was sold to the first couple that looked at it.

During my tour in Melbourne, our son Michael and I developed The Personnel Report, a computerized interpretation of the 16PF for industrial uses. Typically, we collect data from client companies on actual employees before suggesting decision-making algorithms. Michael (like me a diplomate in clinical psychology) and I subsequently rewrote the Karson Clinical Report for the 16PF fifth edition. Michael was senior author, with myself and Jerry O'Dell, of *16PF Interpretation in Clinical Practice: A Guide to the Fifth Edition* (1997), which he dedicated to Dorothy.

BACK IN WASHINGTON, DC,
FOR MY FINAL TOUR (1990–1995)

Robert Gesumaria, who had been a graduate student in psychology at EMU in the 1970s, and whose family I've known for many years, called one day and invited me to meet Dr. Alan Rochlin, the psychologist who served as deputy executive director of Second Genesis, in Bethesda. It developed that the agency, which operates a half dozen residential drug treatment facilities in the Washington, DC, area, was interested in hiring a research consultant for the purpose of helping them to apply for a research demonstration project that had recently been announced by the National Institute of Drug Abuse (NIDA) and the Center for Substance Abuse Treatment (CSAT). With the encouragement of the late Dr. Ken Howard of Northwestern University, I became involved as principal investigator. In early October 1990, we were officially notified that Second Genesis had been awarded a three-year (ultimately, a five-year), six-million dollar grant as part of the DC Initiative. I was back in business with Rob as deputy, Dr. Reginald Nettles as clinical director, and Anne Freeman as administrative assistant. The experience led to two book chapters published with Rob (Karson & Gesumaria, 1995, 1997).

COPING WITH OLD AGE, RETIREMENT, AND FAILING HEALTH (1996–2003)

Approaching my 80th birthday, I now have the consolation of knowing I cannot die young. Neither, it seems, will I leave a good-looking corpse. My biggest adjustment has been spending more time on my body in the last few years than I did in my first seven decades. I have slowly come to accept that the apparatus—especially memory, seemingly invulnerable because of poverty in the Bronx, many wartime bombings, and much intercontinental travel, not to mention academia—like any machine, ultimately wears down and wears out. Numerous time-consuming medical services are required, from which there is apparently no escape, even for an artful dodger. In fact, I considered changing the title of this piece to "Have PhD, Cannot Travel."

After 57 years of marriage, Dorothy and I are still living under the same roof, and still share a mutual interest in politics, friends, movies, our children, and our four grandchildren. Her interest in baseball has outlasted my own. Our daughter Linda is deeply involved in helping the homeless in the Tampa area, where her family moved when Richard accepted an offer a few years ago as a vice-president of TECO. Their children, Paloma, a gifted singer, is studying at Drew University, and Damien is a junior in high school, learning to be a fencing master. Michael and his partner Janna Goodwin recently moved to Denver, where Michael is teaching in the Graduate School of Professional Psychology at DU, and Janna is writing her dissertation in communication and working on original theater pieces. Michael's son Ethan is a software engineer and aspiring comedy writer in Los Angeles. Max, also an aspiring writer, will begin college soon in Massachusetts.

SOME OBSERVATIONS ON ASSESSMENT
AND THE PROFESSION

As a 52-year APA member, I was deeply disappointed by the "resolution" of the Cattell affair by the American Psychological Foundation (APF) principals, who announced his receipt of their Gold Medal lifetime achievement award and then never conferred it (he withdrew his name in response to their inquiry into his racism). I can fully appreciate how wrong, immoral, and outmoded his racial and religious views were. Apparently, higher education and very superior intellect are not sufficient in all cases to eliminate deep biases accumulated over long periods of history, especially for an Englishman in the tradition of Cecil Rhodes. However, I was drawn to Cattell in the first place by his ability to distinguish the personal from the scientific, and I wish APF had been capable of that standard. To no avail, I had proposed to Joe Matarazzo years earlier that APF give APA members some voice in the selection of award recipients, perhaps analogously to the selection of major league baseball all-stars or hall-of-famers. Thus, I was pleased when the Society for Personality Assessment (SPA) recently honored Professor Cattell with the Marguerite Hertz Award for his scientific contributions, even though I know he never had any fondness for the Rorschach.

Second, I am glad to see the SPA making an organized effort to demonstrate the cost-effective value of assessment. Over the years, I have made many decisions and recommendations about pilots, parents, children, air traffic controllers, and Foreign Service personnel. Much of the research I conducted was in an effort to provide a self-check on the validity of what I was doing. Otherwise, I had no way of knowing if my recommendations were any different than those based on common biases. I assumed that my own biases were as invisible to me as others' were to them.

On my last day at the Department of State in 1983, the late Dr. Dustin, then Medical Director, made it a point to tell me that what saved his large budget for medical evacuations (i.e., flying personnel and dependents home for treatment, and shipment of furnishings plus replacement costs) was the data made available to him in "Personality Profiles in the U.S. Foreign Service" (Karson & O'Dell, 1987b). In that chapter, evidence was presented of our ability to distinguish, via psychological testing, differences in severity between psychiatric evacuees and those who could be treated at post. Accurate assessment saved money. And "Dusty" added with a smile, "But when you first proposed an afternoon off every week for research, I thought it was a boondoggle." He rewarded me with a consulting contract that also saved money by computerizing overseas employment interviews.

By now, many are familiar with the amount of influence international drug companies have on funding outcome studies in many medical and psychiatric publications. In clinical psychology, some of the leading assessment researchers (like myself) are financially associated with particular personality tests, whether through outright ownership or through contracts associated with usage, book royalties, or, especially, computerized interpretive systems. Do these potential conflicts of interest need closer ethical scrutiny, especially when some of these researchers repeatedly write supposedly objective evaluations of other companies' products? I believe it is high time for APA to pay more attention to such problems and, at the very least, to require disclosure of all such potential conflicts of interest.

Some 25 years ago, I succeeded in proposing that it was not right for me, as chief psychologist of a government agency, to perform in-house fitness-for-duty evaluations requested by supervisors on agency employees. A system was (eventually) set up allowing such employees to choose between agency clinicians and a list of approved, qualified clinicians from the community. Of course, even then, there was no guarantee of complete objectivity, but the situation was vastly improved over the direct conflict inherent in having employee-clinicians conduct these evaluations. My point is the need to recognize that psychologists are as susceptible to political and financial influences as are any other group of people. I do not expect prescription privileges to have a beneficial effect on this issue. (Generally, though, I favor prescription privileges if adequate professional safeguards can be provided.)

SUMMING UP

After traveling nearly a million miles in my life, it seems I'm ending up fewer than 50 miles from where I was born, at 1100 E. Pratt Street, in Baltimore, Maryland. As noted, my health has faltered, and it serves as a reminder that no one leaves the game of life a winner. I'll keep trying, though, and when the Devil comes for me I'll be tempted to challenge him to an arm wrestling contest before he can take me—that is, if my tendonitis isn't acting up at that moment.

REFERENCES

Butcher, J. N. (1995). *Clinical personality assessment: Practical approaches*. New York: Oxford University Press.

Cattell, R. B., Eber, H. W., & Tatsuoka, M. M. (1970). *Handbook for the Sixteen Personality Factor Questionnaire (16PF)*. Champaign, IL: Institute for Personality and Ability Testing.

Dana, R., Bolton, B., & West, V. (1983). Validation of eisegesis concepts in assessment reports using the 16PF: A training method with examples. *Proceedings of the Third International Conference on the 16PF*, 20–29. Champaign, IL: Institute for Personality and Ability Testing.

Endres, L. S., Guastello, S. J., & Rieke, M. L. (1992). Meta-interpretive reliability of computer-based test interpretations: The Karson Clinical Report. *Journal of Personality Assessment, 59*, 448–467.

Gallatin, J. E. (1982). *Abnormal psychology*. Upper Saddle River, NJ: Prentice Hall.

Karson, S. (1959). The Sixteen Personality Factor Test in clinical practice. *Journal of Clinical Psychology, 14*, 174–176.

Karson, M. (2001). *Patterns of child abuse: How dysfunctional transactions are replicated in individuals, families, and the child welfare system*. New York: Haworth.

Karson, M., Karson, S., & O'Dell, J. (1997). *16PF interpretation in clinical practice: A guide to the fifth edition*. Champaign, IL: Institute for Personality and Ability Testing.

Karson, S. (1965). Group psychotherapy with latency age boys. *International Journal of Group Psychotherapy, 15*, 81–89.

Karson, S., & Gesumaria, R. V. (1995). A comparison of the benefits of two therapeutic community treatment regimens for inner city substance abusers. In J. N. Butcher & C. D. Spielberger (Eds.), *Advances in personality assessment: Vol. X*. Hillsdale, NJ: Lawrence Erlbaum.

Karson, S., & Gesumaria, R. V. (1997). Program description and outcome of an enhanced, six months' residential therapeutic community. In G. De Leon (Ed.), *Community as method: Therapeutic communities for special populations and special settings*. Westport, CT: Praeger.

Karson, S., & O'Dell, J. W. (1974). Personality makeup of the American air traffic controller. *Aerospace Medicine, 45*, 1001–1007.

Karson, S., & O'Dell, J. W. (1975). A new automated computer interpretation for the 16PF. *Journal of Personality Assessment, 39*, 256–260.

Karson, S., & O'Dell, J. W. (1976). *A guide to the clinical use of the 16PF*. Champaign, IL: Institute for Personality and Ability Testing.

Karson, S., & O'Dell, J. W. (1987a). Computer-based interpretation of the 16PF: The Karson Clinical Report in contemporary practice. In J. N. Butcher (Ed.), *Computerized psychological assessment: A practitioner's guide*. New York: Basic Books.

Karson, S., & O'Dell, J. W. (1987b). Personality profiles in the U.S. Foreign Service. In J. N. Butcher & C. D. Spielberger (Eds.) *Advances in personality assessment: Vol. VI*. Hillsdale, NJ: Lawrence Erlbaum.

Karson, S., & Pool, K. B. (1957). The construct validity of the Sixteen Personality Factors Test. *Journal of Clinical Psychology, 13*, 245–252.

Karson, S., & Pool, K. B. (1958). Second-order factors in personality measurement. *Journal of Consulting Psychology, 22*, 299–303.

Karson, S., & Wiedershine, L. J. (1961). An objective evaluation of dynamically oriented group psychotherapy. *International Journal of Group Psychotherapy, 11*, 166–174.

Klopfer, B., Anisworth, M. D., Klopfer, W. G., & Holt, R. R. (1956). *Developments in the Rorschach Technique, Vol. 2.* Fields of application. Oxford, England: World Book.

Lerner, R. M. (1976). *Concepts and theories of human development.* Reading, MA: Addison Wesley.

Philpot, C. L. (1997). The 16PF: Assessing "normal" personality dimensions of marital partners. In A. Rodney Nurse (Ed.), *Family assessment: Effective use of personality tests with couples and families.* New York: John Wiley.

Winder, P., O'Dell, J., & Karson, S. (1975). New motivational distortion scales for the 16PF. *Journal of Personality Assessment, 39*, 533–537.

SELECTED BIBLIOGRAPHY

Karson, S. (1956). Primary factor correlates of boys with conduct and personality problems. *Journal of Clinical Psychology, 21*, 16–18.

Karson, S. (1960). Validating clinical judgments with the 16PF test. *Journal of Clinical Psychology, 16*, 394–397.

Karson, S. (1961). Second-order personality factors in positive mental health. *Journal of Clinical Psychology, 17*, 14–19.

Karson, S. (1981). The return of our American hostages: A psychologist's experience. *American Psychologist, 36*, 420–421.

Karson, S. (1987). The psychologist as an expert witness in Federal hearings. *Psychotherapy in Private Practice, 5*(2), 75–79.

Karson, S. (1997). What is the question? What is the evidence? *Journal of Personality Assessment, 69*, 651–652.

Karson, S., & Haupt, T. D. (1968). Second-order personality factors in parents of child guidance clinic patients. *Multivariate Behavioral Research*, Special Issue, 97–106. (Presented at 1967 Annual Meeting of the Midwestern Psychological Association in Chicago).

Karson, S., & Karson, M. (1995). *Manual for the Karson Clinical Report for the 16PF fifth edition.* Champaign, IL: Institute for Personality and Ability Testing.

Karson, S., & Markenson, D. J. (1973). Some relations between parental personality factors and childhood symptomology. *Journal of Personality Assessment, 37*, 249–254.

Karson, S., & O'Dell, J. (1974). Is the 16PF factorially valid? *Journal of Personality Assessment, 38*, 104–114.

Karson, S., & O'Dell, J. (1974). Personality differences between male and female air traffic controller applicants. *Aerospace Medicine, 54*, 596–598.

Karson, S., & O'Dell, J. (1977). Identifying medical risk factors on the 16PF profile: A clinical approach. In S. E. Krug (Ed.), *Psychological assessment in medicine.* Champaign, IL: Institute for Personality and Ability Testing.

Karson, S., & O'Dell, J. W. (1989). The 16PF. In C. S. Newmark (Ed.), *Major psychological assessment instruments: Vol. II.* Boston: Allyn & Bacon.

Karson, S., & Pool, K. B. (1957). The construct validity of the Sixteen Personality Factors Test. *Journal of Clinical Psychology, 13*, 245–252.

Karson, S., & Pool, K. B. (1958). Second-order factors in personality measurement. *Journal of Consulting Psychology, 22*, 299–303.

Karson, S., Pool, K. B., & Freud, S. L. (1957). The effects of scale and practice on W-BI and WAIS test scores. *Journal of Consulting Psychology, 21*, 241–245.

Karson, S., & Sells, S. B. (1956). Comments on Meehl and Rosen's paper. *Psychological Bulletin, 53*, 335–337.

Karson, S., & Wiedershine, L. J. (1961). An objective evaluation of dynamically oriented group psychotherapy. *International Journal of Group Psychotherapy, 11*, 166–174.

O'Dell, J., & Karson, S. (1969). Some relations between the MMPI and the 16PF. *Journal of Clinical Psychology, 15*, 179–183.

Rahe, R. H., Karson, S., Howard, N., Rubin, R. T., & Poland, R. E. (1990). Psychological and physiological assessments on American hostages freed from captivity in Iran. *Psychosomatic medicine, 52*, 1–16.

Stern, F., & Karson, S. (1954). Motivation and attention: A methodological problem. *Journal of Psychology, 38*, 321–329.

Stern, F., & Karson, S. (1955). A critique of Mowrer's theory of neurosis. *Journal of Psychology, 39*, 71–76.

Winder, P., O'Dell, J., & Karson, S. (1975). New motivational distortion scales for the 16PF. *Journal of Personality Assessment, 39*, 533–537.

Age 18, in the Army Air Corps, Camp Upton, Long Island, New York, 1942

The arm wrestler, 1942. "The ego is a body ego."

With Dorothy and Linda on the move from Miami to Washington, DC, 1962

Enjoying a lobster dinner with Dorothy and relatives, Vinalhaven, Maine, 1976

With Cyrus Vance (then Secretary of State) and Pat Haynes (right), on our way to Wiesbaden AFB, Germany, to evaluate the Iranian hostages, 1980

My life companion, Dorothy Faye Libert, in the U.S. Navy (Waves), 1943

With son Michael at the 2000 APA convention in Washington, DC

CHAPTER 9

From Freud to Gehrig to Rapaport to DiMaggio

Paul M. Lerner
Camden, Maine

Baseball, or the New York Yankees to be more specific, order the decades of my life. When others reflect on their lives, whether in treatment or in writing an autobiography, they often arrange their years in terms of significant events, major moves, or career changes. I organize my memories in terms of where the Yankees finished in the standings and which players comprised their roster.

Baseball is a game of yesterdays. It is played in many venues, from huge stadiums to one's backyard, but also in the diamonds of one's internal world. It excites and constantly fuels one's passion for tradition and encourages one's connection to the past and what is passing. When my mother was pregnant with me, my father, in his attempt to tip the gender scale, presented my mother with a baseball glove. His seemingly innocent gesture fated me to follow a profession steeped in tradition, that looked to the past, and emphasized introspection.

THE DIMAGGIO AND GEHRIG YEARS

I was born in Boston, Massachusetts, in 1937. It was the year after Joe DiMaggio's rookie year, during the heyday of the Bronx Bombers, and two years before Lou Gehrig removed himself from the Yankee starting lineup and played in the last of his 2,130 consecutive games.

With me, and years later with my brother, Howard, my parents were loving and devoted. Unfortunately, they were not well suited for each other. My father had little formal education, having dropped out of high school, was raised in a poor immigrant family that clung to their old world ways, and until mid-life, he struggled to hold a job.

Short in stature, he filled a room with his overbearingness, neediness, and moodiness. His bouts of explosiveness were quickly followed by intense feelings of guilt and remorse and the need to be reassured that he was still lovable. He was opinionated, having a strong and singular view on everything that really counted. His uncanny correctness, however, was often lost in and overshadowed by his alienating bluntness.

Others knew exactly where they stood with him. Ambivalence and indirectness were not part of his makeup. Clearly, he loved my mother, his two sons, New York City, and the Yankees. With no less vehemence and intensity, he hated certain members of his own family, my mother's family, Boston, and the Red Sox. He was an individual who led from his heart, spoke from his gut, and shot himself in his foot.

My mother, by contrast, was college educated, raised in an upwardly mobile family that valued status and culturedness while denying their scrap metal collecting occupation, and was quietly and exceptionally competent. As Lou Gehrig was with Babe Ruth, she was content to remain in the background. She was warm and steady, in counter-distinction to my father's bluntness, as well as tactful and subtle.

Dark complected enough to be mistaken for Spanish, she had dark brown eyes and jet black hair until, in her mid 30s, it turned prematurely gray. I was dazzled by and proud of her beauty. She was also quite somatic, suffering from any number of physical ailments, ranging from a troublesome sacroiliac to painful bouts with rheumatoid arthritis.

Throughout their marriage, my mother was torn between the pull of my father on one side and the appeal and protection of her family of origin on the other side. Her compromise of maintaining one foot in each camp was unsettling for everyone. Because she remained particularly close to her older brother, he became a rival and irritant for my father.

I also remember my mother as frequently tired and depleted, often retreating to her bedroom for an afternoon nap. Only later, as an adult, could I understand her constant fatigue and varying physical complaints as being expressions of an underlying and enduring depression. Unwittingly, I responded to her depressiveness with a sense of wanting to protect her, to lift her heavy burdens, and to refrain from asking too much of her. Unable to ease her suffering, it was inevitable I would aspire to become a psychoanalyst, a profession based on understanding and relieving mental pain and suffering.

I was raised in Brookline, Massachusetts, an incorporated town of 60,000, adjacent to Boston. We lived in an apartment, several blocks from the old Braves Field, home to the then Boston Braves who are now the Atlanta Braves. Although the town and its residents rightfully prided themselves on their exemplary school system, I experienced grade school as boring. Only recess, gym classes, and after school activities held my interest.

In the truest and best sense of the word, I lived in a neighborhood. Automobiles were scarce, it was wartime, and Detroit was building tanks not pleasure vehicles, but stores were within walking distance. Neighbors felt responsible for keeping tabs on each other's children, and one's front steps, not the fenced in backyard, was one's social setting.

In our neighborhood there was a gang of eight of us who were close in age and shared common interests. Our lives, until adolescence, centered around sports; we played football in the fall, basketball in the winter, and baseball in the spring and summer. During the season, in the late afternoon we would walk over to Braves Field. When the attendants would open the gates in the seventh inning for people leaving, we would sneak in, find field-level seats, and pray the game would be tied and go into extra innings. After the game we would wait for the players to come out of their clubhouse to get their autographs. I still collect baseball autographs and my collection includes more than 5,000 signatures.

Books were not my friend; however, radio was. A large and solid Zenith console was the center piece in our living room. At night, as a family, we would sit around that console listening to Edward R. Murrow broadcasting war news live from London, England, or following the chilling exploits of "The Shadow." A small portable, aptly named Tom Thumb, sat on a table next to my bed. I loved radio. It provided a direct link to the world beyond our neighborhood, fired my imagination, and set the stage for the pleasure I experience from listening.

In 1945, a year when ballplayers were returning from overseas and two years before Al Gionfriddo of the Brooklyn Dodgers made his famous catch robbing Joe DiMaggio of a game-tying homerun in the sixth game of the 1947 World Series, my brother Howard was born. Although he claims otherwise, I remember Howard as a head strong, at times cranky, demanding child, who was not hampered by the same built-in restraints and inhibitions that I was. For instance, as a child, if I flagrantly misbehaved, I would be sent to a corner, required to face the wall, and instructed to think about my bad deed. The several minutes in the corner felt like an eternity. When the same punishment was meted out to Howard, he walked toward the wall, spun around, and dashed away. Rather than insisting that he return to the corner, my parents smiled and laughed, clearly enjoying and encouraging his spunk and independence. With the recognition of my own unnecessary obedience, I felt humiliated and wounded.

In the summer of 1952, soon after my father accepted a sales position with *Parent* magazine, our family planned a combined business/pleasure driving trip to Ohio. We methodically covered much of the state, from Cleveland in the northeast to Cincinnati in the southwest. As the trip progressed, my mother became increasingly ill. Now, more than half a century later, I can still vividly recall lying awake in our hotel room at night, listening to her coughing jags, labored breathing, and trips to the washroom to vomit.

Her worsening condition was not discussed. As her symptoms intensified and my concerns were met with silence and denial, I felt increasingly fearful, angry, and helpless. Only toward the end of the trip, when we arrived in Toledo, Ohio, where my mother's younger brother lived, did she see a physician. It was decided that my mother, Howard, and I would immediately return to Boston. My father drove us to Detroit, to the old Willow Run Airport, and put the three of us on a plane. In Boston, we were met at the airport by members of my mother's family. My mother was taken directly to the hospital. Howard and I were placed on a bus to be delivered to a relative's summer cottage on Cape Cod. We would never see our mother again. Even at her funeral her casket was closed.

When you are 14 years old you do not understand death. You regard it as something distant and removed and imagine it as a mysterious dark cloud that descends upon the elderly (grandparents, for instance) and upon those whom you do not know. When it visits your home and takes away your 41-year-old mother, it no longer feels distant and removed. And, when the adults you depend on maintain their conspiracy of silence and are so handcuffed by their own pain as to be unavailable and unhelpful, then you are left alone to wallow in your own agony and loneliness.

Within months of her funeral, our apartment was given up, my father resumed his traveling leaving his two sons feeling orphaned, and Howard and I were separated. He went to live with two aunts, sisters of my father, and I moved in with my paternal grandparents. My grandmother, who claimed that she was the daughter of a famous Russian rabbi and scholar and also claimed that she could speak five different languages, unfortunately could barely speak English, rarely sat still, and was rather disorganized. More importantly, however, I remember her as deeply caring and loving. She taught me, in her actions, not in her words, that what counts is on the inside not the outside.

Because my grandparents lived close to where we had, I was able to maintain the continuity of friends, school, and neighborhood. Howard was less fortunate. His continuity was severely disrupted, and he did not have the availability of a loving caretaker.

As to be expected, I have been compellingly drawn to the phenomenon of loss, especially early loss and its impact on later personality development. From Freud's (1917) *Mourning and Melancholia* to Judith Rosner's (1987) *August*, I have virtually devoured all the psychoanalytic and popular literature on loss that is available. A particular quote from Dylan Thomas continues to make the most sense and holds the deepest meaning for me. Thomas put it this way, "After the first death there is no other."

Of my many publications, the articles I have written on loss (Lerner, 1990), as I have experienced it, are the truest and come from the deepest places within me. When Rita Frankiel (1994) included my paper, "The Treatment of Early Loss: The Need to Search," together with papers on loss by Freud, Abraham, Klein, and Jacobson in her volume *Essential Papers on Loss,* I felt particularly satisfied.

Amid the darkness of the fall of 1952, my mother's vanishing, the separation from Howard, and the loss of familiar surroundings, there was some light—the Yankees won their fourth consecutive American League pennant. Even without Joe DiMaggio, who had retired a year earlier, they defeated the Brooklyn Dodgers and once again were world champions.

THE MANTLE YEARS

In 1954, as Mickey Mantle was coming into his own and increasingly filling Joe DiMaggio's spikes, my father, after a brief courtship, remarried. I was delighted. I even served as best man at their wedding. At that time I did not know my stepmother, up close and personal; nonetheless, I ascribed to her and to her arrival an expectation of permanence, stability, and reuniting.

With the remarriage, my world which had collapsed two years earlier, felt as if it was coming back together. Not only was my senior year in high school joyful and productive, but I was also reassuming the normative tasks of adolescence. I became interested in books and in learning. Like a junior philosopher, as adolescents are, I began to consider and ponder the deeper issues of life. And, it was also at that time that I consciously decided to pursue a career as a psychologist.

In the fall of 1955, several weeks before the Yankees clinched another pennant, I enrolled at the University of Illinois. During freshman orientation week, our entire class of about 8,000 students met with the President of the University in Huff Gym. As part of his welcoming address, Dr. Henry urged us to look around the gym and to take stock of our classmates. He then suggested that each of us work hard, for only 1 in 10, he claimed, would graduate in four years. Of course, he was correct. His remark scared me. Without conscious intent, I transformed his comment into a nagging internal pressure, which, for better and for worse, persisted until I was one of the 10 who did graduate four years later. It was not until the graduation exercises that I saw Dr. Henry again. When it came time for my son to consider college, I encouraged him to select a smaller school with a higher graduation rate whose president was more available and compassionate.

Despite Dr. Henry's warning, during the first two years, my grades were average at best. However, I did play baseball. Several of my teammates became lifelong friends, and two, Bobby Klaus and Tom Haller, eventually played in the major leagues. In the fall, several of us played on an intramural touch football team. One year, we finished first in our league and then defeated the top team in the fraternity league to win the all-University championship. My position involved scouting other teams and maintaining records. I was permitted to play sparingly—only when we had an insurmountable lead or were hopelessly trailing.

During the summer of 1956, between my sophomore and junior years, significant and inexplicable internal changes took place. I returned to school in the fall with a newly acquired sense of self-confidence and a deeply felt determination to excel academically. In the language of hockey, I returned with "fire in my belly." My confidence, then, was not in my intellectual capacities, but in the conviction I could and would work as hard or even harder than anyone else. I earned top grades. Like a pitcher who gets two quick strikes on a batter and then decides how to set the batter up to put him away, I put myself in a position in which graduate school became a realistic possibility.

On occasion, memories of specific undergraduate courses and the teachers will push their way into my consciousness. One such course was Norman Grabener's Diplomatic History of the United States in the 20th Century. Until his course, I had thought of history as a series of unrelated random events identifiable by dates and names. Grabener thoroughly dissuaded me of that more adolescent view of history. With passion and scholarliness, he repeatedly demonstrated the complex yet causal link between historical occurrences. For me, history took on a sense of continuity as Grabener outlined how a particular event was both rooted in previous events and, in turn, gave rise to future occurrences. Although it was not labeled as such, for the first time I was introduced to the concept of historical determinism. This set the stage for my later receptiveness to the notion of psychic determinism, a cornerstone of psychoanalytic theory.

In the final semester of my last year, I enrolled in a counseling course taught by Merle Ohlsen. More than the content of the class, I was taken by my instructor, Dr. Ohlsen the person—his genuineness, warmth, and commitment to his work. Because he was actively treating clients, unlike other professors did, Dr. Ohlsen spoke from his experience and not just from the text. He regarded his students with the same respect and compassion that he extended to his clients.

On occasion, following his late afternoon class, he and I would go for a cup of coffee. I basked in his interest and prized the time we spent together. Over one of those cups of coffee, Dr. Ohlsen asked about my future plans. I told him that I had applied to and had been accepted into a couple of clinical programs, but was concerned with finding financial support. He then inquired if I might be interested in becoming one of his graduate students. He acknowledged that his was a counseling program and not a clinical program, but, as he had done for others, he could tailor a combined course that fit my interests. Furthermore, funds were available for an assistantship to cover my tuition, and he might also be able to arrange a traineeship for me at a nearby VA Hospital.

Despite hoping to leave Illinois, I accepted Dr. Ohlsen's remarkably generous offer. Years later I saw an episode of the television series The Wonder Years, entitled, "Goodbye." The story was of the relationship between an adolescent boy and his teacher. Toward the end of the episode, the narrator reflected, "There are certain teachers we believed in, and if we are lucky, there was one or two that believed in us." When I first heard that remark, I immediately thought of Dr. Ohlsen.

In June 1959, at an outdoor commencement exercise at Memorial Stadium, the field where Red Grange, 30 years earlier, had elevated Illinois football to national prominence, I received my BS in psychology.

In the fall I began graduate study. Dr. Ohlsen delivered on each of his promises. Together, we fashioned an academic program that met departmental requirements but would also provide the practice-based courses that interested me. Both the assistantship and the VA traineeship were secured.

The Counseling Department at that time was practice-based and deeply steeped in a client-centered orientation. Carl Rogers' philosophy and method pervaded all aspects of the program; course content, practical training, research, and method of teaching.

My first clinical exposure, both in practicums and in placements, was to the theory and practice of client-centered therapy. This orientation, with its emphasis on maintaining a respectfulness toward one's clients—by carefully listening, using the therapeutic value of empathy, and attuning to and following affects—provided a solid foundation for my later psychoanalytic training. As well, in later years, I found myself especially open and receptive to the work of Heinz Kohut.

The Clinical Department, by contrast, although adhering to the scientist-practitioner model, held a prevailing commitment to research and to preparing students for academic-research careers. The diagnostic sequence, for instance, was long on test theory and measurement concerns but short on assessment issues such as test usage and test interpretation. The psychotherapy sequence was increasingly moving toward a behavioristic orientation, in part because such an approach lent itself to empirical investigation.

Although the entire Psychology Department had several heavy hitters including O. H. Mowrer, Raymond Cattell, and Ross Stagner, with the exception of Lee Cronbach I was drawn to those teachers whose interests were primarily clinical, held a more psychodynamic orientation, and who, as I experienced them, were decent and caring individuals. Donald Shannon, who directed the psychology clinic and whom I selected to be my principle psychotherapy supervisor—beneath his Cary Grant looks and style—was a uniquely sensitive and skilled clinician.

The traineeship at the VA Hospital provided a much-needed clinical and experiential complement to the academic work. Life was breathed into patients, especially the more severely disturbed ones, whom I had previously only read about. At that time, major tranquilizers were just beginning to be used in the treatment of the psychotic patient. Electroconvulsive therapy (ECT) was still widely and indiscriminately practiced. I can recall seeing patients who had more than 100 shock treatments. Later, when I read Tom Main's (1957) article, "The Ailment," in which he describes the cruel treatment extended to patients who frustrate and disappoint their caretakers by not improving, I thought back to those particular patients.

The experiences at the VA hospital provided the impetus for and direction of my thesis topic. Based on the work of Gregory Bateson, Theodore Lidz, and especially Lyman Wynne, I investigated family processes and schizophrenia. There was also a Rorschach component to the study. I subdivided the schizophrenic sample into a process subgroup and a reactive subgroup, using Wes Becker's genetic level scoring. Several articles (Lerner, 1965, 1968) came from my study and one of them, "Resolution of Intrafamilial Role Conflict in

Families of Schizophrenic Patients 1: Thought Disturbance," was included in Mishler and Waxler's (1968) volume, *Family Processes and Schizophrenia*.

Throughout the study, I again witnessed Dr. Ohlsen's remarkable generosity. My topic was far removed from his own interests and was outside of his areas of expertise. Nonetheless, he remained unflinchingly encouraging and guided me in choosing an especially helpful thesis committee.

At a point when I could see the light at the end of the thesis-writing tunnel, I began to think about life after graduation. Whereas virtually all of my classmates were considering academic positions, that career path did not interest me. My intent was to do direct clinical work and to do it competently. Unfortunately, I felt anything but competent. In baseball terms, I felt myself a raw thrower but not an accomplished pitcher. I could listen well, and I could help patients, through my empathy, to feel comfortable enough to become more open. However, I had no idea of how to think about or organize the material they presented. Clearly, what I lacked was a theory of personality functioning and a theory of treatment. Each new treatment case felt like another trip without a road map. Thus, rather than turn myself loose on an unsuspecting public, I decided to seek postdoctoral training. I applied to several programs including the one at the Menninger Foundation.

Other than an acknowledgment that my application was received, for months I heard nothing from Menninger. Convinced that I had fallen off of their radar screen, literally days before accepting a different postdoctoral, I received a call from Marty Mayman. We hastily arranged a meeting at a railroad station in Chicago. Because he was frantic, he neglected to inform me as to which one of the three stations in Chicago we were to meet. Luckily, I did find him, and several weeks after that interview received a letter informing me of my acceptance to the program.

In the lives of individuals, institutions, and countries, certain years are turning points. The year 1964 was one of those years. In late August I successfully defended my dissertation and was awarded my doctoral degree. After nine years in Champaign, Illinois, with three degrees in hand and a road map, I headed west to Topeka, Kansas.

Two weeks later my brother Howard entered the University of Illinois as a freshman. His road to Champaign had not been an easy one. Several months previously, he, our father, and our stepmother had met with his high school guidance counselor. After reviewing his spotty high school record, the counselor suggested that he apply to junior colleges. Infuriated with her suggestion, my father, with his guns blazing, informed her she knew little about counseling and less about his son. He then stormed out of her office.

Howard worked hard and did exceptionally well his senior year of high school. His all-out effort paid off with his acceptance to the University of Illinois. I am not sure if during his first week in Champaign he heard the same presidential speech I had years earlier, but in any event, he graduated in four years with a major in psychology and the honor of being elected to Phi Beta Kappa.

The year 1964 also marked the end of a Yankee dynasty. The Yankees won the American League pennant that year; however, their loss in the seventh game of the World Series to the St. Louis Cardinals was an ominous sign of what was to come.

THE CBS YEARS

The Yankees of 1965 were a painfully different team from the team of the previous decade, a team that had won nine league championships in 10 years. Mantle's aging and injury-riddled body was betraying him as were other fixtures of those championship teams, including Maris, Berra, Skowron, and Kubeck, who had retired or been traded away. Ownership had shifted to CBS, a giant in radio and television but a midget in baseball, so the franchise entered a period as black as the Dark Ages.

Paradoxically, as the Yankees' fortunes were falling, my fortunes were rising. At Menninger, I found an ambiance that was altogether different from what I had experienced at the University of Illinois. The professional staff did not simply give lip service to clinical work, but in their hearts and souls, were deeply committed to it. From administration to maintenance, everyone's overarching goal was to help patients to get better. The clinical staff—psychiatrists, psychologists, and social workers—all shared the same theoretical concepts and spoke the common language of psychoanalysis. It was a language which at that time I could not grasp but was determined to learn. Excellence was expected and anything less was challenged. The Foundation saw itself as a reclamation center and prided itself in treating patients who could not be worked with elsewhere.

Deriving from the work of David Rapaport, both within and beyond the Foundation, the Psychology Department was regarded as the citadel of individual and individualized psychological testing. Within days of arriving, I was put to work studying Rapaport, Gill, and Schafer's (1945–1946) *Diagnostic Psychological Testing*. Just as Marty Mayman (1976) had described earlier, I saw open before me an incredible landscape in which test responses took on a depth of meaning no one had shown me before. I also saw, first hand, how, in the hands of skilled psychologists, psychological test findings could be elevated from mundane, descriptive, useful statements to a level of interpretation with unbelievable heuristic sweep.

It was months later that I fully appreciated that when I signed on with Menninger, I had also unwittingly agreed to enlist in a particular kind of testing, especially the Rorschach tradition. Beginning with Rapaport, at the heart of the tradition was the marriage he had brokered between psychoanalytic theory and psychological tests. Furthermore, also involved in this tradition was the conviction that there is a "right" way to assess.

The postdoctoral program for psychologists included direct clinical work, intense supervision, workshops, and seminars. For every hour spent in testing a patient, there was an hour given to supervision. And, providing the supervision was a team of outstanding psychologists, including Marty Mayman, Steve Appelbaum, Sid Smith, Howie Shevrin, Len Horwitz, and Irv Rosen.

My first testing supervisor was Steve Appelbaum. Steve was a stickler for detail. One was expected not only to score a test record accurately but also to scour the record meticulously, attending to every response, every phrase, and every word. For Steve (Appelbaum, 1970), the testing report was particularly important. Like Ted Williams demonstrating the art of hitting, Steve taught me how to craft a report that was genuinely helpful, which was more than scientific and technical, but literate and persuasive too.

Steve also shared a deep and abiding interest in baseball. On our psychology team that played and routinely beat the team of psychiatrists on Sundays throughout the summer, Steve was our pitcher and I was his battery mate.

Workshops were devoted to each of the tests that comprised the basic testing battery—the Wechsler-Bellevue Scale, the Rorschach, and the TAT. Most memorable was Marty Mayman's Rorschach workshop. Like his teacher, David Rapaport, Marty was fiery, excitable, and passionate. However, whereas Rapaport's creative energies were ignited by complex theories and lofty abstract ideas, Marty's fire was lit by clinical encounters and raw clinical material. Like an artist, he was at his best sifting through a Rorschach protocol, carefully exploring each and every nuance, teasing out hidden meanings, and then shaping them into a rich and animate portrait of the assessee.

At the beginning of the program, we were presented with a list of seminars to attend. With the exception of one, the syllabus read like a gourmet menu. The one that rankled us, and which we discussed with Mayman, was entitled "Schools of Psychology." We protested that we had chosen Menninger to learn psychoanalytic theory and not to review and rehash what we had studied in graduate school. Mayman patiently listened to our beefs and then, like a good-enough mother who encourages her children to eat their vegetables, suggested that we first attend the seminar and then revisit him.

To our surprise, the seminar was anything but the lima beans we had anticipated. It was a 16-ounce porterhouse steak. Rather than simply reviewing the various schools, the instructor approached each in terms of its relationship to and comparison with psychoanalytic theory. We were awe struck with the teacher's breadth, scholarship, and clearness. As the seminar was drawing to a close, we asked the instructor if he would consider giving us a second helping.

He graciously accepted. He mentioned that he was in the midst of a major project, and that if we were interested, he would use the seminar to test out his ideas. He also warned us that the reading list would be extensive and challenging.

The seminar was beyond our wildest expectations—comparable to an award winning film, an early rendition of Gershwin, or a seventh game of a World Series. We began by reviewing a hefty literature, including the essential writings of the British Object Relations theorists, the early psychoanalytic writings that predated but eventually led to the borderline concept, and all the core papers on narcissism. We were then presented a remarkably comprehensive and innovative psychoanalytic model of psychopathology which, in a narrow sense, explicated and placed the borderline patient and, in a broader sense, represented an attempt to integrate Freud's structural theory with British Object Relations Theory. The instructor, whose initial course we balked at, was Otto Kernberg, and when he presented his theory to us, it was then a work in progress. His second seminar not only made a lasting impression but also, in future years, became one of the foundations for my work.

As my time at Menninger was approaching the later innings, I began applying for a job—embarrassingly, at age 29, for my first *real* job. Having lived in Champaign, Illinois, and Topeka, Kansas, for more than a decade, I ached to return to a large city. With location in mind and looking for a setting with a psychoanalytic orientation, I accepted a position at Sinai Hospital of Detroit, Michigan. Sinai was a mid-sized, general teaching hospital associated with the Wayne State University College of Medicine. I had interviewed with La Mar Gardner, head of the one-person Psychology Department. La Mar was excited about my having trained at Menninger, and I found La Mar inspiring. A Black psychologist born to poor tenant farmers in Mississippi, his path toward becoming a psychologist had been laden with any number of hardships.

When I left Menninger, I was quite different from the green rookie who had arrived two years previously. The earlier feelings of incompetence gave way to a sense of competence and confidence. I had learned how to do things the right way, and I was increasingly achieving a sense of professional identity. More than having the requisite technical skills at my finger tips, I also had the foundations of a theoretical structure to help guide my work. Furthermore, based on my immersion in the Rorschach with Mayman and Appelbaum, as well as Kernberg's seminal seminar, I began to imagine a future direction my work could take. More specifically, building upon Rapaport and Mayman, I had the budding sense of wanting to extend the conceptual basis of the Rorschach by integrating into its assessment the major and exciting shifts that were beginning to occur in psychoanalysis.

Finally—something I did not appreciate at the time—in becoming a Menninger alumnus I was also gaining membership in a professional fraternity whose members were scattered around the globe, and several of whom would become cherished friends and valued colleagues.

In the late summer of 1966, a time when the Yankees were mired in the basement of the standings, I moved to Detroit. Not unlike my earlier move to Kansas, I found the ambiance of Sinai Hospital and Detroit very different from that at Menninger and in Topeka. The headiness and intellectual stimulation were replaced by a blue-collar work ethic in which individuals were more concerned with applying psychoanalytic theory than reinventing it. Position, status, and publications were less important, and everyone, regardless of place, moved to the beat of Motown music.

At Sinai, I provided diagnostic services to a 36-bed, short-term inpatient unit, saw several outpatients in treatment, consulted throughout the hospital, and supervised psychiatric residents and psychology interns. The inpatient unit was exceptional. Two years in the planning, the underlying philosophy was of the therapeutic community. The unit, which featured subtle security provisions, was highly structured. Patients quickly realized what was expected of them, and staff roles were clearly defined and respected. Patients typically stayed for 30 days and invariably improved. The unit worked. It is my understanding that in the 1990s the hospital and the unit were closed, another fatality of our current health care system. Like other deaths, it lives on only in our memories.

Those of us who worked on the unit became quite close; we had lunch together, attended functions together, and shared in each other's successes and setbacks. On Labor Day eve, 1966, I was invited to an informal party at the home of one of the psychiatric occupational therapists. After the others left, Carole and I stayed up the entire night talking and spent the next day together talking too. Our marathon was only interrupted when I had to pick up my brother Howard at the airport. He had planned to spend the Labor Day weekend in Detroit. From that weekend on, beyond work, Carole and I saw each other constantly. We became engaged on Valentine's Day 1967 and were married on May 6th, Freud's birthday!

According to Carole, I was an occupational therapist's delight, a major project. When she initially met me, she was immediately observant of my raincoat. She noticed that apart from its being rumpled, each button had been sewn on with a different color thread. Her need to be needed, resourceful, practical, and competent meshed perfectly with my neediness. In addition, I unknowingly passed her acid test of totally accepting her dog.

More than accepting Carole's dog, I cherished Bogart. He was every man's dream, or, at least my dream; large and handsome (a 75-pound boxer), assertive, playful, mischievous, strident, defiant, self-possessed, and determined. Bogart was the first of our three boxers. When Carole and I married, I was gaining more than a wife. Because of Bogart, I was also gaining a family.

Although Carole wondered, I did not marry her essentially because of her dog. I was drawn to her lovingness, honesty, compassion, relatedness, and attractiveness. During our 36-year marriage, I have discovered her loyalty, supportiveness, integrity, and inner strength.

Two major events occurred soon after we were married. Carole quickly became pregnant and nine months later, in February 1968, our son Brett was born. At our wedding, my father looked ill. Months earlier he had been diagnosed with cancer, and his coloring and weight loss reflected the ravaging effects of the disease. He died seven months later, in December, two months before the birth of our son. At his well-attended funeral, his rabbi and friend emphasized his love of New York and his job, his devotion to his family, and his immense sense of gratitude.

With age, I believe I have become more attuned to the ebbs and flows of life. I see more clearly the delicate balance between success and failure, love and hate, and joy and sorrow. Recognizing that to everything there is a time, I appreciate that the most delicate balance of all is that between birth and death. I mourned the loss of my father, welcomed the arrival of our son, effected the internal shift from son to father, and deeply regretted that my son and father would not have the opportunity to come to know each other.

When our son Brett was one-year-old, I received a job offer from Waterloo, Ontario. The position involved a dual appointment. One part of the appointment involved being the chief psychologist at a community general hospital. The other part of the appointment was as an associate professor in the Department of Psychology at the University of Waterloo. Richard Steffy and Don Meichenbaum, two friends and fellow students at Illinois, and faculty members in the Department at Waterloo, had orchestrated the offer. With great ambivalence, as I truly liked Detroit and our life there, and at Carole's urging, I accepted the offer.

The position was challenging and demanding. At the hospital my first responsibility was to set up a psychology department, including recruiting and hiring. Laden with administrative tasks, doing minimal clinical work, and missing former colleagues and the professional stimulation of Detroit, I began writing a book.

Handbook of Rorschach Scales (Lerner, 1975) was my attempt to bring together in one compendium a host of Rorschach scales that reflected creative and innovative ways in which the instrument was being utilized for research purposes. In addition to hoping that the collection would serve as a useful reference, I also hoped that it would contribute to the Rorschach's theoretical basis.

While working in Waterloo, I established contact with several former colleagues from Menninger who were in practice in Toronto. Desiring to create something of the same working climate we had in Topeka, they would refer me patients for psychological testing and then we would convene for case conferences. Several of these colleagues had completed psychoanalytic training, whereas others were nearing completion.

With the opportunity to establish a practice with these colleagues in Toronto, having already been accepted at the Toronto Psychoanalytic Institute, and recognizing that I needed to live in a city large enough to support a major league team, we relocated to Toronto in 1972. With that move, I felt I had been called up from the minor league.

THE STEINBRENNER YEARS

On January 3, 1973, George M. Steinbrenner, III, head of a limited partnership, purchased the Yankees from CBS. His purchase signaled the end of the dark period. Beginning that day, the Yankees were back on the road to respectability and headed toward reclaiming aspects of their past glory.

In parallel with the Yankees, our move to Toronto signaled the beginning of an especially creative and productive period. Within a short time frame, I established a private practice involving assessment and treatment, began formal psychoanalytic training, was asked to teach a Rorschach course in the Department of Applied Psychology at the University of Toronto, and was appointed a consultant in the Department of Psychiatry at Mount Sinai Hospital. Carole was offered and accepted a position as head of occupational therapy in psychiatry at Mt. Sinai with a cross-appointment at the University of Toronto. Our son, Brett began grade school.

Analytic training served to extend, deepen, and solidify what I had previously learned at Menninger. Because the Institute's faculty, having trained in various locations, represented all points of view, I received topnotch training in classical theory, object relations theory, and self theory. I could readily see how the different models fit together. I felt confident and comfortable, both clinically and theoretically, moving from one model to another.

Of my various supervisors and teachers, the one I felt closest to and who had the most significant impact was Ruth Easser. Tall and gangly, Ruth radiated beauty when she spoke. She was a remarkable clinician, combining an uncanny empathy with an unusual clinical savvy. As a theoretician, her paper, *Empathic Inhibition and Psychoanalytic Technique*, (Easser, 1974) originally presented as the Sandor Rado lecture at the Columbia Psychoanalytic Institute, predated and anticipated several of Kohut's later contributions.

Toward the end of our supervision, Ruth unexpectedly mentioned that she would be having surgery and that we would be missing several sessions. When she returned she had a look about her I was all too familiar with. It was a look I had seen with my father and others dying of cancer. We continued with the supervision—first in her office, then in her home, and finally in her bedroom. When I saw Ruth at her home, her elderly mother would hover in the background. Unfortunately, Ruth treated her mother harshly and with disdain.

Then on one occasion her treatment of her mother changed dramatically. The disdain gave way to lovingness and a willingness to accept her mother's care. I knew that meant the end was near. Ruth died that evening. I felt deeply honored to be selected as a pallbearer at her funeral.

In her life, Ruth was my teacher and I was her student. In her death, I was provided an opportunity—one I had been denied years earlier with my mother—to say goodbye.

The major component of psychoanalytic training is one's own personal analysis. Of my years spent in analysis, what I remember most vividly was our last session. Unintentionally and with no conscious forethought, I spent the entire hour reminiscing about my Tom Thumb radio from childhood. Typically, at the end of an hour, my analyst, Dr. Markson, would close with, "Our time is up." He closed this session differently, simply stating, "Signing off." At that moment and throughout much of the analysis, I felt understood.

With the completion of my formal training, I felt ready to return to my earlier interest in and intent to translate newer psychoanalytic concepts, particularly those issuing from object relations theory, into the language of the Rorschach. In books and in articles (Lerner, 1979, 1986, 1989, 1991), I wrote of a number of these concepts including defense, projective identification, false self, depression, and the depressive position. As I worked with these concepts, out of necessity I began revisiting different features of the Rorschach including specific scores (FCarb, F(c)) and content.

Ironically, as I was following a path laid out by Rapaport, I found myself increasingly moving away from Rapaport's Rorschach conceptualizations and moving closer to those of Schachtel (1966). Psychoanalysis itself was shifting from its earlier interest in drives, energy, and structures to its more contemporary concern with self, object relations, experience, and subjective meanings. It seemed to me that Schachtel's experiential focus was more in harmony with these shifts than was Rapaport's structural focus.

As my interest in Schachtel deepened, I began to see other yet related directions my work could take. For instance, I became interested in extending and broadening Schachtel's formulations regarding an experiential approach to Rorschach assessment. This led to subsequent articles on the clinical inference process, Rorschach interpretation, and the roles of empathy and reflection in interpretation (Lerner, 1992, 1996, 1998). Furthermore, it also seemed to me, that as part of developing a contemporary and comprehensive psychoanalytic Rorschach psychology, one commensurate with the theoretical shifts taking place, Schachtel's work had to be integrated with Rapaport's. That is, a comprehensive theory needed to account for both structure and experience.

In 1978 the Yankees overcame a 14-game deficit and on the wings of a Buck Dent homerun, beat the Boston Red Sox in a playoff game and won their division. They subsequently defeated the Los Angeles Dodgers four games to two and won their twenty-second world championship.

That year I received a call from Jay Kwawer, a psychologist-psychoanalyst in New York. Jay was putting together a symposium involving the Rorschach and the borderline patient that he would be submitting for the APA's annual convention, and asked if I would be willing to participate. I was excited about the opportunity but hesitant to attend the meeting, which would be held in San Francisco.

Carole suggested that I involve my brother Howard as a co-author, as in all likelihood, he would want to attend the meeting. Howard, who was living in Greenwich Village and working at a child guidance clinic on Staten Island at the time, readily agreed. For the next several months Howard and I met regularly, both in Toronto and in New York. After I provided Howard a crash course on Kernberg's theory, we set about writing our paper. In that paper (Lerner & Lerner, 1980), which was based on Kernberg's theoretical formulations, we reported on the development and application of a Rorschach scoring manual designed to assess specific defenses that both underlie and organize the internal object world of the borderline patient.

Kwawer called again several months later. He mentioned that the proposal had been rejected by APA, but that he had resubmitted it to the Society for Personality Assessment (SPA), which accepted it for their mid-winter meeting. Because the meeting would be in Tampa, I decided to attend.

Any number of remarkable and improbable occurrences came from that meeting. The papers were all well received and became the basis of our later book, *Borderline Phenomena and the Rorschach Test* (Kwawer, Lerner, Lerner, & Sugarman, 1980). James Gorney, one of the presenters, who was then at Austen Riggs and is now in Knoxville, over the years has become a valued friend. More concerned with Howard's living arrangement and employment than was he, I spoke with Sid Blatt regarding Howard's possibly doing a postdoctorate at Yale. Having heard Howard's presentation, Sid was quite encouraging. Eventually Howard did apply and was accepted. That was the beginning of Howard's productive and rewarding career.

For me, that meeting marked the beginning of my long and exceptionally rewarding relationship with SPA. I regard SPA as my professional home and its members as my professional family. For each of the past 25 mid-winter meetings, I have had the opportunity to present papers. From Marty Leichtman to Gene Nebel, I have had the opportunity to develop lasting friendships. And, I have had the opportunity to participate in SPA's governance.

Memories of the 1996 meeting in Denver are particularly bitter sweet. Early in the afternoon of the opening day I felt pleased and humbled when presented SPA's Bruno Klopfer Award. Hours later, with tears flowing, I presented a eulogy for my beloved friend Mary Cerney.

In addition to my involvement with SPA, the years in Toronto—that part of the Steinbrenner era—included other beginnings, too. Scott McFaddin had been a student in my Rorschach course at the University of Toronto. As Dr. Ohlsen had done with me, I often met with Scott before class, over a cup of coffee, discussing his future plans. A former hockey goalie in the Boston Bruins organization, he was forced to forego his hockey career because of an injury. He chose psychology as a replacement with an emphasis on sports psychology. Even after completing his doctoral degree, we maintained regular contact.

Scott mentioned to me that he had been approached by the general manager of a National Hockey League team. The general manager, whom Scott knew, was considering an amateur player as his first round choice in the up and coming draft. Questions had been raised, however, involving the young man's character and stability, so perhaps Scott could help answer these questions. Scott and I decided on an assessment battery, and I agreed to interpret blindly the individual's Rorschach and TAT. Based on our assessment findings we recommended that they not draft the player and documented our reasons in a report.

The team did not draft the player. Impressed with the accuracy of several of our specific predictions and pleased that we helped save them about a million dollars, they offered us a contract to assess all their future draftees. We have been involved with several teams but for the past 10 years have been exclusively affiliated with one team. As the National Hockey League has become international, from originally assessing only North American players, we now assess players from Russia, Sweden, Finland, and Slovakia as well.

Soon after I met Scott, I met Tim Gilmor. Tim was a psychology intern at a major Toronto teaching hospital. He would consult with me regarding his more challenging and difficult assessment cases. As with Scott, the relationship became increasingly important to each of us. After completing his doctorate we still stayed in touch. Tim has kept me informed of significant developments in his life, including the birth of his children and job changes.

After several such changes, Tim decided to start his own company. Although the services to be provided came under the umbrella of organizational psychology, a key component was executive selection. Tim included the Rorschach in his assessment and asked if I would be willing to interpret the protocols. Through his prior contacts and hard work, and the quality and accuracy of our assessments, the work has steadily increased. We now provide services to several major Canadian corporations.

On a personal level, the work with Scott and Tim has led to enduring friendships. On a conceptual level, the work reaffirms Rapaport's (1950) dictum that the focus of assessment is personality and not psychopathology. It is my experience that psychological tests, when in the hands of a well-trained assessor, are as helpful in identifying effective hockey players and effective corporate executives as they are in identifying a patient's strengths and vulnerabilities.

During this period, as our son Brett was completing high school, we strongly urged him to consider colleges in the United States. We were concerned with his sense of having an American identity. We visited several schools in Pennsylvania, and he quickly and wisely chose Franklin and Marshall. As much as Carole and I valued and enjoyed living in Toronto, with Brett's going to school in the states, it seemed clearer that we too needed to return.

We considered several places and finally decided on Asheville, North Carolina. Because Toronto was wonderfully cosmopolitan, ethnically rich and diverse, had a major league baseball team, and had afforded us a full and vital social and professional life, we experienced the move as difficult. A level of psychological sophistication I had come to expect was replaced by a deep-seated religiosity; patients needing help often chose between professionals and ministers, and the alternative to psychotherapy was not medication but prayer.

Amid this cultural shock, captured in my wife's referring to herself as Margaret Mead in Samoa, I opened a practice, and Carole began work as a deputy in our county sheriff's department. Having read the Nancy Drew series during her youth, a part of her had longed to do detective work. As I had done in response to earlier relocations and the implicit sense of loss, I began writing another book (Lerner, 1991). Three years later *Psychoanalytic Theory and the Rorschach* was released.

During this early period in Asheville I reestablished contact with colleagues in Knoxville, Tennessee. After several planning meetings, four of us, including Jim Murray, formed a local chapter of Division 39, the psychoanalytic division of APA. The Appalachian Psychoanalytic Society continues to thrive and grow, and is currently one of the most vibrant chapters in the Division. Through the urging and help of Len Handler, I was appointed an adjunct in the Department of Psychology at the University of Tennessee. Because of Len, I met and worked with several former graduate students, including Mark Hilsenroth and Steve Hibbard.

Two years after I moved to Asheville, Jim Gooney relocated to Knoxville. Jim and I had first met in 1978 at SPA and had participated on a panel together. He contributed a chapter to our book, *Borderline Phenomena and the Rorschach*, and, like his other writings, it was exceptional. One day every other week I would see patients and supervisees in Knoxville, and Jim and I shared office space. We also had lunch together, which for me was a special treat.

While still in Asheville I was approached by the publisher of *Braniff* magazine, the in-flight magazine for Braniff Airlines. I agreed to do a monthly column, which essentially involved applying psychoanalytic concepts and formulations to the issues of daily life. After my first article, the airline declared bankruptcy. Undaunted, the publisher quickly secured a contract with Amtrak. Unlike the aborted experience with Braniff, I wrote a monthly column for *Amtrak Express* for five years. In 1994, the articles were awarded a Popular Press Writing Award by the Menninger Foundation.

Writing the articles for Amtrak was pure joy. It was as if someone had presented me with an open forum to express publicly those things that really mattered to me. When my son, Brett, married I wrote about weddings; when a friend questioned why she was socially isolated at her workplace, I wrote about "shunning," and when residents in our town turned to bows and arrows to solve the so-called "deer problem," I wrote of "crossing the line." I found writing magazine pieces very different from, and more to my liking than writing professional articles. I felt less straight-jacketed and freer to express opinions and feelings. In essence, the magazine articles sprang from my heart more than from my head.

Perhaps the most heartfelt of the Amtrak articles involved dealing with the loss of the family pet. The article was prompted by the death of our third boxer, Boca. She was our baby, the daughter we had not had, our son's longest living sibling (we regard our earlier two boxers as siblings too), and the child who never left home.

Boca and I had tied the ribbon of our relationship at obedience school. At graduation, in front of relatives and friends, we skillfully demonstrated all the lessons we had learned—to heel, stay, come, lie down. The final exercise, one we had not done before, called for working with another owner's dog. While heeling a cooperative golden retriever, I felt a tug at the bottom of my pant leg. I looked down and there was Boca. She had broken away from her trainer. Despite screams from the instructor to return her, we clung tight, unabashedly claiming each other.

We elected to bury Boca in a pet cemetery amid apple orchards surrounded by the Blue Ridge Mountains. We also arranged for trees to be planted in her honor—including, of course, a pink dogwood.

After four enriching and full years, Brett graduated from Franklin and Marshall in 1990. He then applied for and was accepted into a combined journalism/business MBA Program at Northwestern University. He fulfilled an internship requirement at Eastman Kodak in Rochester, New York. Upon completion of his degree, he accepted a position in public relations and marketing with Kodak.

Soon after moving to Rochester on a more permanent basis, Brett met Kristine. They were living in separate, converted apartments in what at one time had been a stately mansion. One morning he had taken a shower and used all of his hot water and hers as well. It was not love at first sight. They did begin dating, resolved the hot water crisis, fell in love, and became engaged.

Like my wife, I cried at Brett's wedding. I was not surprised, as Jim Gorney had warned me that weddings were exactly like funerals. Friends tried to reassure me that more than losing a son, I was gaining a daughter-in-law and prospective grandchildren. I heard them with my head but not with my heart. I felt the loss of my son and was filled with nostalgia. Flashing through my mind were the countless experiences we had shared. We had collected baseball autographs together, he had accompanied me to many SPA meetings and was with me when I received the Bruno Klopfer award, and he, my brother Howard, and I had attended a Rose Bowl parade and game. I also recalled his wanting to attend an orthodox religious school after the Seven Days War and after having one beer too many, skiing into a tree. Several months following their wedding, because of cut backs at Kodak, Brett decided to leave the company and accepted a position which involved their relocating to Camden, Maine.

After several visits to Camden, Carole mentioned that in order to be closer to Brett and Kristine, she thought that we too should relocate to Maine. At that point I was finishing the book *Psychoanalytic Perspectives on the Rorschach* (Lerner, 1998). Reflective of my shift away from Rapaport and toward Schachtel, the volume expressed a strong experiential orientation. At the same time, like previous publications, it represented an attempt to integrate contemporary psychoanalytic advances into Rorschach theory and practice.

THE 1998 YANKEES

The 1998 Yankees were a very special team. Despite lacking a superstar of the stature of DiMaggio or Mantle, the team set an American League record by winning 112 games, posted an 11–2 post season record, and swept the San Diego Padres in four games to claim their twenty-fourth world championship. Every player on their roster contributed and, as a team, they played the game as it should be played. Their defense was flawless, they hit in the clutch, and the relief pitching was untouchable.

Because of the Yankees' success in 1998, and earlier in 1997, it felt like a comfortable time to move. Despite that feeling of comfort and Camden's seductive coastal beauty, I was wary of living in a small community. Nonetheless, with the help of two local psychologists, Richard Fisher and Robert Dodge, I quickly established a practice.

As my practice in Asheville was different from my practice in Toronto, my practice in Camden has been unique. Increasingly, I have found myself functioning more like the old family general practitioner rather than as a specialist. I have had to be more flexible, mindful of, but more relaxed with boundaries, and although I do little analysis, psychoanalytic theory, more so than ever, informs my work.

These shifts in the nature of my practice have also prompted me to reflect back upon my relationship with psychoanalysis, including how I have worked as an analyst. At first, I valued the title as an expression of professional identity, relished the institutional affiliations, and clung too tightly to prescribed techniques. This has changed. Over time, I have increasingly been drawn to the values implicit in and underlying psychoanalysis, the incredible breadth and beauty of the theory, and the opportunity the theory provides for working with individuals, both in treatment and in assessment, in as deep a way as possible. Also, I have increasingly appreciated and made use of Kohut's (1959, 1978) view of empathy as a powerful means of coming to know another.

As I see it, psychoanalysis is based on a clinical-humanistic value system that emphasizes the pursuit of truth and meaning. Treatment, not just analysis, as I have experienced it, is not something one does, directs, or steers. Rather, one helps establish its necessary conditions and then allows it to unfold, however it needs to, with its own pace and rhythm.

Several months after our move, at Brett's instigation, he and I bought the local bookstore. The Owl and Turtle Bookshop quickly became a family enterprise. Carole purchases all the non-book items, creates the window displays, and looks after advertising; Brett is responsible for the financial side; and I deal with general administrative matters. Our staff generally numbers 16, and now, after many changes, we have an exceptional group of people who work as a team. For three years consecutively we have been voted the number one independent bookstore in Maine.

Last summer we had a book signing with Richard Russo, a local author who was awarded the Pulitzer Prize in fiction for his book *Empire Falls* (2001). I spotted a distinguished looking man waiting in line to have his book signed. As he approached Russo, they greeted and then Russo arose and escorted the individual over to introduce him to me. Before the introduction, I knew it was David McCollough, the Pulitzer recipient for his nonfiction book, *John Adams* (2001). I thought to myself, "How ironic. Here I am in this quaint, funky bookstore in small-town Maine with two Pulitzer Prize winning authors."

The experience actually reminded me of an earlier one. Decades ago I had attended a Yankee baseball camp with ex-Yankee players including Mickey Mantle, Bill Skowron, and Gene Woodling. On one hot afternoon I was taking extra fielding practice. In between fielding grounders, I looked up from my shortstop post and noticed that Gene Woodling was hitting the balls and that Bill Skowron was receiving my throws at first base. Back then, and again in the bookstore with Russo and McCollough, I asked myself, "Can life get any better?"

The joy of Camden for Carole and myself is not in its scenic beauty, but in our closeness to family. We celebrate holidays together, we see our two granddaughters, Caroline and Claire often, and Brett and I frequently have lunch together.

CONCLUSION

Like other small towns, Camden celebrates civic holidays such as Memorial Day with an annual parade. It is part of the town's tradition. As expressed in my passion for baseball, I revere tradition. Having trained at the Menninger Foundation and having completed psychoanalytic training, it was inevitable I would follow in a Rorschach tradition pioneered by David Rapaport.

Rapaport envisioned the relationship between the Rorschach and psychoanalytic theory as a two-way street. In one direction, he saw theory as offering the Rorschach assessor a vast array of clinical concepts and formulations that could deepen, enliven, and broaden test-based inferences. In the other direction, he saw the Rorschach as providing the psychoanalytic theorist and researcher a means for operationalizing concepts and testing formulations that were elusive and often overly abstract. In time, he saw this as adding to the scientific status and evolving scope of psychoanalytic theory.

For more than three decades, in publications, presentations, and workshops, I have attempted to safeguard, extend, and enrich this tradition. At a time when empirical approaches were making significant contributions and gaining in popularity, it seemed to me that a complementary approach, one which was clinically based and emphasized understanding an individual in his or her uniqueness, complexity, and depth needed to be heard.

On one side of Rapaport's vision, the research side, I believe the work with Howard, my brother, on operationalizing primitive defenses and other borderline phenomena has been a solid contribution. On the other side, I am pleased with having extended psychoanalytic Rorschach assessment in a more experiential-relational direction, bringing overdue attention to the work of Schachtel, and beginning to integrate his conceptualizations with those of Rapaport.

Several years ago I read the acceptance speech of the Pulitzer recipient in photo journalism. He began by pointing out that his mother had died when he was 13 years old. He then, in a deeply personal and reflective way, traced the important aspects of his adult life such as choice of career, investment in his work, and attitude toward family, back to the early loss of his mother. He concluded with the penetrating observation that even though the essence of his life was born of loss, if somehow given the opportunity, he would not wish his life to be any different than it was. His remarks resonated at all levels. Life consists of a series of relationships, later ones are chosen, earlier ones are not. When I consider the relationships in my life—with my parents, Carole, Brett and his family, my brother Howard, our three boxers, the New York Yankees, Seabiscuit, and many others—I feel remarkably lucky and grateful.

REFERENCES

Appelbaum, S. (1970). Science and persuasion in the psychological test report. *Journal of Consulting and Clinical Psychology, 135*, 349–355.

Easser, R. (1974). Empathic inhibition and psychoanalytic technique. *Psychoanalytic Quarterly, 43*, 557–580.

Frankiel, R. (1994). *Essential papers on object loss.* New York: New York University Press.

Freud, S. (1957). Mourning and melancholia. In J. Strachey (Ed. & Trans.), *The standard edition of the complete psychological works of Sigmund Freud* (Vol. 14, pp. 237–260). London: Hogarth Press. (Original work published 1917).

Kohut, H. (1959/1978). Introspection, empathy, and psychoanalysis. In P. Ornstein (Ed.), *The search for the self* (Vol. 1, pp. 205–222). Madison, CT: International Universities Press.

Kwawer, J., Lerner, H., Lerner, P., & Sugarman, A. (1980). *Borderline phenomena and the Rorschach test.* New York: International Universities Press.

Lerner, P. (1965). Resolution of intrafamilial role conflict in families of schizophrenic patients. Part 1: Thought disturbance. *Journal of Nervous and Mental Disease, 146*, 412–416.

Lerner, P. (1968). Correlation of social competence and level of cognitive percetual functioning in male schizophrenics. *Journal of Neuronal and Mental Disease, 146*, 412–416.

Lerner, P. (1975). *Handbook of Rorschach scales.* New York: International Universities Press.

Lerner, P. (1979). Treatment implications of the (c) response in the Rorschach records of patients with severe character pathology. *Ontario Psychologist, 11*, 20–22.

Lerner, P. (1986). Experiential and structural aspects of the (c) Rorschach response in patients with narcissistic personality disorder. In M. Kissen (Ed.), *Assessing object relations phenomena* (pp. 333–348). New York: International Universities Press.

Lerner, P. (1990). The treatment of early object loss: The need to search. *Psychoanalytic Psychology, 7*, 79–90.

Lerner, P. (1991). *Psychoanalytic theory and the Rorschach.* Hillsdale, NJ: The Analytic Press.

Lerner, P. (1992). Toward an experiential psychoanalytic approach to the Rorschach. *Bulletin of the Menninger Clinic, 56*, 451–464.

Lerner, P. (1996). Current perspectives on psychoanalytic Rorschach assessment. *Journal of Personality Assessment, 67*, 450–460.

Lerner, P. (1998). *Psychoanalytic perspectives on the Rorschach.* Hillsdale, NJ: The Analytic Press.

Lerner, P., & Lerner, H. (1980). Rorschach assessment of primitive defenses in borderline personality structure. In J. Kwawer, H. Lerner, P. Lerner, & A. Sugarman (Eds.), *Borderline phenomena and the Rorschach test* (pp. 257–274). New York: International Universities Press.

McCollough, D. (2001). *John Adams.* New York: Simon & Schuster.

Main, T. (1957). The ailment. *British Journal of Medical Psychology, 30*, 129–145.

Mayman, M. (1976). Psychoanalytic theory in retrospect and prospect. *Bulletin of the Menninger Clinic, 40*, 199–210.

Mishler, E., & Waxler, N. (1968). *Family processes and schizophrenia.* New York: Science House.

Rapaport, D. (1950). The theoretical implications of diagnostic testing procedures. *Congres International de Psychiatric, 2*, 241–271.

Rapaport, D., Gill, M., & Schafer, R. (1945/1946). *Diagnostic psychological testing,* 2 vols. Chicago: Year Book.

Rosner, J. (1987). August. New York: Warner Books.

Russo, R. (2001). *Empire Falls.* New York: Vintage Books.

Schachtel, E. (1966). *Experiential foundations of Rorschach's test.* New York: Basic Books.

SELECTED BIBLIOGRAPHY

Books

Lerner, H., & Lerner, P. (1988). *Primitive mental states and the Rorschach test.* Madison, CT: International Universities Press.

Lerner, P. (1991). *Psychoanalytic theory and the Rorschach.* Hillsdale, NJ: The Analytic Press.

Lerner, P. (1998). *Psychoanalytic perspectives on the Rorschach.* Hillsdale, NJ: The Analytic Press.

Kwawer, J., Lerner, H., Lerner, P., & Sugarman, A. (1980). *Borderline phenomena and the Rorschach test.* New York: International Universities Press.

Journal Articles

Lerner, P. (1990). Rorschach assessment of primitive defenses: A review. *Journal of Personality Assessment, 54*, 30–46.

Lerner, P. (1990). The treatment of early object loss: The need to search. *Psychoanalytic Psychology, 7*, 79–90. (Reprinted in R. Frankiel [Ed.], *Essential papers on object loss* [pp. 469–481]. New York: New York University Press, 1994.)

Lerner, P. (1991). The analysis of content revisited. *Journal of Personality Assessment, 54*, 30–46.

Lerner, P. (1992). Toward an experiential psychoanalytic approach to the Rorschach. *Bulletin of the Menninger Clinic, 56*, 451–464.

Lerner, P. (1993). Object relations theory and the Rorschach. *Rorschachiana, 18*, 45–57.

Lerner, P. (1994). Treatment issues in a case of multiple personality disorder. *Psychoanalytic Psychology, 11*, 563–574.

Lerner, P. (1996). Current perspectives on psychoanalytic Rorschach assessment. *Journal of Personality Assessment, 67*, 450–461. (Paper presented as recipient of the Bruno Klopfer Award.)

Lerner, P. (1996). The interpretive process in Rorschach testing. *Journal of Personality Assessment, 67*, 494–500.

Lerner, P. (1996). Rorschach assessment of cognitive impairment from an object relations perspective. *Bulletin of the Menninger Clinic, 60*, 351–365.

Lerner, P. (1998). Schachtel and experiential Rorschach assessment. *Journal of Personality Assessment, 71*, 182–188.

Lerner, P. (2000). Martin Mayman: His work and his place. *Journal of Personality Assessment, 75*, 33–45.

Lerner, P. (2002). A humanistic psychoanalytic approach to assessment. *The Humanistic Psychologist, 30*, 194–208.

Lerner, P. (2004). Further thoughts on an experiential psychoanalytic approach to assessment. *Bulletin of the Menninger Clinic, 68*, 152–163.

Lerner, P. (in press). On developing a clinical sense of self. *Journal of Personality Assessment.*

Lerner, P., & Lerner, H. (1986). Contribution of object relations theory toward a general psychoanalytic theory of thinking. *Psychoanalysis and Contemporary Thought, 5*, 77–115.

Book Chapters

Lerner, P. (1993). The borderline concept: Crossroads of theory and research. In J. Barron, M. Eagle, & D. Wolitzsky (Eds.), *Interface of psychoanalysis and psychology* (pp. 452–463). Washington, DC: American Psychological Association.

Lerner, P. (1998). Training in assessment: Internalization and identity. In L. Handler & M. Hilsenroth (Eds.), *Teaching and learning personality assessment* (pp. 107–118). Mahwah, NJ: Lawrence Erlbaum.

Lerner, P. (2003). Dissociative identity disorder. In I. Weiner (Ed.), *Adult psychopathology case studies* (pp. 183–206). New York: John Wiley

Lou Gehrig (left) and Joe DiMaggio, 1937

Author at right, with Mickey Mantle at a New York Yankees baseball camp, May 1984

The author, far right, with wife Carole and son Brett, at Brett's graduation from Franklin and Marshall College, June 1990

My third boxer, Boca, September 1989

With brother Howard, June 1997

CHAPTER 10

Confessions of an Iconoclast

At Home on the Fringe

Jane Loevinger
Washington University

I was born in 1918 in St. Paul, Minnesota, the middle one of five children. My father, Gustavus Loevinger, was a lawyer who was appointed a district court judge in 1932 while I was in high school. In her spare time, my mother was a gifted amateur pianist and, on occasion, a school teacher. Both of my parents were motherless children, which probably contributed to the somewhat constrained atmosphere in the family. The only grandparent I remember was my mother's stepmother, whom she didn't like, and who was never a close family member.

My father was born in Germany and came with his father to this country as an eight-year-old boy. His mother died shortly after he was born, probably of tuberculosis. Several older brothers had come to the U.S. by themselves. One had settled in Montana, one on a ranch in Texas, one in Mitchell, South Dakota, and one on a farm near Mitchell. My father and his father went to Mitchell, where his brother Joe lived. My father was apparently brought up by Joe's wife and a friendly neighbor. He worked his way through high school and Dakota Wesleyan University, and went on to the University of Minnesota Law School. By then his mastery of the English language was sufficient enough that he taught English.

One thing that distinguished our family from the others was the spelling of our name. The German letter "ö" was translated by various relatives either as an "o" or as "e." My father, teaching himself English as a boy, learned that the correct translation was "oe."

So we had aunts and uncles and cousins, most of whom we rarely saw. I remember mainly my cousin Louise, who came to live with us for several months. Her family lived on a farm, so being with us gave her a chance to see city life while she helped my mother and gave my parents a chance to take a vacation together. Cousin Louise lived with us long enough so that my sister Louise was forever after known by her childhood nickname of Peter.

We were not a typical, warm, family group. There was a lively, somewhat competitive, atmosphere, and a certain family loyalty and pride, but not much overt affection. There were times when we were required to hug and kiss our parents, particularly at arrivals and departures, no matter whether one felt like doing so. I was alienated by the compulsory, pro forma rules for display of affection, and withdrew into myself.

Mother had more spontaneity than Father did. I can remember two occasions on which she danced around the house for joy. One was when her Steinway baby grand piano was delivered. The other was when she got her hair cut. She had always worn her hair long, put up in a large bun that was pinned on top of her head. Her new style was the then-fashionable "boyish bob." My father was as dejected as she was elated. Such was the 1920s version of women's liberation.

My father spent most of his time at work, gladly leaving management of the household, including the children, to my mother. That was a conventional arrangement, so it scarcely seems worth mentioning here, except that my colleagues, Blasi and Hy, tell me that in Italy and Vietnam, the household authority is not the mother but rather the father.

On the whole we were raised in accordance with the childrearing philosophy from which Benjamin Spock rescued the next generation. Parents presided over not only table manners but also what children were expected to eat. My parents were not very punitive, and mother was more lenient than father; only serious infractions, that is, "federal cases," were taken to him.

I was pushed ahead in school, so I was always with older children, and always an outsider. I survived high school by reading through the shelves of poetry in the public library. I considered myself a poet, although I did not succeed in publishing anything. (*Poetry* magazine sent me polite rejections.) But I never surrendered my poetic license.

COLLEGE

With encouragement from my mother I left high school in the middle of my senior year and enrolled at the University of Minnesota (UM). I did not take academics seriously during my freshman year. Instead, I took a course in art history and architecture, and worked on the school paper. Fortunately, the *Minnesota Daily* was the best paper in town; the star reporter was Eric Sevareid. I learned a lot about writing that year. A good city editor does not worry about a cub reporter's feelings. He insists on getting things right.

I did not take courses in English because, in my conceit, I was afraid it would spoil my style. I need not have worried, because statistics soon stole my muse. The country at that time was slipping into a depression, a fact that had a sobering effect on me as well as on other students who were not serious.

I began taking psychology courses because a science was required, and it didn't seem too scientific for me. Vocational counseling was a specialty at UM, and they were considered among the best in that field in the country. So I decided to present myself as a client. Jack Darley, my counselor, told me psychology was too mathematical for me, but I might get by in psychological aesthetics. That was a challenge.

I immediately enrolled in a course in trigonometry. Once I started I continued math through a course in vectors and matrices, where I had a wonderful teacher, Dunham Jackson. I have no gift for mathematics, but I stuck with it. I also had a good statistics teacher, Alan E. Treloar, a biologist.

My psychology teachers included Florence Goodenough in child welfare and Donald G. Paterson in psychology. They both emphasized individual differences in intelligence, and their measurement. There was a leaning towards hereditarian explanations.

When I graduated with an MS degree in psychometrics I was 20. I was turned down for an assistantship by the psychology department, but granted one by the child welfare institute. However, the legislature reduced funding, so one assistantship had to be dropped. Goodenough explained to one of her students why I was the one dropped: "She is too young, too radical, and Jewish." I heard that remark within five minutes of its being made because the other student was a friend of mine; ironically, she was a member of the Young Communist League, which I never considered joining, nor did they want me as a member.

To give more of the flavor of those depression days: The chairman of the psychology department, R. M. Elliot, told me that their best graduate students were Jewish women, and the only jobs for doctoral graduates were in religious schools in rural Minnesota, schools that would not hire either a Jew or a woman. He said, kindly, that he would not want to see me clerk in a dime store; so he recommended that I marry a psychologist. At least he had the grace to smile at that unlikely prospect.

Just as I was about to leave for another school, a senior assistant in psychology got a real job, and so I was offered the assistantship with the understanding that I would leave at the end of the year.

At this time the American Psychological Association had its annual convention in Minnesota. Edward Tolman's presidential address on the behavior of a rat at a choice point displayed his lively, charming approach to science. I was enchanted by the difference between his attitude and that of my Minnesota professors, so I applied for graduate school at Berkeley, unlike other Minnesota students, for whom going away to school meant going East, usually to Chicago. Those were the days of the Dustbowl. Many Midwesterners dreamed of California, but went to Chicago.

BERKELEY

I was "born again" in Berkeley in 1939. At the same time that I arrived, three notable additions to the Berkeley campus were Erik Erikson, Else Frenkel-Brunswik, and Jerzy Neyman. By good fortune I came to know all of them. Neyman was one of the founders of modern statistics. I never mastered his approach, but, by auditing his course, I learned enough to stay a step ahead of my classmates in statistics.

Else Frenkel-Brunswik came to join her husband, Egon Brunswik, who was already on the Berkeley faculty. Else had to leave Vienna on 24 hours notice, not only to come to the U.S., but also to save her life. Else was eager to begin work as a researcher, but most of the usual topics seemed trivial at that time, in the shadow of Hitler and Mussolini. Hence she chose to study the authoritarian personality.

Many of the graduate students joined her research team, including Daniel Levinson, Donald Campbell, and possibly Milton Rokeach and Richard Christie. When Nevitt Sanford joined the faculty, he became part of the research team. Along with many others, I was part of the audience for frequent reports. The research was done in the community using as subjects groups of workers, soldiers, prisoners, and others, rather than solely the usual college students.

Else was deeply committed to psychoanalysis at this time, having interrupted her own analysis when she left Vienna in a hurry. Sanford was himself an analyst.

One of the striking outcomes of this research, after years of work, was that classic Freudian explanations in psychosexual terms did not hold. The common element in authoritarian attitudes and beliefs seemed more like intolerance of ambiguity and intolerance of inner life (Adorno, Frenkel-Brunswik, Levinson, & Sanford, 1950).

International House

Going to Berkeley was my first extended stay away from home. I lived at International House, a kind of dormitory for graduate students and foreign students. I met all kinds of people there. I became friends with some women psychology students. Many of the men were physical scientists. Because of the radiation laboratory and the faculty, Berkeley was a mecca for young physical scientists. I came particularly to know Robert Oppenheimer's students and post docs.

Julian Schwinger would be getting up for breakfast when most students went to bed, but I was hanging out. We often went to a restaurant in the late evening. After the war he was awarded the Nobel Prize. I never saw him after that.

Robert Christy was another friend of that era. He came from Canada; he and I shared a love of ice skating, which was rare among our colleagues in sunny California. He also took me to a couple of parties that "Oppie" (Oppenheimer) gave for his students. After the war Christy became provost of Cal Tech. I have seen him briefly, on occasion, since then, at meetings of the National Academy of Sciences, which I attended as a wife, or later, as a spouse, or, nowadays, as a guest, when I go.

I had an intimate relation with only one physical scientist, Sam Weissman, a post doc in chemistry. We met on a blind date arranged by mutual friends. We are still together, but no longer blind.

The connection between my long association with scientists who needed no further credentials as scientists, and my later work in psychology, is that I gained confidence in my own judgment of what science is. I was not intimidated by the behavioristic experimenters and the followers of Clark Hull, who assumed a "more scientific than thou" stance towards those of us with more humanistic interests and approaches.

Psychology at Berkeley

When I arrived in the psychology department at Berkeley, I felt warmly welcomed. Jean Walker Macfarlane, my advisor, enrolled me in her introductory clinical class and in Erikson's course on Childhood and Society.

At Minnesota just one lecture had been devoted to psychoanalysis, in order to dismiss it as unscientific. One of the older graduate students remarked to me, "Psychoanalysis isn't like they told us. I've been reading Freud; he has a lot to say that's interesting."

More characteristic of student attitudes—they played a game of assigning each other the roles of ego, superego, and id. I was sometimes the ego, often the superego, but never the id.

Erikson's course was a stunning experience, as well as being an introduction to psychoanalysis, which I appreciated more as I read the usual ones later.

For some reason, Macfarlane assigned me to a job as Erikson's research assistant for one semester. Erik was working on configurations in play. The preadolescent girls in the Berkeley Guidance Study would come to his office, one at a time, and he would ask them to construct an exciting scene for a movie, using some small toys on a table. He would either photograph the scene or sketch it, and he would take it down before the next girl came. He could reconstruct it from his sketch and photograph it later.

He showed that the girls usually made somebody or something intruding into a peaceful domestic scene. That contrasted with the responses of the young men he had studied a year earlier at Harvard. They almost always constructed a scene of an automobile accident.

I came in one day when a construction was still standing, and I said that it looked like a model of the girl's body. Erik expressed his annoyance with me. I guess he had been assured that he did not need to worry about me getting caught up in interpretations since I was statistics all the way. Erik leaned back in his chair, with his big yellow sketch pad in front of him, and wrote in large letters, "I C W." That was the acronym of the building we were in. I took it also to mean "I see double you," and as an indirect apology for his angry outburst.

What I was supposed to do for him was unclear, but I gained the impression that he had no interest in scales or quantification. So I have never taken seriously attempts to turn achievement of identity, or any of Erik's other ideas, into a scale.

I was not considered a radical at Berkeley. An *enfant terrible*, perhaps, but not a radical. The other psychology graduate students teased me gently for my naïveté. Three of my friends had a *ménage a trois*, and tried to make me curious about who did what to whom, but I was not much concerned about it.

The War Years
Life changed radically with the advent of war. Many senior faculty members were called to Washington for war-related duties. Despite my lack of a doc-

toral degree, I had teaching opportunities that were not duplicated for many years. I was offered temporary positions at Stanford and Berkeley, for two reasons: I had taken statistics more seriously than the other students had (those being among the main courses to be taught), and, most important, I could not be drafted.

After teaching one year at Stanford I returned to Berkeley to work on my thesis, and do more teaching. In one course my teaching assistant was a fellow student, Betty Goldstein. We became close friends. We agreed that we didn't want to live the kind of lives our mothers did, and we shared vaguely left-wing political sentiments. Although she was an excellent student, Betty left graduate school for the "real" world, at first working on a labor paper, and later writing for women's magazines. She soon married Carl Friedan.

When the women's magazines rejected her articles about discontent among suburban women, and she was fired from a job for becoming pregnant, she collected some rejected essays as a book that she titled, *The Feminine Mystique* (Friedan, 1963/1984). Needless to say, Betty Friedan had a greater impact than did any of us who stayed on to complete our doctorates.

In 1943, "Oppie" and a group of his students and other young scientists, including Sam, left Berkeley to establish a National Laboratory in Los Alamos, New Mexico, which was dedicated to using recent scientific discoveries, particularly in nuclear physics, to advance the Allied war effort.

I remained at Berkeley, teaching and working on my thesis. I was also in analysis at that time. Having become interested in psychoanalysis as a theory of psychology (Loevinger, 1966), I entered analysis in somewhat the same spirit as I consulted a vocational counselor at Minnesota, as a participant observer. Fortunately, the process was more engaging, and the outcome more fruitful, in San Francisco.

Completing My Graduate Degree

My graduate career was upside down, teaching and sitting on committees of students older than myself, when I did not have a degree myself. At Stanford Jack Hilgard was helpful, coaching me when I didn't know what to do. At Berkeley I didn't have a mentor. Robert Tryon was the psychology professor whose topic was psychometrics, the area of my thesis. He was gone when I was working on my dissertation; in fact, it was his courses I was teaching. Even more important, we had opposite ideas about some relevant psychometric issues.

There were, however, faculty members from whom I learned much. I have mentioned several. Else Brunswik was not yet formally faculty, but was esteemed as such by students. Jerzy Neyman was faculty, but not in psychology. Egon Brunswik was important for me and several other students, including Ken Hammond and Don Campbell. Egon had a profound knowledge of the history of psychology, which he presented in terms of his system of probabilistic functionalism. He treated psychoanalysis seriously as a system of psychology. For the graduate language exam, Egon assigned as text Freud's Clark lectures, a gem that I might not have run across for many years if he had not assigned it. Egon did one more thing for me, an unusual one. He went out of his way to express his confidence that I would continue to contribute to psychology, even if I got married and had children.

Psychometrics and Temperament

The topic of my doctoral thesis was construction and evaluation of tests of ability. It began with a critique of the fundamental concept of psychometric theory, test reliability. I proved to my satisfaction that there is no noncircular definition of test reliability. This argument did not endear me to the psychometric establishment. One of my articles came back from a reviewer who said that that sort of thing should not be published. I have had my defenders and my critics over the years, but the role of professional iconoclast is not the royal road to popularity. I no longer do book reviews. My temperament is that of a critic, and I do not need more enemies.

Much of the material in my thesis was later incorporated into my most often quoted article, "Objective Tests as Instruments of Psychological Theory" (Loevinger, 1957). It was turned down for publication everywhere, until I sent it to a vanity journal where I paid to have it published.

While my iconoclasm did not endear me to true believers, it did protect me from some errors, both personal and professional. I think it was Betty Friedan who was told not to associate with me. Her communist friends said that I was a Trotskyite, and her Trotskyite friends said that I was a Communist. I was never tempted to join either group, although I did have some friends of that sort, particularly in Minnesota.

Some true believers used to think that the important core of psychoanalysis lay in cathexis theory. I never accepted the concept of cathexis (Loevinger, 1966), partly because I could not put it into the Queen's English, the only language I had a confident mastery of, and partly because I could not go to bed with an authority on thermodynamics if I embraced psychic energy during the day. Many psychologists who were also trained as analytic therapists, as I was not (notably Robert Holt), also turned away from cathexis theory, and they were soon followed by some analysts.

LOS ALAMOS

As soon as I passed my oral exam and finished my thesis (in 1944), I left Berkeley to join Sam in Los Alamos. We had been married in July 1943. There was no work for psychologists there, but everyone worked at something, clerical or whatever. I was tired from intensive work on my thesis, but did something with punch cards and a primitive computer, whatever I was asked to do.

The doctors and nurses had volunteered for hazardous duty, and were dismayed to find that they were mostly delivering babies for the wives of the young scientists. In a year or so I joined the ranks of the mothers. Los Alamos was a closed community; even mail was censored. Relatives could not come when one went home with a baby. Help consisted mainly of talking to the women in the nearby apartments who had also just delivered. At times the scientists worked around the clock. They could not help at home.

When the bomb was dropped on Hiroshima, there was a brief wave of elation that the secret project had proved its worth. With the dropping of the second bomb, on Nagasaki, the awful nature of what had been done began to sink in among most of the people at Los Alamos, so far as I could observe.

ST. LOUIS

As soon as the war was over we wanted to leave Los Alamos. A group of the Los Alamos chemists came with their families to Washington University in St. Louis, as part of a postwar renewal of the chemistry department. There was no place for me in the psychology department, except for an occasional, small, part-time job. For example, Philip DuBois, Goldine Gleser, and I (Loevinger et al., 1953) were working on a method of homogeneous keying for a biographical inventory for the air force. (My son could not believe I was employed by the air force. I told him I was a test pilot.)

My interest had turned away from psychometrics to the problems of mothers, and of women in general. My personal experiences and those of my friends (in particular, two who had had severe post partum depression) added to the impression that most research in psychology had used male subjects, and that it was time to focus on women. Some other psychologists, including Robert R. Sears and E. J. Shoben, were coming to a similar conclusion at that time.

My initial approach to the field was to construct an objective test of mothers' attitudes. NIMH of the Public Health Service funded my research generously, presumably on the basis of my earlier work in psychometrics.

Not having a position in the psychology department, curiously, had some advantages. Some psychology students who came to Washington University and who found its strict behaviorism uncongenial, drifted over to my small group, which began with Blanche Sweet, a friend from Berkeley, a gifted clinical psychologist. Our group, originally all women, met informally about once a week, often in my home. We began by trying to think of, and write, items covering all of the problems facing mothers and women in general, throughout the day and throughout the life cycle. The items were in dichotomous form, reflecting my psychometric training. Each alternative was an attempt to phrase one position in the phrases a person holding that position would use, thus respecting the person's defenses, reflecting my understanding of Frenkel-Brunswik's (1949) work on the authoritarian personality (Adorno, Frenkel-Brunswik, Levinson, & Sanford, 1950).

After we put together a version of the Family Problems Scale (FPS; Loevinger, 1998), we used it in small studies reflecting interests of the moment and the current students, then we revised as results dictated. That process was repeated through many cycles.

Kitty LaPerriere left Czechoslovakia for Switzerland early in the War. She went from there to Connecticut College, then to Yale, before coming to Washington University to seek a PhD in psychology. She was urged to spend her first summer studying for her language exam. She protested that she was fluent in German, French, and Spanish, to no avail. Thus my group acquired a remarkable clinician.

Our group settled on a semi-final form of the FPS containing 213 items. Various small studies led to testing a variety of women, including, for example, college sororities, mothers' groups of fraternities, church groups, nurses, and women marines. Using the test protocols for the 202 people who had answered every item on the test, we derived homogeneous keys, using the method worked out for the air force (Loevinger, Gleser, & DuBois, 1953). Then we tried to decipher what those results implied about fundamental attitudes. The results led to test revision, which was then used on the next studies. We repeated cycles of that sort until the process converged on a set of items.

Description of this work and elaboration of theoretical implications were the dissertation of Kitty LaPerriere. As I did not have a faculty position, she needed a professor as her advisor, so Professor Abel Ossorio worked well with us and shared our interests (Loevinger, Sweet, Ossorio, & LaPerriere, 1962).

After I had left Berkeley, Ossorio and some others had had a seminar studying the interpersonal psychiatry of Harry Stack Sullivan (1953a, 1953b).

Ossorio told us we were studying ego development. Kitty pointed out that psychoanalysts had appropriated that term, but we could not find a better one for the range of things that had appeared in our results. The Berkeley group had been studying the application of the ideas of Piaget and Sullivan to the problems of delinquency. They came up with a scale for the development of interpersonal relations (Sullivan, Grant, & Grant, 1957). At first I could not read Sullivan (1953a, 1953b), then it was as if I could hear him speak to me. That was less bizarre than it sounds. He did not write his books; they were transcriptions of his lectures, prepared by his students.

Another able clinician, Elizabeth Nettles, joined our group at Washington University, intending to study the relations of adolescent girls and young adult women to their own mothers, and relations to acceptance of their social and biological roles. At the same time, we were all uneasy about the use of the term ego development without some further backup. The usual way of validating such a term was to find another test of ego development and to correlate them. As there was no accepted test for that purpose, we had to create one. Nettles proposed using a sentence completion test, and put together a 36-item measure with stems that led into the topics she wanted to study. It happened to be the case that the Berkeley group studying the development of interpersonal integration had used a sentence completion test. By good fortune, another Berkeley clinician, Virginia Ives, came to St. Louis. She was an expert in judging level of interpersonal maturity from sentence completions. The method had been well worked out by the Berkeley group, but there were no adequate written methods for us to adopt. However, three members of the Berkeley group, Clyde Sullivan, Marguerite Grant, and Douglas Grant, had published an article on development of interpersonal maturity with applications to delinquency (Sullivan et al., 1957). That article became the starting point for constructing our own measure and its scoring manual. We proceeded again by microvalidation; that is, repeated small studies followed by small revisions of the scoring manual.

I had seen expert clinical raters previously whose expertise had vanished when they left. My contribution was a strict rule that everything had to be in writing. This rule went against the grain for clinicians, but it led to our permanent accomplishments.

Expanding the Project

Long before our method had reached its peak, our sentence completion test (SCT; Loevinger, 1993, 1998) began to attract users. Although originally meant for women, it was soon adapted for men and boys. Several men joined our group, some looking for work, some for thesis topics.

A fortunate accession to our group has been several clinicians and others who had the administrative and organizational skills that I lacked. Kitty LaPerriere and Claire Ernhart helped keep the FPS on track (Loevinger, LaPerriere, & Ernhart, 1998). Ruth Wessler and Carolyn Redmore were most important in transition to the SCT scoring manual project (Loevinger & Wessler, 1970).

I cannot in my dotage write a better summary of the process by which our SCT, its scoring manual, and its conception of ego development were shaped by our data than I wrote in "Measurement of Personality: True or False," which was published as a Target Article in *Psychological Inquiry* (Loevinger, 1993).

An Italian-born philosophical psychologist with a classical education might be the last person you would expect to make connections with inner city youths. However, Augusto Blasi (1976) did so. He sorted the boys into ego-level groups, and then gave them age-appropriate conflicts or dilemmas to act out, with observers recording and rating their behavior. This was the boldest and most interesting of several validation projects. Blasi (1998) is, in my opinion, the member of our group with the deepest understanding of ego development, and of its relation to Lawrence Kohlberg's work on moral development, and of its relation to psychoanalysis and the work of Piaget.

Lawrence Cohn (1998) studied age trends in ego development and other measures of personality development. He also helped with administration and keeping records of the project.

The last plane out of Saigon before it fell brought to the United States a remarkable young man, Le Xuan Hy. After a year in a rural day school, he went to St. Louis University for undergraduate training, and thence to Washington University for graduate work.

Heroically devoted secretaries had helped to preserve careful design, so raters were presented with only appropriate information; for example, each item on a person's protocol was rated independently. This process was helped by transforming our records to computers, which became the responsibility of Hy. He also was able to collate results of other users of the test in such a way that they contributed to revision of the scoring manual (Hy & Loevinger, 1996).

The last person to obtain a PhD during my tenure as professor at Washington University, Berkeley was Michiel Westenberg. He has been extending the scope of the work to younger ages, making a new SCT for children and youths, and proposing changes in the conceptions of some of the earliest stages (Westenberg, 1998; Westenberg, Jonckheer, Treffers, & Drewes, 1998).

Vicki Carlson came to the project with an interest in application of the study of ego development to other cultures and other languages. She also helped assemble practice exercises for the revised manual (Loevinger, Carlson, & Hy, 1998). The published practice exercises are a hallmark of our method so that the method is self-teaching in a way unusual for projective tests. Our work has been deeply collaborative (even this *apologia pro vita sua*) and has profited from the wide range of our colleagues.

Teaching

I am not a charismatic undergraduate teacher, but I used my teaching to explore topics that became books. The first and most important looked at ego development from many vantage points (Loevinger, 1976). My second book, not counting the scoring manuals, looked at the major theories of personality through the lens of Kuhn's concept of scientific paradigms (Loevinger, 1987). The surprising outcome is that psychoanalytic theory of personality fits Kuhn's model of a scientific paradigm better than any other theory of personality. It does begin with a major and revolutionary discovery, the dynamic unconscious.

AN AWARD FROM EDUCATIONAL TESTING SERVICE

Over the years I have been fortunate to receive recognition from my peers for my work in personality assessment. One citation that managed to sum things up particularly well came from the Educational Testing Service in 1994. It is printed here as a summary of my work in the area.

1993 ETS Award
for Distinguished Service to Measurement
Citation

Dr. Jane Loevinger

Throughout her long and illustrious career, Jane Loevinger has repeatedly challenged established psychometric practice on rational grounds, arguing that quantitative measures of psychological attributes should be based on sensible underlying assumptions and be consistent with the psychological theory of the attributes assessed.

As instances, she highlighted the paradoxical trade off that increases in reliability beyond a certain point lead to decreases in validity. She argued that test items, unlike persons, are not randomly sampled from populations but rather are constructed to represent domains, thereby questioning the statistical foundation of techniques based on the sampling of items, tests, or testing conditions. She championed the homogeneous keying of item clusters as opposed to the factor analysis of dichotomous items, which in her view is both poorly rationalized and empirically fragile. As a final example, Dr. Loevinger insisted that scoring models should be compatible with what is known about the nontest aspects of the trait being measured, which led her to eschew in her major work on ego development the ubiquitous cumulative linear scoring model in favor of a noncumulative approach that could cope with curvilinear relationships.

This last example brings together the two central lines of Professor Loevinger's life work. The point that scoring models should reflect the psychological theory of the trait being measured typifies the structural aspect of construct validity, which Dr. Loevinger delineated along with substantive and external aspects in an influential monograph that helped galvanize the measurement field to accept construct validity as the whole of test validity for scientific purposes. In addition to immediate implications for test construction practice, this seminal opus had profound theoretical impact. The formal basis of psychological measurement was viewed as part of a broader philosophy of science in which the nature of substantive constructs is taken into account in evaluating the adequacy of their measurement and, in turn, the properties and correlates of the measures help to determine the adequacy and generality of the constructs. Measurement theory thus becomes intertwined with substantive theory, and measurement methodology becomes an integral part and not just an adjunct of psychological science.

When this principle of structural fidelity was applied to the assessment of ego development by means of a sentence completion test, Dr. Loevinger rejected modes of polar dimensions in favor of scoring procedures amenable to milestones or a sequence of qualitatively distinct structures developing over time. In this work, faithful to her principles of construct validity, Dr. Loevinger employed repeated cycles of microvalidation so that the data could shape the theoretical interpretation of ego development and continually reshape the details of the conception as the scoring manual evolved.

For responsibly questioning traditional psychometric practice, for articulating basic principles of personality measurement, for conceptualizing and measuring ego development as a master organizing trait, and for constructing objective tests as instruments of psychological theory, Educational Testing Service is please to present its 1993 Award for Distinguished Service to Measurement to Dr. Jane Loevinger.

Signed, Nancy S. Cole
President, Educational Testing Service
January 19, 1994

NOW

I borrow words of Elinor Wylie (1934) to conclude:

Now let no charitable hope
Confuse my mind with images of eagle and of antelope;
I am in nature none of these.
I was, being human, born alone;
I am, being woman, hard beset;
I live by squeezing from a stone
The little nourishment I get. (p. 65)

REFERENCES

Adorno, T. W., Frenkel-Brunswik, E., Levinson, D.J., & Sanford, R.N. (1950). *The authoritarian personality*. New York: Harper.

Blasi, A. (1976). Personal responsibility and ego development. In R. deCharms (Ed.), *Enhancing motivation: Change in the classroom* (pp. 177–199). New York: Irvington.

Blasi, A. (1998). Loevinger's theory of ego development and its relationship to the cognitive-developmental approach. In P. M. Westenberg, A. Blasi, & L. D. Cohn (Eds.), *Personality development: Theoretical, empirical, and clinical investigations of Loevinger's conception of ego development* (pp. 13–25). Mahwah, NJ: Lawrence Erlbaum.

Cohn, L. D. (1998). Age trends in personality development: A quantitative review. In P. M. Westenberg, A. Blasi, & L. D. Cohn (Eds.), *Personality development: Theoretical, empirical, and clinical investigations of Loevinger's conception of ego development* (pp. 133–134). Mahwah, NJ: Lawrence Erlbaum.

Frenkel-Brunswik, E. (1949). Intolerance of ambiguity as an emotional and perceptual personality variable. *Journal of Personality, 18*, 108–143.

Friedan, B. (1984). *The feminine mystique*. New York: Dell. (Original work published 1963).

Hy, L. X., & Loevinger, J. (1996). *Measuring ego development* (2nd ed.). Mahwah, NJ: Lawrence Erlbaum.

Loevinger, J. (1957). Objective tests as instruments of psychological theory. *Psychological Reports, 3*, 635–694.

Loevinger, J. (1966). Three principles for a psychoanalytic psychology. *Journal of Abnormal Psychology, 71*, 432–443.

Loevinger, J. (1976). *Ego development: Conceptions and theories*. San Francisco: Jossey-Bass.

Loevinger, J. (1987). *Paradigms of personality*. New York: Freeman.

Loevinger, J. (1993). Measurement of personality: True or false. *Psychological Inquiry, 4*, 1–16.

Loevinger, J. (Ed.). (1998). *Technical foundations for measuring ego development: The Washington University Sentence Completion Test.* Mahwah, NJ: Lawrence Erlbaum.

Loevinger, J., Carlson, V., & Hy, L. X. (1998). Appendix B. Notes on WUSCT rating practice exercises. In J. Loevinger, J. (Ed.), *Technical foundations for measuring ego development: The Washington University Sentence Completion Test* (pp. 101–102). Mahwah, NJ: Lawrence Erlbaum.

Loevinger, J., Gleser, G. C., & DuBois, P. H. (1953). Maximizing the discriminating power of a multiple score test. *Psychometrika, 18,* 309–317.

Loevinger, J., LaPerriere, K, & Ernhart, C. (1998). Appendix A. The Family Problems Scale as a measure of authoritarian family ideology. In J. Loevinger, (Ed.), *Technical foundations for measuring ego development: The Washington University Sentence Completion Test* (pp. 95–100). Mahwah, NJ: Lawrence Erlbaum.

Loevinger, J., Sweet, B., Ossorio, A. G., & LaPerriere, K. (1962). Measuring personality patterns of women. *Genetic Psychology Monographs, 65,* 53–136.

Loevinger, J., & Wessler, R. (1970). *Measuring ego development I: Construction and use of a sentence completion test.* San Francisco: Jossey-Bass.

Sullivan, H.S. (1953a). *Conceptions of modern psychiatry.* New York: W. W. Norton.

Sullivan, H.S. (1953b). *The interpersonal theory of psychiatry.* New York: W. W. Norton.

Sullivan, C., Grant, M., & Grant, J. D. (1957). The development of interpersonal maturity: Applications to delinquency. *Psychiatry, 20,* 373–386.

Westenberg, P. M., Blasi, A., & Cohn, L. D. (Eds.). (1998). *Personality development: Theoretical, empirical, and clinical investigations of Loevinger's conception of ego development.* Mahwah, NJ: Lawrence Erlbaum.

Westenberg, P. M., Jonckheer, J., Treffers, P. D., & Drewes, M. J. (1998). Ego development in children and adolescents: Another side of the impulsive, self-protective, and conformist ego levels. In P. M. Westenberg, A. Blasi, & L. D. Cohn (Eds.), *Personality development: Theoretical, empirical, and clinical investigations of Loevinger's conception of ego development* (pp. 89–111). Mahwah, NJ: Lawrence Erlbaum.

Wylie, E. (1934). *Collected poems of Elinor Wylie.* New York: A. A. Knopf.

SELECTED BIBLIOGRAPHY

Hy, L. X., & Loevinger, J. (1996). *Measuring ego development* (2nd ed.). Mahwah, NJ: Lawrence Erlbaum.

Loevinger, J. (1957). Objective tests as instruments of psychological theory. *Psychological Reports, 3,* 635–694.

Loevinger, J. (1966). Three principles for a psychoanalytic psychology. *Journal of Abnormal Psychology, 71,* 432–443.

Loevinger, J. (1976). *Ego development: Conceptions and theories*. San Francisco: Jossey-Bass.

Loevinger, J. (1987). *Paradigms of personality*. New York: Freeman.

Loevinger, J. (1993). Measurement of personality: True or false. *Psychological Inquiry, 4*, 1–16.

Loevinger, J. (Ed.). (1998). *Technical foundations for measuring ego development: The Washington University Sentence Completion Test*. Mahwah, NJ: Lawrence Erlbaum.

Loevinger, J., Gleser, G. C., & DuBois, P. H. (1953). Maximizing the discriminating power of a multiple score test. *Psychometrika, 18*, 309–317.

Loevinger, J., Sweet, B., Ossorio, A. G., & LaPerriere, K. (1962). Measuring personality patterns of women. *Genetic Psychology Monographs, 65*, 53–136.

Loevinger, J., & Wessler, R. (1970). *Measuring ego development I: Construction and use of a sentence completion test*. San Francisco: Jossey-Bass.

Jane Loevinger (second from right behind the man) at a campaign rally for Eugene McCarthy, Washington University, St. Louis, Missouri, circa 1968

Jane Loevinger as Stuckenberg Professor of Human Values in Psychology, Washington University, circa 1985

CHAPTER 11

Speak, Memory,
or Goodbye, Columbus

Joseph Masling
State University of New York at Buffalo

The best opening line I know in all of literature—even better than Melville's "Call me Ishmael," or Kafka's "As Gregor Samsa awoke one morning from uneasy dreams he found himself transformed in his bed into a gigantic insect"—is from James Agee's autobiographical *A Death in the Family* (1957): "We are talking now of summer evenings in Knoxville, Tennessee in the time that I lived there so successfully disguised to myself as a child" (p. 3). Agee's opening sets the stage perfectly for what follows: an attempt to describe and recreate a self-disguising human being many years after the crucial events. Agee suggests that self-disguise is a continuing process and has not yet given it up. It implies what we now commonly accept—that history, particularly personal history, is a construction, a present-day point of view imposed on early events by someone living at some historical distance from those events. Further, the early incidents recalled may not have happened and surely have been altered by self-serving memory. Others in the writer's life would have recalled different events and would have different versions of the same event. The Japanese film *Rashomon* describes the same story four times, each as recalled by one of its key participants; at the end of the film what is described is not a single incident but four incidents with some overlapping details. Spence (1982) stated this recounting of history well: "We have come a long way from the naïve illusion that recalling the past is a simple act of going back to an earlier time and distance and reading off the contents of the scene that emerges. . . . The past, always in flux, is always being created anew" (p. 93).

Modern ideas of psychotherapy agree that when patients and therapists talk they construct narratives, building a set of statements that help explain and free one from the past and that allow greater alternatives for leading better lives than had existed under the narrative that patients had built alone. Presumably a good narrative has some strong relationship to the truth, but a short story can evoke different meanings from different readers (Holland, 1975) and even the same photograph draws different interpretations. To paraphrase Oscar Wilde, the historical truth is rarely pure and never simple. The best we can hope for either in our own lives or in our therapeutic efforts is to create a narrative that allows us to live comfortably and to work and love successfully.

My attempt to fulfill the request of the editors of this series to provide autobiographical data that "focus primarily on events that relate to the individual's most important contribution to personality psychology" runs afoul of the need for the self-disguise Agee wrote about. What I can bring to this process obviously and necessarily is subject to the vicissitudes of selective memory in the clutch of defenses. My mirror provides no more accurate a reflection than does a teenager's. Providing these autobiographical notes is an imprecise process, but when I recalled (and revised) an Oscar Wilde observation that every teacher "nowadays has his disciples and it is always Judas who writes the biography," I decided it would be prudent to present my flawed version rather than some one else's.

It is, of course, no accident that I began this piece by quoting from James Agee, with his observation that self-perception may be distorted. What an appropriate way to describe the two fields in which I have worked, projective assessment methods and psychoanalytic theories, both of which declare that what you see is not always there, that there may be things there you do not see, and that these unseen things influence behavior. Freud, after all, believed that practicing psychoanalysis was similar to uncovering ruins.

When I was a young man, madly running about teaching, collecting data, writing, doing clinical work, engaged in the crucial tasks of earning tenure and gaining academic promotions, I had no grand scheme in my head of what guided my research interests or selected my psychotherapeutic methods. My choices were sufficiently interesting and the reinforcements sufficiently frequent to ward off the necessity of dealing with such a vexing question. It was only much later, when I had time to sit back, breathe easily, and enjoy the luxury that comes from being a tenured professor whose children's education has been paid for that I could think back to the motives that led me to the choices I made. Like behavior at all major choice points, my decisions were over-determined, influenced partly by innate talents and deficiencies, partly by the chance of being in a particular place at a particular time, partly by the infantile past reaching into the present to push and shove me here and there, and of course, partly by the ability of my ego functions to assess and determine appropriate behavior.

HELLO, COLUMBUS

To begin, the place where I landed more or less by chance was Ohio State University in Columbus, where in 1947 I began my training in clinical psychology, opting for Ohio State for no better reason than that my brother had graduated from there and that I had once visited the campus. Thus it was that I was exposed to the ideas and personalities of Victor Raimy, Boyd Mc-Candless, Julian Rotter, and George Kelly. My arrival at Ohio State, because of some administrative error, was unanticipated and not at all welcomed. Already enrolled was an extremely large class of first-year graduate students, probably 25 to 30, and now another body had shown up. (As best as I can recall, fewer than 10 of us achieved the PhD.) On my first day, I was taken to a faculty office and interviewed (grilled would be a more accurate description of that interaction) by a rather large man who did not try to hide his irritation at having yet another student in the program. I had never heard of George Kelly, I was not particularly interested in knowing George Kelly, and I did not know why he was giving me such a hard time.

One exchange in that interview remains with me. When he asked about my military service during World War II and how long I had been in the armed forces, I answered with the exact number of years, months, and days, prompting him to inquire why I knew this figure so precisely. After a long, difficult silence, I told him that if he had to ask, there was no way he could understand my answer. I did not know it at the time, but that was the best way of dealing with Kelly: If he sensed weakness, he attacked. My response to him was instinctive, not calculated.

Because my postwar academic record and test scores were superior to some of the students officially on the list, Kelly had no alternative but to accept me. Fortunately, the only academic record Ohio State evaluated was from the four semesters I spent at Syracuse University following my discharge from the service. The one and a half years I spent prewar at the State University of Iowa were ignored, including the two Ds I earned in ROTC and the D I got in Psychology 101, where I was much more taken by the pretty woman sitting next to me than by the lecture.

The atmosphere at Ohio State in that period was fiercely competitive among both faculty members and students. It included a rivalry between two students for the number of reprints they could collect, and competition between faculty members for the quality of students they could attract. We were given broad training in psychology at Ohio State in those days, with only an occasional course in clinical psychology. Our preliminary exams, extending over a period of five or six days, tested our knowledge of the entire subject matter of psychology. Following the written preliminaries, we were subjected to an oral examination based on our answers to the written questions.

This broad training served me well. I recall two classes in particular—Arthur Melton's course in learning and Julian Rotter's in projective assessment, where I was taught the Beck system of scoring the Rorschach. By the time I left graduate school, I could read and understand at some level every major journal in psychology except *Psychometrika*. When I became a faculty member I was able to teach Psychology 101 with little difficulty and some pleasure. Today I can't even keep up with all the major psychoanalytic journals.

One aspect of that training program was not particularly useful. The pejorative of the day was the word naïve and being accused of naiveté in choice of theory or research interest caused immediate drop in status. In those days, Ohio State was one of the exemplars of dust bowl empiricism, and any one who preferred ideas for which there were no extant confirming data was seriously out of step with the local zeitgeist. Psychoanalytic concepts obviously fell into that forbidden category. Carl Rogers' concepts were marginal, but clearly not the first choice of the deep thinkers among faculty or students. I drank from the same waters as the others, though I was unaware for many years of the extent to which that notion permeated my thinking.

One observation of Kelly's impressed me strongly, and I have taken great care to pass it on to my own students: When American psychologists have data that conflict with their theories, they retain the theories and discard the data. Clearly, no sensible person should do that. It was a "tough guy" approach to psychology, in a way not a bad thing, because it emphasizes the legitimacy and primacy of data. Not immediately apparent is the potential cost of such an attitude—it can discourage flights of imagination and creativity. Tough minds can create foolproof research designs, but the quest for a pure design may hamper risk-taking and daring. "Safe" dissertation topics can get by a doctoral committee but may not investigate an interesting, vital problem. I am reminded of an aphorism by an unknown wit: Researchers can be placed on one dimension, with the simpleminded at one end and the muddleheaded at the other.

Two extremely important theories of personality were being written when I was a graduate student—Rotter's Social Learning Theory and Kelly's Personal Construct Theory. Each theory influenced clinical psychology for a number of years; Kelly's theory in fact earned him a considerable international reputation. Although most students gravitated toward one or the other of these men, I stayed away from both because I wanted to work with material that was more immediately clinically relevant than either seemed to offer, so I went first to Raimy for research tutelage and then to McCandless when Raimy moved to Colorado. Both Kelly and Rotter built grand, formal theories, complete with corollaries and subcorollaries. Each theory was scientific to a fault, Rotter in fact even including mathematical formulae with his, and each was built on the laudable notion that their ideas could be subject to empirical test. For me, these theories were so highly intellectualized, so determined to be "scientific" that anything remotely human had been relentlessly squeezed from them. I could find no description in them of what Farber (1976) referred to as lying, despair, jealousy, envy, sex, suicide, drugs, and the good life."

To illustrate the highly abstract way both Kelly and Rotter described behavior, I provide (highly selected) examples of their descriptions of behavior:

> The occurrence of a behavior of a person is determined not only by the nature and importance of goals or reinforcements but also by the person's anticipation or expectancy that these goals will occur. Such expectancies are determined by previous experience and can be quantified (pp. 102–103). . . . The potential for behavior x to occur in situation 1 in relation to reinforcement a is a function of the expectancy of the occurrence of reinforcement a following behavior x in situation 1 and the value of reinforcement a. (Rotter, 1954, p. 108)

> The variations in a person's construction system is limited by the permeability of the constructs within whose range of convenience the variants lie. (Kelly, 1955, p. 77)

ENCOUNTERING CARL ROGERS
AND BRUNO BETTLEHEIM

These ideas seemed sterile and unrelated to any interesting clinical problem, and because there was no reason for me to anticipate that therapy supervision would be appreciably better, I began to look for alternative clinical training. The Public Health Fellowship I had been awarded gave me the freedom to travel to other programs for further training if the opportunity arose. When

Carl Rogers came to Columbus to give a professional address, I told him I was interested in being supervised in client-centered psychotherapy and asked if I could go to the University of Chicago as a one-semester special student and see clients in the Counseling Center there. He immediately agreed. After I arrived in Chicago, I went to the Counseling Center, introduced myself to the director, and asked about taking on cases. He was stunned at my request. Rogers had not informed him that a vagabond from Ohio State would be left on his doorstep, and the director looked extremely unhappy at the prospect. He asked if I could return to Ohio State and at some future date arrange to work at the Counseling Center, a strange request to be made by an advocate of client-centered therapy whose goal is to understand the needs of the other. I told him I had undergone considerable trouble to move to Chicago and that I expected him to honor Rogers' verbal promise to me.

We finally reached an impasse. I inferred it was my duty to understand his discomfort and to spare him the difficult decision to turn me away, but I had no intention of doing this. Finally, I told him that it was his responsibility to accept or reject my application and that I was not going to make the decision for him. He finally took a deep breath and told me I could not work at his Counseling Center that semester. I was to learn later that rigid embrace of ideology characterizes other psychologists as well, including behaviorists and psychoanalysts.

As a consolation prize, I was allowed to audit a graduate seminar led by Rogers, also attended by several faculty members. I was the outsider, watching as students and faculty members, all bright, all highly verbal, alternated between trying to attract Rogers' attention and attack his position. Rogers was unrattled by all this and handled the seminar with facility and tact. He seemed the least rigid, the least dogmatic, the most willing to see another point of view in the entire group. My attempt to become a believer failed when I sensed the quasi-religious undertones of some parts of Rogers' theory and saw that it could not account for either impulse or evil.

With time on my hands, I decided, more or less on whim, to attend Bruno Bettleheim's graduate course in psychoanalytic theory. Up to that point all I knew about psychoanalysis was what any curious undergraduate could easily pick up from unguided reading. Bettleheim introduced me to Fenichel and to classical psychoanalytic texts. As great teachers can, he illuminated difficult material and gave life to abstract ideas. But the cost was considerable because he was a cold, authoritarian instructor whose method of teaching was to induce fear in his students. He began his class by asking for questions. At first there were many, but Bettleheim's general method of dealing with questions was to demand of the questioners why they expected him to do their reading for them. Predictably, after the first few sessions no one asked a question. Then Bettleheim would declare that in the absence of questions he would question us. Taking out his grade book and calling on students at random, he would ask what Fenichel meant by this or that, appearing to write some evaluation of the student's response, though this may have been a sham. Woe to the hapless student who did not know the answer exactly, because Bettleheim would become visibly angry, declaring that if he could not be fooled by schizophrenics he could not be fooled by someone who only guessed at the answer and did not know the material fully.

In all my years of schooling, that class with Bettleheim was the most stressful I had encountered. Although he did not provide a comfortable environment for learning, he surely provided ample incentive to learn and master the assigned material. When he did lecture, he was superb in clarifying and extending the material, illustrating it nicely from his own experiences; his reading list served me well for years. When after his death he was accused of sometimes acting brutally against his staff members and patients at the Orthogenic School, I was not surprised.

FRITZ REDL AND AN "INTERNSHIP"

I returned to Ohio State to complete my course work and take preliminary exams. At some point the American Psychological Association (APA) decreed that all clinical students should complete an internship year, but the definitions of an acceptable internship had not yet been promulgated. I knew almost from the start that I did not have the talent, patience, or interest to work with institutionalized patients, so I suggested that I be allowed to find an internship that emphasized research. Now that the rules of internships have been codified, 50 years after the fact, it seems incomprehensible that the clinical program at Ohio State gave me permission to seek such an "internship." The year was 1949 and I found two possible placements: one working with Bettleheim at the Chicago Orthogenic School and one working with Fritz Redl and Ronald Lippitt on a research project studying behavioral contagion in children's groups. Redl's name is not often mentioned nowadays, but at one point he was a central figure in psychoanalysis with children, and his two books with Wineman (Redl & Wineman, 1951, 1952) describing theory and practice in work with delinquent children were often cited.

When Bettleheim interviewed me, he asked if I had other offers and I told him about the possibility of working with Redl. He told me that Redl was a nice man but that he knew little about children and their pathology. When I was interviewed by Redl, he pressed a cigar on me, although I was reluctant to accept it because I knew all about the symbolism of a cigar and was uncomfortable with having to snip off its end while being observed by the famous psychoanalyst. Redl, too, asked about my other offers, and when I told him about Bettleheim, he immediately described Bettleheim's excellent work and said I could learn much from him. It did not take great clinical acumen to know which offer to accept.

Working with Redl, Lippitt, and the project director, Norman Polansky, was the mirror opposite of my experience as a graduate student. I learned to be careful as a graduate student but to be adventurous with ideas on my internship. Kelly and Redl could not have been more different. Kelly was austere, formal, and the very correct son of a Presbyterian minister; one sensed he cared, but the evidence for this was indirect and had to be assumed. Only years later did it occur to me that all those barriers might have served to hide shyness. Several years after I received my PhD, Kelly presented a paper at Syracuse University when I was on the faculty. He stayed with my wife Annette and me in our small apartment, and after he went to bed that first night, my wife, whom I had met after I left graduate school said, "It is a little like having God in the apartment." In contrast, Redl was open, effusive, and a talented raconteur, whose caring was undisguised. His ability to free associate about clinical issues was stimulating, and I regret now that I was not wise enough then to have recorded his ideas after our sessions. Both Kelly and Redl had considerable clinical skills, though it took me some time to realize this about Kelly; each took clinical responsibilities very seriously, and each communicated deep commitment to the welfare of their clients.

Halfway through that year, Kelly called me somewhat apologetically to say that the clinical faculty members thought it might be useful for me to get some clinical experience and supervision during my internship. That phone call was the first time Kelly slipped from his usual manner of addressing each graduate student as Mister or Miss by inadvertently calling me Joe, though by the end of the call I was again Mr. (Only after the completion of the dissertation oral examination did he call students by their first name; one assumes he was prepared for us to call him George then, but that intimacy was feigned, not genuine, for most of us.) Acquiring supervision for clinical work was not an unreasonable request to make of a future clinical psychologist, and so I began to do group therapy with delinquent boys, supervised by Redl and members of his staff.

These were tough kids to work with, street wise, and hardened by a series of broken promises, disappointments, poverty, and neglect. I did the best I could, but the results were negligible and surely less than I had hoped for. During one supervisory session with Redl, I began by discussing the children one by one. Finally, I said, "And then there is Ronny." "What about Ronny?," asked Redl. "Well," I said, "he is a challenge." Redl smiled and said, "It's OK. You don't have to like him if you don't want to." He was, of course, absolutely correct—one does not refer to favored people as challenges—but I did not know then that for defensive reasons some clients go to considerable trouble not to be liked (Ronny successfully rebuffed my efforts to be therapeutic with him). and that such a dislike was occasionally professionally acceptable.

Sometime during the year, Redl took my group of children for an outing. Afterward, all these boys could talk about was "Uncle Fritz." They had bonded with him as they never had with me, despite all my earnest therapeutic efforts. Envious, I asked him how he managed to get these wary, tough kids to develop such affection for him after only a few hours. He laughed and told me that when I had his income I could do the same: He had taken them to an ice cream shop and told them they could have anything they wished and as much of it as they could eat. I don't think Fenichel (1945) mentions ice cream therapy in his book. One of Redl's insights makes so much sense that I have repeated it to all my classes and to a fair number of my clients: "It ain't your pathology, it's the way you use it." He meant there was no point in claiming neurosis as an excuse for inappropriate behavior because neurosis of one sort or another is universal; the difference between people is the extent to which they use their neurosis to get on with their lives. Only when I began to write this article did I realize that through Redl and his mentor, August Aichhorn (1925), I am separated from Freud by only two teachers.

The research project during my internship studied the way behavior spread from child to child. The idea had its origins in Lewinian field theory and was concerned with both the circumstances of the behavioral contagion and the personalities of the children who initiated the behavior the others imitated. For two summers I worked at the University of Michigan's Fresh Air Camp, clipboard in hand, following children in their activities, checking off appropriate behavioral categories. I used this opportunity to develop and complete my dissertation research. I noted that some boys (all the campers were boys) showed more flexibility and variability in their behavior than others. I tried to predict behavioral rigidity by using a variation of the Einstellung effect. Alas, I did not have the foresight to conduct a pilot study of that test. Much too late for it to matter, I learned that most of the boys scored at one end of the distribution. With little scatter in my main variable, I found few significant results. Kelly generously agreed to be my dissertation supervisor, though the topic was not central to his interests. The dissertation was neither a happy nor successful experience but it taught me a valuable lesson: Pilot testing the independent variables and the hypotheses saves both time and ego.

FIXED ROLE THERAPY

I returned to Columbus to analyze my data and to write the dissertation and was given the most senior assistantship in the clinic run by the psychology department. For the first time I was immersed in doing psychotherapy, though I scarcely knew what I was doing. Kelly supervised one of my cases and had me doing fixed role therapy, much to my discomfort. The general goal in this treatment is to break the logjam of neurosis by inducing the client to try new behavior. Kelly did not believe that insight alone is sufficient to get people to experiment with new methods of dealing with the world and that some nonthreatening device might make behavioral change more likely. He devised the idea of having clients play roles, much as actors do. Although giving advice did not work, role playing might illustrate different ways of interacting with the world.

Based on the information we had about a client, whom Kelly (1955) called Ronald Barrett, he and I wrote a new role for Barrett, one which bypassed his crippling social anxiety by having him act as someone who was skilled in getting others to talk about themselves. We hoped that as he gained some reinforcement for being a good listener, his feelings about being socially inept and his anticipation of being rejected would be reduced. I had considerable misgivings about interfering so directly in a client's life and Kelly knew it. He described this case at length in his book (Kelly, 1955, pp. 392–397) and said about me, "The therapist had never attempted this type of therapy before and was somewhat skeptical of its appropriateness to the case and its professional respectability in general" (p. 392).

In rereading the case notes that Kelly (1955) had reproduced, I note with considerable embarrassment that fixed role therapy led us to decide which topics were relevant for therapeutic discussion and which were irrelevant, and so I steered the conversation toward goals Kelly and I had preselected, even though Barrett occasionally wanted to talk about other issues. For a variety of reasons I would not do that today. Despite my misgivings and lack of experience in this kind of therapy, Barrett showed considerable progress and movement. He was making new friends, sabotaging his own efforts less frequently, and was more able to experiment with new behaviors—and all without what would usually be called insight. It is yet another example of the wisdom of the old, cynical observation about psychotherapy: No matter what you do in therapy, some people will get better; no matter what you do, some people won't.

Several of Kelly's clinical observations remain with me still. He often described what he called "threshhold therapy." For example, at the end of a session the client, with one foot out the door, turns to the therapist and says,

"Oh, I almost forgot to tell you—I tried to kill myself last week." I have heard statements like this several times. He also had a useful analogy for change when he sensed that clients believed that Kelly wanted them to alter their behavior in an unacceptable direction. "Imagine you are an onion of infinite size," he would say, "and therapy begins to peel away some of the layers. But no matter how many layers are removed, what is left is still you, not someone else. It will just be another aspect of you, a part now hidden." Finally, Kelly thought therapy was a matter of alternating between tightening and loosening the client's constructs. Constructs are loosened when the therapist is neutral, silent, and asks open-ended questions. Constructs are tightened when there is danger of decompensation and they are accomplished by lack of therapeutic ambiguity and by frequent, direct interventions.

Sometime during this period, (e.g., early 1951) Kelly began an obvious campaign to alter his own behavior. He felt sufficiently comfortable with me to have invited me to his office one day to ask my opinions about the clinical program. I was astonished at the request because it was such a radical change in his behavior, but I was even more surprised when he insisted that I take his chair behind the desk rather than the visitor's chair. Evidently he believed that one determiner of role was the furniture one used. And so I sat in Kelly's chair and he sat in the other and I told him something about the clinical program. It was during this same period when he confessed to me some personal failings and his efforts to correct them. In his honesty about himself and his insistence on maintaining the highest personal and professional standards for himself and his students, he was an admirable model. He was a good, loyal friend. All his students knew Kelly carried a small notebook with him at professional meetings in which he had listed both job openings and the names of his students who might be job hunting. In those simpler days, he worked as a one-man job placement agency. As could be expected, he arranged for my first professional position, pairing me with one of his former students.

Years after I left Ohio State, I bundled up a series of my reprints and sent them to Kelly, though I was unsure what he would make of my turn toward psychodynamic thinking. By return mail I received a two-sentence reply. The first thanked me for the reprints. Then he added this laconic statement: "Every student has the obligation to make his teacher a wise man." I was so impressed and pleased with this comment that I have laid the same responsibility on all of my own students, most of whom have complied enthusiastically to that request with ease and uncanny speed. And as my own path differed from Kelly's, at least three of my students, Robert Deluty, Sandra Harris, and Lillie Weiss found behavioral psychology congenial and have made substantial contributions to that field.

THE RELATIONSHIP BETWEEN PSYCHOTHERAPY
AND THE TESTING SITUATION

The position Kelly made possible for me was at the short-lived Institute for Research in Human Relations, a research group established to investigate important social problems. When it became obvious that the only funding sources interested in sponsoring research on psychological issues were the armed forces, I joined the faculty at Syracuse University as assistant professor, understanding full well that I was expected to do research and publish but with no commitment to any particular topic. I also did a good deal of clinical work and clinical supervision. My work with children convinced me that the key to successful treatment was in the therapeutic relationship. Rotter had introduced me to the ideas of Frederick Allen, a student of the social worker Jessie Taft, who in turn had been trained by Otto Rank. Allen emphasized the importance of the need for separation and independence and the frequent conflicts that occur around this dimension. My concern with the subtleties in the therapeutic relationship raised my interest in the nuances of the relationship in the psychodiagnostic examination. At about this time I read Roy Schafer's *Psychoanalytic Interpretation of Rorschach Testing* (1954), in which he described psychological testing as a two-person relationship, listing the various roles and needs enacted when a psychologist and test subject interact.

I combined these interests to document the examiner's contribution to the end product of a psychological test. I employed two attractive undergraduate women as experimental accomplices, trained them to act either warmly or coldly to a test administrator, and had them memorize prepared responses. As I hypothesized, when these women acted in a warm manner their responses to a sentence completion test were interpreted more favorably than when they gave the same responses but acted coldly (Masling, 1957), and their responses to an IQ test were given more credit when they were warm to the examiner than when they were cold (Masling, 1959). I produced a number of studies, all demonstrating the unique contribution of the examiner to the final test protocol, and a *Psychological Bulletin* article (1960) which reviewed the considerable literature showing interpersonal and situational influences in projective assessment.

In the *Bulletin* article and in a subsequent review paper (Masling, 1966), I attacked the naïve belief, then rather widely held, that a projective instrument worked as a psychological X-ray, revealing the innards of a subject without being influenced by external elements. In doing so I was proving how thoroughly indoctrinated I was in the ethos at Ohio State. Not only was I not naïve, I declared that the emperor wore no clothes, no matter what the believers said. In a sense I was correct: Test protocols invariably reflect the circumstances in which the test is administered, including the room, examiner gender, and examiner characteristics. At that time discussion of projective testing, aside from Schafer's book (1954), rarely raised this possibility. As I wrote at the time, we were witnessing "a proliferation of projective methods, most of which are greeted with enthusiasm and validated by endorsement" (Masling, 1960, p. 65). What I did not emphasize then was that these situational and interpersonal influences, while ubiquitous, were rarely substantial. Statistically significant effects were there and were easily demonstrated but had little impact on final results.

I might have gone on with this work forever, demonstrating that projective assessments were oversold and were not as pure as proponents promised, but for two events. The first was a comment by a colleague, Paul Diesing, a philosopher of science, who said about my research that any discipline that devotes all that energy to self-examination was in trouble. I recognized the truth in that statement at once and realized that there would be more satisfaction in exploring new areas than continuing to find flaws in the research of others.

STUDIES OF ORALITY

The second event was a Fulbright award in 1964–65 to the Hebrew University in Jerusalem where I was asked to help construct the first PhD program in clinical psychology in Israel. Israel is a complex, intriguing society, but one of its aspects is rarely discussed—its emphasis on food and dependence. My first effort to investigate a psychoanalytic proposition, born from my experiences in Israel, was designed to test the relationship of orality to obesity. Again borrowing from Schafer (1954), I lifted nearly intact his listing of oral and dependent signs in Rorschach responses. I also devised a list of oral and dependent content in TAT stories. My Israeli research assistant, Lillie Rabie, later Lillie Rabie Weiss, tested 34 patients at an outpatient metabolic clinic at the Hadassah Hospital, 18 of them obese and 16 non-obese controls. I scored both Rorschach and TAT protocols for oral dependent responses, blind to patient diagnosis. Orality scores on the two tests correlated .58, a highly significant figure but one accounting for only about 1/3 of the variance. We found that the obese patients reported more oral dependent responses on both the Rorschach (p = .01) and the TAT (p = .05) than the controls. In a further analysis, we examined the records of those subjects who were consistently high or low in oral responses on both tests, discarding those who were high on one test and low on the other. This left us with a "pure" sample of 21 subjects. In this group, there were 9 consistently high oral responders and they were all obese, while 10 of the 12 low oral responders were control subjects (e.g., the combined use of both tests allowed us to predict correctly the diagnosis of 19 of the 21 subjects; Masling, Rabie, & Blondheim, 1967).

I was unprepared for those results because I had expected to find that the psychoanalytic notion underlying the hypothesis had no merit. My motive for the experiment was political: I wished to demonstrate what I had learned in graduate school, that psychoanalytic thinking was without a scientific basis. In a sense I was disappointed with my positive findings. I was fond of repeating one of Kelly's maxims: "When the history of psychology in the United States is written, there will be a debate whether it was a greater aid in the 19th century than a hindrance in the 20th." My simple, off-the-cuff study made me reconsider the wisdom of Kelly's observation.

On my return to America I moved to the State University of New York at Buffalo where Sharon Bertrand, a graduate student, hypothesized that alcoholics might show the same oral dependent needs as the obese. She examined the files of VA inpatients for whom there were Rorschach records and located 20 with a primary diagnosis of alcoholism, which she then matched with 20 control patients. Again, the results were significant, p = .01 (Bertrand & Masling, 1969). At the same time, Lillie Weiss, now a graduate student at Buffalo, searched the files of a local Catholic outpatient mental hygiene clinic to identify patients who had been administered the Rorschach Test. Our analysis of these records (Weiss & Masling, 1970) replicated the positive findings obtained with the Israeli obese and Buffalo VA alcoholic groups, as well as showed that ulcer patients and those who stuttered reported (at the .05 and .01 significance levels, respectively) more oral responses than the controls. In addition, following up a suggestion of Fromm (1947) that for oral people, the source of all good is external, two of my students and I (Masling, Weiss, & Rothschild, 1968) showed that subjects who yielded to the majority in an Asch conformity experiment reported more Rorschach oral imagery than nonyielding subjects. This study may have been the first investigation of the personalities of yielders, previous explorations having examined the conditions under which yielding occurs but not the kind of person who yields.

Thus, the first four studies I conducted all produced statistically significant results, despite my expectations to the contrary. I began this work with the avowed purpose of burying psychoanalysis, but my data succeeded in honoring it. My Ohio State training to respect data before conjecture refused to allow me to disallow what I had found. Now I was hooked. Psychoanalytic conceptions evidently had more merit than I had been taught or had allowed myself to realize. I knew that if I wished to follow the lead of these studies I had to learn more about psychoanalysis, but it was not a labor of love. With my training and empirical orientation, it was difficult to embrace psychoanalytic theory with its ornate, reifying, imprecise, parsimony-violating language. Psychoanalysts, so often sophisticated and witty in person, frequently write as though their first language is German and their translator is unfriendly. See for example what Leites (1971) says about psychoanalytic writing. My personal analysis in the early 1960s in Syracuse showed me the wisdom and clinical competence of a well trained analyst, but it did not occur to me then that psychoanalytic construct ideas could be put to empirical test.

THE GROUP RORSCHACH

These four studies relied on data gathered by individual administration of the Rorschach. To extend my research into other areas I had to find a quicker, more efficient way of collecting data because I had neither the manpower nor, more importantly, the temperament, to rely exclusively on such a time-consuming method. Instead, I used a technique first brought to my attention by Seymour Fisher (Fisher & Cleveland, 1968)—the group administered Rorschach. Fisher had used this method in a variety of studies and assured me that neither reliability nor validity suffered. Slides of the inkblots are shown on a screen and subjects are asked to describe in some detail 25 percepts, 3 each on cards 1, 2, 3, 8, and 10, and 2 responses each to the other 5 cards. I compiled a one-page scoring manual, deviating only slightly from the Schafer (1954) discussion. It is essentially a lexical system, giving credit for key words from these 16 categories of oral and dependent responses: foods and drinks; food sources; food objects; food providers; passive food receivers; beggars and those asking for help; food organs; oral instruments; nurturers; gift and gift givers; good luck symbols; oral activity; passivity and helplessness; pregnancy and reproductive organs; baby talk in the subject's speech; negations of oral percepts. Any explicit reference to these categories is scored once, with a total possible score of 25. This system, described in Masling (1986), explicitly rules out clinical hunches and subjective judgment. Acceptable interscorer reliability is easily reached and usually ranges from 89% to 95% agreement.

By using explicit rules for scoring, examiner experience and intuition are rendered irrelevant. A lengthy, detailed rich response is given the same credit as an afterthought. This feature is bothersome to many clinicians who believe they are more sensitive to clinical nuances than a rigid formula. This is undoubtedly true, but what is lost in intensive analysis of a single protocol is more than gained from the ability to collect data easily. I was not interested in phenomena so subtle they could only be found with intensive examination of a protocol. I was also aware that clinical intuition, so often wise, can also be incorrect. I sensed early on what Garb (1998) has recently demonstrated—that sometimes clinical inferences have little merit. He states:

> Psychologists who were thought to be experts did not make more valid judgments than other psychologists . . . Judgments made by psychologists were generally not more valid than those made by graduate students. . . . Confidence was not positively related to validity when clinicians made ratings using projective test results. . . . Research on illusory correlations indicates that clinicians may believe that they are basing their judgments on their clinical experiences, but instead they may be responding to the verbal associations of test indicators. This has been demonstrated for clinicians using the Rorschach and the Draw-A-Person test. (Garb, pp. 36–37)

Neither the Rorschach test nor psychoanalysis had good standing in American academia. At about the time I was beginning this work, Jensen (1965) wrote this about the Rorschach: "The rate of scientific progress in clinical psychology might well be measured by the speed and thoroughness with which it gets over the Rorschach" (p. 509). Psychoanalysis had even a worse reputation. Fortunately, I was sufficiently practical not to have discovered these interests until I had become a tenured full professor. Protected by tenure and without the need for external funds, I was free to study what I wanted and to teach what I wanted. Although the chairman of my department was unhappy with my proposal to offer an undergraduate course in psychoanalytic theories, because he thought undergraduates were "too young for that sort of thing," I taught the course anyway, as well as a graduate seminar in psychoanalytic theories.

The disrepute of psychoanalysis had one important paradoxical effect: The brightest and most imaginative of the graduate students were drawn to it. I learned that a number of our graduate students had a secret interest in psychoanalysis but had been savvy enough not to mention this when they were applying to graduate schools. But my leaving the psychoanalytic closet enabled them to leave theirs. Thus I had the good fortune of being able to work with a group of creative, intellectually gifted students. The research studies we created were almost always jointly conceived, though the fun of corralling subjects and collecting data was left to them. Over a period of years we demonstrated empirically that those who report many oral dependent images on the Rorschach test, in contrast to those who report fewer such images, are more sensitive to interpersonal cues; show more physiological arousal when placed alone in a sound-proof chamber; show more physiological arousal when placed in a sound-proof chamber with an unfriendly experimental confederate; are more willing to touch an experimental confederate on the arm or hand; are more dependent in a difficult puzzle situation; are more apt to be child abusers; are more likely to try to confirm the experimental hypothesis; give a group leader better evaluations; volunteer to participate in required experiments in Psychology 101 earlier in the semester; and after four therapy sessions can describe their therapists more accurately.

Robert Bornstein (1996) estimated that over 50 studies using the Rorschach oral dependence (ROD) scale were published between 1967 and 1995. He has demonstrated the ROD's construct validity (Bornstein, 1996) and extended knowledge of the dependent personality considerably (Bornstein, 1993). With his colleagues (Bornstein, Hilsenroth, Padawer, & Fowler 2000), he recently reported that personality disorder (PD) inpatients had higher ROD scores than PD outpatients, antisocial PD outpatients, and college students; and with O'Neill he found that various samples of depressed patients had higher ROD scores than matched controls (O'Neill & Bornstein, 1990, 1991).

Concurrent with this research activity, I began to read Freud and other analysts seriously, always trying to translate their statements into operational terms. A surprising number of Freud's observations can easily be turned into testable hypotheses (e.g., that orderliness, parsimoniousness, and obstinacy form a unitary trait; Freud, 1959, p. 169), or that the superego in women is never as strong as it is in men (Freud, 1961). Those who wish to reserve psychoanalysis for hermeneutics ignore Freud, the amateur statistician, who was frequently not content to confine his observations to a single case but extended them to groups of cases, e.g., his remarks about the differences between hysterics and obsessives, or his generalizing from the dynamics of the Schreber case to paranoids in general. Any number of testable hypotheses can be derived by simply lifting statements directly from Freud's writing and finding suitable operational definitions.

Along with my self-guided reading, I had the good fortune to become a member of an informal group of faculty members on campus interested in psychoanalytic thought. The Group for Applied Psychoanalysis was begun and led by Norman Holland, a psychoanalyst and professor of English. A number of faculty members from diverse units in the University participated in the group, with a relatively large contingent from English and Comparative Literature. As could be expected, psychoanalysis held little interest for anyone in psychology except for Marvin Feldman and myself, and after Feldman's death, only myself. The group met monthly to discuss a variety of topics, from ideas about jurisprudence to Richard Nixon, group process, and the inevitable problems of literary interpretation.

As a nonbeliever I was impressed that this group of bright, verbal faculty members, some of them internationally known scholars, would give up evenings to discuss psychoanalytic ideas. As an empiricist, I was impressed by the apparent lack of interest among any of the group members in whether what they were saying was true or not. They were engaging in extending psychoanalytic concepts into their academic areas; it was fun, it was frequently exhilarating, but no one seemed concerned with whether the ideas could be tied to some external criterion. Internal consistency of the argument, particularly for those in the English department, seemed to be all that mattered. I recall one meeting where the guest speaker discussed his recent book on schizophrenia, a rather remarkable achievement given that his degree was in the arts and that he had never worked with a schizophrenic. In one lively session, we debated whether Hamlet was psychotic, apparently unaware that he was a fictional character. Putting one's splendid ideas to the test did not seem to be a chief concern for those in disciplines other than psychology, despite my frequent reminders that at some point, testing against an external criterion was crucial for the establishment of the merit of an idea.

A YEAR AT THE ANNA FREUD CLINIC

After I completed a number of studies on oral dependence, I began an intensive review of the experimental literature on orality and anality. Aware that I did not have sufficient fluency in psychoanalytic theories to complete that project to my satisfaction, I applied for, and was given, a one-year grant from the Foundations' Fund for Research in Psychiatry to study at the Hampstead Clinic, the training and treatment institution that Anna Freud had established in London. I simultaneously applied for, and was given permission, at the Hampstead Clinic to take classes and generally participate as an observer. Although the work of the governing committee of the Clinic was never made public, it was rumored that my application received only one positive vote— Miss Freud's—and it won the day. Only Miss Freud appreciated the value of helping train psychoanalytic allies in the scientific community.

That year, 1972–73, was a splendid one for me. I had just completed a three-year term as chairman of the psychology department at Syracuse and was eager to return to scholarly activities. A staff member, Jack Novick, served as personal mentor, tutor, and general go-between for me and the institution. I was immersed in a psychoanalytic culture, participating in regular meetings of several of the working groups—the nursery school group and the ongoing case group among them—and also attended the large weekly case conference session. That year, Miss Freud offered a weekly seminar at the Hampstead

Clinic in which she discussed her 1936 book, *The Ego and the Mechanisms of Defense*. This was a very special treat, and the sessions were eagerly attended. Two other Americans were with me at the Clinic for the full year, and the Clinic administration decided we could attend providing we "did not ask too many questions." I don't think we asked even one.

Miss Freud was then 77 years old, physically frail but mentally at the top of her game. Her intellectual skills were extraordinary, and her ability to answer questions by constructing exactly the right image or analogy was without equal. I kept reminding myself of the miracle that put me in the presence of the daughter of Sigmund Freud, who herself was an enormous force in contemporary psychoanalysis. Hearing her speak unselfconsciously about "my father," as she did several times, was particularly memorable. Her memory was astonishing. Every therapy case seen in the Clinic, perhaps 50 to 60, was summarized in a weekly report sent to her. All the many discussion groups had a member assigned to report each session, those notes going to Miss Freud, too. In addition, she had a busy analytic practice and supervisory duties. And there must have been a flood of administrative details and local and international mail requiring her attention. Yet on more than one occasion I recall hearing her ask a staff member why she had not yet received the weekly report on a particular therapy case.

I was surprised to learn from that seminar with Miss Freud that many of the confusions and ambiguities in psychoanalytic theory arose from faulty translation from the German. Miss Freud was once asked to comment on the difference between primary and secondary repression, a controversy that had sparked a number of lively debates in the literature. She laughed a bit and then explained that the concept of secondary repression originated from a bad translation and that there was no such phenomenon; such are the problems that accrue to a discipline based exclusively on clinical intuitions. At another point she said that the concept of acting-out also resulted from a bad translation; she preferred the term enactment. As for the references she cited in *The Ego and Mechanisms of Defense*, those were added, she said, only after she had written the book and then only for political purposes. It was clear that this work was entirely her own and any acknowledgments of the work of others were included only for diplomatic reasons. In fact, she rarely mentioned other psychoanalytic authorities in that seminar other than those in the small circle around her and her father, with one exception—Wilhelm Reich. She thought his concept of character armor had merit.

I had free use of the excellent library at the Clinic and profited from the many hours of Jack Novick's tutoring in the fine points of psychoanalysis. Because his degree was in psychology he could appreciate my strong belief that the long-term health of psychoanalysis rested on its being able to demonstrate scientific merit. In contrast, other faculty members could not understand my interest in empirical evidence. When the leader of the nursery school group regretted not having data to show the effectiveness of his program, I offered to show him data I had collected years before on the long-term effects of nursery school experiences. He said he was not interested. He had been referring to case histories, not to numbers and statistical tests. I once commented to a seminar leader that just as IQ was a construct in psychology, so were ego, id and superego in psychoanalysis. "Oh, do you think of id, ego, and superego as constructs?" was his answer. My general demeanor in the seminars must have differed from that of the analytic trainees because at one point a senior staff member complimented me, though the comment took a unique form: "Joe, I am glad you are here," she said, "you always say what is on your mind." It was a strange remark and said a good deal about the interpersonal climate at the Clinic.

The Clinic provided first rate, intensive training in psychoanalytic theory and practice, but it did not provide an atmosphere where one could openly challenge established authority. It was a place to learn the established doctrines but not a place to ask if these doctrines were valid. The Clinic provided high quality care for its patients and intensive supervision of its analytic candidates. Impressive improvements were achieved in extremely difficult cases. During the course of the year, I noted an interesting difference between American and English child patients. Without an exception—every little girl being treated at the Clinic eventually realized that she had once had a penis and lost it and was now angry about the loss. In contrast, in the United States I had never once encountered such a child in my own cases or in those I supervised. My unsolicited efforts to explain this fact in terms of reinforcement of selected content categories of a child's speech and behavior were not welcomed.

I took the opportunity of being in proximity to Miss Freud to clarify a problem I had been unable to solve on my own. In discussing obsessions and compulsions, Fenichel (1945) wrote, "The anal-erotic drives meet in infancy with the training for cleanliness, and the way in which this training is carried out determines whether or not anal fixations result. The training may be too early, too late, too strict, too libidinous. If it is done too early, the typical result is a repression of anal eroticism . . . ; if it is done too late, rebellion and stubbornness are to be expected . . ." (p. 305). This entire passage of 11 lines is indented, set in smaller type, and attributed to Freud's paper on female sexuality, strongly suggesting this is a direct quotation. That passage was crucial for the review paper I was preparing on orality and anality, and I had to deal with it. Yet I could not find that quotation in the paper of Freud's that Fenichel had cited or for that matter in anything else Freud had written. I therefore wrote a note to Miss Freud and asked where her father had written it. Back came her response: Her father had never made such a statement. Evidently, Fenichel had made it up and used Freud's name as the authority. As it turns out, the claims found in that "quotation" are not empirically true.

OUT OF THE PSYCHOANALYTIC CLOSET
AND INTO SUBLIMINAL PERCEPTION

Back in the United States I continued to examine psychoanalytic constructs experimentally, convinced more than ever that psychoanalysis could not survive if its only source of support was accounts by various authorities of their clinical experiences. That these authorities differed among themselves about what these experiences demonstrated did not seem to bother the great majority of practicing clinicians, the field witnessing a series of mitotic splits as one group after another broke off from the main body to announce its own version of psychoanalytic truth. A turning point in my research interests occurred after I heard Lloyd Silverman lecture on his experimental work on subliminal stimulation. I was intrigued by this research because I could not understand it. Silverman had demonstrated that a stimulus presented below the level of conscious awareness altered behavior. The results seemed paradoxical: How is it possible to respond to a message that one does not know is there? After his presentation, I vigorously challenged Silverman about this research. His response was typically Lloyd—nondefensive and open: He invited me to spend a semester in his lab at New York University where he would share all his data and procedures with me.

In 1980 I did that and was convinced that the phenomenon (or perhaps phenomena) he described was authentic. I did not understand and still do not know how it worked, and because it was so mysterious and counter-intuitive, I was drawn to the problem in an effort to explain it. The issue is vital to psychoanalysis because it underlies the dynamics of defense mechanisms (i.e., the ability to ward off a threatening idea before it becomes conscious). With the aid of departmental equipment and several generations of bright graduate students, I began to examine subliminal stimulation. A number of experiments, most of them doctoral dissertations, were completed for this purpose. The first study, truly a joint effort (Masling, Bornstein, Poynton, Reed, & Katkin, 1991) succeeded because Edward Katkin allowed us to use his psychophysiological lab, and Robert Bornstein persisted until we knew how to present the message properly. We demonstrated that the message, NO ONE LOVES ME, presented on a tachistoscope below the level of conscious awareness, resulted in physiological arousal, though a control message, NO ONE LIFTS IT, did not, nor did the experimental message when presented supraliminally. Somehow the autonomic nervous system responded to the experimental message but not the control message, even though the central nervous system could not identify either statement from a multiple choice list.

In Bornstein's dissertation experiment (Bornstein, Leone, & Galley, 1987), male subjects were shown photographs either subliminally or supraliminally of a male confederate. Following this manipulation, the subject and two confederate males, one of them whose photograph had been shown, were asked to judge the gender of the writer of various lines of poetry. When the two confederates disagreed, the subject formed an alliance with the person whose face had been previously exposed; this effect occurred only in the subliminal condition. Jackie Hansen's dissertation (1988) provided evidence that a fairly long sentence, MY LOVER AND I ARE ONE, can be processed and assimilated at the subliminal speed of four milliseconds, despite the belief in academic psychology that such a long sentence could not possibly be processed at subliminal speed. Kihlstrom (1999), for example, wrote that humans "simply do not have the cognitive capacity to extract the meaning of complex stimuli like whole sentences" (p. 377). He was wrong—they do.

Cynthia Patton (1992) investigated the dynamics of bulimia by presenting either an experimental message, MAMA IS LEAVING ME, or a control phrase, MAMA IS LOANING IT, either subliminally or supraliminally, to female bulimic-like and control subjects. Following the tachistoscopic exposure, the subjects were asked to sample and rate crackers in a bogus tasting situation. The experimental subjects who saw the experimental message at a subliminal speed ate more than twice as many crackers (19.40) as any of the other groups (who ate a mean of 9.6 crackers). In Nancy Talbot's dissertation (Talbot, Duberstein, & Scott, 1991), male subjects were shown either the experimental sentence, MOMMY IS LEAVING ME, or a control sentence, MONA IS LOANING IT. Following the tachistoscopic presentation, the men completed two different measures of self-confidence in winning an attractive woman's affection. The experimental message lowered the subjects' belief in themselves—those subjects exposed to it at a subliminal speed showed less self-confidence than any of the other subjects.

One of Freud's more esoteric hypotheses is that a woman's wish for a penis can be replaced by a desire for a baby. Lindy Jones (1994) was convinced that both this conjecture and a previous study by Greenberg and Fisher (1980) purporting to support Freud's penis = baby notion were faulty. Using much better equipment than Greenberg and Fisher had available and adding an additional control group, she presented an audio tape of either a pregnancy or a sexual penetration message to male and female subjects. Some of the subjects received the message at a volume below the level of conscious awareness and some received it within normal hearing range. The experimental manipulation was sandwiched between administrations of the Holtzman ink blots. To our surprise, the earlier results of Greenberg and Fisher (1980) were replicated: At the .005 level, those women who were exposed to the pregnancy message reported a greater increase in phallic imagery from pre- to posttest than did the women exposed to the sexual penetration message. The male subjects' Holtzman responses were not affected by any message at any speed. Those data make a more meaningful statement than a priori speculations.

These studies of the effects of subliminal stimulation as well as my earlier work on the oral personality demonstrated to my satisfaction that psychoanalytic hypotheses could be successfully investigated empirically, contrary to the widely held belief that this was not possible. (Many psychoanalysts thought this was both unwise and superfluous.) Furthermore, many Freudian hypotheses were confirmed through this process. The data from the subliminal stimulation studies are more consistent with Freud's second theory of unconscious processing (Freud 1955, 1959) than with his first (Freud, 1953). The first theory suggests that the unconscious is disorganized, chaotic, and governed only by the need for immediate discharge of tension, while the second discusses the unconscious as organized, purposeful, and directed to rather complex goals. Our data show that subjects can discriminate between relevant and irrelevant messages presented below conscious awareness and that bodily processes show differential responses to stimulation presented subliminally. "The unconscious," whatever it is, is evidently capable of screening incoming messages with some discernment and can reach into and alter bodily processes and cognitive judgments. Moreover, Bornstein (1990) demonstrated that subliminal stimuli have greater effect on behavior than supraliminal stimuli. Given the remarkable ability of stimuli presented below the level of conscious awareness to affect behavior, including the response of the autonomic nervous system (Masling et al., 1991), a most desirable next step would be to attempt to bolster and enhance the efficiency of the immune system through appropriate messages presented subliminally.

EMPIRICISM AND PSYCHOANALYSIS

What was sufficient proof for me was not proof for much of academia. The old stereotypes of psychoanalysis persisted, aided and abetted by the psychoanalytic old guard who found no need to establish a scientific basis for their theories. In the face of rapidly expanding research in cognitive and behavioral theories and therapies, psychoanalytic theories appeared to be an outmoded, hopelessly complicated set of antiquated ideas. While behavioral therapies were being investigated and their usefulness empirically demonstrated, psychoanalytic treatment had to rely on support based almost exclusively on testimonials provided by its practitioners. I was asked any number of times by friends, who thought me to be otherwise reasonable and rational, why I would waste my time exploring psychoanalytic ideas experimentally. A great many clinical psychologists probably agreed that the description of the sexual act ascribed to Lord Chesterfield also characterized psychoanalysis: "The pleasure is momentary, the position is ridiculous, and the expense damnable." In the case of psychoanalysis, public behavior is not always identical to private behavior as Lazarus (1971) learned when he asked 20 of his behaviorist friends who were in personal therapy to describe the theoretical orientation of their therapists. He reported that seven were in psychoanalytically oriented therapy, five in Gestalt therapy, four were being seen by an existentialist therapist, three were in psychoanalysis, one was in "group dynamics" therapy, and one in bioenergetics therapy, a neo-Reichian treatment method. Even more striking were the comments these behaviorally oriented psychologists made about their therapists: "Let's face it, if you can afford it in terms of time and money, psychoanalysis is still the treatment of choice" (p. 349); "my therapist is to me a beautiful human being and that means more to me than his theoretical orientation" (p. 349).

The general hostility expressed toward psychoanalysis prompted a number of us to propose that we establish our own journal. Thus Helen Lewis became editor of the new journal, *Psychoanalytic Psychology*, and for the first time those of us who were engaged in research on psychoanalytic topics no longer needed to explain to journal editors why we wished to work empirically with psychodynamic ideas. At about the same time, with the encouragement of Seymour Fisher and Lloyd Silverman, I launched the book series, *Empirical Studies of Psychoanalytic Theories* (Masling, 1986). These volumes review the empirical work in a variety of content areas—developmental, object relations, psychopathology, unconscious processes, the psychoanalytic hour, etc. I was sole editor of three volumes, Paul Duberstein had co-edited one volume (on health psychology), and Robert Bornstein had co-edited five others. The tenth volume, on gender differences, will be published in late 2001 or early 2002. Although the reviews of these books have been more favorable than sales, I am told the volumes are frequently stolen from libraries, a statement of a sort about their value. These books demonstrate the vitality of psychoanalytic thought and the vigorous research programs they have inspired. Indeed, it is likely that psychoanalytic ideas have generated more research than any other theory of personality.

My attempts to uncover the self-disguise Agee described has culminated in the investigation of the theory that accepts self-disguise as a natural and useful mechanism of coping with a difficult, complex world. As I have reported throughout this paper, I have had considerable help in this work—wise teachers, a department that allowed me to do the work I wanted with minimal interference, a publisher who was more concerned with a book's quality and importance than with a balance sheet, and a series of very talented, energetic research assistants, all of whom began as students, quickly became colleagues, and soon thereafter my teachers. We all agree that the world of human behavior and its disguises needs to be examined.

REFERENCES

Agee, J. (1957). *A death in the family*. New York: Grosset & Dunlap.

Aichhorn, A. (1925). *Wayward youth*. New York: Viking.

Bertrand, S., & Masling, J. M. (1969). Oral imagery and alcoholism. *Journal of Abnormal Psychology, 74*, 5–53.

Bornstein, R. F. (1990). Critical importance of stimuli unawareness for the production of subliminal psychodynamic effects: A meta-analytic review. *Journal of Clinical Psychology, 46*, 201–210.

Bornstein, R. F. (1993). *The dependent personality*. New York: Guilford.

Bornstein, R. F. (1996). Construct validity of the Rorschach Oral Dependency Scale, 1967–1995. *Psychological Assessment, 8*, 200–205.

Bornstein, R. F., Hilsenroth, M. J., Padawer, J. R., & Fowler, J. C. (2000). Interpersonal dependency and personality pathology: Variations in Rorschach Oral Dependency scores across Axis II diagnoses. *Journal of Personality Assessment, 75*, 478–491.

Bornstein, R. F., Leone, D. R., & Galley, D. J. (1987). The generalizability of subliminal mere exposure effects: Influence of stimuli perceived without awareness on social behavior. *Journal of Personality and Social Psychology, 53*, 1070–1079.

Farber, L. H. (1976). *Lying, despair, jealousy, envy, sex, suicide, drugs, and the good life.* New York: Harper Colophon.

Fenichel, O. (1945). *The psychoanalytic theory of neurosis.* New York: W. W. Norton.

Fisher, S., & Cleveland, S. (1968). *Body image and personality* (2nd ed.). New York: Dover.

Freud, A. (1936). *The ego and the mechanisms of defense.* New York: International Universities Press.

Freud, S. (1953). The interpretation of dreams. In J. Strachey (Ed. & Trans.), *The standard edition of the complete psychological works of Sigmund Freud* (Vols. 4–5). London: Hogarth. (Original work published 1900).

Freud, S. (1955). Beyond the pleasure principle. In J. Strachey (Ed. & Trans.), *The standard edition of the complete psychological works of Sigmund Freud* (Vol. 14). London: Hogarth. (Original work published 1914).

Freud, S. (1959). Inhibitions, symptoms and anxiety. In J. Strachey (Ed. & Trans.), *The standard edition of the complete psychological works of Sigmund Freud* (Vol. 20). London: Hogarth. (Original work published 1926).

Freud, S. (1961). Some psychical consequences of the anatomical difference between the sexes. In J. Strachey (Ed. & Trans.), *The standard edition of the complete psychological works of Sigmund Freud* (Vol. 19). London: Hogarth. (Original work published 1925).

Fromm, E. (1947). *Man for himself.* New York: Rinehart.

Garb, H. N. (1998). *Studying the clinician.* Washington, DC: American Psychological Association.

Greenberg, R. P., & Fisher, S. (1980). Freud's penis-baby equation: Exploratory tests of a controversial theory. *British Journal of Medical Psychology, 53,* 333–342.

Hansen, J. (1988). *The relationship of subliminally activated psychodynamic conflict to anorexic performance on a lexical decision task.* Unpublished doctoral dissertation, State University of New York at Buffalo.

Holland, N. (1975). *Five readers reading.* New Haven: Yale University Press.

Jensen, A. R. (1965). A review of the Rorschach. In O. K. Buros (Ed.), *Sixth mental measurements yearbook* (pp. 501–509). Highland Park, NH: Gryphon.

Jones, R. L. (1994). An empirical study of Freud's penis-baby equation. *Journal of Nervous and Mental Disease, 182,* 127–135.

Kelly, G. A. (1955). *The psychology of personal constructs* (Vol. 1). New York: W. W. Norton.

Kihlstrom, J. (1999). A tumbling ground for whimsies? *Contemporary Psychology, 44,* 376–378.

Lazarus, A. (1971). Where do behavior therapists take their troubles? *Psychological Reports, 28,* 349–350.

Leites, N. (1971). *The new ego.* New York: Science House.

Masling, J. M. (1957). The effect of warm and cold interaction on the interpretation of a projective protocol. *Journal of Projective Techniques, 21,* 377–383.

Masling, J. M. (1959). The effect of warm and cold interaction on the administration and interpretation of an intelligence test. *Journal of Consulting Psychology, 23*, 336–341.

Masling, J. M. (1960). Interpersonal and situational influence in projective testing. *Psychological Bulletin, 57*, 65–85.

Masling, J. M. (1966). Role-related behavior of the subject and psychologist and its effects upon psychological data. In D. Levine (Ed.), *Symposium on motivation.* Lincoln: University of Nebraska Press.

Masling, J. M. (1986). Orality, pathology, and interpersonal behavior. In J. Masling (Ed.), *Empirical studies of psychoanalytic theories* (Vol. 2, pp. 73–106). Hillsdale, NJ: Lawrence Erlbaum.

Masling, J. M., Bornstein, R. F., Poynton, F. G., Reed, S., & Katkin, E. S. (1991). Perception without awareness and electrodermal responding: A strong case of subliminal psychodynamic activation effects. *The Journal of Mind and Behavior, 12*, 33–48.

Masling, J. M., Rabbie, L., & Blondheim, S. H. (1967). Obesity, level of aspiration and Rorschach and TAT measures of oral dependence. *Journal of Consulting and Clinical Psychology, 31*, 233–239.

Masling, J. M., Weiss, L., & Rothschild, B. (1968). The relationship of oral imagery to yielding behavior and birth order. *Journal of Consulting Psychology, 32*, 89–91.

O'Neill, R. M., & Bornstein, R. F. (1990). Oral dependence and gender: Factors in help-seeking response and self-reported psychopathology in psychiatric inpatients. *Journal of Personality Assessment, 55*, 28–40.

O'Neill, R. M. & Bornstein, R. F. (1991). Orality and depression in psychiatric inpatients. *Journal of Personality Disorders, 5*, 1–7.

Patton, C. J. (1992). Fear of abandonment and binge eating: A subliminal psychodynamic activation investigation. *Journal of Nervous and Mental Disease, 180*, 484–490.

Redl, F., & Wineman, D. (1951). *Children who hate.* New York: The Free Press.

Redl, F., & Wineman, D. (1952). *Controls from within.* New York: The Free Press.

Rotter, J. B. (1954). *Social learning and clinical psychology.* Englewood Cliffs, NJ: Prentice Hall.

Schafer, R. (1954). *Psychoanalytic interpretation in Rorschach testing.* New York: Grune & Stratton.

Spence, D. P. (1982). *Narrative truth and historical truth: Meaning and interpretation in psychoanalysis.* New York: W. W. Norton.

Talbot, N., Duberstein, P., & Scott, P. (1991). Subliminal psychodynamic activation, food consumption, and self-confidence. *Journal of Clinical Psychology, 47*, 813–823.

Weiss, L., & Masling, J. M. (1970). Further validation of a Rorschach measure of oral imagery: A study of six clinical groups. *Journal of Abnormal Psychology, 76*, 83–87.

SELECTED BIBLIOGRAPHY

Bornstein, R. F., & Masling, J. (1985). Orality and latency of volunteering to serve as experimental subjects: A replication. *Journal of Personality Assessment, 49*, 306–310.

Bornstein, R. F., & Masling, J. (Eds.). (1998). *Empirical perspectives on the psychoanalytic unconscious: Empirical studies of psychoanalytic theories* (Vol. 7). Washington, DC: American Psychological Association.

Bornstein, R. F., & Masling, J. (Eds.). (1998). *Empirical studies of the therapeutic hour: Empirical studies of psychoanalytic theories* (Vol. 8). Washington, DC: American Psychological Association.

Bornstein, R. F., & Masling, J. (Eds.). (2002). *The psychodynamics of gender and gender role: Empirical studies of psychoanalytic theories* (Vol. 10). Washington, DC: American Psychological Association.

Bornstein, R. F., & Masling, J. (Eds.) (2005). *Scoring the Rorschach: Seven validated systems*. Mahwah, NJ: Lawrence Erlbaum.

Duberstein, P. R., & Masling, J. (Eds.). (2000). *Psychodynamic perspectives on sickness and health: Empirical studies of psychoanalytic theories* (Vol. 9). Washington, DC: American Psychological Association.

Masling, J. (1983). *Empirical studies of psychoanalytic theories* (Vol. 1). Hillsdale, NJ: Lawrence Erlbaum.

Masling, J. (1986). *Empirical studies of psychoanalytic theories* (Vol. 2). Hillsdale, NJ: Lawrence Erlbaum.

Masling, J. (1990). *Empirical studies of psychoanalytic theories* (Vol. 3). Hillsdale, NJ: Lawrence Erlbaum.

Masling, J. (1997). On the nature and utility of projective tests and objective tests. *Journal of Personality Assessment, 69*, 257–270.

Masling, J. (2001). Empirical evidence and the health of psychoanalysis. *The Journal of the American Academy of Psychoanalysis, 28*, 665–686.

Masling, J. (2002). How do I score thee? Let me count the ways or some different methods of categorizing Rorschach responses. *Journal of Personality Assessment, 79*, 399–421.

Masling, J. (2003). Stephen A. Mitchell, relational psychoanalysis, and empirical data. *Psychoanalytic Psychology, 20*, 587–608.

Masling, J., & Bornstein, R. F. (Eds.). (1993). *Psychoanalytic perspectives on psychopathology: Empirical studies of psychoanalytic theories*. Washington, DC: American Psychological Association.

Masling, J., & Bornstein, R. F. (Eds.). (1994). *Empirical perspectives on object relations theory: Empirical studies of psychoanalytic theories*. Washington, DC: American Psychological Association.

Masling, J., & Bornstein, R. F. (1996). *Psychoanalytic perspectives on developmental psychology: Empirical studies of psychoanalytic theories*. Washington, DC: American Psychological Association.

Masling, J., Bornstein, R. F., Fishman, I., & Davila, J. (2002). Can Freud explain women as well as men? A meta-analytic review of gender differences in psychoanalytic research. *Psychoanalytic Psychology, 19*, 328–347.

Masling, J., & Cohen, I. S. (1987). Psychotherapy, clinical evidence, and the self-fulfilling prophecy. *Psychoanalytic Psychology, 4*, 65–79.

Masling, J., O'Neill, R., & Katkin, E. S. (1982). Autonomic arousal, interpersonal climate, and orality. *Journal of Personality and Social Psychology, 42*, 529–534.

Masling, J., Shiffner, J., & Shenfeld, M. (1980). Client perception of the counselor and orality. *Journal of Counseling Psychology, 27*, 294–298.

Masling, J. M., & Schwartz, M. (1979). A critique of research in psychoanalytic theory: Orality and anality. *Genetic Psychology Monographs, 100*, 257–307.

Faculty-student soccer game, Hebrew University,
Jerusalem, Israel, 1964

With tachistoscope, circa 1985

Speaker at psychology department graduation, SUNY at Buffalo, 1991

With my wife and best friend, Annette, "in disguise" for a Halloween party, Buffalo, 2000

CHAPTER 12

A Blessed and Charmed
Personal Odyssey

Theodore Millon
Institute for Advanced Studies in Personology
and Psychopathology, Coral Gables, Florida

The invitation to write this autobiography came a few days after the horrific events of 9/11/01. I put pen to paper soon thereafter (my usual first draft style), a difficult task owing to growing feelings of sadness, if not despair, and the gnawing fear that the tragedy may have brought an end to a unique and wondrous period in humankind's history—the open and free humanistic democracy of twentieth century America—a time when persons of all backgrounds could retain not only their sense of invulnerability, but the freedom to become whatever they may have aspired to, that is, "to actualize their potentials" as my old mentor, Kurt Goldstein, may have put it.

   Once more we must brace ourselves to live life as my forebears had for centuries past, to survive in the face of unrelenting hostility and degradation. Our vision of impregnability has forever been blinded by an adversary so pernicious that nothing, not even the extraordinary goodwill and opportunities of the past several decades, could prepare us sufficiently to withstand, that is, to keep us from recognizing that nothing will ever be the same. Both a tangible and a psychological barrier have been irrevocably breached; our continental shores have been penetrated and our psychic structures destabilized. Our sturdy bastions of physical safety and secure futures have been forever pierced. Our sense of material and psychological inviolability has naïvely been taken for granted, and our innocence has protected us from having to deal with an unblemished future that might come to an end. The assumption that all things will continue to be well has been revealed as a fantasy. We have not only been felled by an attack from beyond our shores, but our inner sense of optimism has been undermined from within. Worse yet, the suicide attacks on the World Trade Towers and Pentagon may merely have been a dry run for something far more devastating, a monstrous assault on humankind and civilized history—one we can only begin to imagine that may be perpetrated by Osama bin Laden or Saddam Hussein's acolytes.

I am not by nature a Cassandra whose prophecies should best be disregarded. As a person in his eighth decade, I can let myself be less troubled about our future than most. But the events of 9/11/01 have assuredly and will forever alter the lives of our children and grandchildren. Thus, on a personal note, three of my four good-natured and thoughtful children, Diane, Andy, and Adrie, (I consider all thousand or so of my past psychology students also to be children of mine), as well as five of my seven lovely and affectionate grandchildren, Lissy, Katie, Elizabeth, Matt, and Annie, reside in the metropolitan New York area; daughter Carrie and her children, Molly and Livia, reside near my wife, Renee, and I in Florida. None has been harmed physically by the catastrophe, but all have been shaken psychologically.

Sympathetic as we all are to the economically wretched and inescapably anomic world of the perpetrators, their cruel and malicious effort to find scapegoats for perennial resentments and confused ambitions are especially frightening to me, for they are reminiscent of similar barbarities that sought out and identified my Jewish ancestors as ostensibly justified objects for plunder and vilification. Those who trace their origins to the victims of anti-Semitic pogroms and Nazi annihilation know all too well the history of Jews as readily employed emblems of cosmic evil, contrivances of religious calumny and economic malevolence from the demonizing days of the ancient crusaders to the paranoid displacements of modern Arab dictatorships.

In no small part, the awesome horror of 9/11/01 has led me to redouble my desire to reconnect with my ancestral heritage in this essay; it is reason also to acquaint my children and grandchildren to more than their father and grandfather's professional history, but also to its ancient and valued family roots.

FAMILY

What little I learned about my family's ancestry was told to me by my paternal grandfather, in his 70s, who had resided with my parents from the mid-1930s to the mid-1940s, when I was six until I was 14. A rabbi (R) by training, Zayde, as I called him, was the youngest of nine sons of a Talmudic scholar and Yeshiva teacher, all of whose male children were educated and became rabbis at the Volozhyn (Lithuanian) Yeshiva. Zayde's father, my great-grandfather (GGF), R. Elizier Isaac Millon (1812–1881), served in his early adulthood as a rabbi in Bryansk, Russia, until he received an invitation to join in teaching at the Volozhyn Yeshiva in 1844; there he remained for almost 40 years through its periodic travails until his death. GGF was the son of Rachel Zalman (1780–1833) and R. Avrum Millon (Milan?) (1775–1827), the latter a rabbi for most of his life in the city of Pinsk, Russia; R. Avrum traced his family of origin to R. Judah ben Eliezer, who headed Yeshivas in both Padua and Milan, Italy, in the fifteenth century. Rachel, a dutiful wife, was the daughter of R. Arieh Leib Zalman (1752–1810), who was the first son of R. Elijah ben Judah Solomon Zalman (1720–1797), a distinguished Talmudic scholar known throughout the Pale of Russia as the Vilna Gaon.

Following his formal education, Zayde [his actual name being R. Jacob Millon Bernstein (1864–1955)] was assigned in 1886 to a synagogue as an assistant rabbi in Bialystok, Poland, where he married and had his first son, during whose birth his mother died. Shortly thereafter, in 1889, Zayde was transferred to oversee a modest synagogue in the shtetl (small Jewish village) of Sokoly, Poland, where he settled and married his second wife, Temma (after whom I was named Tevya). Repeated pogroms and Russian edicts in the early 1890s, that forced Jews out of St. Petersburg and Moscow led Zayde to contemplate leaving the Russian Pale of Jewish settlement for more hospitable environs. Hence, in 1895 he left for London, England, where his eldest brother, R. Judah Millon, had emigrated to take advantage of the receptivity of that city's mayor to educated Jewish immigrants. After a two-year London period and a visit back to Poland with his family, Zayde left for the United States, returning every other year to Sokoly to visit his growing family, inevitably followed shortly thereafter by his wife's pregnancy and another child. Unable to establish a position at a temple in the United States, Zayde wandered from Boston to New York to Chicago as an itinerant leather merchant, returning to Poland in 1910 and again in 1912 to bring his then-eldest child back with him to the United States. When his third son's (my father's) turn to emigrate was scheduled in 1914, the First World War suddenly erupted, leaving my father, his mother, and three younger siblings behind in Europe, until the mid-1920s.

His education effectively terminated, my father (Tata, as I called him in my childhood, Pop in later years), Abraham Millon (1900–1970), now the eldest male, assumed full responsibility to provide for his family. This he undertook as a tailor's assistant in my future maternal grandfather's modest, but successful clothing factory in Sokoly. Here, he met my mother who, among her other daughterly roles, surreptitiously provided my father with the factory workers' "lunch leftovers" to feed what would otherwise have been my father's rather impoverished family. Both of my parents emigrated to the States in the mid-1920s, marrying shortly thereafter in New York City, where they resided for the next 40+ years. I was born on August 18th, 1928; the number eight was considered in the mysticism and numerical acrobatics of the Gematria, a component of the medieval Jewish Cabbalah, to be a lucky number; hence, I was seen to be a triply blessed child with a charmed future.

My father, sans a formal education, became the co-owner in the Depression of a small clothing manufacturing business. However, owing to his intrinsic language and mathematical skills, he also wrote "replies" to weekly *Bintel Brief* letters regularly published in the *Jewish Daily Forward*, a major Yiddish newspaper in America; he also served for a year or so as a civilian cryptographer during the Second World War, a "classified" activity I did not learn of until some years thereafter. The most significant memory of my youth (apart from the periodic loneliness of being an only child) was my father's all-consuming affection for me (the roots of my secure narcissism, I am sure), most charmingly illustrated by the fact that he brought home a gift for me (toy, game, book) every working day from the time I was two until I turned 13. A warm, reflectively intelligent, and socially-concerned idealist, he was regarded highly as a supportive friend to the underprivileged, as well as an outspoken union activist, despite remaining a factory "boss" throughout his life.

My mother (Mama early, Mom later), Molly Gorkowitz Millon (1902–1982), had a family background and temperament substantially different from my father's. Hasidic in religious orientation, emotionally intense and expressive, musically gifted, physically zestful and courageous, she was sporadically sick from numerous ill-defined ailments, distinctly hypochondriacal, and would be "diagnosed" today as affectively bipolar. My lifelong relation with her was composed of a mixture of warmth and deep attachment, but also fraught with her erratic and unpredictable moods. Notably, she was among the first in the late 1930s to undergo both electroconvulsive and insulin coma "therapies" by the earliest promulgators of these techniques in the States.

EARLY SCHOOL YEARS (1934–1945)

An early talker and late walker, my parents never failed to inform new visitors in my childhood that from nine to 18 months, I would sit in my highchair "telling them" not only what they could do for me, but also how they should do it. All my talk for the next several years was in Yiddish, my only language until first grade when I entered a special class for Yiddish-speaking young-sters who were to be taught English, a language we all became quite adept at within a matter of weeks, albeit most with an "accent" such as mine that did not fade for more than a decade or two. Notable in this first grade year was my Zayde's effort to teach me mathematics, not just basic arithmetic, but both algebra and geometry, subjects that appeared to intrigue me greatly and served me well throughout my entire academic career.

In third grade I was invited to attend elementary school in a "gifted pro-gram" at Hunter College, a school located on the upper east side of Manhattan in New York City. Although I could "hold my own" quite well in mathematics and the "physical sciences," I was clearly outclassed by my program peers in almost all the humanities and "social sciences." It was not an especially grati-fying period for a youngster who otherwise felt quite special. Moreover, the daily trip to and from Hunter from our home in Brooklyn proved both tiring and expensive for my economically-strained father, who would not let his eight-year-old son travel to the "city" on his own, having therefore to arrange taxicab rides to and from the Manhattan subway station he used himself to travel to work.

Somewhat advanced in my education, I returned to the fifth grade in Brooklyn, spending the better part of the year "buddying" with a fellow youngster by the name of Maurice Sendak; together we would draw on large charts and posters placed on the back blackboards of all the classrooms of the school. Here I proved second best again; talented as I was artistically, Maurice achieved the representations we sought (e.g., Washington crossing the Delaware, Civil War battles such as in Gettysburg) more effectively than I. Nonetheless, fifth grade proved to be a great joy with a wonderfully sensi-tive homeroom teacher, Mr. Greenspan. Also notable that year were close friendships with Wally Robinson, the only African American youngster in our neighborhood, nephew of the "super" of our apartment building, and Marvin Immelman, a quiet and intelligent boy who suffered a rather severe speech and hearing impairment. Both were *persona non grata* kids, and were poked fun at or completely shunned by both local peers and adults. It was not any humanistic impulse or deviance on my part that drew me to them; I simply found both interesting and thoughtful peers with whom Maurice and I shared wild and Harry Potter-like stories on the front steps of our homes, mystical tales of ancient and future fantasies. Much to my joy, both Tata and Zayde not only tolerated these friendships with Wally and Marvin, but went out of their way to encourage them. I then began an almost meteoric growth spurt in my tenth year; in sixth grade I grew from 5'3" to 6'2", a progression that stirred my mother to take me to numerous "hormone" specialists. As usual, there was no reason to worry; I simply stopped my height advance the next year or two, remaining about 6'4" from age 12 on. I towered over all other males at my Bar Mitzvah, much to the approval of my Tata and Zayde, both only 6 feet tall.

Junior high was another buoyant experience. In New York City's RA (rapid advance) Program, I thoroughly exulted in the company of fellow students of high motivation and ability, especially "Izzy" Mandelbaum, a life-long neighborhood friend who always was tops in our shared classes, from early Heder (Hebrew school) days to being ranked first in his graduating medical school class. Izzy was my very closest and dearest friend through early schooling years, a superego "nudge," however, who spent many an afternoon seeking to dissuade me from my inclination to forgo serious study and drift instead into adolescent sports, art "doodles," or music and song, not that he himself was ill-equipped to star in these pursuits as well. But Izzy was committed from his earliest years "to be a doctor," which he became, ultimately as professor and chief of cardiovascular surgery at Indiana University's School of Medicine by his late thirties (more about Izzy later).

Not unexpectedly, high school proved to be a period of identity diffusion, if not confusion, one lasting well into my college years. Two problematic matters stand out in this period. First, and despite numerous self-generated distractions from study, I remained a stellar math student, the only one in my high school senior class of 1,300 students to have attained 100s in all New York State Regents math exams. Arrogantly, I assumed I would receive the math medal at graduation, but learned to my consternation that it was to be awarded elsewhere, to a fellow by the name of Ed Murray, who I was to meet up with some 30 years later when I joined the psychology faculty at the University of Miami; much to my pleasure, Ed became my best and most highly esteemed colleague during our 20-plus years there together.

Returning to my high school days, Dr. Freilich, chair of the math department, told me with acerbity, and in no uncertain terms, that I had wasted my "questionable" talents, and in no way did I deserve the medal owing to being "both irresponsible and immature" because of my frivolous involvements with girls and extra-curricular activities, the latter stemming from my "preoccupation" with acting and singing in school plays and shows. In this second problematic aspect of my high school career, I had joined my more lighthearted friends in a variety of high-spirited merriment, particularly the art of imitating the voice and style of the famous singers of the day; my forte was that of impersonating Bing Crosby, Perry Como, and Danny Kaye. Another mime at the time was a chap named Vito Farinola, later known and somewhat famous as the singer Vic Damone, who was quite apt at imitating Frank Sinatra; here, again, I proved second best.

I was tempted in high school, albeit briefly, to consider a theatrical or singing career, but was told firmly by my parents (and Izzy) that efforts such as these invariably failed; more importantly, that these vocations were not befitting "a nice Jewish boy." Other career fantasies of the time were likewise derided; to seek a future as a "serious artist" was quickly dismissed by my parents, as well as by relatives whose similar aspirations proved to be sorrowful decisions. Similarly, the more respectable thought of becoming a mathematics teacher was discounted as a vocation with limited financial possibilities. However, along similar lines, and owing to the growing successes of the Lasser brothers (J. K. and S. J.), distant family relatives who served then as my father's accountants, they were put forward as career models well-worth emulating.

COLLEGE AND GRADUATE SCHOOL YEARS

And so I entered the City College of New York (CCNY) in the spring of 1945 as an accounting major, a career to which I took an instant dislike in the first weeks of the first course. Dropping that vocational goal was followed by a carnival of miscellaneous majors, each proving ephemeral. Drawn into the socialistic but anti-communist ideals then rampant in cafeteria talk at CCNY, I was intrigued and enticed to explore the field of economics, majoring seriously but briefly in what was called "mathematical financial management," a precursor to what is referred today as econometrics. I then wandered into both philosophy and physics majors. By chance and curiosity, I scored impressively on exams in my introductory psychology course. The instructor, Dr. Max Smith, sought then to seduce me into pursuing this subject further by enticing me to hear a series of lectures by a professor Gardner Murphy. The lectures proved quite compelling and the seduction into psychology was successful, at least for a few years.

My CCNY period was an increasingly joyous and exhilarating one personally, socially and intellectually. I met my lovely wife Renee when she entered CCNY as a freshman in 1948; we have been together for almost 54 years as of this writing. Friendships were established with Phil Teitelbaum, Shel Taylor, Bob Lifton, Elliot Valenstein, Zanwil Sperber, Wally Mandell, and Herb Spohn, as we competed for the few "A"s given in courses by stellar teachers such as Murphy, Joe Barmack, John Peatman, Dan Lehrman, Herb Birch, and Kenneth Clark. At the same time, I was able to serve as art editor of the college newspaper, associate editor of its yearbook, and vice president of the student council, reveling in the awesome academic schedule I sought to maintain while transported into a bevy of weekend activities of serious social import in a New York young person's intelligentsia.

Toward graduation I accepted a research assistantship with I. E. Farber in the graduate clinical psychology program at the State University of Iowa. However, I found it too difficult to tear myself away from my many involvements in greater New York, and decided to forgo the questionable lures of the Midwest and to stay on at CCNY in its master's psychology program. Fortunately, I was offered an unusual assistantship arranged in both the psychology and sociology/anthropology departments, serving as a part-time experimental lab assistant for Dan Lehrman, as a chauffeur and "bodyguard" for Professor Kurt Goldstein, and as a grader and occasional lecturer in sociology/anthropology for Dr. Stan Chapman. Among the many highlights of my master's year was time spent with Gardner Murphy and Larry K. Frank, then a leader in New York's Ethical Culture Society, perhaps best known for having coined the term "projective methods." For several months I joined both Murphy and Frank in Sunday morning gatherings at Margaret Mead's home in the Village. Notable also was my experience over several months as an analysand in Professor Ernst Kris' "creatively gifted" research study. Likewise following class, I learned more during our drive to Professor Goldstein's home on the upper east side of New York, where I was introduced and had several evening talks with another New York "idol" of mine, Goldstein's good friend and neighbor, Professor Meyer Schapiro, an eminent art historian.

In the spring before completing my master's degree, I received an acceptance to attend Harvard's then relatively new Social Relations Program, no doubt owing to my unusual mix of psychology/sociology/anthropology coursework. The Viking Fund Fellowship I was then awarded meant I would work as an assistant to Gordon Allport, a good friend of my mentor Gardner Murphy. I was taken aback, however, by the fellowship requirement that I engage in research for the better part of several summers in Africa, a prospect I did not relish at all. After a few weeks of reflection, as well as a disabling and extended bout of mononucleosis, I decided to withdraw from the fellowship offer and stay on in New York, perhaps to explore courses at the New School and to give my moribund artistic aspirations an opportunity to be stirred and flourish or, at least, to be tested in reality while living in Greenwich Village.

Reality took another course, however. In late June 1950, the United States entered into a war with North Korea. I soon learned that men in 1-A draft status would be called into service unless they were bona fide full-time students. I was disposed to "take my chances," but my parents and bride-to-be implored me to regain my graduate school standing. But where? City College did not have a doctoral program at that time. I called Allport in Cambridge a week or so after Independence Day. Kind as he was, the fellowship had been awarded elsewhere, but he would do his best if I would reapply for admission—the following year. I contacted both Murphy and Joe Barmack, who served as acting chair of psychology at CCNY summer sessions, and "pleaded" for their assistance. Several frantic weeks passed following applications and letters in late July and early August to a number of psychology and philosophy programs at northeastern universities. Only the University of Connecticut (UConn) program in personality/social was fully responsive, offering both acceptance and a much-needed assistantship, given that I would live away from my New York home. Whether it was Murphy's good word or my first cousin, Sylvia (Tookie) Bernstein, then an assistant to the dean of the UConn graduate school, that was instrumental in gaining this late support, I never was able to determine. My family, however, breathed a sigh of relief as I went on to UConn that early September.

My reception and history at UConn was a mixed blessing. A number of new and able graduate students in the personality/social program had been told that assistantships were unavailable to them. I came upon the scene the week before classes with the prize they all had aspired to. I did not receive a cheerful welcome, especially from one student who had very much sought to gain admission to Harvard's Social Relations program and learned that I had "stupidly" turned down such an offer. This situation became more problematic when they learned that I carried a less than full load so that I could audit courses in philosophy at Yale (Professors Carl "Pete" Hempel and Henry Margenau seminars) where I had also been accepted, but without financial support. The special arrangements that the UConn faculty permitted me only added to my troubled relationship with my personality/social/and clinical peers, although I did become a member of a comfortable network of experimental and developmental students. Fortunately, in the following two years, my good CCNY friend, Shel Taylor, entered UConn's personality/social program, Renee and I got married, and I turned my full academic effort to a dissertation on the "authoritarian personality," a subject with which I had been deeply intrigued, owing to my immersion in issues of social morality, especially the role of national character in the origins of the Nazi holocaust. My New York years with Larry Frank discussing "society as the patient" became the undergirding theme of my doctoral research.

Completing the dissertation in October 1953, I prepared myself to enter the army later that fall, a non-appealing prospect as far as I, an ambivalent pacifist, was concerned. The Korean War had been brought to an end, however. Rather shockingly, when the day came for me to be inducted, I was "rejected" at the final health examination, assigned a 4-F status owing to a physical problem that previously had been an insufficient cause for nonacceptance to the service. Disoriented momentarily, but frankly elated, I walked out the door of the induction center, feeling charmed again, to see Renee waiting to bid me goodbye near the bus that was to leave for Fort Dix; not speaking a word, lest I suddenly be called back, we took the subway, saying nary a word, to my parent's home, where the night before we had held a "celebratory" farewell party.

Unhesitatingly, I sought to start life anew that fall; realistic in my expectations, I nevertheless was able to find a few part-time opportunities that New York friends brought to my attention. Without flattering my credentials, I began what I knew would be the arduous task of searching for *any* academic position. The most memorable event of this six-month search was a telegram from Professor M.O. Wilson, psychology chair at the University of Oklahoma; he asked if my wife and I, native New Yorkers, would consider accepting a position at Oklahoma. Would I? Of course! Wilson's telegram was the very first job offer to come my way. I wrote back immediately with an enthusiastic letter, indicating not only my willingness to accept his offer, but also my joy at the prospect of collaborating with Professor Muzafer Sherif of Oklahoma's faculty, whose autokinetic work I had drawn on extensively in my dissertation. Renee and I then waited for a reply; a week or two passed, we waited, and waited, and waited, finally giving up as other opportunities began to appear. Some seven or eight years later my then three children came running up the stairs from the basement of our home with a request to tear off the unmarked stamp on a letter they found. And there it was—to my embarrassment and somewhat to my chagrin—the unmailed letter addressed to Professor M. O. Wilson. Somehow, Renee and I both overlooked sending the missive to Oklahoma. How different the turn of life's events would have been had we not forgot (unconsciously desired?) to post the letter properly.

THE PENNSYLVANIA YEARS (1954–1970)

Opportunities arose in April 1954 to consider similar positions at both Swarthmore College and Lehigh University in Pennsylvania. The salaries, however, for these assistant professorships differed substantially; my penchant was to accept Swarthmore, but I had no realistic choice but to select Lehigh at the then princely sum of $4,200, some $900 more than Swarthmore offered for the academic year. It turned out that the position at Lehigh was one for which I was especially well suited. The department had lost two members that spring, a retiring social psychologist and a suddenly resigned clinical/personality psychologist. Given my not inconsiderable background in both subjects, I seemed to fit their teaching needs quite well, although I had a devil of a time preparing six new courses in my first academic year.

Teaching became my professional *raison d'être*, one which I loved from the start and one I continue to cherish to this waning day of my academic career. Owing to my enthusiasm for the teaching role, a benign power to provoke and enlighten, I explored numerous course options over the years; most notable was an opportunity that came my way to instruct a course entitled "Creative Concepts," one open only to students in the top 2% of the university's junior and senior classes, and taught by only four professors for a year or two. I was able, as stated by the Arts and Science dean, to "teach anything," and so I did, wandering through themes such as cosmogony, evolution, consciousness, the future of mankind, etc., subjects that were both challenging and exhilarating to me owing in no small measure to the gifted academic students I taught from diverse fields such as engineering physics, econometrics, molecular biology, and so on.

Despite internecine departmental politics, particularly the then-intense schism between clinicians and experimentalists, as well as my outspoken "radical" anti-Vietnam polemics, I managed to survive at Lehigh, owing to a respectable publishing record, a not-to-be-dismissed position on campus as a teacher of note, and an unusual stature as a mental health leader in both the community and the state. Let me turn to this latter role in public health.

In many regards, my Pennsylvania years were characterized most significantly by activities that would appear secondary to my position as a university professor. It was in my first year at Lehigh that I was required to teach abnormal psychology, a course that entailed taking students to the local Allentown State Hospital (ASH), enabling them thereby to observe "live" case presentations. It was early in October 1954 that we made our first visit to ASH; it consisted of a hospital tour, a not untypical initial segment of such courses. The experience proved appalling, disheartening, terrifying, and unnerving. Of my 30-plus students in the class, half withdrew from the tour after walking through the first or second building; three or four more were revolted and nauseated following a brief stay at the hospital cafeteria. I, myself, despite considerable prior acquaintance with a number of state hospitals, was sickened at the conclusion of the visit.

Coincidentally, an electoral campaign for state governor was in progress that fall. The Democratic candidate, a young man by the name of George Leader, had commented to the press about the failure of previous Republican administrations to care adequately for Pennsylvania's citizens, especially the mentally ill. Little did he know! I took it upon myself following our wrenching experience at ASH to write him a five-page, single-spaced letter beseeching him to visit the revolting ASH, to see for himself tangibly how horrifying and cruel the conditions were at this institution. To my surprise and pleasure, his campaign manager, a former state senator by the name of Harry Shapiro, phoned me the week following my letter to invite me to come to the hospital in a few days to meet Mr. Leader and, at his side, to join him on a tour of the institution. And so, at the appointed time and day, along with more than a 100 reporters and photographers from throughout the state, I met Mr. Leader, and we walked through the harrowing dungeons of ASH, a place many would term "a snake pit" and a "cuckoo's nest." The public uproar was overwhelming. Leader was elected, the first Democratic governor in over 30 years. Shortly after his inauguration in January, I was invited by Shapiro to become a member of the newly appointed ASH Board of Trustees. The fact that I was the only member of the new board with a mental health credential (most were physicians, ministers, rabbis, liberal businessmen), I was chosen president of the board (age 26), a post I retained for more than a decade. During this period the hospital, which housed 2,100 patients in 1955, had been rated as 22nd of the 22 state hospitals in Pennsylvania on a series of health service criteria; at the same time, Pennsylvania had been ranked 47th of the 48 states in the U.S. on these same criteria (second from the bottom only to Mississippi). In the ensuing decade, ASH progressed to rank first in the state, while Pennsylvania advanced to third in the nation. During the 15 years of my involvement with the hospital, given its vastly enhanced staff and improved facilities, we built superb clinical services and genuine research programs, designed, for example, to evaluate experimental pharmacological agents, as well as to establish the then-novel outreach community mental health centers.

In my personal efforts to explore the lives of patients more insightfully and compassionately than was otherwise available to me, I frequently ventured incognito through the hospital, at times clothed in typical hospital garb overnight or for entire weekend periods, conversing at length with patients housed in a variety of acute and chronic wards. Let me digress for a moment and recount a brief episode of what proved to be my final overnight stay at the hospital. Early that Sunday morning I bolted up in my cot, one of over 30 lined up in the ward. I broke out in a cold sweat, and began to obsess over whether I was, in reality, a psychology professor and a hospital board member. Was I not just another deranged patient, a paranoid who cleverly deluded others *and* himself? Had I fashioned a self-entrapping disguise akin to those about me who asserted they were Christ or the Pope, but were no more "mad as a hatter" than I? Unable to shake the confusion and fear that overtook me, I got to a phone quickly, called my staff co-conspirator, Dr. Shettel, who came to my rescue in what seemed like an interminable 10 minutes, and quieted down my sudden and inexplicable delusional thought.

I learned much in these hospital wanderings; they served me well as I began to contemplate writing about the shortcomings of our mental health profession, its diagnostic concepts, its scientific base, its therapeutic approaches. These visits became, in effect, the motivation and substantive foundation of my first major book, entitled *Modern Psychopathology* (MP), an advanced text that initiated my serious career as a so-called "thinker" in the field, a career that ultimately led to the development of new diagnostic tools (e.g., Milton Clinical Multiaxial Inventory; MCMI), theoretical models (e.g., evolutionary psychology), and therapeutic approaches (e.g., psychosynergy). But I am getting ahead of my story here.

I wrote in the preface of MP (Millon, 1969) that the book began, quite simply, as an exercise in self-education, an attempt on my part to gather and to render the disparate facts and theories of psychopathology into a coherent and orderly framework; such a venture, it was hoped, would enable me to pursue my future research, teaching and clinical responsibilities more effectively. Little did I know that the tasks of authorship would force me to think more presumptuously that I cared—even worse, to feel a measure of pride and vanity in these presumptions. Faced repeatedly with the obscurities, contradictions and confusions that beset the field, I found myself formulating novel "clarifications" and "solutions" to old and perplexing problems. In short, an act of modest self-education became an act of intellectual audacity. I stated further, and most presumptuously, that the time had come for the development of a new and coherent theoretical framework, one that interwove both psychological and biological factors, and from which the principal clinical syndromes could be derived and coordinated. Instead of rephrasing traditional psychiatric categories in the language of modern theories, as several able psychopathologists had done, I sought to devise a new classification schema, one constructed from its inception by coalescing what I considered to be the basic principles of personality development and functioning. MP set forth what I then termed a "biosocial theory of maladaptive learning and functioning."

I should say a word about a wonderful group of affectionate and enduring friends from my Pennsylvania days, many of whom are still with us, now well into their seventies and eighties, and whom I still strive to visit or have as guests at least once a year, namely: Flo and Jack G., Norma and Herb F., Addi and Howard A., Rose and Tommy W., Viv and Len R., Edie and Josh

E., Myra and Jerry F., Dorothy and Ferdi L., Naomi and Sam G., Renee and Eli S., Shirley and Mike L., Sylvia and Joe D., Ruth and Victor V., Carol and Marshall A., Bunny and Dick D., and Thelma and Adi G. However, despite the warmth and my attachment to these cherished friends, no sooner had the MP text appeared than I found myself approached by several universities urging me to consider leaving Lehigh to joining their faculties.

THE CHICAGO YEARS (1969–1977)

The opportunity that attracted me most was a chief psychologist's position at the Neuropsychiatric Institute (NPI) of the University of Illinois Medical Center in Chicago. The head of psychiatry, Melvin Sabshin, struck me as a genuine "mensch." Though only three or four years my senior, he felt like a good "father-figure," a kindly, socially liberal, and highly intelligent person of genuine egalitarian spirits, one in whom the MD/PhD distinction would be of no significance. Happily, my initial impressions proved correct; Mel and his chosen staff—psychiatrists, psychologists, social workers, sociologists, anthropologists, neurophysiologists, statisticians—composed a highly congenial team of mental health clinicians, scholars and researchers. My tenure at NPI, while Mel "ran the shop," was a joy, a highly productive and collaborative period. Unfortunately, when Mel left to head the American Psychiatric Association in Washington, DC in late 1974, life at NPI became tense and divisive; the new chair set forth the preeminent "rights" of biological psychiatry, one that was to rule over all other professional disciplines and activities. To counter the hegemony of biological psychiatry, I pressed forward a proposal that Mel and I had begun to develop for a novel Doctorate in Mental Health degree to be implemented in a separate School of Mental Health Sciences at the University's vast Medical Center campus. Achieving only modest support for this innovative venture, I then vigorously sought, with the initial approval of the University's executive dean, to sever psychology's subservient tie to psychiatry at NPI. This latter venture ultimately also failed, and rather miserably, leaving me no alternative but to explore other academic options.

Relationships in the sophisticated psychological environment of Chicago were nonetheless exceptionally rewarding, notably opportunities to share (and disagree over) analytic ideas with Heinz Kohut, Mert Gill, and George Pollack at the Chicago Institute of Psychoanalysis; wonderful substantive discussions with Len Eron and I. E. Farber of the Circle Campus faculty of the University of Illinois (UI), as well as seminars taught with doctoral clinical students at both UI and the University of Chicago. Memorable also was reuniting with my old childhood schoolmate, Izzy Mandelbaum. He visited from Indiana two or three times in 1971, 1972, and 1973; we would get together at what was popularly known in Chicago as Greek Town, having lunch or dinner in one of its superb ethnic restaurants. When I did not hear from him for several months after our last visit, I became concerned, called his University Surgery Division in Indianapolis, only to learn to my terrible shock and grief that Izzy failed to survive a sudden and massive coronary while performing an operation some months previously.

Two accomplishments of note distinguished my professional activities in the early and mid-periods of my tenure at NPI: first, the central role that Mel and I played in establishing a "forward-seeking," contextually-oriented and empirically-grounded Diagnostic and Statistical Manual of Mental Disorders (DSM-III) (American Psychiatric Association, 1980) and, second, the opportunity I had to develop with younger colleagues a series of "modern" psychodiagnostic tools. I'd like to comment on each of these in turn.

I wrote in a review of the DSM-III venture (Millon, 1983) that the implicit charge to the American Psychiatric Association's Task Force on Nomenclature and Statistics in May 1974 was the expectancy that it would revamp the DSM-II (American Psychiatric Association, 1968) in a manner consonant with the then current empirical knowledge, theory, and practice. Also implicit was the assumption that the product would be viewed by allied mental health professions as having been cognizant of their diverse interests and orientations.

The basic conceptual schema and the distinctive innovative features of the DSM-III were set well in place by the end of the first full year of deliberation, for example, the use of "operational" criteria, the contextually-oriented multiaxial format that also separated clinical (Axis I) from personality (Axis II) disorders, the systematic and comprehensive description of disorders, and the plan to implement extensive and formal field trials. What proved especially gratifying, as well as fruitful in achieving a strongly shared consensus, was the open and egalitarian spirit that prevailed in the Task Force's early deliberations. Not that there was a paucity of vigorous disagreement or that impassioned polemics were invariably resolved, but these divergences and spirited controversies did not result in group discord, traditional academic schisms, or professional power struggles; for example, the psychologists on the Task Force not only had full voting rights—when votes were necessary— but also provided more than their share of ideas, disputations, and formal content drafts. Owing to my prior writings, my primary assignment was to construct complete and detailed texts for each of the personality disorders.

The Task Force agreed to take an explicitly nondoctrinaire approach, evident not only by avoiding the introduction of particular theoretical biases concerning the nature and etiology of mental disorders but also by actively expunging them wherever they were found in the DSM-II, actions which evoked the ire of several deeply mortified professional organizations, such as the American Psychoanalytic Association. The Task Force was equally committed to the goal of syndromal inclusiveness. The intent here was to embrace as many conditions as were commonly seen by practicing clinicians, thereby maximizing the opportunity of future investigators to evaluate the character of each condition as a valid syndromic entity.

Lest the reader think otherwise, let me assure my psychology colleagues that I was no apologist for the DSM-III's (or the DSM-IV's; American Psychiatric Association, 1994) shortcomings; nor did I have especially fond illusions about the altruistic or power and economic interests of the psychiatric profession. I continue to maintain a long agenda of unfinished work concerning how best to advance future diagnostic enterprises (e.g., Millon, 1991b, 2002), specifically to further promote the rigorous empiricism (e.g., diagnostic criteria) and contextual orientations (e.g., multiaxial schema) that characterize modern psychological thought.

The second seminal activity of my Chicago years was the work I undertook to strengthen both the theoretical and psychometric grounding of psychological assessment (see Millon, 1997). As I noted elsewhere, a year or two after the publication of MP, I began with some regularity to receive letters and phone calls from graduate students who had read the book and thought it provided ideas that could aid them in formulating their dissertations. Most inquired about the availability of an "operational" measure they could use to assess or diagnose the pathologies of personality that were generated by the text's theoretical model. Regretfully, no such tool was available. Nevertheless, they were encouraged to pursue whatever lines of interest they may have had in the subject. Some were sufficiently motivated to state that they would attempt to develop their own "Millon" instrument as part of their dissertation enterprise.

As the number of these potential "Millon" diagnostic progenies grew into the teens, my concern grew proportionately regarding both the diversity and the adequacy of these representations of the theory. To establish a measure of instrumental uniformity for future investigators, as well as to assure at least a modicum of psychometric quality among tools that ostensibly reflected the theory's constructs, I was prompted—perhaps "driven" is a more accurate word—to consider undertaking the test construction task myself. At that time, in early 1971, I was directing a research supervision group composed of psychologists and psychiatrists-in-training during their internship and residency periods. All of them had read MP and found the proposal of working together to develop instruments to identify and quantify the text's personality constructs to be both worthy and challenging.

The initial task was that of exploring alternate assessment instruments for gathering relevant clinical and personologic data. About 11 or 12 persons were involved in that early phase. Some were asked to analyze the possibilities of identifying new indexes from well-established projective tests, such as the Rorschach and the Thematic Apperception Test; others were to investigate whether we could compose relevant scales from existing objective inventories, such as the Sixteen Personality Factor Questionnaire (16PF) and the Minnesota Multiphasic Personality Inventory (MMPI). Another group examined the potential inherent in developing a new and original structured interview. After four or five months of weekly discussions, the group concluded that an entirely new instrument would be required if we were to represent the full scope of the theory, especially its diverse and then-novel "pathological" personality patterns (this work, it may be recalled, preceded by several years that undertaken by myself and others on the DSM-III Task Force).

Naïvely, it was assumed that the construction task could be completed in about 18 months, a time period that would allow several members of the research group to participate on a continuing basis. Despite the fact that we "postponed" developing a possible Personality Interview Schedule after a brief initial period, the "more limited" task of building an adult clinical inventory took seven years to complete.

We did see our way, however, to also construct an adolescent-oriented inventory, the Millon Adolescent Personality Inventory (MAPI) (and later its revision, the Millon Adolescent Clinical Inventory MACI), as well as a medically-oriented tool, the Millon Behavioral Health Inventory (MBHI) (and later its replacement, the Millon Adolescent Medicine Diagnost MBMD). Especially gratifying in these early years was working with a group of young clinical research associates, most notably Robert B. Meagher, Jr., Catherine J. Green, and my daughter Diane B. Millon. More recent test development colleagues of similar talent and congeniality include Roger D. Davis, Larry Weiss, Sarah E. Meagher, Seth D. Grossman and, not to be overlooked, my daughter Carrie N. Millon.

Despite an extensive Chicago friendship network, and the exceptional cultural qualities of Chicago (its stunning art institute and superb symphony orchestra), both Renee and I had serious illnesses in late 1976 (she, colon cancer, and I, one of the first of the five-vessel coronary artery bypass graft (CABG) surgeries), and decided that it would be best to "stop making every second count," and to seek a physically warmer and psychologically more nurturant environment for our later years. Several opportunities arose, especially one beckoning us to join Stanford's distinguished psychiatry and psychology departments, but we chose simply to move straight south to the Miami area of Florida, not the least owing to the presence there of our equally beckoning elderly parents. The rapid-talking and energetically ambitious atmospherics at Stanford were intimidating, more than I felt I could comfortably deal with, owing in part to a post-surgical realization that I no longer could cognitively process simple algebraic equations in my mind, as I had been able to do since childhood. Certain abstract capacities simply appeared to have evaporated, a fact later found to be a rather common sequel to surgical procedures requiring extended periods on the heart-lung machine.

THE MIAMI AND BOSTON YEARS (1977-PRESENT)

I thought initially of the post I accepted as Clinical Psychology Director at the University of Miami as a "retirement position," a place where I would slow my usual hectic pace of professional activity. How wrong I was, but how vigorous and happy I became over the following two or three years as my health and normal optimistic outlook came once more to the fore.

I mentioned earlier my delight with reuniting at UM with my high school math competitor, Ed Murray, but I also found satisfaction elsewhere at the university. Early in my tenure, Neil Schneiderman, a physiological psychologist, joined me in establishing a doctoral clinical health psychology program in the department, one of the first two or three in the nation. Other colleagues of note were Clyde Hendrick and Paul Blaney, both of whom came to the UM faculty the same year I did. Numerous graduate and post doctoral students of extraordinary academic and clinical talent became a pleasure to mentor; among those not already mentioned in this essay are George Everly, Steve Strack, Mike Antoni, Sally Kolitz-Russell, Neil Bockian, and Robert Tringone. Tempted as I was in the early 1980s to consider leaving UM for chief of psychology appointments at Langley Porter Institute of the UCSF and at the Connecticut CMHC of Yale University, I concluded that it would be wisest to stay put at UM. A part-time visiting professorship, however, was extended to me by the Psychiatry Department of Massachusetts General Hospital (MGH) of Harvard Medical School, one I later transferred to its affiliated McLean Hospital. Here I saw an opportunity again to play a part in influencing the course of psychiatric thinking; I carried this teaching role for more than a decade.

At MGH, I teamed up with Gerry Klerman, who previously had overseen NIMH during the Carter presidency. He returned to Harvard in 1981 for a few years before moving on to Cornell Medical Center, his alma mater, in New York City. Unknown to me initially, it turned out that Gerry was a distant relative of mine; our mothers were cousins, both bipolar and neurotic depressives from nearby shtetls (Lomza and Sokoly) in Poland. After Gerry and I completed a book in the mid-1980s (Millon & Klerman, 1986), I continued at Harvard's McLean Hospital, lecturing and advising psychiatric residents, as well as participating in later years with John Gunderson's DSM-IV-related New England Personality Disorder Group, a professional seminar setting as stimulating and congenial as one could find, composed of informed and innovative participants from several of Harvard's affiliated hospitals, as well as from Tufts, Yale, and Brown universities.

Despite an initial measure of self-enforced isolation and academic hesitation owing to what I saw as my brain's oxygen-depleted and lessened capacities, I was encouraged by several colleagues and by Herb Reich, psychology editor at John Wiley and Sons, to undertake a book that focused solely on the personality disorders (Millon, 1981). In justifying the volume, I wrote in its preface that the recently published DSM-III, on whose Task Force I had been an active member, was far more comprehensive descriptively than its predecessors, but was not designed to provide detailed clinical presentations nor the competing theories and etiologies of the syndromes it encompassed. The lack of such materials was especially problematic to those seeking information on the personality disorders. As I saw it, these syndromes had suddenly "come of age," transformed from a class of impairments possessing only incidental relevance to the diagnostic enterprise into one that was central, if not crucial, to the new DSM-III multiaxial format. Although clinicians and researchers could find a substantial literature on most syndromes in psychological and psychiatric texts and journals, such was not the case, even to a modest degree, for the personality disorders. And now that these syndromes were advanced to the status of major clinical conditions, the need to develop a literature to fill the void was all the more acute. The book set out to bring together the sparse, widely scattered, and highly doctrinaire clinical literature on all of the personality disorders, seeking in a single sourcebook to both coordinate and evaluate what had been written on the subject. To maximize scholarly and practical utility, it contained contrasting historical and theoretical viewpoints, serving thereby as a reference guide of alternate conceptions of these disorders. To enhance its value as a textbook, a full and separate chapter was devoted to each condition. Of particular interest were sections in each chapter that quoted the important historical forerunners of contemporary ideas. In addition to providing comprehensive reviews of each of the new personality syndromes—avoidant, narcissistic, borderline, and schizotypal—many "mixed" personality types were also extensively illustrated. Of special utility to clinicians were detailed discussions of frequent Axis I and Axis II comorbidities, that is, clinical and personality syndromes that coexisted with great regularity. And to compensate for the lack of etiologic hypotheses in the DSM-III, significant portions of each chapter were devoted to describing the syndrome's most plausible developmental origins and dynamics.

The success of the first edition of *Disorders of Personality* was immediate and substantial (21 printings); it led another publisher, Seymour Weingarten of Guilford Press, to ask if I would like to edit a handbook of personality disorders. I demurred, saying that there simply were not enough scholars around, nor were there sufficient solid scientific data available to justify such a volume. Instead, I proposed that he underwrite a new journal that might lead ultimately to a body of literature to serve as a foundation for the handbook. Seymour assented, and Gerry Klerman and I recommended that he ask a young psychiatrist then at Cornell Medical School, Allen Frances, to join with me to co-edit what we then entitled *The Journal of Personality Disorders*, a clinically and scientifically successful periodical with both an impressive subscription list and an editorial board composed of most of the major players in the field. Allen and I remained the journal's co-editors for over a full decade, turning responsibility for running the journal over to John Livesley, then psychiatry head at the University of British Columbia.

Throughout the eighties and nineties, I characteristically refused to conform to popular taste and to seek opportunities for "creative" expression. Thus, I continued to write and develop both my idiosyncratic theoretical model (Millon, 1990) and its correlated assessment tools (Millon, 1997; Strack, 2002). Further, I worked on the second edition of my *Disorders of Personality* book (Millon, with Davis, 1996), which proved to be a substantially expanded version of the first, approximately twice its length. In its preface I wrote that, given the many advances in conceptual and empirical research of the previous two decades, the time had come for a far-reaching theoretical model that would interweave not only psychological and biological factors, but also coordinate that knowledge to more fundamental and adjacent fields of scientific endeavor. Toward that end I sought to devise a classification schema that coalesced several principles drawn from evolutionary theory. Thus, in addition to reviewing historically diverse conceptions of classification, I set out to provide a rationale and logic for an "evolutionary approach" to pathological styles of behavior. Not only did the schema connect personality and clinical pathology to other realms of scientific thinking, but it also sought to demonstrate the developmental continuity of pathological functioning throughout the life span, as well as the interconnections that existed among ostensibly unrelated syndromes. To make this developmental continuity explicit, an organizational sequence was constructed to show that more severe stages of disorder are problematic extensions of less serious personality impairments (e.g., schizotypal viewed as a more severe variant of basic schizoid and avoidant patterns).

My work had progressed through the years from what I originally labeled a "biosocial framework" to an "evolutionary model." Despite their changed terminology and conceptual base, these two schemas were both consistent and consonant. The former derived its constructs largely from learning theory and served to undergird developmental ontogenesis, whereas the latter's constructs derived from evolutionary theory and served to explicate the phylogenesis of human adaptive styles. Readers inclined to pursue these more speculative, but perhaps scientifically more fruitful, ventures were advised to read another of my books, *Toward a New Personology: An Evolutionary Model* (1990), a treatise that reviewers generally lauded, though one or two scoffed at my ideas as "too sociobiologic," or found them to be forbiddingly opaque. To show that I was not speaking metaphorically, I drafted a series of formal analyses for constructing classification systems in fields such as normal personality (1991a, 1994) and psychopathology (1991b, 1996).

The profession's acceptance of my upgraded assessment tools, especially the MCMI-III (Millon, Millon, & Davis, 1994), has been exceptionally gratifying; it ranks now third only to the MMPI and the Rorschach as the most frequently employed of the psychodiagnostic tools in this country, mirroring the "objective" psychometric features of the former, and interpreted in line with the "projective" clinical richness of the latter. Similarly, the MACI (Millon, Millon, & Davis, 1993) has become *the* most frequently used adolescent inventory throughout the clinical world. And the recently completed MBMD (Millon, Antoni, Millon, Meagher, & Grossman, 2000) has already surpassed the earlier MBHI (Millon, Green, & Meagher, 1982) as the comprehensive instrument of choice for medical patients in whom psychological factors are likely to be of clinical significance. Comparable levels of acceptance have been extended to a normal personality inventory, the Millon Index of Personality Styles (MIPS) (Millon, Weiss, Millon, & Davis, 1994), and a clinician's checklist of pathological attributes (Tringone, 1997). It was in the mid-1990s that I began to hear references to "Millon," not as a person, but as a brand name, like Kleenex or Chevrolet. A confused and preternatural feeling overtook me. My substantive reality had been replaced (deposed?); I had become a dehumanized (deified?) object; shades of "the Rorschach."

Along with current colleagues and students, I have continued to author or edit numerous articles, chapters, and books that have gained respectable, if not laudatory reviews, notably volumes such as the graduate and professional tome, the *Oxford Textbook of Psychopathology* (Millon, Blaney, & Davis, 1999); an advanced undergraduate text, *Personality Disorders in Modern Life* (Millon,

Davis, Millon, Escovar, & Meagher, 2000); a collection of my selected papers, entitled *Personality and Psychopathology* (Millon, 1996), and a comprehensive statement of my views concerning treatment, called *Personality-Guided Therapy* (Millon, 1999). Under the aegis of the American Psychological Association (APA), I have recently enjoyed and learned much while authoring a wide-ranging history of the mental health field, entitled *Masters of the Mind* (Millon, Grossman, & Meagher, 2004), as well as editing a new APA series of 21 books to be authored by different psychologists and psychiatrists, tentatively under the general title, *Personality-Guided Psychology*.

As mentioned earlier, teaching has always been a joy for me, occasions to improvise extemporaneously, to stir an audience's empathic sensibilities, if not to "melt their minds," so to speak. I have been asked and have been delighted to speak in any number of settings beyond my university home base on diverse theoretical, diagnostic, and therapeutic subjects, but always anchored to the key role I have continued to see for personality and its disorders. By now, I have given somewhat over 750 such addresses at APA and at most state and regional psychological associations through the years. A member of several "professional circuits" and "speaker stables," such as IRE, STS, and the Cape Cod Seminar group, I have enjoyed many occasions to vacation travel with my family, visiting friends across the nation. A recent innovation has been the National Computer Systems' inspired "Millon Conferences"; these comprise extended workshops by some 15 speakers each year on a variety of "Millon" topics, held at annually changing cities around the country.

Over a decade ago I had the pleasure of working with a Danish group of psychologists and psychiatrists, particularly Niels Strandbygaard and Erik Simonsen, to establish the *International Society for the Study of Personality Disorders*, whose first biennial conference was held in Copenhagen in 1988, a meeting attended by over 400 participants from 22 nations. It has subsequently met with equally numerous and enthusiastic participants in cities such as Oslo, Cambridge, Milan, Vancouver, and Geneva; its seventh conference was set for New York in early October 2001, but was canceled owing to the tragedy of 9/11/01. My 1970s entrée into the European community owes much to Professor Strandbygaard, whom I fondly refer to as a great Dane; he not only translated my work for much of Scandinavia, but led the first "Millon Study Group" for several years in the 1980s. I've cheered from the sidelines as Niels' European study group model expanded to the United States, where more than 40 similar clinical associations have been established, assembling for a one or two-year period in a number of States, such as Indiana, Minnesota, New Jersey, California, Florida, and elsewhere, as well as in Canada.

Reception to my writings has brought me numerous international invitations to settings where I have been impressed by mental health clinicians and scholars of exceptional talents, notably in diverse countries such as Norway, England, Japan, Germany, Canada, Spain, the Netherlands, Ireland, Italy, Sweden, Argentina, Belgium, Israel, and beyond. There are more esteemed and cherished colleagues around the world who have been generous and hospitable than I can name in a brief essay such as this.

Recent years have enabled me to semi-retire to what is called the Institute for Advanced Studies in Personology and Psychopathology in Florida; here I have been able to reflect, write, and carry out research together with local graduate students and international post doctoral colleagues. The Institute's diverse activities are ably and comfortably managed by its executive director, Donna Meagher. Here also I have been able to tie together the threads of my professional work these past years. Thus, my recent writings have stressed the need for mental health disciplines to rise from their stasis of spirit, and begin to coordinate (synergize is the term I like) their professional roles and functions. As elaborated in recent talks and papers (Millon, 1999b, 2002), I assert that heretofore unconnected components of our field's classical activities should be synthesized, specifically as follows: (1) that our guiding principles be grounded in the universal laws of nature, notably those of evolution; (2) that our personologic theories and pathological concepts be formulated as one of nature's many expressions (e.g., physics, biology) of these universal laws; (3) that our profession's formal classification system and nosology be derived logically from these personologic theories; (4) that our assessment instruments be sufficiently sensitive quantitatively to test these theories empirically, and to serve clinically to identify/measure our personological dimensions and diagnostic categories; and (5) that our therapies be focused on target areas that are accurately and relevantly appraised by coordinated assessment tools, and be themselves fully integrated and composed of synergistically combined modalities.

In closing this brief, but inclusive memoir, I should like to raise my Sabbath wine glass to all my children, both biological and psychological, in the wish that their futures be as blessed and charmed as mine has been, one free and untroubled, joyful and productive, as it can be in a socially caring and humanistic world.

REFERENCES

American Psychiatric Association. (1968). *Diagnostic and statistical manual of mental disorders* (2nd ed.). Washington, DC: Author.

American Psychiatric Association. (1980). *Diagnostic and statistical manual of mental disorders* (3rd ed.). Washington, DC: Author.

American Psychiatric Association. (1994). *Diagnostic and statistical manual of mental disorders* (4th ed.). Washington, DC: Author.

Millon, T. (1969). *Modern psychopathology: A biosocial approach to maladaptive learning and functioning.* Philadelphia: W. B. Saunders.

Millon, T. (1981). *Disorders of personality: DSM-III, Axis II.* New York: Wiley Interscience.

Millon, T. (1983). The DSM-III: An insider's perspective. *American Psychologist, 38,* 804–814.

Millon, T. (1990). *Toward a new personology: An evolutionary model.* New York: Wiley Interscience.

Millon, T. (1991a). Classification in psychopathology: Rationale, alternative & standards. *Journal of Abnormal Psychology, 100,* 245–261.

Millon, T. (1991b). Normality: What may we learn from evolutionary theory? In D. Offer & M. Sabshin (Eds.), *The diversity of normal behavior* (pp. 100–150). New York: Basic Books.

Millon, T. (1996). *Personality and psychopathology: Building a clinical science (selected papers).* New York: Wiley Interscience.

Millon, T. (Ed.). (1997). *The Millon inventories: Clinical and personality assessment.* New York: Guilford.

Millon, T. (1999a). *Personality-guided therapy.* New York: Wiley Interscience.

Millon, T. (1999b). Reflections on psychosynergy: A model for integrating science, theory, classification, assessment and therapy. *Journal of Personality Assessment,72,* 437–456.

Millon, T. (2002). Assessment is not enough: The SPA should participate in constructing a comprehensive clinical science of personality. *Journal of Personality Assessment, 78,* 209–218.

Millon, T., Antoni, M., Millon, C., Meagher, S., & Grossman, S. (2000). *Millon Behavioral Medicine Diagnostic (MBMD) Manual.* Minneapolis: National Computer Systems.

Millon, T., Blaney, P., & Davis, R. (Eds.). (1999). *Oxford textbook of psychopathology.* New York: Oxford University Press.

Millon, T., with Davis, R. (1996). *Disorders of personality: DSM-IV and beyond.* New York: Wiley Interscience.

Millon, T., Davis, R., with Millon, C., Escovar, L., & Meagher, S. (2000). *Personality disorders in modern life.* New York: John Wiley.

Millon, T., Green, C. J., & Meagher, R. (1982). *Millon Behavior Health Inventory (MBHI) Manual.* Minneapolis: National Computer Systems.

Millon, T., with Grossman, S., & Meagher, S. (2004). *Masters of the mind.* Washington, DC: American Psychological Association.

Millon, T., & Klerman, G. (Eds.). (1986). *Contemporary directions in psychopathology: Toward the DSM-IV.* New York: Guilford.

Millon, T., Millon, C., & Davis, R. (1993). *Millon Adolescent Clinical Inventory (MACI) Manual*. Minneapolis: National Computer Systems.

Millon, T., Millon, C., & Davis, R. (1994). *Millon Clinical Multiaxial Inventory-III (MCMI-III) Manual*. Minneapolis: National Computer Systems.

Millon, T., Weiss, L., Millon, C., & Davis, R. (1994). *Millon Index of Personality Styles (MIPS) Manual*. San Antonio: The Psychological Corporation.

Strack, S. (Ed.). (2002). *Essentials of Millon inventories assessment* (2nd ed.). New York: John Wiley.

Tringone, R. (1997). The MPDC: Composition and clinical applications. In T. Millon (Ed.), *The Millon inventories* (pp. 449–474). New York: Guilford.

SELECTED BIBLIOGRAPHY

Davis, R., & Millon, T. (1993). The five-factor model: Apt or misguided. *Psychological Inquiry, 4*, 104–110.

Millon, T. (1969). *Modern psychopathology: A biosocial approach to maladaptive learning and functioning*. Philadelphia: W. B. Saunders.

Millon, T. (1983). The DSM-III: An insider's perspective. *American Psychologist, 38*, 804–814.

Millon, T. (1984). On the renaissance of personality assessment and personality theory. *Journal of Personality Assessment, 48*, 450–466.

Millon, T. (1987). On the prevalence and genesis of the borderline personality disorder: A social learning thesis. *Journal of Personality Disorders, 1*, 354–372.

Millon, T. (1990). *Toward a new personology: An evolutionary model*. New York: Wiley Interscience.

Millon, T. (1991). Classification in psychopathology: Rationale, alternative & standards. *Journal of Abnormal Psychology, 100*, 245–261.

Millon, T. (1991). Normality: What can we learn from evolutionary theory? In D. Offer & M. Sabshin (Eds.), *Normality: Context and theory*. New York: Basic Books.

Millon, T. (1996). *Disorders of personality: DSM-IV and beyond*. New York: Wiley Interscience.

Millon, T. (1999). *Personality-guided therapy*. New York: Wiley Interscience.

Millon, T. (1999). Reflections on psychosynergy: A model for integrating science, theory, classification, assessment and therapy. *Journal of Personality Assessment, 72*, 437–456.

Millon, T. (2000). Reflections on the future of DSM Axis II. *Journal of Personality Disorders, 14*, 17–29.

Millon, T. (2000). Toward a new model of integrative psychotherapy: Psychosynergy. *Journal of Integrative Psychotherapy, 10*, 37–53.

Millon, T. (2002). Assessment is not enough: The SPA should participate in constructing a comprehensive clinical science of personality. *Journal of Personality Assessment, 78*, 209–218.

Millon, T., Blaney, P., & Davis, R. (1999). *Oxford textbook of psychopathology*. New York: Oxford University Press.

Millon, T., & Davis, R. (1995). The development of the personality disorders. In D. Ciccetti & D. Cohen (Eds.), *Developmental psychopathology*, Vol 2: Risk disorder, and adaptation (pp. 633–676). New York: Wiley Interscience.

Millon, T., & Davis, R. (1995). Conceptions of personality disorders: Historical perspectives, the DSMs-IV, and future directions. In W. J. Livesley (Ed.), *The DSM-IV personality disorders* (pp. 3–28). New York: Guilford.

Millon, T., & Davis, R. (1996). An evolutionary theory of personality disorder. In J. Clarkin & M. Lenzenwenger (Eds.), *Major theorists of personality disorder* (pp.). New York: Guilford.

Millon, T., & Diesenhaus, H. (1972). *Research methods in psychopathology*. New York: John Wiley.

Millon, T., et al. (2004). *Masters of the mind: Exploring the story of mental illness from ancient times to the new millennium,* New York: John Wiley.

Millon, T., et al. (2004). *Personality disorders in modern life* (2nd ed.). New York: John Wiley.

The author at age 1, early 1930   Working on Modern Psychopathology at home in Pennsylvania, 1966

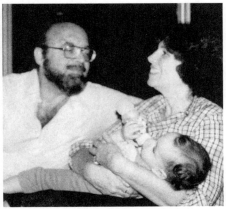

With Mel Sabshin in Chicago, 1973   With wife Renee, and granddaughter Katie, in Miami, 1982

Celebrating the 20th anniversary of the Millon clinical inventories, Minneapolis, 1998

Enjoying the good life in Coral Gables, Florida, 2003

CHAPTER 13

Ideas from My Undergraduate Years

An Autobiographical Fragment[1]

Edwin S. Shneidman
University of California, Los Angeles

As a preface I should like to provide an overview of this chapter and make a social introduction between myself and the reader as two sentient human beings. It occurs to me that the quickest way for me to introduce myself is through a one-paragraph curriculum vitae (CV), the kind that all professors carry around in their academic hip pockets. CVs have always sounded to me like applications for a job—at least like petitions for promotion (or self-promotion). But it is a way to cut though prolixity and to save space. Here is what I look like—the skeleton of my career—in a single paragraph:

Curriculum Vitae

Edwin Shneidman, PhD, was born in 1918 in York, Pennsylvania. He is Emeritus Professor of Thanatology at the University of California at Los Angeles (UCLA). During World War II he served in the army from private to captain. In the 1950s he was co-founder and co-director of the Los Angeles Suicide Prevention Center. In the 1960s he was the charter Chief of the Center for the Study of Suicide Prevention at the National Insti-

---

[1] *Author Note*: These remarks, in modified form, were first made at the Fourth Annual Distinguished Alumnus Award, Department of Psychology, UCLA, in 1998. Portions of these pages were published previously as "Suicidology and the University" in *Suicide and Life-Threatening Behavior*, 2001, 31, 1–8.

tute of Mental Health (NIMH) in Bethesda. He has been Visiting Professor at Harvard and at the Ben Gurion University of the Negev in Beersheva. He has been Research Associate at the Karolinska Hospital in Stockholm and Fellow at the Center for Advanced Study in the Behavioral Sciences at Stanford. In 1968 he founded the American Association of Suicidology. He is the founding editor of the journal *Suicide and Life-Threatening Behavior*. He is the editor or co-editor of eight books, including *Thematic Test Analysis* (1951). He is the author of *Deaths of Man* (1973; nominated for a National Book Award), *Voices of Death* (1980), *Definition of Suicide* (1985), *The Suicidal Mind* (1996), *Comprehending Suicide* (2002; winner of a CHOICE Award), and *Autopsy of a Suicidal Mind* (2004). He is a member of the Melville Society. He is widowed and has four sons (all health professionals) and six grandchildren.

I have an immediate impulse to put some flesh on these bones. It is accurate to say that my intellectual life as a psychologist has revolved around my relationship with Henry A. Murray, MD, PhD, surgeon, psychiatrist, personologist, head of the Psychological Clinic at Harvard, Melville scholar, gentleman, towering intellect, and the most complicated and interesting—generous and difficult—human being I have ever met outside the pages of a great novel. I studied with him for two extended periods in my life, in 1961 and 1969. In addition, I am the recipient of 170 extraordinary letters from him. Here following is a letter I received in late 1966 when I was 48. I had just moved to the NIMH as the chief of the newly formed Center for the Study of Suicide Prevention, and I had attended an American Psychological Association (APA) meeting—and apparently I was running around like a chicken with two heads.

22 Francis Avenue
Cambridge, MA 02138
December 30, 1966

Beloved Ed,
I was greatly disturbed by what I saw and heard of you in New York. In addition I was stunned to see your Achilles heel for the first time (although I always have a mind that every tragic hero has one). Now in retrospect, I recall previous intimations of essentially the same prideful sin against Nature. I am somewhat biased on this score, because of my experiences in the great outdoors, in athletics and physical adventure, in biology and surgery—all of which conspired to endow me with a profound veneration for life in all its manifestations—especially the wisdom of the body. Interrelated it seems to me are: your sleeplessness, your absolutely unique conception of sleep as somehow comparable to suicide, your dashing off in the morning without breakfast, and your incessant restlessness of body,

thought, wit, enterprise and intention. And then your decision not to consider for a moment the possibility (I would say the hardly disputable occurrence) of a rational and defensible suicide. And yet all the while you seem to be intent on over-expending and abusing the large reservoirs of energy that Nature has vouchsafed you, as though they were inexhaustible, as if your soaring ambition and indomitable will could triumph over the aging process which begins at conception. Actually you are racing toward the depletion of these priceless energies, or so it seems. In any event, you are unfortunately and miserably confronted by a diaphragmatic hernia, the severity of which I cannot, of course, appraise; and so I am in no position to urge you to do anything but find a highly recommended doctor whom you like and trust, and don't let any pride or fears (in you) keep you from taking his advice. Personally I wouldn't trust him if he didn't insist on a complete rest for at least a fortnight. Granted that you were born with a rapid tempo of energy release, can do five times more than other persons in a day, have a brilliant and witty mind, and a loving kindness that is perpetually brimming over and much else beside, *still* there is a limit. Your being is so precious to me that it makes me sick at heart to witness your defeat in wisdom by a juvenile (in my scales) prideful determination to continue in perpetual motion.

Con Amore,
Harry

That precious letter illustrates to me at least two points: That human personalities are enormously complicated and that it is critically important to have, if possible, a central inspirational figure in one's life—a mentor, an intellectual parent. I have always felt that I was at least 20 IQ points brighter when I was in his presence or writing with him specifically in mind. My two best papers are *Orientations Toward Death* (about subintentioned death), written for Harry's *festschrift* in 1963, and *The Deaths of Herman Melville* written for presentation at the Melville Society at Williams College when Harry was president of the society in 1968.

I have some thoughts about *assessment*. I have always believed that some ongoing assessment was propaedeutic to effective intervention; that it is best to understand what one is faced with before one acts. It seems common sense to me that one ought to know what a thing is before one tinkers with it. And I have never been keen on simple diagnostic labels in psychiatry and psychology. I have taken seriously Harry's injunction to me that one should never disparage a fellow human being in fewer than 200 words. I must confess that I am not enamored of the word "assessment" as used in contemporary psychology. The dictionary tells us that an assessment is an evaluation of a man, his worth, for tax purposes. It is a monetary figure, an amount, a single number. In this sense, perhaps the truest assessment book on record is that of Louis I. Dublin (1930)—first statistician for the Metropolitan Life Insurance Company—entitled *The Money Value of a Man*. What we psychologists mean when we use the word assessment is comprehension, understanding, conceptualization and reconceptualization. Assessment sounds too much, in my ears, like a Wechsler Adult Intelligence Scale (Wechsler, 1955) IQ number or a Minnesota Multiphasic Personality Inventory (MMPI; Hathaway & McKinley, 1943) diagnostic score. I would prefer that this journal[2] were called *Journal of Personality Comprehension*, the official publication of the Society for Personality Comprehension.

MY UNDERGRADUATE DAYS AT UCLA, 1934–1938

Inasmuch as this is an intellectual autobiography focusing on the (relatively brief) personality assessment segment of my professional life, it is directly relevant to narrate the main *ideas* that activated my undergraduate life and all of my career subsequent to those formative years. In 1934 I was a rather immature 16-year-old, a *tabula rasa*. In retrospect, I muse that there were five professors at UCLA who played important roles in shaping my mind and in helping to make me the kind of assessment psychologist I have become. Let me introduce them.

Joseph A. Gengerelli: The Method of Difference

In a figurative way, Professor Gengerelli saved my life. Ginger was a dapper and handsome man who possessed a beautiful intellect. When he passed me on campus or in a hallway, he would come up to me and put his face an inch or so from mine and say to me, "Shneidman, have you had any clear and distinct ideas?" With that searching question, we were, of course, talking about Descartes, who begins the *Discourse on Method* (Descartes, 1956). Descartes' clear and distinct idea was that he could think and introspect about his thinking. Everybody knows "Cogito ergo sum" (I think therefore I am). And I would reply to Ginger, "No sir, not lately, but if I have any I'll surely come directly to you." And he would throw back his leonine head and roar with laughter.

---

[2]The journal that this autobiography first appeared in was *The Journal of Personality Assessment*.

I took every course I could from him. Once there was a midterm examination that he returned to me. On the cover he had written: "100%. A distinguished paper. Your handwriting leaves something to be desired." In a burst of adolescent temerity and sheer happiness, I went up to him and said, "Professor Gengerelli, I can read the first phrase, but I can't quite make out what these other words say." And he looked at me, and he looked at the blue book, and he looked at me and then he exploded into laughter. That anecdote, of my happy chutzpah and my authority's happy acceptance of it—is somehow paradigmatic of my life. What a joy it is for a young mind to be nurtured like that!

But that is not the point that I wish to make. Ginger was a keen believer in John Stuart Mill's methods of inductive science, how one gets from a number of particular observations—in nature, in the laboratory, in the clinic, or in a coroner's vault—to some reasonable inductive generalization. He taught me—and I learned as only an eager adolescent can learn—the methods of agreement, of difference, of agreement and difference, of concomitant variation, and of residue, but especially the method of difference. The method of difference is the heart of experimental inductive science.

One day, 15 years down the temporal road—after service in a world war, marriage and fatherhood, and a doctoral degree—when I was an employee of a local neuropsychiatric hospital, the chief of the hospital called me in and asked me to write letters for his signature to two young women whose husbands had recently committed suicide in the community. I read their clinical folders and talked to a few nurses and then decided to go to the coroner's office and see what they had.

So early one morning I drove into downtown Los Angeles, intending to complete this chore in a half hour and get back to work. I obtained their case numbers, and descended into the vaults of the coroner's office and found the first folder. There was the expected grisly material: a death certificate, an autopsy report, a police report, and some photographs. But there was something I had never seen before, a suicide note. The second folder did not have a suicide note, and because I was a UCLA, Gengerelli-trained psychologist and not a clerk, I stayed and looked at folders that they had been keeping since early in the previous century. I spent the whole day there.

When I picked up that first suicide note, there was a buzz in my head and a voice that said, "Don't read it. Be able to state that you had not read this note. It is a genuine suicide note." And John Stuart Mill's voice said to me, "The contrast with *genuine* suicide notes is *simulated* suicide notes. You must obtain simulated suicide notes from nonsuicidal people." In the next several days I reproduced a couple hundred suicide notes—and did not read them.

But in the coroner's office that first day, figuratively speaking, Gengerelli came to my side, reminded me of the method of difference—and handed me a career. You don't gain much more at a university than that.

With the thought that two heads might be better than one, within a short time I called a former fellow VA-trainee, Norman Farberow, who had done his dissertation on suicidal patients using my Make-A-Picture-Story (MAPS; Shneidman, 1950, 1952) test. Together we obtained suicide notes from matched male nonsuicidal people at labor unions and fraternal groups. Then both the genuine and simulated notes were typed by a third party, and Norman and I began to analyze them, "blind" as to the identity or status of each of the note-writers. If I had taken only genuine notes, we would have found what we were looking for, what was *au courant*—probably hostility toward the father—and it would have been over. Someone has said that on that first day in the coroner's vaults a scientific suicidology was born. I had used the method of difference in a real experiment in a natural setting in the real world on a topic that really mattered.

People at the university seem not to be impressed by publications or committee service or teaching skills, but they are impressed by money. In 1956, Norman and I published a five-page article in *Public Health Reports*. There was an unexpected telephone call from Bethesda, Maryland—where I later went to head the national program in suicide prevention, and where I founded the American Association of Suicidology in 1968—suggesting that we apply for a small grant. Within months we had an NIMH grant for five thousand dollars. What is more impressive is that within a few years of that we received a grant that extended over several years and amounted to $1.6 million. Robert Litman, who had joined us as chief psychiatrist, looked at the award and suggested that it be rounded to the nearest million. That NIMH grant supported the Los Angeles Suicide Prevention Center, a pioneer enterprise that had research, training and clinical segments. Unremittingly, Norman, Robert, and I have been professionally suicidal ever since. For me, my commitment to the study of suicide dates from that fulcrum morning in the coroner's vaults when I was guided by the spirit of John Stuart Mill.

Franklin Fearing: The Multidimensionality of Causation

Franklin Fearing was a marvelous man and a wonderful professor. Of course, I did not have the kind of relationship with Professor Fearing that I had with Gengerelli. It just couldn't be achieved. Fearing was a large man. He was called Buddha, but not to his face. In the 1930s at UCLA, he taught a very popular course on psychology and the social sciences. The textbook—by

J. F. Brown (1947) of the Menninger Foundation—was *Psychology and the Social Order*, a book calculated to pop open the eyes of any youthful reader. It was an amalgam of the enthusiasms of the 1930s, of Kurt Lewin and his topological psychology, of Karl Marx, and of Sigmund Freud. It is painfully out of date today, but at that time it was the most exciting book I had read in psychology before I was overwhelmed by Murray's (1938) *Explorations in Personality*—which is still marvelously applicable today.

What Fearing taught me was there was multidimensionality to human life. In his course on physiological psychology I learned that whatever the mind is, it functions within a living brain. No brain, no mind. But although understanding the brain and its physiology was a marvelous thing for its own sake, it did not in itself teach one about the workings of the mind.

But there is more than one requirement. For *cogito*, you have to have a mind within a brain, and a brain within a body that supports and feeds that brain, and that body, with its own history, walking in a culture. Think of walking through a large central square in a culturally-rich, old European city, and in that square there is the cathedral with its mores, the university with its library, the courts with its laws, the Palace of Justice, the state opera, the national theater, the newspaper building, and the hall of records with family genealogies—all the institutions which shape and color who a local citizen is, and all the beliefs, values, enthusiasms, sentiments, prejudices that he embodies.

This concept helps us understand suicide: No one commits suicide without a mind and a living brain and a body existing in a complex culture that has taught them the mores and folkways of their time and that defines the threshold at which a person finds their psychological pain intolerable.

As I say, Fearing indirectly taught me the multidimensionality of suicide. As a psychologist I leave it to others to speak their own points of view. In my view, there are three major approaches to understanding one particular case of suicide and the topic itself. These are the genetical and biological approaches, the sociological approach embracing demography, epidemiology and statistics (including the indispensable insights of Durkheim and Morselli), and the psychological approach, where I believe the most relevant action is, specifically in the drama in the mind.

Edgar Lazier: The Importance of Taxonomy

Lazier was professor of zoology and dean of Letters, Arts and Science. His undergraduate zoology lectures were given to a class of 300 students. I am not sure that I ever spoke to him personally. Beyond the earthworm and the frog in the lab sessions, what I learned of signal importance was about the eighteenth century Swedish naturalist, Carols Linnaeus, and the way he has imposed order on all the living world. What an intellectual coup! There were two kingdoms, plants and animals, and every living animal could be placed in one of 16 animal phyla, and then classified precisely. The schoolboy's mnemonic device was "King Phillip, come out for God's sake," namely kingdom, phylum, class, order, family, genus, and species. There is not a living creature that is not classifiable within this system. You learn very quickly that a flying squirrel is not a bird and that a whale is not a fish, and there is no creature you can discover who does not have its ordered place in Linnaeus' (and Nature's) taxonomy. That power of a taxonomic system was enormously impressive to me. I realized that the taxonomist had great intellectual authority. That is, he ordered the world for others and established the outline and vocabulary in terms of which others had to think. The omnipotent power of a comprehensive taxonomy flooded my adolescent mind.

I now recognize that Henry Murray's grand ambition was to create a taxonomy of the *psychological* aspects of human life. His efforts served as a cautionary for me and I was always thereafter somewhat cautious about grandiose classifications of primarily *mental* phenomena. For me, the primary example of this error was Kraepelin's taxonomy that, alas, has come to dominate contemporary American psychiatry.

The other major taxonomy that floated through my head in those early years was the periodic table of Dimitri Mendeleyev, the nineteenth century Russian chemist. Mendeleyev arranged the basic chemical elements in a periodic table according to their atomic weights. In those days there were 92 elements that encompassed the inorganic and organic world. In my head there was the aspiration of bringing better order to other dimensions of the universe, the psychological dimension, to be specific.

As I say, about that time I read Emil Kraepelin's seminal book, *Psychiatry*, first published in 1883, and revised numerous times to this date. Kraepelin tried to do for psychiatry and the human mind what Mendeleyev had done for chemistry, and what Linnaeus had done for living things. It was apparent to me—a feeling which I hold to this day—that Kraepelin's taxonomy did not have the same epistemological status as Mendeleyev's or Linnaeus's. A phobia or obsession does not have the same reality status as an opossum or a hunk of gold. Mental syndromes are not as "real" as animals or elements. Regrettably, Kraepelin's classification became the official classification of American psychiatry and of the *Diagnostic and Statistical Manual of Mental Disorders* (DSM; American Psychiatric Association, 1994).

Methodologically, they confused Kraepelin with Linnaeus and Mendeleyev. I believe that in the DSM there is too much specious accuracy built on a false epistemology. The categories simply do not have the same veridicality as those of biological phyla or chemical elements. To build a profession on this base is to put a city of skyscrapers on sandy soil. Billions of dollars rest on this grandiose intellectual endeavor: the drug industry, third-party payments, HMOs, and most of academic psychiatry and abnormal psychology. Nowadays, one cannot function in a psychiatric residency or in a clinical psychology training program without memorizing the DSM. I see it as warmed-over Kraepelin. That sounds like a recipe for Sunday breakfast. It certainly has been a recipe for vast economic success.

My being peripheral, as I think I am, has inured me. It saved me from the mainstream of erroneous thinking. It gave me the freedom to think original thoughts in an original vocabulary. I have this mild iconoclastic view of the prevailing contemporary nosology of the human mind. And it led me to different and I believe refreshing views of suicide.

When I entered (and labeled) suicidology, there were four main categories: attempted suicide, threatened suicide, committed suicide, and nonsuicidal. Later, when I worked on the wards of the Los Angeles County Hospital and at our own Suicide Prevention Center, it was apparent to me that attempts at suicide ranged in their possible lethality from no lethality to very high lethality, and that the four categories could be more obfuscatory than clarifying. I came to eschew those four categories and began, instead, to use ratings of lethality and ratings of perturbation of each person. I came to think of intentioned, unintentional, and subintentioned deaths.

And, of course, every living sentient person could be rated, say from 1 to 9, for perturbation and separately for lethality. I believe, for example, the currently-touted biochemical markers of "suicide" can be more accurately understood as reflections of heightened general perturbation within the psychosomatic living system.

At rock bottom, no discipline can be more rigorous than its subject matter will allow. We err to pretend it is otherwise, such as the attempts of psychiatry and psychology to emulate physics and chemistry. In all scientific endeavors, there is always a trade-off between precision and relevance, and we should be very wary of losing relevance for specious accuracy (even if it brings kudos and money).

Knight Dunlap: The Iconoclastic Approach

This is the most painful segment of retrospective for me; indeed, it is the only painful segment. Knight Dunlap, who was chairman of the department of psychology at UCLA in the 1930s, didn't like me, and I feared him. But there were also positive things about him that I borrowed. His love for the academic life was palpable. I have had that same love. The university has been my home; it is where I belong.

Dunlap's buddy at Johns Hopkins had been John Watson. Watson's enormously influential, mindless, scientific view of psychology as the study of only observable behavior shifted American psychology (and UCLA's department), which would be like flicking a switch to change William James's embracing view of mind, brain, and behavior to an ungenerous view of a baby as a robot. But one thing I liked about Dunlap's texts was that each had a glossary; many of the words were built with prefixes and suffixes. There was also a discernable negativity, almost perversity, about his ideas. Nonetheless, there was a certain elegance to his writing, and he had a penchant for neologisms. I learned all these aspects of style from the nuances of his books. His pleasure with language was memorable.

My own career is in part marked, pockmarked if you will, by a whole string of serious neologisms. I made up the word "suicidology," which is now in the *Oxford English Dictionary*. I coined words and phrases like "psychological autopsy," "subintentioned death," "postvention," and "post-self." "Psychache" is my current favorite. It is meant to describe the psychological essence of suicide. Psychache is not an earache, not a toothache, and not a headache. It is a pain or perturbation in the mind. When it occurs, its introspective reality is undeniable, and usually identified by the common names of the negative emotions such as shame, guilt, loneliness, grief, abandonment, helplessness, hopelessness, and so on. There is an enormous amount of psychache in the world in the absence of suicide, but I believe that for all practical purposes there is no suicide without introspectively-felt unbearable psychache.

I think that indirectly I got the freedom to challenge established language from Dunlap. What troubled me about him was the anti-Semitic menace that I felt from him.

I sought for wisdom and comfort elsewhere. In the late 1930s I discovered a newly published book—unheard of at UCLA and probably taboo—Henry Murray's (1938) *Explorations in Personality,* which changed my life and showed me what psychology, that glorious discipline, ought to be.

Somehow my conflict with Dunlap and his junior partner Roy Dorcus reflected the larger issues of proactivism and acquiescence in my life. Again, a book played an important role. Joyce's *A Portrait of the Artist as a Young Man* also made a profound impression on me. It is written in Joyce's early and completely accessible style and presents his life's core dilemmas in an unforgettable way: to be safe or free, at home or in exile, to belong to the Other or to the Self. These basic choices were put in a searing and electric way. Joyce's great book articulated what I wanted to know.

To the extent that I have been negative in my life, I was critical *within* my home, religion, workplace, profession, university, and country. I never felt independent enough to say, as Joyce did, *non servium*. I certainly wanted to have a great amount of independence, but I was not willing—nor did I see the need—to dwell apart or to go into geographic or intellectual exile, although I am currently willing to function at the margin if I feel my ideas are sound enough. I am happy to note that apparently I do not have the passion for truly radical intellectual destruction that is propaedeutic to asserting a totally new view—although sometimes I deeply wish that I had.

George Shelton Hubbell: The Interrelationship of Art and Science

George Shelton Hubbell was a professor of English at UCLA. As a sophomore, I had the privilege of taking his course on American Literature. I think I must have sat in his class with my jaw agape. On occasion, I felt almost overcome with intellectual joy. Along with Poe, Hawthorne, Emerson, Whitman, and Dickinson, he featured Melville.

Later, I was reintroduced to Melville, who has practically dominated my adult life. In 1991, the centenary of Melville's death, my eldest son David—who is a double UCLA alumnus, literature and medicine—and I gave our Melville collection of about 160 volumes, many of them first editions, to UCLA. I started collecting Melville as an undergraduate. My very first purchase was a first edition copy of *Moby Dick*. Henry Murray gave me the even rarer three-volume *The Whale,* also published in 1851. All of these books are now comfortably berthed in the Special Collections unit of the UCLA University Research Library.

Hubbell read Melville to the class. I had never heard language like that before. Melville's language is unlike any other. What Melville teaches, among many other things, is the complexity of the human personality. He seems to focus especially on the pivotal concept of ambivalence. Melville writes of ambiguities, dualities, duplicities, false appearances, confidences and scams, complexities, "the little lower layer" of personality. In 1851—six years before Freud was born—Melville comfortably used the word "unconscious" in its contemporary meaning.

George Shelton Hubbell helped to move me from the science of psychology to the more embracing science *and* art of psychology. The world's greatest psychologists are not Wundt or Titchener or Skinner but Melville and Dostoevsky.

MY ASSESSMENT YEARS, 1946–1951

The postwar Veterans Administration (VA) program to train clinical psychologists was the single greatest influence on American clinical psychology in the second half of the twentieth century. The VA program shifted the basic paradigm for clinical psychology from Binet to Freud. Psychologists were not only permitted to do psychotherapy with veterans, they were trained to do so. One of the textbooks in my VA training period, 1946–1948, was Otto Fenichel's (1945) *Psychoanalitic Theory of Neurosis*. I also read Fromm-Reichman, Sechahaye, and Rosen. At the VA hospitals and clinics where I interned I had psychoanalytic supervisors. And on the assessment side, the big guns were the Rorschach technique and Murray's (1935) *Thematic Apperception Test* (TAT), both of which derived their intellectual permissiveness from the basic notion of unconscious processes. (There was, of course, the MMPI, which had one foot in Midwestern empiricism and one foot in Kraepelin's nineteenth-century psychiatric typology.) The psychologist's report was more often a paragraph or two of prose (however strangled) rather than quotients and percentiles. Psychologists, by the hundreds, practiced the art and science of therapy. The changing structure of the mother organization, the APA, reflected this sea change.

The most influential director of the VA program was the youthful, gifted James Grier Miller, MD, PhD, whose doctoral dissertation (1942; at age 21) was *Unconsciousness*. (I know, from correspondence, that Henry Murray was offered that post, but declined.) One of Miller's successors was Harold Hildreth, who, after he moved to NIMH, became my personal guardian angel and the NIMH "patron" of the Los Angeles Suicide Prevention Center. (After Hal prematurely died, I went to the NIMH.) I got my PhD under the GI Bill at the University of Southern California, in a hurry, in 1948, and moved to the staff of the Brentwood (West Los Angeles) VA Hospital, where I worked and worried mostly with acutely schizophrenic veterans. My ambition was to crack that nut. (Schizophrenia, whatever it is, remains a tough nut to crack.)

In those days, the honest-to-goodness clinician I got to know best, and who influenced me the most, was that sweet and magical Viennese refugee, Bruno Klopfer, a wizard of ink blots.

A few words about Bruno: Klopfer was not at UCLA when I was there as an undergraduate, but he was there after the war, and I knew him when I was a VA trainee in the 1940s. He was hired by the UCLA psychology department because they wanted a clinical program and they needed a clinician. He was never made to feel welcome by the department and he was treated rather shabbily. I revered him and he liked me.

The Rorschach technique, Bruno's specialty, is a magnificent instrument if used as Herman Rorschach intended it to be. The insight that Rorschach, a young physician who died at age 32, had was that each of us has an idiosyncratic perceptual style. You come into any new situation and you "case the joint," you look it over. You do this every moment of your life. Some people focus on the whole scene and some see parts, and some are taken with tiny details; some people see the figurative color of the scene; some see its black-and-white architecture. But there is a certain furtive, vigilant, and survival-oriented aspect to all perception. Inasmuch as each individual perceives and misperceives the world through his brain, his responses to a set of amorphous ink blots furnish us with a paradigmatic template of his modal perceptual style. It is not a trivial idea.

One important lesson I learned from Bruno was that while it is rather easy for any tyro to see pathology in the Rorschach record, it takes a skilled psychologist to see the assets and the strengths and coping mechanisms. Bruno taught me that in writing up a report I should look at various aspects of psychological functioning, the stimulus, the stressor, the emotion, the cognitive state, the perceptual state, common actions, interpersonal patterns, and consistencies in lifestyle. Indirectly this led me some years later to posit the 10 commonalities of suicide. In the 1940s and 1950s I was keenly interested in projective techniques. I was especially interested in Henry Murray's (1935) TAT. I developed my own MAPS test (Shneidman, 1950, 1952).

In the 1950s I was associate executive editor of *The Journal of Projective Techniques* which mutated (especially after it began publishing articles on the MMPI) into the *Journal of Personality Assessment*. I remember sitting around a table in a screen-enclosed veranda in Bruno's Pasadena home, with Bruno and Walther Joel and Bert Forer, discussing the next issue of the journal. Picture-thematic assessment techniques, the TAT, and van Lennep's (1930/1948) *Four Picture Test*, from the first, had a special appeal for me. They had to do with stories, narratives, plots, thema, wishes, fears, obsessions, emphases, secrets, significant dyads, the threads of life. They overtly combined literature and psychology. For me, the premier psychological technique was the TAT. I believe that it is not possible for a person to tell stories to a series of somewhat ambiguous, complicated pictures without betraying or mirroring or explicating some of his own basic intra- and interpersonal complexes and orientations. To quote from the TAT *Manual* (Murray, 1943): "The fact that stories . . . reveal significant components of personality is dependent on . . . the tendency of people to interpret an ambiguous human situation in conformity with their past experiences and present wants, and the tendency of those who write stories to do likewise: draw on the fund of their experiences and express their sentiments and needs, whether conscious or unconscious. (p.1)" During this period, for a while, I was editor of the *TAT Newsletter*, and I was especially pleased to be associated (in my own mind at least) with the eighteenth-century literary tradition of Addison and Steele and their newsletters *The TATler* (1709–1711) and *The SpecTATor* (1711–1712).

One day while administering the TAT, the idea occurred to me to separate the figures and the backgrounds. By the end of that day I had developed the MAPS test (Shneidman, 1950, 1952). There were 21 backgrounds—living room, street scene, bedroom, bridge, cave, cemetery, etc.—and 67 figures—male, female, children, animals, etc. The subject's task is to take one or more of the figures, put them on a background as they might be in real life, and tell a story regarding the situation they have created. I felt the MAPS test was the TAT plus the objective indicia of which figures had been placed on which backgrounds. The Figure Location Sheet, by itself, contains a good deal of assessment information. I wrote my PhD dissertation (1948) on *Schizophrenia and the MAPS Test*. Three years later, in 1951, with Walther Joel and Kenneth Little, I edited *Thematic Test Analysis*, about the TAT and the MAPS test. For me, the principal outcome of that whole enterprise was the Foreword by Henry A. Murray who wrote, "Surely this book is an original . . ." (Shneidman, 1951, p. ix). My subsequently rich relationship with him was the highlight of my intellectual life. With the MAPS test, I thought that I was launched into the field of projective assessment as a life career, and that is what consumed me for a few years until the day I "discovered" the research potential in the topic of suicide—or, more accurately, suicide discovered me. But the assessment thread is deep within me and has guided my attempts to understand human self-destruction over the past half century. I still view a suicide note as an individual's response to TAT card No. 16.

In 1961 (as research associate) and again in 1969 (as visiting professor) I sat at Henry Murray's table at the Harvard Psychological Clinic. I had the head-turning opportunity to interact with the stars of the Social Relations and Psychology firmament: Gordon Allport, Jerome Bruner, Erik Erikson, Talcott Parsons, I. A. Richards, B. F. Skinner, and Robert White. It was as though I were in the epicenter of personality theorizing and personality comprehension. I felt that I had died, gone to intellectual heaven, and had safely emerged with a born-again consciousness, as a new and improved psychologist.

In the past few years, I have gone back to assessment testing. I am obsessed with the challenge to objectify, scientize, metricize, and put numbers around *psychache*. Just as there are measures of physical pain, I wonder: Why can't there be measures of psychological pain—the psychache that is central to suicide? Not unexpectedly, I turned to my old favorite, the picture-thematic format, and developed the *Psychological Pain Assessment Scale* (Shneidman, 1999) that attempts to rate an individual's perception of psychological pain by his or her reactions to a set of a half dozen pictures, and then relate those ratings to previous suicidal history, if any. So, toward the end of my life, I return to some of my earlier efforts.

Over the past 65 years, since those seminal days at UCLA, I have become a suicidologist. That is what I am today, formed in no insignificant part, by my university instructors and by my experiences in assessment psychology.

Time for a summary of my career: Six books (about suicide and death); eight edited books (about thematic techniques, about Henry Murray, and about self-destruction). I started, and for 11 years, was editor of the quarterly journal *Suicide and Life-Threatening Behavior*, which is the official journal of the American Association of Suicidology. Along the way, in my turn, I was president of the Division of Clinical Psychology (Div. 12); the Division of Psychologists in Public Service (Div. 18); of the Society for Protective Techniques; and of the American Association of Suicidology. I have had my share of awards, and I jest that if I get any more plaques I am in danger of contracting leukemia.

Two references can be cited that contain significant contents of my life and work: C. Eugene Walker (Ed.), *The History of Clinical Psychology in Autobiography* (Shneidman, 1991). Walker's book contains my autobiographical chapter, "A Life in Death: Notes of a Committed Suicidologist"; and Antoon Leenars (Ed.), *Lives and Deaths: Selections from the Works of Edwin S. Shneidman* (Leenars, 1999), which contains reprints of 37 of my previously published articles and chapters, as well as a complete bibliography of my works through the year 2000.

To repeat: I feel lucky to have been at UCLA in my teens and to have absorbed some concepts and orientations that have nourished the intellectual aspects of my subsequent life. The five worthies at UCLA were the sub-mentors of my life. They prepared me for Henry Murray some 20 years later, who gave me a different voice by enriching the texture of my perceptions and, in a direct way, the texture of my personality, and the texture of my life.

NOW

It is 2004 and I am 86. I am unhappily widowed (after 56 beatific years of marriage to my wife Jeanne), I have four sons who love me, six radiant grandchildren, a health care worker who keeps me alive, and a cadre of peerless friends. I recently published a book centering around the psychological autopsy of the suicide of a 33-year-old physician-lawyer, with multiple interviews of family members and several consultations with experts—a kind of *Rashomon*. I love enigmas that remain so—like when and how I will die. To the extent that I am invested in my post-self—quite a bit I would say—I am grateful for this opportunity to pen these words about myself and to speak, eventually *ex cathedra*, from my urn of ashes.

REFERENCES

American Psychiatric Association. (1994). *Diagnostic and statistical manual of mental disorders* (4th ed.). Washington, DC: Author.

Brown, J. F. (1947). *Psychology and the social order*. New York: McGraw-Hill.

Descartes, R. (1956). Discourse on method (L. J. LaFleur, Trans.). Indianapolis: Bobbs-Merrill.

Dublin, L. I. (1930). *The money value of a man*. New York: Ronald Press.

Fenichel, O. (1945). *Psychoanalytic theory of neurosis*. New York: W. W. Norton.

Hathaway, S. R., & McKinley, J. C. (1943). *The Minnesota Multiphasic Personality Inventory*. Minneapolis: University of Minnesota Press.

Kraepelin, E. (1883/1902). *Textbook of psychiatry for students and physicians: Abstracted and adapted from the 6th German edition of the Lehrbuch der Psychiatrie*. New York: Macmillan. (Original work published 1883).

Leenars, A. (Ed.). (1999). *Lives and deaths: Selections from the works of Edwin S. Shneidman*. Philadelphia: Brunner/Mazel.

Miller, J. G. (1942). *Unconsciousness*. Oxford, England: Nijhoff.

Murray, H. A. (1935). *Thematic Apperception Test manual*. Cambridge, MA: Harvard Corporation.

Murray, H. A. (1938). *Explorations in personality*. New York: Oxford University Press.

Murray, H. A. (1943). *Thematic Apperception Test manual* (2nd ed.). Cambridge, MA: Harvard University Press.

Shneidman, E. S. (1948). Schizophrenia and the MAPS test. *Genetic Psychology Monographs, 38*, 145–223.

Shneidman, E. S. (1950). *The Make-A-Picture Story (MAPS) test*. New York: Psychological Corporation.

Shneidman, E. S. (Ed.). (1951). *Thematic test analysis*. New York: Grune & Stratton.

Shneidman, E. S. (1952). Manual for the MAPS test. *Projective Techniques Monograph, I* (Whole No. 2), 1–92.

Shneidman, E. S. (1963). Orientations toward death. In R. White (Ed.), *The study of lives* (pp. 200–227). New York: Atherton Press.

Shneidman, E. S. (1968). The deaths of Herman Melville. In H. P. Vincent (Ed.), *Melville and Hawthorne in the Berkshires* (pp. 118–144). Kent, OH: Kent State University Press.

Shneidman, E. S. (1973). *Deaths of man*. New York: Quadrangle/New York Times.

Shneidman, E. S. (1980). *Voices of death*. New York: Harper & Row.

Shneidman, E. S. (1985). *Definition of suicide*. New York: Wiley.

Shneidman, E. S. (1991). A life in death: Notes of a committed suicidologist. In C. E. Walker (Ed.), *The history of clinical psychology in autobiography* (pp. 225–292). Pacific Grove, CA: Brooks/Cole.

Shneidman, E. S. (1996). *The suicidal mind*. New York: Oxford University Press.

Shneidman, E. S. (1999). *The Psychological Pain Assessment Scale: Toward operationalizing psychache—A preliminary report*. Unpublished manuscript.

Shneidman, E. S. (2002). *Comprehending suicide: Landmarks in suicidology*. Washington, DC: American Psychological Association.

Shneidman, E. S. (2004). *Autopsy of a suicidal mind*. New York: Oxford University Press.

Shneidman, E. S., & Farberow, N. L. (1956). Clues to suicide. *Public Health Reports, 71*, 109–114.

van Lennep, D. J. (1948). *Four Picture Test*. Oxford, England: Nijhoff. (Original work published 1930.)

Wechsler, D. (1955). *Manual for the Wechsler Adult Intelligence Scale*. New York: Psychological Corporation.

SELECTED BIBLIOGRAPHY OF AUTHOR'S WORKS

Shneidman, E. S. (1943). An experimental study of the appraisal interview. *Journal of Applied Psychology, 27*, 186–205.

Shneidman, E. S. (1948). Schizophrenia and the MAPS Test. *Genetic Psychology Monographs, 38*, 145–223.

Shneidman, E. S. (1951). *Thematic test analysis*. New York: Grune & Stratton.

Shneidman, E. S. (1960). Psych-logic: A personality approach to patterns of thinking. In J. Kagan & G. Lesser (Eds.), *Current issues in thematic apperceptive fantasy*. Springfield: C. C. Thomas.

Shneidman, E. S. (1962). Projections on a triptych; or a hagiology for our time. *Journal of Projective Techniques, 26*, 379–387.

Shneidman, E. S. (1963a). The logic of politics. In M. May & L. Arons (Eds.), *Television and human behavior*. New York: Appleton.

Shneidman, E. S. (1963b). Orientations toward death. In R. White (Ed.), *The study of lives* (pp. 200–227). New York: Atherton Press.

Shneidman, E. S. (1965). Projective techniques. In B. Wolman (Ed.), *Handbook of clinical psychology*. New York: McGraw-Hill.

Shneidman, E. S. (1967). (Ed.). *Essays in self-destruction*. New York: Science House.

Shneidman, E. S. (1968). The deaths of Herman Melville. In H. Vincent (Ed.), *Melville and Hawthorne in the Berkshires* (pp. 118–144). Kent, OH: Kent State University Press.

Shneidman, E. S. (1971). Perturbation and lethality as precursors of suicide in a gifted group. *Life-Threatening Behavior, 1*, 23–45.

Shneidman, E. S. (1973a). *Deaths of man.* New York: Quadrangle/New York Times.

Shneidman, E. S. (1973b). Suicide. *Encyclopaedia Britannica.* Chicago: Benton.

Shneidman, E. S. (1973c). Suicide notes reconsidered. *Psychiatry, 16,* 379–395.

Shneidman, E. S. (1976a). (Ed.). *Death: Current perspectives.* Palo Alto: Mayfield.

Shneidman, E. S. (1976b). (Ed.). *Suicidology: Contemporary developments.* New York: Grune & Stratton.

Shneidman, E. S. (1977). The psychological autopsy. In L. Gottschalk (Ed.), *Guide to the investigation and reporting of drug abuse deaths.* Washington, DC: Government Printing Office.

Shneidman, E. S. (1980). *Voices of death.* New York: Harper & Row.

Shneidman, E. S. (1981). (Ed.). *Endeavors in psychology: Selections from the personology of Henry A. Murray.* New York: Harper & Row.

Shneidman, E. S. (1984). Personality and success among a selected group of lawyers. *Journal of Personality Assessment, 48,* 609–616.

Shneidman, E. S. (1985). *Definition of suicide.* New York: John Wiley.

Shneidman, E. S. (1986). MAPS of the Harvard Yard. *Journal of Personality Assessment, 50,* 435–447.

Shneidman, E. S. (1989). The Indian summer of life: A preliminary study of septuagenerians. *American Psychologist, 44,* 684–694.

Shneidman, E. S. (1991). A life in death: Notes of a committed suicidologist. In C. E. Walker (Ed.), *The history of clinical psychology in autobiography* (pp. 225–292). Pacific Grove, CA: Brooks/Cole.

Shneidman, E. S. (1993). Suicide as psychache. *Journal of Nervous and Mental Disease, 181,* 147–149.

Shneidman, E. S. (1996). *The suicidal mind.* New York: Oxford University Press

Shneidman, E. S. (1998). Suicide on my mind; Britannica on my table. *American Scholar, 67,* 93–104.

Shneidman, E. S. (2002). *Comprehending suicide.* Washington, DC: American Psychological Association.

Shneidman, E. S. (2004). *Autopsy of a suicidal mind.* New York: Oxford.

Edwin (age 37) and wife Jeanne (age 34) at the dedication of the Suicide Prevention Center, Los Angeles, 1955

Henry A. Murray (age 70), Cambridge, MA, 1963. Photograph by Bachrach

Edwin (age 51) and Henry A. Murray (age 76) at Murray's home in Cambridge, Massachusetts, 1969

Make-A-Picture-Story (MAPS) test materials, 1949

Edwin (age 76) in Los Angeles, 1994. Photograph by Devra Breslow

CHAPTER 14

Chance and Choice:
Change and Continuity

That's Life

Norman D. Sundberg
University of Oregon

Writing now in my 80's, I find myself mentally reviewing many scenes in my life: reciting in a one-room country school, marching on a hot blacktop, flying alone as a low line of distant clouds transform into the great snowy Alps, saying "oui" with other couples in a civil ceremony in Paris, holding new baby boys in wonder, driving west through the magnificent Columbia Gorge, dealing with a disturbed student in an Abnormal class, interviewing parents of an autistic child, seeing a ragged man eat the inside of a banana peeling he picked off the street in Delhi, lecturing about the Rorschach in Karachi, and typing and pecking on old typewriters and calculators—and now a computer. These and many other images race randomly across my awareness as I start writing this autobiography. Chance and choice, change and continuity—how to encapsulate such a journey of memories?

EARLY CHANGES AND CHOICES:
GROWING UP IN NEBRASKA

In this journey of memories, I must start with one for which I have no memory: I was born on September 15, 1922, in an old house serving as a hospital in Aurora, Nebraska. My parents, Cedric and Nellie Sundberg, and my brother, Donald, two years older, lived on a farm nine miles northeast of Aurora, where I stayed the first 15 years of my life. All four of my grand-parents were immigrants from Sweden in the 1870s and 1880s. Among my grandparents, I knew best my maternal grandmother, Mary Larson Akerson, with whom we lived in Aurora for several years. At age 12 she had arrived in Chicago shortly after the Great Fire of October 1871—supposedly started when Mrs. O'Leary's cow kicked over a lantern in a barn. Grandma Akerson and her family settled on a farm near Stromsburg, Nebraska, where they lived in a sod house with Indians still around. Grandma never went beyond four grades in a school in Sweden. She was a small, kindly lady, and knowing her helped me become interested in other times and places. I wish now that I had learned much more of her life story.

I remember my father bouncing me on his knee to the Swedish tune "Rida, Rida, Ranka" (ride-o, ride-o, upon a horse astride-o). I remember sitting in my mother's lap on a warm summer evening on the porch while she read *Swiss Family Robinson* to me. Mom and Dad had finished eight grades at a one-room country school, and then, as was common with farm families at that time, they were expected to work, not to get further education. Like them, Don and I went to a one-room country school, walking a half mile sometimes through snowdrifts, sometimes stopping to catch frogs in the creek in the spring. (Figure 1 shows me with my brother in bright winter sunshine.) The number of students during my eight grades ranged from 14 to 23, and there were only 14 books in the school's library. At school I wasn't very good at baseball, but I did well in studies thanks to an excellent high school graduate who was our teacher, Ellen Andersen Friesen, with whom I still exchange letters.

My most traumatic memory is from May 1, 1930, when I was seven years old. That morning I hung lilac-filled May baskets on my parents' chairs before school. Mid-morning the teacher answered a knock at the door and called my brother and me to come outside. Our uncle took us home, telling us on the way that our father had died. He had shot himself in the barn. Was it accident or suicide? There was no evidence of intention to commit suicide, but the insurance company decided it was suicide, thereby saving money by cutting the benefit payment in half. The mystery of his death still haunts. When I was young, I used to think irrationally that I would die at age 36 too. Dad's death must have entered into my decision to become a psychologist, hoping for help in my search for the meaning of life and death. My mother was a great support in those difficult times after his death, but she had bad dreams. She would wake up hearing him call her. Our dog howled for many nights thereafter. Mom lived until 1982 and died at age 89.

The 1930s also brought the Great Depression and terrible droughts and dust storms to the Great Plains. We were poor, but somehow held on to the farm, and with income from a renter's help, we survived. In those times before the current monocultural farming, farms were much more independent and self-sufficient. We had chickens, pigs, cows, and a garden. Horses provided the power for planting and harvesting the corn and wheat. We didn't have electricity, but we did have a party-line telephone. Since everybody nearby was in the same situation, we didn't feel especially poor.

Soon after I started high school, Mother, Don, and I moved to Aurora (population 2,500) to live with Grandma Akerson. After high school, Don got a job in Lincoln working for a lumber company and ultimately after military service became an engineer—a "dam engineer" as he liked to joke. Though I am taller, he still calls me "little brother." At Aurora High School my 1940 graduating class had only 38 students. In a small school, as Roger Barker has shown in his research in Kansas, students are likely to have many opportunities and pressures to participate in activities. I was president of the drama club and student editor of the annual, and I helped organize cheering for football games. I took typing, shorthand, and bookkeeping classes expecting that they would help me find work when I graduated. My first paid job in Aurora was working for 15 cents an hour transplanting tomato plants in a greenhouse. That was boring! Working with people was more interesting. I sold shoes and other things at Penney's and took tickets and ushered at the one theater in Aurora, where I saw *Gone with the Wind* five times. As the valedictorian at my high school graduation, I gave a commencement speech entitled "The American Way," which was printed on the front page of the weekly newspaper—my first publication!

Having placed second on the statewide Regents examinations, I received a scholarship to the University of Nebraska. There, to support myself, I also took a job for $20 a month under the NYA, the National Youth Authority, one of the many creations of the Roosevelt era that provided useful work for students during the Depression. First, I worked in chemistry supplies, then in psychology. One summer I helped to build a defense plant near Aurora for the grand sum of 60 cents an hour. To work there, I had to join the Hod Carriers Union, but I haven't kept up my membership!

Why psychology? Why that important choice? One part of the answer is my predisposition to seek understanding of that important death early in my life. Also an interest in observing and describing people developed early. While on the farm we went to town on Saturdays to buy a week's provisions. There, waiting with my brother or cousin in a car parked on the town square, we chatted about people passing by, imagining what they were doing or saying. I remember reading Dale Carnegie's book, *How to Win Friends and Influence People*, and most of the tales and poems of that master of the mysteries of the human mind, Edgar Allan Poe. An important influence toward psychology was counseling. Coming to UN in Lincoln being unsure of what major to choose, I went to the University counseling center. On the Kuder I was high on artistic and social service interests, both reflected in subsequent years. (Service values had been encouraged during my early Methodist church attendance.) With results of the Strong Vocational Interest Blank, too, we talked about various possibilities, psychology being one of them. Strangely, freshmen were not allowed to take psychology courses, but the next year, reinforcement came when I was awarded the Psi Chi prize for the highest grades as a sophomore. The prize was a psychology dictionary, which turned out to be very useful for a long time. (Many years later I contributed entries to *Corsini's Dictionary of Psychology*.) For my introductory psychology course, the textbook was by J. P. Guilford who, I later discovered, also had family connections in Aurora. In my personality course, the 1937 text was by Gordon Allport, who is often considered the founder of personality psychology. I liked the book very much, and later as a graduate student, on my return trip from Europe I stopped at Harvard to see Allport. He was friendly and was probably important in my admission to Harvard after receiving my master's at the University of Minnesota, though I decided not to go to Harvard.

While I was an undergraduate, Don Dysinger, then head of the UNL Psychology Department, and Charles Harsh, my advisor, hired me to administer performance tests in a research project, further extending my interest in psychology. Both seemed to take a personal interest in me, and knowing my limited finances, Dysinger occasionally hired me to do odd jobs at his house. For my minor I chose mathematics, and I also ultimately got enough credits to minor in English and German. For the mandatory courses in ROTC (Reserve Officers Training Corps), I chose Field Artillery, as did a close friend from Aurora. Along the way, Harsh suggested, "Since you'll probably go on for graduate work, choose a variety of elective courses that will enrich the rest of your life." So I felt free to take classes in art, history of architecture, music appreciation, physiology, and swimming in addition to the required courses. All of these subjects have played their parts in my later life. I've often thought of that long-range view of the field of choices when meeting with my students who are starting to make their own way in the world.

MILITARY SERVICE AND GERMANY

On December 7, 1941, at a dance in the Student Union, news about the Pearl Harbor attack quickly spread around the floor, and the session was stopped. Walking back to my room, I knew my life would be forever changed. In the army's roundabout way, I was not called into service until April 1943, and after field artillery basic training in California, our ROTC group was returned to Lincoln (to mark time, I think, until there were openings in officer training). Others were assigned to engineering classes in the Army Specialized Training Program (ASTP), but I was chosen for the ASTP German Area and Language Program (intended for military government). In the few months we were held in Lincoln, I met some lifelong friends in that program and developed considerable skill in German.

In March 1944, the ASTP in Lincoln was disbanded. My friends in the German program were sent to England to be used in the landings in France in June. Some were killed and wounded in the advance through France and Belgium, and others eventually did serve in military government in Germany. Our ROTC group was sent to Fort Sill, Oklahoma, for training in Officer Candidate School. After completing that, I was assigned to a communications course. Then I volunteered and was accepted for artillery liaison pilot training. Liaison pilots flew small two-seater planes and had minimal instrumentation. These low-flying observation posts were important but easy targets in combat. (See Figure 2 taken while in training at Rattlesnake Field in Fort Sill.) In May 1945, while I was still in flight training, the conflict with Germany ended, and then in August, Japan surrendered.

In late 1945, I was on a troop ship to France. I spent a year in the American zone of Germany moving from assignment to assignment, replacing pilots going home. In addition to some field maneuvers, I mainly flew senior officers to various places. A beautiful memory is the experience, while flying for the first time to southern Bavaria, of seeing the snow-capped Alps for the first time and flying around Germany's highest mountain, the Zugspitze. Another strong memory is flying back to my unlit grass landing strip as night fell. My life was saved by the quick thinking of my African American sergeant who ringed the little field with lights from Army trucks to show me where to land. Incidentally, the military wasn't desegregated until President Truman ordered it in 1947, and the only Whites in that battalion were officers. I got to know African Americans, as I had not been able to in predominantly White Nebraska.

An interesting experience resulted from getting a day off to attend the nearby Nuremberg trials. From the small visitor gallery I could see Goering and other Nazi officials sitting grimly on the left and the four Allied judges (British, French, Russian, and American) sitting opposite. Admiral Doenitz, who negotiated the surrender of Germany, was on the stand that day. He later served a 10-year sentence. Of the 22 on trial, 10 were hanged, and Goering committed suicide the day before his scheduled hanging. A Web site on the trial lists the IQs of the defendants as ranging from 106 to 143 with a median of 130. There is a lesson for today in how a highly educated and industrious citizenry can be led into war and horrendous acts against chosen minorities. Goering said at the trial,

> It is the leaders of the country who determine the policy, and it is always a simple matter to drag the people along, whether it is a democracy, or a fascist dictatorship, or a parliament, or a communist dictatorship. Voice or no voice, the people can always be brought to the bidding of the leaders. That is easy. All you have to do is tell them they are being attacked, and denounce the peacemakers for lack of patriotism and exposing the country to danger. It works the same in any country. (Gilbert, 1947, pp. 278–279)

Now there's a challenge for research!

Looking back on my military experience, I ask myself, "Were there lasting benefits of my army experience?" I haven't found any use for "cannoneer's hop" (the training exercises moving through different positions for shooting a howitzer), and I don't march or fly a plane any more. But I do know that those three and a half years were important in learning about people from all socio-economic levels and backgrounds. Later, "knowledge of others" became one of my interests in psychology. Also since "hurry up and wait" could be the motto of the military, I learned a lot about boredom, a topic that I researched later. Of course, travel in the army provided much important cultural learning in the U.S. and Europe. Being abroad helps one see one's home country differently and to learn about attitudes of others towards Americans. I remember one German woman telling me in a contemptuous tone that our country was a "Mischvolk" (mixed population). I'm sure she reflected Hitler's attitude that Americans were badly mixed racially. I was fortunate to survive those years. My two closest friends in grade school and high school were killed in the Pacific during World War II.

BECOMING A PSYCHOLOGIST:
MINNESOTA, OREGON, AND BEYOND

The postwar GI Bill was one of the greatest methods ever for enriching the human capital of the United States. Along with many veterans, it enabled me to continue my education. So in early 1947 I found myself in Lincoln again, finishing my undergraduate degree in psychology. I suppose I could have gone in many occupational directions after that, but psychology was firmly embedded in my mind, clinical psychology especially. I applied only to the University of Minnesota for graduate work and was admitted to the clinical program. Minnesota provided an excellent variety of courses and clinical experiences necessary to become a psychologist. The department helped me by providing appointments as a teaching assistant and then instructor. At that time, clinical students were required to take medical school courses in neuroanatomy and neuropsychiatry. My internship was at the University of. Minnesota Hospital where I was supervised by Starke Hathaway and Bill Schofield. Very importantly, I came to know them and other outstanding professors including Paul Meehl, Donald Paterson, Kenneth MacCorquodale, William Heron, and others, and I had topnotch fellow graduate students. Richard Elliott was head of the department, and I came to appreciate his dignity and broad-ranging intelligence. Later, he served as the editor for my first book.

I was Schofield's first or second PhD dissertation advisee. The research topic I chose was psychotherapists' "knowledge of others," defined as the ability to predict verbal responses of normal groups (Sundberg, 1952). To measure knowledge of others, I developed six tests. Four were composed of items asking subjects to indicate responses showing sex differences, age differences, and student preferences. I chose the items from the MMPI, the Strong and the Jurgensen tests, and based scoring on the norms or previous research results. The fifth test I constructed was for preferences of cartoon humor, and the sixth, partially originated by Hathaway, involved the implied meaning of spoken statements. Using Minnesota's famed "dustbowl empiricism," I learned a great deal about test construction while doing studies of reliability, validity, and composite scores for the six tests. On comparisons of 85 introductory psychology students with 46 psychotherapists, the therapists were significantly higher on four tests, but not on judging the cartoon preferences of students. With the freshmen and sophomore students, the composite score showed a low correlation with entrance scores and high school ranks. The psychiatrists, social workers, and psychologists taking the tests showed no significant differences among themselves except on knowledge of interests. Clinical trainees scored as well as professional staff members. I published only one part of the dissertation—the interesting test of implied meanings—in a Dutch journal after a talk I gave at Nijmegen University in the Netherlands (Sundberg, 1966). In that article I reported additional findings, suggesting that the test was related to empathic ability.

I have fond memories of the faculty at Minnesota in those times. Among many, here are a few. I remember Starke Hathaway with mustache and tousled hair at a staff case conference. Knowing only the MMPI profile and a mere introduction to the case of a murderer, he correctly interpreted: "I'd say the murder weapon must have been a blunt instrument." I never understood what MMPI clues he used. I also remember noticing once that he had come to class wearing one black shoe and one brown shoe. Later in life, as a professor, I was shocked in class one morning to look down and see I had done the same thing. I remember Paul Meehl in his Rorschach class asking us students to raise our hands to choose what the scoring should be. Just then Donald Paterson, going to his office next door, stuck in his head and said, "Science by ballot—humf!" Among many other memories, there were also patients I worked with at the U of Minnesota hospital; among them was a lobotomized nurse who had a normal IQ on the Wechsler. Another was of a young mother who had smothered her baby and was obviously psychotic and suicidal. I remember therapy cases, too, and wonder what happened to them.

Important life events occurred in those years in Minnesota (1947–52). For the summer of 1948, I was one of a small group of students who received scholarships to do research in Germany. The program was sponsored by a new organization, Student Projects for Amity among Nations (SPAN), which is still commendably sending Minnesota students to do research projects in other countries. I had two projects. Starting in the University of Marburg and going to other universities, I did interviews about student services in German universities, which I reported in my master's thesis. In addition, with the help of Marburg sociology and medical students, I translated the MMPI for the first time into German and administered it to about 120 Marburg university students. The results were a good learning experience in cross-cultural research. The German students averaged high or very high on D (Depression), Pd (Psychopathic Deviate), Ma (Hypomania), and Sc (Schizophrenia). Why? One is tempted to speculate on the personal difficulties of living in Germany during the war, and during its defeat and occupation. However, I reasoned that this was a normal German student sample, and my conclusion was that translated items were milder and therefore more easily endorsed than those in English, thus raising MMPI scores (Sundberg, 1956). Later Otfried Spreen revised my German version, which was then published by Hans Huber in Switzerland.

During the 1947–48 academic year, I met Donna Varner, a graduating senior in psychology, and we became engaged. When I went to Germany for the summer, we decided to get married in Paris. With French friends present, we first said "Oui" with a group of strangers in the first arrondissement opposite the Louvre, and then "I do" in the American Church of Paris. Altogether we spent three wonderful and educational months traveling in France, Germany, Switzerland, Italy, and England. I remember in that fall of 1948 that American planes were taking off from the airport near Frankfurt every three minutes with food and coal to keep the German population in the Soviet blockaded areas alive. In those uncertain times, the American dollar was worth much more in Europe than it is now. We traveled and lived well on $5 a day and sailed back to New York on the Queen Mary. Back in Minnesota, Donna was a great help with the statistics and typing my dissertation. Also by the time my PhD at Minnesota was finished in 1952, we had two small boys, Charlie and Greg.

As with all PhD graduates, there are major choices about what to do next. I was offered positions working at the VA in Minnesota and teaching at the universities of Iowa, Penn State, and Oregon. Heeding the advice of Horace Greeley in an earlier century, "Go west, young man," we decided to move to a place we had never been. Eugene, Oregon, was a small town then (35,000 on the 1950 census) with a small university (about 4,500), both of which have grown considerably. In the fall of 1952, I became one of six faculty members in the Department of Psychology at Oregon. I had met only Leona Tyler who had stopped in Minneapolis to interview me on her way home from a London sabbatical. The head of the department, Howard Taylor, retired within a year. Bob Leeper became head, and I was interested in his perceptual view of personality and sat in on his seminar while he was writing a book with Peter Madison from Arizona. Dick Littman was another fellow faculty member whom I got to know well, and we worked with a student on the study of a psychosexual scale (Littman, Nidorf, & Sundberg, 1961). Leona Tyler became a close family friend and with her interest in writing on individual differences and counseling, she was a natural colleague for collaboration on many projects.

The choice of Oregon proved to be a good one for my family and professional development. However, in 1952 my salary was $4,500 for the nine academic months, and I necessarily had to supplement it by teaching evenings and summers. Within a few years, Donna and I added Scott and Mark to our family. (Figure 3 shows our four sons ages 4 to 12 with Santa Claus.) Over many early years at Oregon, I taught a variety of courses such as abnormal personality, introductory clinical, and testing, as well as large introductory courses. I remember taking my classes in abnormal personality to visit the state hospital in Salem. In those days they brought patients onto a stage to tell about their problems. We also saw the rooms where they subjected patients to hydrotherapy and insulin shock therapy. I remember many students fondly, and others for difficulties. One student became unusually argumentative in class, and I had sessions in my office to explore his obvious anger and other problems. I remember another student who stopped in the middle of an exam and started crying. I talked with her about a personal problem, and let her take the exam again soon, and she did very well. In the early 1960s, Lew Goldberg, with his strong interest in personality research, came to take over some of my courses.

I also worked part time in the Counseling Center, but in 1954–55, my main job was to start a clinic and the doctoral clinical program at the University of Oregon. Previously the psychology department had given only master's degrees, except for one PhD in 1938. The second PhD was my advisee in 1955. With helpful consulting from a Portland clinical psychologist, Bob Boyd, I became director of the new University Child Guidance Center, which later was renamed the University Psychology Clinic. Starting the clinic involved establishing and maintaining community connections, something that had not been stressed in my graduate work in Minnesota, and I came to appreciate the importance of context in institution building. The location in a small community 110 miles from the medical school in Portland necessitated the use of nearby resources for clinical activities. At that time there were no PhD psychologists in private practice and only one psychiatrist in Eugene; now there are many. The prevailing clinical model then was the treatment team of a psychologist working with a medical doctor, preferably a psychiatrist, and a social worker. Before World War II, psychologists, mostly with master's degrees, primarily gave tests. In our new clinic, students were trained to be therapists as well as assessors. (Figure 4 shows me administering the Blacky story-telling test to a child.) The Clinic is still housed with the department on campus and has acquired a strong research emphasis with Don Tucker, Scott Monroe, Anne Simons, Gordon Hall, Tom Dishion, and others.

SPREADING A WIDE NET IN PERSONALITY ASSESSMENT: REVIEWS, FAKEABILITY, AND CREATIVITY

In developing the clinical program, I read widely, conducted surveys, and published reviews. Some were useful enough to be reprinted in other publications (e.g., Sundberg, 1960). One account was a spoof I gave at a meeting of the Oregon Psychological Association in 1956, called "A Completely Blind Analysis of the Case of a Veteran." Without knowing anything about the case, other than that the man was a patient in the VA hospital in Roseburg where I had been consulting, I assumed he was schizophrenic and presented what seemed like a bona fide psychological report with such phrases as "considerable inadequacy in interpersonal relations" and "his sex life has been unsatisfactory." In a study, I showed that the report-writing psychologist could go a long way with vague statements and generalizations (Sundberg, 1955). These kinds of reports are the opposite of those emphasizing life histories, which are highly individualized. I also wrote reviews of many books and tests, including a first on the Myers-Briggs. For four years (1957–60) I wrote chapters covering projective methods and psychological assessment for *Progress in Neurology and Psychiatry*. I have continued writing reviews throughout my professional career.

Such a broad search in psychology—particularly in clinical and personality psychology—was compatible not only with program-development responsibilities but also with learning experiences in Minnesota. Theoretically, I had a strong introduction to Hullian learning there as well as a bit of an introduction to psychoanalysis, and later I wrote reviews of books of relevance to those theories. In counseling and therapy, I found myself leaning most toward the ideas of Carl Rogers, although he was not highly regarded in Minnesota. The nondirective or client-centered approach with its strong emphasis on careful listening to clients and checking one's perceptions suited my style. In research, too, I like to do interviews in addition to collecting quantitative data. My appreciation for behavioral learning theory helped in recruiting Gerald Patterson, another Minnesota PhD, who had received his master's in Oregon. Jerry worked with families in the UO Clinic and went on to found the now well-known Oregon Social Learning Center (OSLC). The general psychological research climate in Eugene has been also stimulating and productive outside the university. Three major psychological research institutes emerged: OSLC, the Oregon Research Institute, Electrical Geodesics and Decision Research—all relevant to programs at the University and helpful for employing students and part-time faculty.

My search led me to apply for an NIMH year of support at the Institute of Personality Assessment and Research (IPAR, subsequently renamed the Institute of Personality and Social Research, IPSR) at UC Berkeley. In 1959, ten years after IPAR's start, the founders, Donald MacKinnon and Nevitt Sanford were still there, and I was fortunate to become acquainted with them and with Harrison Gough (whom I'd known a little at Minnesota), Richard Crutchfield, Ravenna Helson, Frank Barron, Wallace Hall, and others, and to participate in some of their extensive assessments in that delightful, former fraternity house on Piedmont Avenue. IPAR was well known for using self-report, interviews, and observation on such topics as creativity, with architects, writers, military officers, engineering students, and women mathematicians. At Berkeley I sat in on a psychology seminar given by Ted Sarbin on group interaction and became impressed with his ideas of role theory. Jack Block in the UC Psychology Department invited me to write a book for the series on personality that he was editing. IPAR invited me to stay on a second year, and my family was glad to do that.

While at Berkeley, I had an opportunity to conduct an unusual study on creativity after a call from a friend of ours, Will Martin. Will was an architect and artist in Portland, who had won the competition for designing the Pioneer Courthouse Square in Portland, a much-used downtown gathering place. On the telephone, Will asked if I would be interested in studying whether people would become more creative in going without sleep. I got in touch with Walter Klopfer in Portland, and he and Sheridan McCabe organized a team of psychology students to help around the clock. We observed, photographed, and interviewed Will, and administered the TAT and other tests to him by his easel in a bar in northeast Portland. He somehow managed to go without sleep for 88 hours, but the hypothesis did not pay off. Instead of becoming imaginative and creative, Will got more fatigued and befuddled. But he did report a strange experience, which we hadn't known before. We called the phenomenon the "snowfall illusion." Severely sleep deprived, he described seeing snow or sand moving vertically down walls and objects making them seem to be dripping down. We presented our findings at an APA meeting (Sundberg & McCabe, 1962). After it was all over, Will gave me a painting I treasure, "The Bridges of Portland," which he finished early in his long ordeal. Unfortunately, a few years later he was piloting his plane with his son in the Grand Canyon and could not get back over the rim; and they both died.

Back in Eugene in the fall of 1961, I resumed teaching and part-time clinical work, and with Leona Tyler, completed our introductory clinical book (Sundberg & Tyler, 1962). It was well received, and later with one of my doctoral students, Julian Taplin, published new editions in 1973 and 1983. (See Figure 5 for a picture of the three of us.) Recently with another ex-student, we published the fourth edition (Sundberg, Winebarger, & Taplin, 2002). Unfortunately, Leona died in 1993 and was not one of the last book's authors. For the obituary of Leona Tyler, who was the fourth woman president of APA, see Sundberg and Littman (1994).

Growing out of my IPAR experience, I wrote the book for Jack Block's series (Sundberg, 1977), broadly covering personality assessment. Like the early clinical books, this was widely used. About that time, too, colleagues and I published a chapter in the *Annual Review of Psychology* that brought out another broad theme in my psychological interests—the relation of person assessment to situations (Sundberg, Snowden, & Reynolds, 1978). In Ellensburg, Washington, and Portland, Oregon, over many years I also participated in a series of summer training programs for those seeking or having the diploma of the American Board of Professional Psychology (ABPP). (I had passed my ABPP examinations in clinical in Los Angeles in 1958, and subsequently served on the national board and received a distinguished service award in 1992.) Part of the work involved preparing psychologists for the national ABPP exams.

CROSSING CULTURES: INDIA AND ELSEWHERE

Growing up in the Midwest patchwork of immigrant settlers as well as my personal travel experiences predisposed me early to an interest in the wider world. With Leona Tyler in the mid-sixties, I entered earnestly into what became extensive studies in other cultures. She had obtained a grant from the U.S. Office of Education, entitled "Factors Affecting Career Choices of Adolescents," and during her second sabbatical, she had collected data in Enkhuizen, a Dutch town north of Amsterdam. We had worked together in planning that Dutch study, and then we gathered a group of psychology students to help carry out a parallel study in North Bend, a coastal town in Oregon. Then in 1965–66, with a Fulbright award to India and the help of Indian colleagues there, principally Pritam Rohila and Perin Mehta, we extended our research to a very different part of the world, focusing on Palwal, a small town south of New Delhi. Later in 1976, while teaching at LaTrobe University in Melbourne, Australia, I collected further comparative data with Millicent Poole. The subjects were ninth grade boys and girls (roughly 15 years old) in small towns in the different countries. The research covered a broad range of topics, such as awareness of choices (Sundberg & Tyler, 1970; Tyler, Sundberg, Rohila, & Greene, 1968), values (Sundberg, Tyler, & Rohila, 1970), family cohesiveness and autonomy (Sundberg, Sharma, Rohila, & Wodtli, 1969), originality (Chartier & Sundberg, 1969), and problem solving (Bates, Sundberg, & Tyler, 1970). In regard to family relations, clearly the American adolescents viewed themselves as more independent and free to make decisions by themselves than did the Indians, thereby reflecting the American emphasis on individualism. This finding was confirmed by interviews with Indian parents who preferred parent-arranged marriages to "love marriages." Another of the interesting findings was that, although the American and Indian adolescents differed statistically on many items, they showed much in common. Both items were on opposite sides of the 90-item values Q sort on only two items. These referred to greater Indian need for social approval, which is in line with the interdependence or collectivism often noted among Asians as compared with Westerners. Australian adolescents were more similar to the Americans than to Indians in expectations about future events (Mehta, Rohila, Sundberg, & Tyler, 1972; Sundberg, Poole, & Tyler, 1983). However, in the content of listed events, all the adolescents showed strong similarities; they anticipated education and marriage in their futures. Unfortunately in cross-cultural research, to disprove the null hypothesis, we tend to emphasize differences, so much that we overlook the great similarities across cultures.

My own cross-cultural work preceded and followed this large Adolescent Research Project. Readers will recall that I had started cross-cultural psychological research during graduate years in Minnesota with a German translation of the MMPI. In studies in the 1950s and 1960s, my Oregon Art Department friend, Tom Ballinger, and I investigated children's drawings in a large sample of elementary schools in Nepal. The findings showed Goodenough "IQ" scores equivalent to those of Americans at early ages and a steady decrease into the early teens, which we interpreted as a reflection of the lack of equivalent schooling (Sundberg & Ballinger, 1968). My two Fulbrights to India (1965–66 and 1973) involved lecturing and consulting at Indian universities on the development of student services. I edited a special edition of the Fulbright newsletter in the winter of 1973, and I published several articles in the Indian *Student Services Review* (e.g., Sundberg, 1973). Among reviews of cross-cultural research in American publications, one was on counseling (Sundberg, 1976), which was revised in three subsequent editions of *Counseling Across Cultures* by Paul Pedersen and colleagues, the latest two being with David Sue. Our more recent cross-cultural research and writings have covered community prevention approaches in Southeast Asia (Sundberg, Hadiyono, Latkin, & Padilla, 1995), and Hong Kong students' views of the future (Sundberg, French, Lee, & Scott, 2001). While teaching at the University of Hong Kong, I also started a survey of test usage in Hong Kong (Tsoi & Sundberg, 1989). Through my travels, including a pleasant time as a lecturer on a cruise in the South China Seas, I developed an interest in what tourists learn about other cultures, and have published an informal article on "tips for tourists" (Sundberg, 2001). With a colleague, Gerald Fry, we have explored the importance of tourism, which is one of the world's largest industries. On a professional visit to Indonesia in 1988, my wife and I met Johana Hadiyono in psychology at Gadjah Mada University in Yogyakarta and sponsored her for a Fulbright. She has returned to Oregon several times and has become a close friend. Hadiyono and I arranged for seven of her colleagues to spend research time at the University of Oregon.

It is frequently said that the world is getting smaller, but do we understand each other better? Undoubtedly much about globalization is positive.

But shocking reminders of negative aspects must be recognized in terrorist attacks in the United States, the bombings in Bali and elsewhere, and the war with Iraq. One is led to ask: Is there such a characteristic as international identity? Recently a UO colleague, Holly Arrow, and I have been exploring the issue raised by Socrates (469–399 BC) when he said "[I am] not an Athenian, nor a Greek, but a citizen of the world" (attributed to Socrates by Plutarch in *Of Banishment*). We have identified three different kinds of identity that transcend national boundaries: (a) global identity exemplifying what Socrates said, (b) selective cross-national category memberships such as being European or Muslim or a psychologist, and (c) networks of personal linkages such as friends, many facilitated now by computerized methods (Arrow & Sundberg, 2004). Much more needs to be done to develop a measure of international identity and answer the question: To what does it relate, and how is it exemplified in action?

BOREDOM!

Perhaps it was my experience in the military that led me to wonder about the measurement of boredom. Perhaps it was from observing some of my students in large classes. While I was teaching in Australia in the mid-seventies, Herb Bisno (a UO colleague who had moved to Melbourne) and I discussed this emotion extensively and did exploratory interviews. Boredom must have been in the air then, although we had not read the 1975 book *Beyond Boredom and Anxiety* by Czikszentmihaly. Paradoxically, we found the phenomenon of boredom to be extremely interesting. Boredom can be seen as the opposite of interest. However, most of what is formally called research on the topic of interests has to do with occupational choice, rather than daily involvement in life activities, and there was relatively little research on boredom as of the seventies.

Going through life reacting with different environments, people are interested in this and bored with that. Boredom is a common emotional experience, but many people don't recognize the condition of being bored. When a person states that he or she is never bored, if you press on in conversation, you can often find periods in which the person faces idle periods and wonders what to do. Most people are bored when waiting in long lines. There seem to be three kinds of general behavioral manifestations: restless boredom, listless boredom, and hidden boredom. One can also differentiate endogenous (self-related) and exogenous boredom (situation-related). Boring situations are often ones in which one has limited control—except perhaps over one's own reactions. If one leans toward an existential philosophy, there is another distinction—between existential boredom (the general lack of meaning of life, i.e., life-boredom) and neurotic boredom (often related to the failure to confront and cope with life's problems). Also there is the state-trait distinction—short-term boredom (related to a limited time and place) versus more pervasive boredom—the trait of boredom proneness.

Returning to Oregon, I found that one of my students, Rich Farmer, was also interested in boredom. Intending broad coverage, we located and wrote about 200 items on boredom proneness. Examples are "Time always seems to be passing slowly" and (scored oppositely) "I find it easy to entertain myself." Through studies of reliability, validity, and factor analysis, we boiled the scale down to 28 true-false items which take 5 to 10 minutes to answer. We published the Boredom Proneness Scale (BPS) in the *Journal of Personality Assessment* (Farmer & Sundberg, 1986), and for this article, the Society for Personality Assessment gave us the first annual Walter Klopfer Award. I have had more requests for this publication than any other. Later, we also found that there are gender and cultural aspects to boredom proneness (Sundberg, Latkin, Farmer, & Saoud, 1991). Stephen Vodanvich has constructed a Likert-type scale for the BPS items (Vodanovich & Kass, 1990), and in a recent review of measures of boredom (Vodanovich, 2003), he lists over 30 studies using the BPS. The relation of boredom proneness to depression is frequently found. An interesting future study would be to explore boredom and the ability to meditate. One might think that there is no more potentially boring situation than sitting alone paying attention only to one's wandering mind. Yet my experiences suggest that meditation is not boring at all.

SEEING RED:
RESEARCH ON RAJNEESHPURAM

One of the strangest episodes in the history of Oregon was that of Rajneeshpuram. From late 1981 to early 1986, a remote ranch in the central part of the state was "invaded" by people dressed in red—the followers of Bhagwan Shree Rajneesh. (Bhagwan can be translated in various ways—as a god, spiritual leader, or lord.) Rajneesh was born in 1931 in India to a Jain-Hindu family. A student of philosophy in college, he experienced what he called an enlightenment in 1953, and by 1964, he was holding meditation camps and attracting followers. As with several spiritual gurus in India at the time, people came from Europe, America, Australia, and Japan. In 1974, Rajneesh and his followers opened an ashram in Pune in the Western hills near Bombay (now called Mumbai). Running into opposition in India, Rajneesh and his followers looked for a place to establish a new center, and his chief spokesperson, Ma Anand Sheila, found a large ranch near the small town of Antelope in central Oregon (a three- to four-hour drive from Eugene or Portland). They energetically began building a commune in 1981–82. Starting from the ranch house and barn, they constructed cabins and houses and a small town with a restaurant, hotel, and shopping mall. They set up a large bus system and built an airport for Learjet landings. They dammed a creek to create a lake for irrigation and swimming, and farmed the ranch with considerable environmental sensitivity. There were training courses in meditation and self-improvement, and in their large hall, Bhagwan would speak in his slow, whispering, almost hypnotic voice. The requirements for initiated followers (called sannyasins) were to adopt a new name usually, engage in daily meditation, wear a necklace with Bhagwan's picture, and wear clothes the colors of the sunrise—primarily shades of red. Though not required, many gave up their savings when they joined the group. At its peak, 4,000 people resided in Rajneeshpuram. For summer festivals, as many as 15,000 came from around the world. Followers started giving Bhagwan diamond watches and Rolls Royce cars. Before the commune folded in the mid-eighties, he had received over 90 of these cars. Every day he would slowly drive one of the Rolls Royces through Rajneeshpuram with cheering, singing, and dancing red-clothed followers lining the roads. (Figure 6 shows Bhagwan driving among sannyasins in Rajneeshpuram.) Followers recorded his words and edited them into hundreds of volumes. His message was a mix of Indian spiritual writings, Buddhism, aspects of Christianity and Islam, and New Age or "pop psychology." He asserted that society promotes misery and neuroses, and fulfillment comes from meditation and freedom to love, but that wealth was not bad. In many ways, however, he preached the opposite of Gandhi's concern for simple living and service.

My interest derived from several sources. At that time I was teaching community psychology, and here was an opportunity to see a community in the making. Also, experience in India had led me to an interest in this movement with its roots in Indian thought. Though personally skeptical of all religious belief systems, I know that religion is very important in the lives of many people and important in all cultures. Furthermore, the Rajneeshee processes of self-exploration and training in meditation were relevant to clinical psychology and personality change. Of particular interest to me was an invention of Rajneesh called "dynamic meditation." This, as other investigators and I later experienced in the large lecture hall, involved listening to Indian music for an hour while going through a succession of different activities such as shouting to get out one's feelings, sitting silently in a meditative mood, and dancing by oneself.

My first visit was in spring 1982 to the little developed ranch, followed by 10 more visits spread over the years, usually with students and colleagues. My psychology colleague, Dick Littman, was particularly interested in the Rajneeshee socialization of the children. Although it was not easy to get the confidence of the leadership, we were eventually allowed to do research, and together with a set of students, carried out focus groups, surveys, interviews, and testing sessions. Part of our agreement was to give feedback to the Rajneeshees about our findings. Marion Goldman, who teaches the sociology of religion at Oregon, also conducted interviews there, and we collaborated on a study. One psychology graduate student, Carl Latkin, lived on the ranch for a month as a participant observer and made numerous additional visits while working on his PhD dissertation. He led the way in authoring many of our publications (e.g., Latkin, Hagan, Littman, & Sundberg, 1987; Latkin, Littman, Sundberg, & Hagan, 1993; Latkin, Sundberg, Littman, Katsikis, & Hagan, 1994).

One clear finding was that the devotees of the Bhagwan were much better educated than the general population (64% through college, 35% with a master's or higher degree); many were professionals, including psychiatrists and psychologists. The large early survey, comprised about equally of men and women, showed an average age of 34 years, a majority married (74%), and reports of high levels of psychological well-being and self-esteem, and low levels of stress and depression.

We were able to administer two widely known tests, the CPI and the TAT. The sample taking the California Psychological Inventory (Sundberg, Latkin, Littman, & Hagan, 1990) included 34 women and 33 men. The CPI showed scores particularly high on In (Independence) and Fx (Flexibility), and they manifested strong norm-doubting. On a Narcissism scale, the Rajneeshees come out higher than any other group in the CPI manual. (One could speculate that the eventual downfall of Rajneeshpuram in Oregon may have been due not only to leadership problems and arrogance toward locals but also to the imbalance of lifestyle types among the Rajneeshees themselves.)

The Thematic Apperception Test also produced interesting results in a study of 22 high-achieving Rajneeshees matched with 22 non-Rajneeshees of the same professional backgrounds, such as counselors, lawyers, and accountants (Sundberg, Goldman, Rotter, & Smyth, 1992). Six TAT cards (1, 2, 3 BM, 4, 13 MF, and 16) were administered during interviews. The blank card (16) was most productive of differences. We trained coders to rate each story on the familiar characteristics of achievement, power, affiliation, and intimacy. In addition, we developed ratings on narcissism and quest (i.e., religious seekership). We found significant differences, with Rajneeshees being higher on quest, narcissism, and unusual conditions in stories. Some examples of Rajneeshee thinking are as follows: A Rajneeshee man in response to card 1 said that the parents are "not allowing the boy to flow and flower naturally in his own way and his own time, to come to the music. . . . It's a violation of his being." A woman's story for card 3 said, "This person looks like she really enjoys being miserable. People being miserable don't realize they enjoy being miserable. This person is just completely reveling in being miserable, indulging that sort of thing, indulging in it." These responses reflect emphasis on personal freedom and on responsibility for one's own feelings.

Intense opposition developed between Rajneeshees and their Oregon neighbors, who perceived them as arrogant, expansionist, advocating free love, and in general, alien to their way of life. That quiet, high desert country hadn't been so disturbed since the struggle between the cowboys and sheep men at the turn of the century. The "red people" took over little Antelope by outnumbering the voters and renaming it Rajneesh. For a county election, they bused in several hundred homeless people to increase the vote (though that didn't succeed). Just before the election, in an action worthy of terrorists, Sheila and a few cohorts secretly slipped salmonella into salad bars at restaurants in the Dalles, the county seat, causing an outbreak of illness. There were threats to Bhagwan's life, and the commune members became fearful of attacks and had machine guns at entrances and even a helicopter flying over Bhagwan's drive-by route. Several other questionable and illegal activities by the Rajneeshees were investigated by state and federal law enforcement. Conflicts within the leadership on the Ranch arose. By the summer of 1985, Rajneesh had repudiated Sheila, who had already fled. (She was arrested and sentenced to two years in prison.) He attempted to flee but was caught and brought to trial in Portland. After admitting to a charge of staging marriages to enable foreigners to stay in the U.S. and paying a large fine, Rajneesh left and moved back to India. A large number of his followers expanded the former Pune commune and developed better relations with the local people. Shortly after changing his name to Osho, Rajneesh died in January 1990. The Osho Commune still conducts self-exploration courses and meditations, and attracts people from around the world. A book by Goldman (1999) provides an interesting account of why successful women became followers. The article "The Pitfalls and Pratfalls of Research on an Experimental Community" (Latkin et al., 1993) recounts our approach and findings in this challenging field study.

My feelings about the whole experience are mixed. I appreciated their cooperation and liked some of the Rajneeshees, but the behaviors of Sheila and a few of her followers were reprehensible and downright stupid. The development and death of Rajneeshpuram were fascinating for students of human behavior. More details about Rajneesh, the Oregon commune, and the Osho center in India can be obtained from the Worldwide Web. A large amount of material on Rajneeshpuram has been placed in the Special Collections of the University of Oregon Library for the use of scholars.

PERSON, COMMUNITY, AND ADMINISTRATION

A fundamental question for personality psychologists is, "How well does an individual fit into his or her surroundings?" Erikson's identity question, "Who am I?" includes "What is my place in the world?" In writing *Assessment of Persons* (Sundberg, 1977), I dealt with questions about times and places in chapters on life history, persons in context, and society's future. These chapters represented my growing appreciation for the importance of developing ways of representing and studying the interactive influence of situations with individuals over time. One of the ways I attempted to do this was by using roles as metaphors. Shakespeare, in writing "All the world's a stage, and all the men and women merely players," suggested different roles a person might play over a lifetime. By interviews or more time-consuming observations (as those by Roger Barker and his colleagues), one can identify places and social situations, and then specify the roles a person plays in the important scenes. Another concept for connecting persons is the idea of networks. With whom does a person communicate in person, on the telephone, or by e-mail? One can then draw a chart showing those connections and their frequencies. In a sociometric network, a person may be an isolate standing alone or a node through which much information flows. An interview technique is to have people list major personal events in one column and major community or world events in another column, and then discuss possible connections. A variation on that is to have clients draw a line from birth to the present time, showing points of change and decision, and relating these to the environment at the time.

Beyond direct personal interactions and roles, there is a larger geographical locale—the community. The personal-community orientation is something we find difficult to relate to according to common personality categories. Perhaps the closest we come is with such concepts as extraversion. In regard to careers, John Holland's extensive work (1997), with its six personality characteristics, ties vocational satisfaction to environmental characteristics. Clinical concern for post-traumatic stress also calls for recognition of social support and neighborly cohesion in the surrounding community. In understanding a person, whether in research or clinical assessment and therapy, a person's sense of control and attitudes about the future are important. Colleagues and I have asked subjects to write down future events they expect in their lives, and on a separate sheet future societal or world events they expect. In rating both lists on pleasantness, the majority of subjects think personal events will be pleasant and societal events unpleasant (Sundberg, French, Lee, & Scott, 2001). Events close to home and community would receive more favorable ratings than those further from one's sense of control and interaction.

In 1967, my involvement with trying to understand communities and train for community work had become intensive when I was asked to be the founding dean of the Wallace School of Community Service and Public Affairs (CSPA) at the University of Oregon. The school was named after Lila Acheson Wallace, who was a 1927 UO graduate and had founded *The Readers Digest*, along with her husband. During Arthur Flemming's presidency at the University, she donated one million dollars to start CSPA. Prior to that, as already mentioned, I had some administrative experience in institutional development in establishing the University Clinic and the Clinical Psychology Program, and in consulting with universities in India. I had also served as president of the Oregon Psychological Association when state certification and licensing were first being attempted. During the summer of 1963, before Kennedy was assassinated, I had also been an assessment officer for the second Nepal Peace Corps Training Program. (Later, I was invited to consider the job of director of Peace Corps assessment in Washington, DC, but after extensive interviews and a good dinner with Sargent Shriver, I was not hired.) In starting CSPA, I asked Oregon colleagues, Herbert Bisno, Jarold Kieffer, and Clancy Thurber, to head the three primary specialties: social service, public management, and international activities. Another less prominent branch was leisure services. A key element in all was experiential learning through undergraduate community placements in relevant organizations. The School attracted many students with a service orientation and strengthened university linkages with the community and state.

Several publications describe those early years of the School and its community concerns (e.g., Sundberg, 1970). With a core faculty of about 10 to 15, CSPA attracted an enthusiastic response on campus and in the state, and during its existence, graduated about 1,600 students. Several other universities began similar programs across the U.S. My years as dean came at exciting times in the late sixties and early seventies, which saw the continuing remnants of Johnson's ambitious Great Society, combined with student protests about the Vietnam War. I particularly enjoyed planning and developing programs, and I started personal courses on Behavioral Ecology and The Future and its Social Alternatives. A CSPA colleague, Dick Fehnel, and I obtained a grant to develop assessment procedures for giving mature students, especially women, credits for life experiences.

Does being a clinical psychologist prepare one for administration? In some ways, yes. A clinician is likely to be sensitive to nonwork problems and is inclined to listen readily. In other ways, no. The clinician may be misled into seeing administrative problems as personal. A prominent realization was that there is often a sharp difference between people in different roles, for instance, those of friend and university faculty. Even those with whom you have strong personal friendships may argue or lobby strongly against your administrative position. Another important learning was about the way the administrator is involved in both internal and external politics. The dean stands between two worlds—that of the faculty and students and that of the upper echelons of administration—and communication over that divide is important and often difficult. A special problem for CSPA was that the University of Oregon as a research university emphasized the graduate level, and CSPA was almost entirely undergraduate with few research grants. Also, on the national scene, during the early Nixon era and with Vietnam protests intensifying, the national mood shifted away from concern for poverty and human services. Using budget cuts in 1982 as a reason, new university leadership disbanded CSPA, and the programs were dispersed within the university. Public affairs and international studies still continue at Oregon fortunately, but the loss of the community service specialty left many people disappointed.

After my five years as CSPA dean, James G. Kelly, who had been the second president of the APA division of community psychology, succeeded me. I changed to part time in both CSPA and Psychology. In addition to Kelly, I looked to George Albee and his Vermont series to help me appreciate the importance of prevention in community and ecological psychology. In the UO Psychology Department with Ed Lichtenstein, I obtained an NIMH training grant for prevention programs, working on projects in nearby rural towns, and we started courses in community psychology in the department. As part of that program, we developed an introductory method for assessing students' knowledge of the community (Nettekoven & Sundberg, 1985). Colleagues and I also did a follow-up of rural adolescents' views of life possibilities (Sundberg, Tyler, & Poole, 1984) and published articles on prevention (e.g., Sundberg, 1985). In teaching one hopes to help develop long-range thinking and a concern for the common good (despite problems Garrett Hardin warned about in his 1968 *Science* article, "The Tragedy of the Commons"). I returned to being director of the clinical program in the psychology department, defending it against attempts by the department's "basic researchers" to cut the number of clinical students admitted (though they had the highest scores of all applicants) and keeping clinical faculty. From many of APA clinical site visits to other universities, I knew ours was not alone in the split between basic and applied psychology. APA itself still faces this unfortunate divisiveness.

Throughout these periods of administration, I continued to keep a broad outlook on personality, and social and clinical psychology, by attending conferences and doing reviews of books and chapters on assessment, and by writing entries for the editions of *Corsini's Encyclopedia of Psychology*. I've taught a variety of courses in psychology, including ones on personality, using Dan Adams' excellent books. Administrative experience reinforced the belief that personality assessment must relate in some way to the situations in which the person lives. I am often reminded of the "fundamental attribution error," which states that the observer often tends to blame the person for a problem that the person sees as due to the situation. One must also question the adequacy of psychiatric diagnosis as codified by the DSM manuals. We have yet to fulfill the challenge posed a half a century ago by Kluckhohn and Murray (1953): Every person is in certain respects (a) like all other persons, (b) like some other persons, and (c) like no other person. This triad of sharing in personhood is useful in looking for the relation of persons to communities and settings that influence the course of lives.

THE IMPORTANCE OF PERSONAL
AND FAMILY LIFE FOR A PSYCHOLOGIST

How important for professional development is one's non-professional experience? Intuitively the answer is obvious—very important, especially for a clinical psychologist. (Surprisingly, there is little research on this question.) Certainly a person's most important learnings about people are often in the family. I am grateful to my mother and brother who supported and taught me much when I was growing up, including our brotherly fights that were repeated by my sons. For me, nothing is more important than having Donna as a spouse for over 55 years and seeing our four children move through the developmental stages. One great advantage of having a partner, as opposed to living alone, is not only the social support but also having someone to check on ideas and plans when they get too far out. Knowing how to relate to community resources and institutions, especially children's schools and the medical establishment, is another aspect of personal learning. One must remember, of course, that one family's experiences provide only a limited sample of the variety among the other families.

It is useful to keep a diary or at least a personal appointment book to help recall times of pleasure and difficulty, and to identify the circumstances around important decisions. I recommend to students and clients with writing inclinations that they record their feelings to gain perspective on their lives. Wright and Chung (2001) reported evidence that writing therapy is useful, probably including e-mail exchanges. Reviewing my life, I've discovered that I have not always been very rational and organized about the important decisions of life, which my good friend, Barry Anderson (2002), wisely recommends. The big decisions such as getting married and moving west were mixtures of thought and feeling, and turned out to be excellent choices. My father's death and World War II were not my doing, but how one reacts to whatever one encounters is crucial. In the process of living, the clinician naturally has in some way experienced many of the problems discussed by clients. Having heart surgery in 2002 deepened my appreciation of patient–caretaker relationships. Being in the role of a client is important to understand. I encourage clinical graduate students to seek counseling or therapy themselves, if they can do it conscientiously.

Times of relaxation are as important as times of work. For me, gardening, walking, and hiking are helpful, not only for physical exercise but also for "working off steam." I remember with great pleasure ambling along the beach or climbing in Oregon's beautiful mountains. (Figure 7 shows three of my sons aged 11, 15, and 19, with me on the summit of the South Sister east of Eugene. In the background are the Middle and North Sisters.) Now, as with many busy fathers, I wish I had done much more with them when they were growing up, but the professional 'rat race' was a powerful force.

For our family, travel has provided many important cross-cultural learning experiences. Starting with our three-month honeymoon in Europe, Donna and I have learned to adjust to the vicissitudes of travel around the world with our sons, and after that, with my teaching and research sojourns in India, Australia, France, Spain, Hong Kong, and Southeast Asia. Our sons were deeply affected too. All are interested in other cultures and history. We have five grandchildren, and their parents have already begun to share the value of personal learning about the big world and its variety. Our sons have followed their own paths, and none became psychologists, but each has expressed himself well in his own way: Charlie is a landscape architect working in historic preservation in Seattle; Greg has a graphic design business in New York City; Scott headed a large Oregon State University project on developing an atlas identifying native Oregon plants and their locations, and Mark is an economist with the World Bank and is currently involved with developmental programs in India. (Sadly, Scott died of cancer at age 50.)

After retiring fully from teaching in 1993 (after 5 years teaching part time), I continued to work on projects, finishing the fourth edition of the clinical book, writing up research, and serving on a few committees. I carried out a follow-up of all the department PhD graduates (over 400), and Dick Littman and I recorded interviews with all retired and leaving faculty members for the use of future scholars. Recently, the UO Psychology Department honored me with a conference, and some of my students have established a scholarship in my honor. Even within the past few weeks, while completing this autobiography, I've received a request for comments on clinical program development in Hong Kong, an inquiry from a student in China, a doctoral dissertation from Karachi to evaluate, and an e-mail interview for a seventh-grade project from one of my granddaughters.

Donna and I attend local lectures and see many plays. We have continued our travels, many of them in Asia. (Figure 8 shows the two of us in Hong Kong.) We have done various community volunteer jobs, including work at the Museum of Natural History on campus for several years, and I have given many community lectures. Donna has been interested in international cooking and has helped edit a Chinese cookbook. (Incidentally, our World Bank son says the easiest way to get acquainted with people in other countries is to share food and talk about it.) Also, I sometimes tell others that my wife was in jail for three and a half years. As a volunteer, she interviewed and arranged placements there for people who were sentenced to community service. So family learning is part of continued psychological learning.

CHANCE AND CHOICE, CHANGE AND CONTINUITY

How to conclude this journey of memories? Life is certainly a mixture of chance and choice, change and continuity. Looking back, I must conclude that it has been a lot of fun as well as frustration. I failed to accomplish many things I would like to have done, but I was fortunate enough to be in some situations where I got support for expressing whatever talents I had. I have often thought about what my life history would have been had I been sent into World War II battles, as were friends in the Pacific and Europe, or if I had never met my wife that day in Minnesota, or for that matter if I had been born in China or Germany. I think too of the many changes in psychology over the last half century—the increasing specialization, the proliferation of technology, globalization and demographic changes, and I wonder about their impacts on the future of the field. If any values have been strengthened over the years, they are the importance of a deep interest in people, a skillful willingness to listen to others, and respect for the importance and dignity of each individual, recognizing the person's roles and situations.

The areas in which I have worked leave much important work to be done and many questions of conceptualization. I still would like to see a thorough attempt to assess knowledge of others and its usefulness in clinical and counseling work. I would like to see the important emotion of boredom explored much more completely. I would be pleased if community and cultural elements would be usefully included in assessment. How to understand and categorize life histories? There is much to be learned about life stories and narratives, building on the excellent work of McAdams, Runyan, Sarbin and others.

In older age, one's world of action narrows with decreasing energy and physical ability. But how rich and varied life can still be! I am looking forward to interesting opportunities in my remaining future; I only hope I can see possibilities and seize them creatively for my personal world and for the profession that has been so important and rewarding.

REFERENCES

Anderson, B. F. (2002). *Three secrets of wise decision making.* Portland, OR: Single Reef Press.

Arrow, H., & Sundberg, N. D. (2004). *International identity: Definitions, development ands some implications for global conflict and peace. In B.N. Setiadi, A. Supratiknya, W. J. Lonner & Y. H. Poortinga* (Eds.). *Ongoing themes in psychology and culture.* Proceedings of the Sixteenth Congress of the International Association for Cross-Cultural Psychology, Yogyakarta, Indonesia, July 15–19, 2002.

Bates, B. C., Sundberg, N. D., & Tyler, L. E. (1970). Divergent problem solving: A comparison of adolescents in India and America. *International Journal of Psychology, 5*, 231–244.

Chartier, G. M., & Sundberg, N. D. (1969). Commonality of word listing, predictability, originality and chunking: An analysis of American and Indian ninth graders. *International Journal of Psychology, 4*, 195–205.

Farmer, R., & Sundberg, N. D. (1986). Boredom proneness: The development and correlates of a new scale. *Journal of Personality Assessment, 50*, 4–17.

Gilbert, G. M. (1947) *Nuremberg Diary.* New York: Farrar, Straus.

Goldman, M. S. (1999). *Passionate journeys: Why successful women joined a cult.* Ann Arbor: University of Michigan Press.

Holland, J. L. (1997). *Making vocational choices: A theory of vocational personalities and work environments* (3rd ed.). Odessa, FL: Psychological Assessment Resources.

Kluckhohn, C., & Murray, H. A. (1953). Personality formation: The determinants. In C. Kluckhohn & H. A. Murray (Eds.), *Personality in nature, society and culture* (pp. 35–48). New York: Knopf.

Latkin, C. A., Hagan, R. A., Littman, R. A., & Sundberg, N. D. (1987). Who lives in Utopia? A brief report on the Rajneeshpuram Research Project. *Sociological Analysis, 48*, 73–81.

Latkin, C. A., Littman, R. A., Sundberg, N. D., & Hagan, R. A. (1993). Pitfalls and pratfalls in research on an experimental community: Lessons in integrating theory and practice from the Rajneeshpuram Research Project. *Journal of Community Psychology, 21*, 35–48.

Littman, R. A., Nidorf, L. J. & Sundberg, N. D. (1961). Characteristics of a psychosexual scale: The Krout Personal Preference Scale. *Journal of Genetic Psychology, 98*, 19–27.

Latkin, C. A., Sundberg, N. D., Littman, R. A., Katsikis, M. G., & Hagan, R. A. (1994). Feelings after the fall: Former Rajneeshpuram commune members' perceptions of and affiliation with the Rajneeshee movement. *Sociology of Religion, 55*, 65–73.

Mehta, P. H., Rohila, P. K., Sundberg, N. D., & Tyler, L. E. (1972). Future time perspectives of adolescents in India and the United States. *Journal of Cross-Cultural Psychology, 3*, 293–302.

Nettekoven, L., & Sundberg, N. D. (1985). Community assessment methods in rural mental health promotion. *Journal of Rural Community Psychology, 6*, 21–44.

Sundberg, N. D. (1952). The relationship of psychotherapeutic skill and experience to knowledge of other people. *Dissertation Abstracts International, 12*, 390–391.

Sundberg, N. D. (1955). The acceptability of "fake" versus "bona fide" personality test interpretations. *Journal of Abnormal and Social Psychology, 50*, 145–147.

Sundberg, N. D. (1956). The use of the MMPI for cross-cultural personality study: A preliminary report on the German translation. *Journal of Abnormal and Social Psychology, 52*, 281–283.

Sundberg, N. D. (1960). Basic readings in psychology. *American Psychologist, 15*, 343–345.

Sundberg, N. D. (1966). A method for studying sensitivity to implied meanings. *Gawein (Journal of Psychology, Nijmegen, Netherlands), 15*, 1–8.

Sundberg, N. D. (1970). The community concern of the university. In F. R. Paulsen (Ed.), *Higher education, dimensions and directions* (pp. 157–169). Tucson: University of Arizona Press.

Sundberg, N. D. (1973). Cross-cultural advising and counseling. *Student Services Review, 7* (2), 6–12.

Sundberg, N. D. (1976). Toward research evaluating cross-cultural counseling. In P. Pedersen, W. Lonner, & J. Draguns (Eds.), *Counseling across cultures* (pp. 139–169). Honolulu: University Press of Hawaii.

Sundberg, N. D. (1977). *Assessment of persons.* Englewood Cliffs, NJ: Prentice Hall.

Sundberg, N. D. (1985). The use of future studies in training for prevention and promotion in mental health. *Journal of Primary Prevention, 6*, 98–114.

Sundberg, N. D. (2001). Tips for tourists. *International Psychology Reporter (APA Division 52 Newsletter), 5* (2, Summer), 17 & 20.

Sundberg, N. D., & Ballinger, T. O. (1968). Nepalese children's cognitive development as revealed by drawings of man, woman and self. *Child Development, 39*, 969–985.

Sundberg, N. D., French, D. A., Lee, H-c., & Scott, B. (2001). Hong Kong students' views of the future before the handover. *International Psychology Reporter, 4* (1), 11–12.

Sundberg, N. D., Goldman, M. S., Rotter, N. J., & Smyth, D. A. (1992). Personality and spirituality: Comparative TAT's of high achieving Rajneeshees, *Journal of Personality Assessment, 59*, 326–339.

Sundberg, N. D., Hadiyono, J. P., Latkin, C. A., & Padilla, J. (1995). Cross-cultural prevention program transfer: Questions regarding developing countries. *Journal of Primary Prevention, 15* (4), 361–376.

Sundberg, N. D., Latkin, C. A., Farmer, R. F., & Saoud, J. (1991). Boredom in young adults: Gender and cultural comparisons. *Journal of Cross-Cultural Psychology, 22*, 209–223

Sundberg, N. D., Latkin, C. A., Littman, R. A., & Hagan, R. A. (1990). Personality in a religious commune: CPI's in Rajneeshpuram. *Journal of Personality Assessment, 55*, 7–17.

Sundberg, N. D., & Littman, R. A. (1994). Leona Elizabeth Tyler (May 10, 1906—April 29, 1993). *American Psychologist, 49*, 211–212.

Sundberg, N. D., Poole, M. E., & Tyler, L. E. (1983). Adolescents' expectations of future events: A cross-cultural study of Australians, Americans and Indians. *International Journal of Psychology, 18*, 415–427.

Sundberg, N. D., Sharma, V., Rohila, P. K., & Wodtli, T. (1969). Family cohesiveness and autonomy of adolescents in India and the United States. *Journal of Marriage and the Family, 31*, 403–407.

Sundberg, N. D., Snowden, L. R., & Reynolds, W. M. (1978). Toward assessment of personal competence and incompetence in life situations. *Annual Review of Psychology, 29*, 179–221.

Sundberg, N. D., & Tyler, L. E. (1962). *Clinical psychology: An introduction to research and practice.* New York: Appleton-Century-Crofts.

Sundberg, N. D., & Tyler, L. E. (1970). Awareness of action possibilities of Indian, Dutch and American adolescents. *Journal of Cross-Cultural Psychology, 1*, 153–157.

Sundberg, N. D., Tyler, L. E., & Poole, M. E. (1984). Decade differences in rural adolescents' views of life possibilities. *Journal of Youth and Adolescence, 13*, 45–56.

Sundberg, N. D., Tyler, L. E., & Rohila, P. K. (1970). Values of Indian and American adolescents. *Journal of Personality and Social Psychology, 16*, 374–397.

Sundberg, N. D., Winebarger, A. A., & Taplin, J. R. (2002). *Clinical psychology: Evolving theory, practice and research* (4th ed.). Upper Saddle River, NJ: Prentice Hall (574 pages).

Tsoi, M. M., & Sundberg, N. D. (1989). Patterns of psychological test use in Hong Kong. *Professional Psychology: Research and Practice, 20,* 248–250.

Tyler, L. E., Sundberg, N. D., Rohila, P. K., & Greene, M. M. (1968). Patterns of choices in Dutch, American and Canadian Adolescents. *Journal of Counseling Psychology, 15,* 522–529.

Vodanovich, S. J. (2003). Psychometric measures of boredom: A review of the literature. *Journal of Psychology, 37,* 569–595.

Vodanovich, S. J., & Kass, S. J. (1990). A factor analytic study of the Boredom Proneness Scale. *Journal of Personality Assessment, 55,* 115–123.

Wright, J., & Chung, M. C. (2001). Mastery or mystery? Therapeutic writing: A review of the literature. *British Journal of Guidance & Counselling, 29,* 277–291.

SELECTED BIBLIOGRAPHY

Farmer, R. F., & Sundberg, N. D. (1986). Boredom proneness: The development and correlates of a new scale. *Journal of Personality Assessment, 50,* 4–17.

Mehta, P. H., Rohila, P. K., Sundberg, N. D., & Tyler, L. E. (1972). Future time-perspectives of adolescents in India and the United States. *Journal of Cross-Cultural Psychology, 3,* 293–302.

Nettekoven, L., & Sundberg, N. (1985). Community assessment methods in rural mental health promotion. *Journal of Rural Community Psychology, 6,* 21–44.

Sundberg, N. D. (1955). The acceptability of "fake" versus "bona fide" personality test interpretations. *Journal of Abnormal and Social Psychology, 50,* 145–147.

Sundberg, N. D. (1956). The use of the MMPI for cross-cultural personality study: A preliminary report on the German translation. *Journal of Abnormal and Social Psychology, 52,* 281–283.

Sundberg, N. D. (1957). Projective methods. In E. A. Spiegel (Ed.), *Progress in Neurology and Psychiatry:* Vol. 12 (pp. 571–583). New York: Grune & Stratton.

Sundberg, N. D. (1960). Basic readings in psychology. *American Psychologist, 15,* 343–345. Reprinted in the *Bulletin of the British Psychological Society, 42,* (1960) 47–50.

Sundberg, N. D. (1961). The practice of psychological testing in clinical services in the United States. *American Psychologist, 16,* 79–83. Reprinted in *Bulletin of British Psychological Society, 44,* (1961) 1–9.

Sundberg, N. D. (1977). *Assessment of persons.* Englewood Cliffs, NJ: Prentice Hall.

Sundberg, N. D. (1981). Historical and traditional contributions to cognitive assessment. In T. V. Merluzzi, C. R. Glass, & M. Genest (Eds.), *Cognitive assessment* (pp. 52–76). New York: Guilford.

Sundberg, N. D., & Ballinger, T. O. (1968). Nepalese children's cognitive development as revealed by drawings of man, woman and self. *Child Development, 39,* 969–985.

Sundberg, N. D., French, D. A., Lee, H-c., & Scott, B. (2001). Hong Kong students' views of the future before the handover. *International Psychology Reporter, 4*(1), 11–12.

Sundberg, N. D., Goldman, M. S., Rotter, N. J., & Smyth, D. A. (1992). Personality and spirituality: Comparative TATs of high achieving Rajneeshees. *Journal of Personality Assessment, 59,* 326–339.

Sundberg, N. D., Latkin, C. A., Littman, R. A., & Hagan, R. A. (1990). Personality in a religious commune: CPI's in Rajneeshpuram. *Journal of Personality Assessment, 55,* 7–17.

Sundberg, N. D., Snowden, L. R., & Reynolds, W. M. (1978). Toward assessment of personal competence and incompetence in life situations. *Annual Review of Psychology, 29,* 179–221.

Sundberg, N. D., & Tyler, L. E. (1962). *Clinical psychology: An introduction to research and practice.* New York: Appleton-Century-Crofts.

Sundberg, N. D., Tyler, L. E. & Taplin, J. R. (1973). *Clinical Psychology: Expanding Horizons.* New York: Appelton-Century-Crofts.

Sundberg, N. D., Taplin, J. R. & Tyler, L. E. (1983). *Introduction to clinical psychology: perspectives, issues, and contributions to human service.* Englewood Cliffs, NJ: Prentice-Hall.

Sundberg, N. D., & Tyler, L. E. (1970). Awareness of action possibilities of Indian, Dutch and American adolescents. *Journal of Cross-Cultural Psychology, 1,* 153–157.

Sundberg, N. D., Tyler, L. E., & Poole, M. E. (1984). Decade of differences in rural adolescents' views of life possibilities. *Journal of Youth and Adolescence, 13,* 45–56.

Sundberg, N. D., Tyler, L. E., & Rohila, P. K. (1970). Values of Indian and American adolescents. *Journal of Personality and Social Psychology, 16,* 374–397.

Sundberg, N. D., Winebarger, A. W., & Taplin, J. R. (2002). *Clinical psychology: Evolving theory, practice, and research* (4th ed.). Upper Saddle River, NJ: Prentice Hall.

Tyler, L. E., Sundberg, N. D., Rohila, P. K., & Greene, M. M. (1968). Patterns of choices in Dutch, American and Indian adolescents. *Journal of Counseling Psychology, 15,* 522–529.

My brother, Donald, and I as young boys in bright winter sunshine, circa 1925

In training at Rattlesnake Field, Fort Sill, Oklahoma, July, 1945

Our four sons, ages 4 to12, with Santa Claus, circa 1960

Administering the Blacky Test to a child, circa 1956

Leona Tyler, Julian Taplin, and I, spring 1981

Bhagwan driving in Rajneeshpuram, 1985

Three sons and I on the summit of South Sister, Oregon, July 1969

My wife Donna and I in Hong Kong, circa 1990

CHAPTER 15

The Shaping of Personality

Genes, Environments, and Chance Encounters

Marvin Zuckerman
University of Delaware

In 1996, Ebstein and his colleagues in Jerusalem reported the first discovery of a major gene associated with a personality trait. The gene was for the Dopamine D4 receptor and the personality trait was "novelty seeking." Novelty seeking is assessed by a scale devised by Cloninger. The content of his scale is closely related to the test for sensation seeking that I first devised in the 1960s. The most current form of the test, Impulsive Sensation Seeking, correlates very highly with Cloninger's Novelty Seeking (Zuckerman & Cloninger, 1996). Robert Plomin, one of the primary behavior geneticists, alerted me to Ebstein's pioneering study. Excited by this finding, I decided to spend my last sabbatical before retirement at Plomin's laboratory at the Institute of Psychiatry in London. I wanted to learn more about the new science of molecular genetics and possibly look for other genes associated with sensation seeking.

I had spent my first sabbatical at the Institute with Hans Eysenck in 1976. One of our projects was a twin study of sensation seeking and impulsivity to determine the heritability of sensation seeking (Fulker, Eysenck, & Zuckerman, 1980). The heritability of sensation seeking was quite high (58%) and at the upper limits of the range found for other personality traits. Since then, the genetical findings have been confirmed in a study of twins separated at birth and raised apart (Hur & Bouchard, 1997), as well as one using twins raised together (Koopmans, Boomsa, Heath, & Lorenz, 1995).

When I was in college at mid-century, the gene was still a hypothetical construct, but by the year before I received my doctoral degree, Watson and Crick (1953) had described the structure of the DNA molecule. Over the remaining half of the century, techniques were developed for identifying specific genes and investigating their relationships with disease, psychopathology and biological and psychological traits.

Soon after arriving at the institute in London, I asked them to analyze my own DNA for the presence of the form of the D4 gene associated with high or low novelty seeking. For years people have been asking me if I am a high sensation seeker on the assumption that there is a relationship between areas of psychological interest and personality. This is a dubious assumption to begin with. Are all investigators who study schizophrenia schizoid? Are all those who study anxiety, anxious? Are those who do research on aggression, aggressive? My observations of colleagues in these areas revealed no invariable associations of topic with investigator. Nevertheless, I felt I should answer the question. The problem is that the main definition of the trait comes from the scale that I devised. So here was a chance to answer the question in terms of a portion of the genetic basis for the trait.

The D4 receptor gene comes in two primary forms, depending on the number of repeats of the base sequence: a short form and a long form. The long form is associated with high sensation seeking and the short form with average or low sensation seeking. My DNA revealed that I had the long form. This confirmed some of my life-history data when I was younger, but sensation seeking falls with age even though the genes don't change. As I told my colleagues in London, sensation seeking for me at age 70 consisted of riding on the top deck of the double decker bus in London (at the very front seat, though). Genes are not destiny and their influence varies at different ages and in different environments.

Let me begin my personal story, however, with my ancestors whom I did not know or only knew when they were older, and my parents who supplied both genes and environment during my formative years. Sensation seeking, like most other personality traits, shows little influence of the shared family environment, but a major influence of the nonshared environment outside of the home. The latter includes the environments we create for ourselves in our choices of friends and activities, and the "chance encounters" that may significantly influence our destinies, like the person who we happen to meet at a party whom we become involved with and marry. If we had not gone to that party, would we have met and married someone else who would have had the same kind of influence on our personality development? There is an "uncertainty principle" in personality explanation, analogous to that in physics (Zuckerman, 1979a).

Ancestors

I suspect that most Jewish psychologists who have won some distinction in the clinical or scientific areas have rabbis in their ancestry. What other vocation was there in Russia for a person with a scholarly disposition and an interest in human experience? Secular universities were not open for Jews. My great-grandfather on my father's side was a rabbi. Figure 1 shows him with a flowing and full white beard and yarmulke. His son and my grandfather are pictured in a Russian type cap and military style jacket with a more trimmed beard (something like mine). He was a teacher in a Hebrew school.

My father came over from Russian before World War I when he was 17. He wanted to go to a secular college—impossible for a Jew in Russia. He taught himself English out of a Hebrew-English bible. I always wondered why he did not speak in the King James dialect. When they asked him what he wanted to study in college, he said, "maybe engineering." When they told him that there were no Jewish engineers, he replied, "Now I know that is what I will be." He had neither beard nor mustache and dressed in a natty American style with suit and tie. Note the progression in the male line from devoutly religious to secular in both dress and occupation. Even though my father was president of his local synagogue, I became an atheist just before my bar mitzvah, although I can remember questioning the existence of an omnipotent god when I was only five years old in Sunday School. At the same time, I identify strongly as a Jew. A Jewish atheist (Freud was one) may seem a contradiction to some, but being a Jew means an ethnic identification with the history of a people, a pride in their accomplishments, and a refusal to conform to the mandate of the majority by conversion or denial of one's ethnic background. Other than this, there is a taste for pastrami and a special appreciation of Woody Allen's humor.

On my mother's side her father, my grandfather, emigrated from Romania—with a stay in England—to the United States. While in England he met and married my grandmother (Figure 2). His father, my great-grandfather, was a rabbi, and he left the old country as much to escape from his destiny as a rabbinical student as to escape the Czarist military draft. After he settled in Cincinnati and acquired a dry-goods store, he ran for alderman on the socialist ticket and, of course, lost.

My lack of mention of the women in the family, mother and grandmothers, is not due to misogyny. These were strong, loving, and traditional women who held the family together through feuds and fights, and made sure everyone was well fed, if not contented. They ruled in the home and in the rearing of the children.

Adolescence

My father gave me two important values: the importance of education and finding a kind of work you really loved. During the late 1960s my son, then in high school, asked me how would I feel if he didn't go to college but just wandered around the country for a time earning his "bread" at odd jobs. I replied that first I would cry for a couple of months and then accept it. He went to college and became a leader in the revolutionary movement on campus, did some drugs, but never missed a class, and got top grades. But more on my children later.

Strangely enough, I had a similar crisis with my father. Graduating from high school at 16 years of age during the last years of World War II, I wanted to enlist in the navy rather than go to college. But he would not give his permission, insisting that I go at least a year to college before going into the military. I finally gave in and went to the University of Kentucky (my father's college) where I reached my full sensation-seeking potential through drinking, sex, and hitchhiking around the country. My first love affair with an "older" (19-year-old) woman lifted me to a state of euphoria, only to plunge into the depths of melancholy when the affair ended. In the latter state, I wrote a great deal of adolescent mawkish poetry, some of which was actually published in a college magazine. By the time the draft caught me, the war was over and at 18, I reluctantly entered the peacetime army. Several months of basic training in the swamps of Louisiana followed by a long, boring year of garrison duty in Texas put an end to any military ambitions I might have had.

Tracing the origins of my interest in psychology, I remember coming across a book on graphology while in high school. I went around analyzing the character of friends and family through their handwriting, perhaps a portent of my interest in personality assessment. Nasty questions of reliability and validity did not disturb my confidence in my ability to read character from scrawls. This kind of "faith validity" carried me through my early years of clinical training when we were taught projective techniques.

During my melancholic period at the University of Kentucky, I read Freud's great works on *The Interpretation of Dreams* and *The Psychopathology of Everyday Life.* Oddly enough, I left the book on the train, but despite this "slip," I overcame my repression and obtained another copy. I began to interpret my own dreams, and in an English course I wrote a term paper on "Sexual Symbolism in Dreams." My prissy instructor told me that this was not a fit topic for an English course, but I went over his head to the chair of the department who gave me permission. Of course, I got only a "C" grade for my first paper in psychology. I also took courses in Introductory and Personality Psychology.

After discharge from the army, I returned to college but now at New York University. In my first college year, I had majored in journalism with the idea of becoming a writer but earning a living as a reporter. Some years later I actually returned to Kentucky to give a talk on sensation seeking at a conference sponsored by Lew Donohew in the communications department. Communications is the new term for journalism, now more broadly defined. My visit was a lesson in the futility of nostalgia. I could not find my old drinking and dancing places or the secluded grassy places where we would make love under the stars. Everything was paved over with housing and highways. Stick with the dreams, time travel is impossible.

Graduate School

I finished my undergraduate work at NYU starting as a major in pre-med with the ultimate goal of psychiatry. At this time NYU had started one of the early PhD programs in clinical psychology and I decided to pursue a career in psychology. At this point in my life I married at too young an age for the wrong reasons, such as the need to concentrate on my studies without the distractions of "dating" (the term we used for short-term mating strategies). The marriage lasted 12 years and the marital relationship was not a happy one, but despite the defects in the shared environment, it produced two great children and four grandchildren. Who can comprehend the mysteries of assortative mating?

In graduate school I patched together a living from the GI Bill educational allotment, a teaching assistantship in experimental psychology, and research assistantships. The TA, under the supervision of Margaret Tresselt, was a major influence in my subsequent career. I became interested in experimental methods and theories based on research rather than on clinical anecdote. Clinical students like myself had multiple personalities. On the one hand, we had Dr. Jekyll: learning theory, logical positivism, comparative and physiological psychology or, in sum, science. Then there was Mr. Hyde: psychoanalytic theory, Rorschach, and other projectives, and insight-oriented psychodynamic psychotherapy. Remember, this was before the alternatives of behavior and cognitive therapy and, except in Minnesota and a few other places, training in objective test assessment. For a time, I resolved my cognitive dissonance through the book by Dollard and Miller (1950), *Personality and Psychotherapy*. Miller, a learning theorist in the Clark Hull model, translated all of the fuzzy Freudian constructs into the terms of learning theory, no mean trick considering that Hull's theory was entirely behaviorist, even when describing mental events as stimuli and responses inside the head. Still, the elegant analogue between conflict behavior in the rat—approach, avoidance, and inhibition—and the human gave the illusion of a scientific basis for psychodynamic theories. But one cannot generalize across species unless there are common methods of investigation, and the exploration of conflict in humans happened almost entirely on the couch.

While still in graduate school, I did my first study (Zuckerman, 1951), which was published in the *Journal of Abnormal and Social Psychology*, and which I presented as a paper at the 1953 meeting of the American Psychological Association. This was the last meeting of the APA held at a college campus (Penn State). Presenting a paper before an audience of distinguished psychologists (in those days they actually went to hear the papers) was a highly rewarding experience, much more so than a clinical presentation. Then there were the drinking parties organized by the various university departments. One could wander from party to party with free booze at each. At one point I found myself at a party exchanging dirty jokes with my idol Neal Miller. The campus police eventually came around and closed down the loud, raucous parties bordering on riot. This is one reason the APA stopped having parties on college campuses. The other is that the organization grew too big.

During the third year, I went on an internship to Wayne County General Hospital outside of Detroit. Wayne County was an old type hospital consisting of an admissions building, where most of the evaluation and therapy was done, and a number of custodial buildings where the old chronics were kept for many years. The latter were "snake-pits," where one rarely ventured with one's black box containing Wechsler-Bellevue Intelligence kits and Rorschach cards, unless there was a rumor of recovery in one of the chronics. The young residents were all imbued with Freudian psychoanalytic theory and were just putting in their time until they could go into psychoanalytic training and practice. The older staff doctors were a mélange of alcoholics, bipolars, and simply apathetic types. The first antipsychotic drugs were just starting to be used. The therapy was largely electric and insulin shock, lobotomy, and hydrotherapy, with a very few patients being given some kind of psychotherapy.

I couldn't help noticing that it was largely the young attractive women who were selected by the male residents for dynamic therapy that went beyond "so how are you feeling today?" Psychological reports at staff meetings were embraced as scientific confirmation if they supported the diagnosis of the chief of staff, and derided as hocus-pocus if they conflicted with his infallible conclusions. The total atmosphere was disillusioning and depressing. I began to question my career goals.

I remember taking a day off to go to the library at the University of Michigan, just down the road, to do some preliminary library research for my dissertation. It was a beautiful, crisp fall day; the leaves had turned to glorious oranges and reds. I could hear the crowd cheering in the football stadium. The thought occurred to me that this would be a pleasant place to work as an academic clinical psychologist.

I returned to school and began work on my dissertation. By that time I had two children. Living conditions were difficult. I worked at three part-time jobs, including my TA, attended some classes, and collected the data for my dissertation. My workday went from 8 a.m. to 11 p.m.

My first idea was to work in the area of conflict using human subjects. However, the methodology using the conflict board and reaction times seemed a poor way of testing conflict dispositions. One simply could not develop the kind of strong conflict motivations that were possible by using rats. Reward points were not the same as food versus shock for a hungry rat. I then became interested in what was being called the "New Look" in research on perception.

Personality traits and values were associated with perceptual thresholds for words with relevant content. My idea was to measure aggressiveness as a trait, using the Rosenzweig Picture Frustration Test, a projective test based on responses to cartoon pictured situations. Aggression or hostility as a state was supposedly induced by a frustration with criticism using manipulated failure on an "intelligence test." After the induction of negative emotion, the subject's perceptual thresholds for aggressive and neutral words were measured using a tachistoscope. My hypothesis was that frustration would lower thresholds for aggressive words, particularly in those with high levels of trait aggression. Frustration increased thresholds for all words, but there was no interaction between content of words and the personality of the subject. In retrospect, the failure of the research could have been in the measure used for a personality trait and the lack of a state measure of affect. Disappointment in the outcome of this research for a time left me disillusioned with research as well as with clinical work. I began to read outside of the field in archeology and anthropology.

Life after Graduate School

My first clinical job during and after my PhD work was at Norwich State Hospital in Connecticut. Norwich was another old snake pit. My only compensation was my delightful colleagues, Bud Orgel and Peggy Scales, and a weekly trip to the outpatient clinic in Hartford. I remember a patient I saw there who raised doubts about the dynamic theories that guided my therapy efforts. He was a depressed, middle-aged man who only wanted to talk about his wife's extravagant spending habits and how they angered him, rather than their general relationship dynamics. Finally, I gave up the search for insight and helped him devise a reasonable budget to present to his wife. A week later he showed a dramatic improvement and thanked me for his "cure." In contrast, other patients developed profound insights but remained as depressed as ever. I think dynamic therapists must maintain a great deal of faith in their theories and never ask the question "What really helped this patient to recovery?" A bit of practical suggestion may go a long way even though patients are supposed to develop their own solutions to life problems including the interpersonal ones. Of course, this was all before cognitive therapy.

In 1954 I moved to a more modern hospital, Larue D. Carter Memorial Hospital in Indianapolis. Arnold Buss was the chief psychologist and he was the one who decisively turned my interests back to research. Arny ran the psychologist section like a university department, with research seminars and discussions of new techniques. During my orientation with other new employees, he appeared (reluctantly) to discuss the role of the clinical psychologist in the hospital. He said, "Clinical psychology is assessment, therapy and research, and other than that, it is a black art," and then stalked out of the room.

Arny was an intellectually provocative and skeptical person with an extraordinary level of activity, sociability, and enthusiasm. He was always challenging his colleagues to games of tennis, chess, impromptu discussions of current films, books, and even dramatic plays in which we all took parts. Our informal seminars were augmented by trips to Indiana University in Bloomington to attend their seminars. We enjoyed spontaneous parties thrown by Arny and his wife Edith. I began doing research again and conceived of life outside of clinical settings. I realized that I enjoyed doing and talking about research more than testing and treating patients. It is not that I didn't sometimes become engrossed with particular patients or gratified by their improvement, I just did not find the process intellectually satisfying. I became convinced that the answers to basic questions about the sources of behavior must come from controlled research.

In 1956 one of those chance events happened that determine our destinies. An institute for psychiatric research opened in the medical center next door to Carter Hospital. I was hired by the director, John Nurnberger, a research-oriented psychiatrist, to join an interdisciplinary team of biochemists, microbiologists, and experimental psychologists. I trace my interest in psychobiology to these years, although it only came to full expression in my theorizing and research years later. However, despite some efforts at collaboration, my four years there were largely spent studying problems in personality assessment, including direct (questionnaire) vs. indirect (projective) methods in the assessment of dependency, anxiety, and affect traits, response set influences in tests, and the measurement of trait and state emotions. Dr. Nurnberger asked my help in developing measures of affect to be used in a study of pregnancy over time. I realized the state-trait problem in such research and developed the first real trait-state test for anxiety (Zuckerman, 1960), later expanded into a three-factor test (anxiety, depression, hostility), the Multiple Affect Adjective Check List (Zuckerman & Lubin, 1965). The current form of this test includes scales for positive affects as well as the three negative affects (Zuckerman & Lubin, 1985; Lubin & Zuckerman, 1999).

During my last year at the Institute I began doing experimental research in the area of sensory deprivation. In this research, volunteers are placed in dark, soundproof rooms with tactual and movement as well as visual and auditory restriction. The reactions to such deprivation are varied and include anxiety, panic, hallucinations, complaints of cognitive inefficiency, boredom, and restlessness. My research in this was primarily directed at finding the sources of these reactions in otherwise normal subjects by experimentally varying the physical components of the complex situation and the expectations induced by different kinds of instructions to the subjects. A group of investigators in Boston had used an iron lung to confine movement in their subjects. We found an old one in the storehouse of the medical center and began to use it for 8-hour studies of perceptual isolation. Both sensory deprivation and social isolation without sensory deprivation proved to be significant factors in producing anxiety and stress in subjects (Zuckerman, Albright, Marks, & Miller, 1962). Perceptual deprivation and set interacted to produce hallucinations. Subsequent experiments were done using an ordinary bed in a dark soundproof room. The degree of movement restriction also proved to be a significant source of stress.

I finally made the move to academia in 1959, joining the faculty at Brooklyn College. The move coincided with a drastic change in my life—a divorce, personal therapy, and a period of turmoil and growth. I could not afford a car in New York, so I buzzed around town on a Vespa motor scooter (Figure 3). After a period of living in the old home with my parents, I got my own place in a loft near the beach in Brooklyn. Dating is difficult after a long period of marriage, particularly when one is short on money. It was during this period that I got the idea for the trait called "sensation seeking."

I was interested in personality as a predictor of responses to sensory deprivation. Sensory deprivation has been called a "walk-in ink-blot," an ambiguous situation in which personality might shape responses. It was clear that persons high on neuroticism or trait anxiety might feel particularly anxious in such an undefined situation, particularly if the procedures and instructions led to an expectation of stress in the situation.

Sensory deprivation is for most persons well below an "optimal level of stimulation" (OLS) at which they feel good and function well. The OLS theory dates back to Wilhelm Wundt, the founder of psychology at the end of the nineteenth century. Freud, in his early paper with Breuer, had suggested that individuals might vary in their optimal levels of "cerebral excitement." The construct was revived in the early 1950s with the discovery of the reticular activating system, a system for regulating cerebral arousal to keep it within optimal limits for effective functioning. But no one had developed a personality trait measure based on the OLS construct. Because of its possible relevance to reactions to sensory deprivation, we developed the first sensation seeking scale in the early 1960s (Zuckerman, Kolin, Price, & Zoob, 1964).

The first scale was based on a general factor with items reflecting the need for novel, complex, exciting, and intense experience, and susceptibility to boredom when stimulation was constant, repetitive, and dull. Later research showed that there were essentially four factors in the total scale: Thrill and Adventure Seeking, Experience Seeking, Disinhibition, and Boredom Susceptibility (see Zuckerman, 1971, 1979b; 1994a for descriptions).

The scale was first applied to prediction of responses to sensory deprivation and a study of those volunteering for the experiment. Would the results support an optimal level of stimulation theory of individual differences in response to sensory deprivation? The main difference between high and low sensation seekers in sensory deprivation was that over time the highs became more bored and restless, as measured by random movements on the mattress to which they were confined. There was no difference in affective responses. Trait anxiety predicted who would have negative affective reactions.

In 1962 I moved to Adelphi University where I continued the sensory deprivation experiments and development of the Sensation Seeking Scale (SSS). During my years in Indianapolis, I had become an activist in the civil rights movement. The head of the local Civil Liberties Union was a black lawyer who set up his cases for violations of civil rights ordinances with sit-in challenges. Several of us psychologists from the I. U. Medical Center went on these sit-ins in restaurants, bars, and even an amusement park. These encounters in the late 1950s were not yet accepted, even in the North, and once we were confronted with a pistol by an irate owner of a bar. We left. Letting oneself be arrested is one thing, being shot is another.

When I moved to Adelphi, I joined the local chapter of the Congress for Racial Equality (CORE). I got tired of walking a picket line one evening and joined the "lie-in" in the lobby of an apartment house in Long Beach that had refused to rent to African Americans. I spent an evening in the local jail. The bail money arrived before I had much time to acclimate myself to my cell or the other inmates who were engaged in a card game of whist (!) when I arrived. The Long Island paper published a picture of me lying prone in the police station with the caption "Adelphi professor arrested in demonstration." There was another picture of me being taken off to prison in handcuffs looking unshaven and belligerent (Figure 4). Needless to say, the administrators of Adelphi were not thrilled with this publicity and as I did not have tenure my stay there was guaranteed to be short.

Fortunately, a colleague from the Institute in Indianapolis, Harold Persky, a biochemist, was in the process of moving to the research laboratories of the Department of Endocrinology and Human Reproduction at Albert Einstein Medical Center in Philadelphia. He invited me to join the group there and collaborate with him in a project on the experimental induction of different emotions using hypnosis and the measurement of psychological, physiological, and endocrine reactions that might distinguish one emotion from another. I was also able to move my soundproof room once again and continue my studies in sensory deprivation with the addition of psychophysiological and endocrine measures of stress. This was a particularly productive period for me during which we managed to identify many of the variables influencing responses to sensory deprivation and further explore the role of personality. One particular finding made us reconsider our conceptions of the sensation seeking. We found that the persons volunteering for the hypnosis and the sensory deprivation studies scored high on the SSS. We could understand why they volunteered for hypnosis, but why were sensation seekers volunteering to be deprived of sensory stimulation and activity for reasons other than the money paid to all participants? During the post-experimental questioning, we found that because of media sensationalism they expected to have unusual experiences, including hallucinations, without the aid of drugs like LSD. Low sensation seekers regarded the experiment as risky but came just for the money. This led us to amend the definition of the construct: "the need for novel, complex, and intense sensations and experiences *and the willingness to take risks for the sake of such experience.*" Not all sensation seeking activities are risky, but it takes a great deal of risk appraisal to deter a high sensation seeker from engaging in such activities. We also found that high sensation seekers tend to have lower risk appraisals of activities they have never tried than low sensation seekers. Lows are not necessarily fearful, they just do not see the sense in taking risks they don't have to for the sake of the dubious rewards of novel experiences.

At the end of the 1960s I faced another work and relationship crisis. Albert Einstein Medical Center was entirely funded on soft money with no institutional back up. When I started there, my salary was funded partly on Persky's grant and partly on my own, but by 1968 my salary was entirely derived from my own grant. After 10 years of support from the NIMH for sensory deprivation research, they decided that there was nothing more to be learned about the topic. I wanted to pursue the individual difference aspects, but I suddenly realized the difference between "hard" and "soft" money. Looking for an appropriate level position at the age of 40 can be a demoralizing experience. In addition to my job desperation my second marriage was in trouble and ended in divorce.

Fortunately, I got a job at the University of Delaware where they were starting a new program in clinical psychology. Once again my massive double-wall sensory deprivation room was disassembled, moved, and reassembled in Delaware. Without a grant, however, sensory deprivation research was too expensive to pursue. One has to pay subjects to spend eight hours in sensory deprivation and cannot rely on the free subject pool. I decided to concentrate on sensation seeking research to see what else could be predicted other than volunteering and sensory deprivation behaviors. The 1970s were a good time for sensation seeking research using college students. This was the time of the sexual, drug, and political (anti-war) revolutions on campuses. People were beginning to engage in extreme sports like parachuting, hang gliding, and scuba diving. Sexual experience, drug use, liberal beliefs, and participation in extreme sports were all related to sensation seeking. But the phenomenal expressions of sensation seeking were much broader. Tastes in music, art, media, humor, and food were influenced by the trait. Risky driving habits, health risks, and gambling were correlated with sensation seeking. The trait played a role in vocational preferences and choices, social, premarital and marital relationships, and mate choices. Cognitive styles, fantasy, and creativity were correlates. Although the SSS was developed with the narrow goal of predictive validity for sensory deprivation, it became apparent that it also had broad construct validity.

The Biological Roots of Sensation Seeking: I—Psychophysiology

My first sabbatical in 1976 was spent at the Institute of Psychiatry with Hans Eysenck. Eysenck is regarded as the father of the biological approach to personality. The first time I met him was on the way to the 1966 International Psychology Conference in Moscow. I wanted to tell him about my idea that sensation seeking was based on individual differences in the optimal level of sensation. He listened quietly to what I had to say. After a long pause, he said "Yes I have already made that the fundamental basis for extraversion." But that was no problem to Hans, he simply regarded sensation seeking as a subtrait of extraversion.

Eysenck described himself as a stable introvert, and indeed he was. When asked a question, he thought long on it until one began to think that he had not heard the question. But his answer was well framed. He delighted in controversy and was anti-authoritarian, whether of the left or right. He was the opposite of politically correct and incurred a great deal of hostility because of his views on heredity. But he believed in the open marketplace of ideas and that all points of view that had some backing from data deserved to be heard. He believed science would eventually sort out the incorrect from the correct hypotheses. His faith in data made him gullible to dubious research on pseudoscientific areas such as astrology.

Eysenck pioneered the behavioral genetic approach to personality using identical and fraternal twins. While I was on sabbatical we developed a new and shorter form of the SSS (form V), and with David Fulker and Sybil Eysenck, we did a genetical analysis of the SSS using subjects from the Maudsley twin bank. Our results are described in the early part of this chapter. The high heritability for the trait found in this study convinced me that sensation seeking was not just a minor subtrait of personality but one with a strong evolutional-biological source. But what was inherited? Genes do not make personality traits. Genes only make proteins, including those that shape neuronal systems and neurotransmitters in the brain.

My first studies of the biological basis of sensation seeking were in psychophysiology. Richard Neary and I found that high sensation seekers had a strong orienting reflex, an indication of interest in novelty features of stimuli. This finding was extended from skin conductance to heart rate responses. When stimuli were novel, high sensation seekers showed greater arousal than lows, but as soon as stimuli became familiar, their responses did not differ. In collaboration with Jerome Siegel, a colleague, and Thomas Murtaugh, then a graduate student, we found a relationship between the strength of the cortical visually evoked potential (EP) in reaction to increasing intensities of stimulation and sensation seeking (disinhibition). High sensation seekers were augmenters, i.e., their EPs increased in amplitude in proportion to increases in stimulus intensities; low sensation seekers tended to be reducers, i.e., their EPs showed little increase in amplitude with increasing stimulus intensity and sometimes showed reduction at the highest stimulus intensities. Some replications and failures of replication by others of these psychophysiological experiments are described in Zuckerman (1990).

I view sensation seeking as a trait with a biological basis and an evolutionary history expressed in other species and human infants in terms of explorativeness and approach responses to novel stimuli (Zuckerman, 1984, 1991). It is therefore important to show that the kind of individual differences observed in humans can be seen in other species. If this similarity is only based on behaviors of a similar sort, then it is only metaphorical and even anthropomorphic. Neal Miller's comparison of experimentally induced conflict in rats and conflict in humans was an example of this kind of comparison. But if we find a common biological link between the differences observed in humans and other species, we are on more solid ground.

One of the more gratifying aspects of an academic career has been the opportunity to work with colleagues on problems of mutual interest. My work on the biological basis of sensation seeking has been somewhat limited because of the lack of a medical school and the absence of interested biologists at the University of Delaware. However, I had the good fortune to have a colleague and close friend who is an outstanding neuroscientist, Jerome Siegel. We recently retired at the same time and now share an office at the University. Jerry extended our work on human augmenting-reducing of the cortical EP first to cats and then to rats (Siegel & Driscoll, 1996). In cats he found that those showing the augmenting EP pattern were more exploratory, active, and aggressive, and more likely to approach novel stimuli than the reducer cats, who were more generally passive and avoidant of novel stimuli. In experimental tasks, the augmenter cats more easily adapted to the experimental situation and responded more for a simple fixed-interval rewarded bar-pressing task. But the reducer cats were superior on a task in which reinforcement was contingent on a slow rate of responding. The augmenter cats were too impulsive and could not adapt to the demand for restraint in responding. At the human level, impulsivity as well as sensation seeking has been related to EP augmenting.

Siegel and Driscoll studied two strains of rats, one actively avoidant and aggressive in response to shock, and the other tending to freeze and slow to learn avoidance in the shock situation. Members of the actively avoidant strain were nearly all moderate to strong EP augmenters, whereas nearly all of the fear-inhibited strain were EP reducers or very weak augmenters. The low-avoidant, EP reducer rats are less exploratory and more fearful in the open field test, and the females are more nurturing of their pups. The high-avoidant, augmenter rats are more likely to develop a taste for alcohol, and are less nurturing of their pups. The augmenters are more responsive to high intensity brain stimulation in the "reward centers" of the lateral hypothalamus. Under stress, the augmenters show more dopaminergic response in the frontal lobes while the reducers show more endocrine stress response in the hypothalamic-pituitary-cortical pathway.

The Biological Roots of Sensation Seeking: II Biochemistry
The search for the biological roots of sensation seeking went deeper with the finding of biochemical correlates. The psychophysiology depends upon psychopharmacology because neurons react through chemical mediators and regulators. In the 1970s, Reid Daitzman, a former student, undertook studies of sensation seeking in relation to gonadal hormones. The fact that males are higher than females on sensation seeking and that the trait declines with age (as does testosterone) suggested the possibility of a hormonal connection. The disinhibitory type of sensation seeking was related to levels of plasma testosterone in males, as were a variety of other personality traits, including sociability, dominance, extraversion, and activity. Then an even more exciting finding changed my entire course of theory.

Monte Buchsbaum developed the EP augmenting-reducing paradigm when he was at the NIMH. In 1974, I received a call from him informing me that investigators, including Dennis Murphy and himself, had discovered a relationship between the enzyme monoamine oxidase (MAO) and sensation seeking in two samples of males. The correlations were negative: high sensation seekers had low levels of MAO, and low sensation seekers had high levels.

Realizing the importance of this finding, I began a crash course for myself in psychopharmacology that continues to this day. Most replications in diverse populations (summarized in Zuckerman, 1994) have confirmed the MAO-SSS finding; although the actual relationship is a relatively weak one, it is fairly reliable (9 of 13 studies). MAO, as indicated by its name, regulates the monoamine neurotransmitters. More recently, it has been discovered that the type B MAO is a preferential regulator of dopamine, whereas the type A MAO regulates both serotonin and norepinephrine. MAO-B is a reliable biological trait with many correlates in psychopathology and normal behavior extremes, such as drug and alcohol use, and sensation seeking analogous behavior in monkeys (Zuckerman, 1984, 1979, 1994a; Zuckerman, Buchsbaum, & Murphy, 1980). Generally, things that are related to MAO are also related to sensation seeking. The convergent validity pointed to further research on the role of the monoamine neurotransmitters in sensation seeking.

Eysenck was an important influence in my research and theory of my earlier years. However, with the shift in attention to brain neurotransmitters, I looked to another psychologist, and neuroscientist, Jeffrey Gray, at Oxford University. Jeffrey was "bottom up" theorist in contrast to Hans, who was a "top-down" type. Both believed in the importance of comparative psychology, genetics, and neuropsychology, but Jeffrey actually did neuropsychological experiments on rats whereas Eysenck's work was primarily based on psychophysiological and behavioral research on humans. Jeffrey developed a theory linking brain neuronal systems and neurotransmitters in the brain to motivational mechanism governing sensitivities to signals of reward and punishment. The motivational mechanisms, in turn, affect the basic personality traits: anxiety, impulsivity (approach), and aggression (fight-flight). In 1983, I spent a sabbatical in Oxford with Jeffrey during which I learned a great deal about Jeffrey's theory and its applicability to my own theoretical model.

Oxford is a cloistered, medieval university both architecturally and academically, using the tutorial system instead of regularly scheduled class lectures. I lived with my then partner, Mary Hazard, on the last cobblestone street in Oxford behind the university. I remember one night after dining and drinking at "high table," reeling home through the narrow university streets under the spires of the colleges and thinking of the centuries of drunken scholars who preceded me down these streets. When I got back to the United States, I began to work on my book, *Psychobiology of Personality*, which was finally published in 1991 in Gray's series with Cambridge University Press, *Problems in the Behavioral Sciences*. Gray's guidance on this book was invaluable.

As I said before, my own collaborations in this field were limited by the lack of collaborative opportunities in Delaware. Fortunately, other laboratories began to use sensation seeking as a model for some of their work on individual differences in humans and other species. Murphy, Post, and Ballenger at NIMH studied CSF monoamine metabolites, personality, and psychopathology. Petra Netter and Rammsayer at the University of Giesen in Germany did research on the effects of monoamine agonists and antagonists on different types of personality, including sensation seeking. Dellu, LeMoal, and Simon at the University of Bordeaux in France studied "novelty seeking in rats" with the goal of establishing relationships to sensation seeking in humans. At the University of Kentucky, Bardo studied the role of dopamine in the preference for novelty in rats, while Lewis Donohue has used sensation seeking to design effective ads to discourage drug use and safe sex in adolescents.

It is particularly gratifying at this late stage of my career to see the influence of my work on such an international group of distinguished scientists. It is not exactly immortality, but it is more than I anticipated when I ventured into this new world of the "psychobiology of personality" (Zuckerman, 1991). My model for impulsive sensation seeking (Zuckerman, 1994b, 1995, 1996) may be wrong in most aspects, or at least proven grossly over simplified by future research, but it will have stimulated a great deal of comparative research.

My work has not gone unnoticed in the media and I now find the term "sensation seeking," which I believe I devised, being used in popular publications without attribution. Contributing a new word to the lexicon is a kind of tribute even if the context is not always appropriate.

International Society for the Study of Individual Differences (ISSID)

We all belong to large organizations like APA or APS, but every psychological scientist needs a smaller group in which he or she can exchange views with others of like interests at paper and symposium sessions, and informal chats in restaurants and lounges. As portrayed in David Lodge's book *Small World*, once or twice every year we leave the small quiet world of our academic homes, flying around the world to meet the same colleagues in varied exotic settings. We are the academic "jet-set."

Hans and Sybil Eysenck founded the journal *Personality and Individual Differences* in 1980. Ernest Barrett, Robert Stelmack, and I, at a bar somewhere at some conference, came up with the idea of forming a society for the study of individual differences that could be associated with the journal. We presented the idea to Hans and Sybil, and they enthusiastically agreed. Hans asked for my advice about a name for the society. I suggested the Individual Difference Society. I think he liked it until he realized that the acronym was IDS. Hans had an intense antipathy to Freud and psychoanalysis. We compromised on the name International Society for the Study of Individual Differences.

It is a truly international society with members from many countries around the world. We decided to hold our meetings alternatively in North America and Europe. Eysenck was acclaimed as the first president in 1983, and I was elected as the second one in 1985. Subsequent presidents include foremost researchers in the field of individual differences: Gordon Claridge, Ernest Barratt, Robert Stelmack, Jan Strelau, Paul Costa, Nathan Brody, Ian Deary, T. Vernon, and Adrian Furnham. The society and its journal have fostered the growth of the science of individual differences. Sadly, its founder

Hans Eysenck who led and nurtured the psychobiological approach to individual differences died in 1997. His memory is honored in all of our work.

Personality Structure

During the preparation for my 1991 book *Psychobiology of Personality*, I realized I had to construct the book around the scaffolding of some personality trait theory. This was prior to the development of the Big-five in the Costa and McCrae version. Besides, the early versions were based on lexical analyses of adjectives mostly applicable only to human personality, and my own approach was a comparative one. Factors like "conscientiousness" are not useful in describing nonhuman species. I decided to do a factor analysis of scales which had been used in psychobiological research with several markers for each of the hypothesized basic personality traits. Several factor analyses of scales yielded five replicable factors: Sociability, Neuroticism-Anxiety, Impulsive Unsocialized Sensation Seeking, Aggression-Hostility, and Activity. We called this the Alternative Five-Factor Model (Zuckerman, 1994b). Using the items in the tests that were the best factor markers, we developed our own five-factor test: the Zuckerman-Kuhlman Personality Questionnaire (ZKPQ). The ZKPQ has been used in our own research and in translated versions around the world (Zuckerman, 2002).

Within the ZKPQ is a scale for Impulsive Sensation Seeking (ImpSS). Our factor analytic studies scales for impulsivity and sensation seeking were closely related and always loaded on the same factor, if one limited the analysis to the five primary factors. Sensation seeking is a subtrait of extraversion whereas impulsivity is a subtrait of the psychoticism factor in Eysenck's last structural model. In Costa and McCrae's Big-five, "excitement seeking" is also regarded as a subtrait of extraversion, but impulsiveness is considered a subtrait of neuroticism. Of course, what you get out of a factor analysis depends on what you put into it. I included the several subscales of the SSS and several types of impulsivity scales in my analyses, whereas others included only one general scale for each of these factors. If you have only one marker, you cannot identify a broader factor. Which are primary and which are secondary factors depends upon both your theory and the number of possible markers included in the analysis. We considered sensation seeking to be an important primary factor because of its high heritability, comparative analogues, and strong biological connections. Our surprise was in how closely it was linked to impulsivity. In actual fact, Buss and Plomin (1975) included sensation seeking as a subtrait of impulsivity in their earlier temperament theory. Some of these arguments about which are the primary dimensions of personality may be resolved by research in molecular genetics.

Descendents

I started this chapter with an account of my ancestors. Please indulge me in some words of pride about my children and grandchildren. This section illustrates the problems of applying concepts from population-derived genetics to individual families. My son Steven was a true sensation seeker, particularly when he was younger. He was a political rebel in high school and college, an experimenter in the drug and sex scene of the 1970s in college, a world traveler by foot and bicycle, but also a fine student. He studied anthropology in graduate school and with his wife Paula went off to the highlands of New Guinea to live among the Papuan highlanders. His wife, Paula Gorlitz, got her degree in clinical psychology and set up a practice in Chicago. Steve found a position in family practice hospitals training residents and doing psychotherapy. He took further training in family therapy and now has a part-time private practice in addition to his regular hospital job.

Steve and Paula made two extraordinary children: Ariel and Eric. Ariel, the elder, is a superb tennis player and plays the cello, piano, and guitar. She shows signs of developing the empathy of a "shrink," but who knows where her interests will develop. Like his father and grandfather when they were his age, Eric loves to play action and war games. He has an impressive arsenal of toy weapons and soldiers. Unlike his father and grandfather, he is great at sports, particularly soccer. The whole family goes skiing together and they travel together in Europe. Steve goes fly fishing in Colorado. He has come far from his days as a wild-haired revolutionary. When we go out, I defer to his choice of wines. He also advises me on my clothes. His ideology is unchanged but his lifestyle has markedly expanded.

April as a child could be described as a cautious sensation seeker (a rebuke to my linking of the two traits). Steve clamored up the monkey bars, sometimes slipping and falling. April went up carefully, watching her foot placements before going to the next level. During anti-war demonstrations while they were in college, Steve would be at the front of the demonstration, taunting and confronting the police, while April would hang toward the rear of the crowd, noting the possible escape routes in case the police should charge.

April had two children by her first marriage. Veronica, the eldest, achieved some fame as a child, appearing in a television program on child prodigies. She read at a very early age and wrote adult quality poetry. She is now in graduate school in English literature. Genevieve showed impressive artistic talents. I have a painting she did of me, which hangs in my apartment. She is now going to college and majoring in women's studies.

April was what I used to call a "Jewish dropout," meaning she stopped her education after winning her bachelor's degree and devoted herself for many years to raising her children. However, after her divorce she decided to get a master's degree in social work and took on a responsible job as the assistant supervisor of a community-based center for psychiatrically disturbed individuals. Like my son, she took further training in family therapy and now has a small part-time private practice outside of her job. She is remarried to a great guy, an English professor. He is more of a sensation seeker, a scuba diver. They take trips to the Caribbean where she snorkels or sits under a palm tree while he goes on deep dives. They like to travel in France. She is an experience seeker when it comes to food. We can detect the presence of a genetic taste for chocolate, passed from father to mother to granddaughter. Unlike her parents, she is a dedicated exerciser. She gets up at 5 a.m. in order to go for a workout before she goes to her job. Where does she get this kind of discipline? Not from her parents.

Retirement: On the Beach

In September 2002 I finally retired (Figure 5). At 74 it was overdue. I had some trepidation about retirement. I have seen some notable psychologists who simply disappeared from the scientific scene after retirement. I am not the type to retire to Florida and play golf. However, I can relax at the beach in Delaware where I have a house (Figure 6). But when I am at the beach, I spend my mornings writing and afternoons on the beach, swimming, reading and just watching the waves.

Retirement is simply an extended sabbatical. I loved my sabbatical years spent in Europe. A major part of this pleasure was the opportunity to write, study, and talk to colleagues, freed of the pressures of teaching schedules, boring faculty meetings, and trivial academic politics. Undergraduate teaching has its rewards, but I was no "Mr. Chips." What I sometimes regarded as a brilliant digression from the main topic, the students described in evaluations as "rambling." Afterwards they asked that question that infuriates teachers, "Is this going to be on the test?"

When I was a young sensation seeker, I imagined that after I retired I would do all kinds of adventurous things like hang gliding, parachute jumping, and learning to fly an airplane. These are the furtherest things from my plans now. But whereas thrill and adventure seeking and disinhibition fall rapidly with age, experience seeking does not change. I have moved to Philadelphia where there is more social life and cultural opportunities. My apartment is on the 40th floor with great views (not for acrophobics). I have season tickets to the symphony, chamber music groups, and theaters. There is a jazz club nearby and many good restaurants. Most importantly, I spend my mornings and even part of the afternoon writing. I have recently revised my 1991 book, *Psychobiology of Personality*. I have kept an office at the University of Delaware where I am still engaged in some research. I also have an appointment as a research professor at the Jefferson Medical University in Philadelphia. I plan to collaborate on some research there. In the summer I will be making short trips to Europe to give talks and visit friends. I have a loving lady friend whom I am with on weekends.

How long I can keep this up is a question, but for now life is stimulating and productive. I plan to continue writing and I try to keep up with the latest advances in my field. This is an exciting period in psychobiology. The advances in methods such as neuroimaging and molecular genetics have allowed research we never dreamed of mid-century. Whereas these methods were once restricted to studies of pathology, they are now starting to be used in the study of personality.

I started my research program in personality assessment. The controversies over response sets, consistency, state versus trait, person versus situation, engaged me for a time, but I always felt that the goal of assessment was to define meaningful personality traits. Reliability is a requisite but construct validity is the goal. Personality traits should define constructs within a theory and should not be mere items in a catalogue of traits.

REFERENCES

Buss, A. H., & Plomin, R. (1975). *A temperament theory of personality development*. New York: John Wiley.

Dollard, J., & Miller, N. E. (1950). *Personality and psychotherapy: An analysis in terms of learning, thinking, and culture*. New York: McGraw Hill.

Fulker, D. W., Eysenck, S. B. G., & Zuckerman, M. (1980). The genetics of sensation seeking. *Journal of Personality Research, 14*, 261–281.

Hur, Y., & Bouchard, T. J., Jr. (1997). The genetic correlation between impulsivity and sensation seeking traits. *Behavior Genetics, 27*, 455–463.

Koopmans, J. R., Boomsa, D. I., Heath, A. C., & Lorenz, J. P. D. (1995). A multivariate genetic analysis of sensation seeking. *Behavior Genetics, 25*, 349–356.

Lubin, B., & Zuckerman, M. (1999). *Manual for the Multiple Affect Adjective Check List*. San Diego, CA: Educational and Industrial Testing Service.

Siegel, J., & Driscoll, P. (1996). Recent developments in an animal model of visually evoked potential augmenting/reducing and sensation seeking behavior. *Neuropsychobiology, 34*, 130–135.

Watson, J. D., & Crick, F. H. C. (1953). Genetical implications of deoxyribonucleic acid. *Nature, 171*, 164–167.

Zuckerman, M. (1951). The effect of threat on perceptual affect in a group. *Journal of Abnormal and Social Psychology, 46*, 529–533.

Zuckerman, M. (1960). The development of an affect adjective check list for the measurement of anxiety. *Journal of Consulting Psychology, 24*, 457–462.

Zuckerman, M. (1971). Dimensions of sensation seeking. *Journal of Consulting and Clinical Psychology, 36*, 45–52.

Zuckerman, M. (1979a). Traits, states, situations and uncertainty. *Journal of Behavioral Assessment, 1*, 43–54.

Zuckerman, M. (1979b). *Sensation seeking: Beyond the optimal level of arousal.* Hillsdale, NJ: Lawrence Erlbaum.

Zuckerman, M. (1984). Sensation seeking: A comparative approach to a human trait. *Behavioral and Brain Sciences, 7*, 413–471.

Zuckerman, M. (1990). The psychophysiology of sensation seeking. *Journal of Personality, 58*, 313–345.

Zuckerman, M. (1991). *Psychobiology of Personality.* Cambridge, UK: Cambridge University Press.

Zuckerman, M. (1994a). *Behavioral expressions and biosocial bases of sensation seeking.* New York: Cambridge University Press.

Zuckerman, M. (1994b). An alternative five-factor model for personality. In C. F. Halverson, Jr., & R. P. Martin (Eds.), *The developing structure of temperament and personality from infancy to adulthood* (pp. 53–68). Hillsdale, NJ: Lawrence Erlbaum.

Zuckerman, M (1995). Good and bad humors: Biochemical bases of personality and its disorders. *Psychological Science, 6*, 325–332.

Zuckerman, M. (1996). The psychobiological model for Impulsive Unsocialized Sensation Seeking: A comparative approach. *Neuropsychobiology, 34*, 125–129.

Zuckerman, M. (2002). Zuckerman-Kuhlman Personality Questionnaire (ZKPQ): An alternative five-factorial model. In B. DeRaad & M. Peruginini (Eds.), *Big five assessment* (pp. 377–396). Seattle: Hogrefe & Huber.

Zuckerman, M. (2005). *Psychology of Personality.* (2nd ed.), revised and updated. New York: Cambridge University Press.

Zuckerman, M., Allbright, R. J., Marks, G. S., & Miller, G. L. (1962). Stress and hallucinatory effects of perceptual isolation and confinement. *Psychological Monographs, 76* (30, Whole No. 549).

Zuckerman, M., Buchsbaum, M. S., & Murphy, D. L. (1980). Sensation seeking and its biological correlates. *Psychological Bulletin, 88*, 187–214.

Zuckerman, M., & Cloninger, C. R. (1996). Relationships between Cloninger's, Zuckerman's, and Eysenck's dimensions of personality. *Personality and Individual Differences, 21*, 283–285.

Zuckerman, M., Kolin, E. A., Price, L., & Zoob, I. (1964). Development of a sensation seeking scale. *Journal of Consulting Psychology, 28,* 477–482.

Zuckerman, M., & Lubin, B. (1965). *Manual for the Multiple Affect Adjective Check List.* San Diego, CA: Educational and Industrial Testing Service.

Zuckerman, M., & Lubin, B. (1985). *Manual for the Multiple Affect Adjective Check List- Revised (MAACL-R)* San Diego, CA: Educational and Industrial Testing Service.

SELECTED BIBLIOGRAPHY

Books and Manuals

Zuckerman, M. (1979). *Sensation seeking: Beyond the optimal level of arousal.* Hillsdale, NJ: Lawrence Erlbaum.

Zuckerman, M. (1991). *Psychobiology of personality.* Cambridge, UK: Cambridge University Press.

Zuckerman, M. (1994). *Behavioral expressions and biosocial bases of personality.* New York: Cambridge University Press.

· Zuckerman, M. (1999). *Vulnerability to psychopathology: A biosocial model.* Washington, DC: American Psychological Association.

Zuckerman, M. (2005). *Psychology of Personality.* (2nd ed.), revised and updated. New York: Cambridge University Press.

Zuckerman, M., & Lubin, B. (1985). *Manual for the MAACL-R: The Multiple Affect Adjective Check-list, Revised.* San Diego, CA: Educational & Industrial Testing Service.

Journal Articles

Zuckerman, M. (1960). The development of an affect adjective check list for the measurement of anxiety. *Journal of Consulting Psychology, 24,* 457–462.

Zuckerman, M. (1971). Dimensions of sensation seeking. *Journal of Consulting and Clinical Psychology. 36,* 45–72.

Zuckerman, M. (1984). Sensation seeking: A comparative approach to a human trait. *Behavioral and Brain Sciences, 7,* 413–471.

Zuckerman, M. (1989). Personality in the third dimension: A psychobiological approach. *Personality and Individual Differences, 11,* 343–353.

Zuckerman, M. (1990). The psychophysiology of sensation seeking. *Journal of Personality, 58,* 313–345.

Zuckerman, M. (1995). Good and bad humors: Biochemical bases of personality and its disorders. *Psychological Science, 6,* 325–332.

Zuckerman, M., Buchsbaum, M. S., & Murphy, D. L. (1980). Sensation seeking and its biological correlates. *Psychological Bulletin, 88,* 198–214.

Zuckerman, M., Eysenck, S. B. G., & Eysenck, H. (1978). Sensation seeking in England and America: Cross-cultural, age, and sex comparisons. *Journal of Consulting and Clinical Psychology, 46,* 139–149.

Zuckerman, M., Kolin, B. A., Price, L., & Zoob, I. (1964). Development of a sensation seeking scale. *Journal of Consulting Psychology, 28*, 477–482.

Zuckerman, M., & Kuhlman, D. M. (2000). Personality and risk-taking: Common biosocial factors. *Journal of Personality, 68*, 999–1029.

Zuckerman, M., Kuhlman, D. M., & Camac, C. (1988). What lies beyond E and N? Factor analyses of scales believed to measure basic dimensions of personality. *Journal of Personality and Social Psychology, 54*, 96–107.

Zuckerman, M., Kuhlman, D. M., Joireman, J., Teta, P., & Kraft, M. (1993). A comparison of three structural models for personality: The Big Three, the Big Five, and the Alternative Five. *Journal of Personality and Social Psychology, 65*, 757–768.

Zuckerman, M., Kuhlman, D. M., Thornquist, M., & Kiers, H. (1991). Five (or three) robust questionnaire scale factors of personality without culture. *Personality and Individual Differences, 12*, 929–941.

Zuckerman, M., Levitt, E. E., & Lubin, B. (1961). Concurrent and construct validity of direct and indirect measures of dependency. *Journal of Consulting Psychology, 53*, 316–323.

Zuckerman, M., Murtaugh, T., & Siegel, J. (1974). Sensation seeking and cortical augmenting- reducing. *Psychophysiology, 11*, 535–542.

Zuckerman, M., Persky, H., Eckman, K. M., & Hopkins, T. R. (1967). A multitrait multimethod measurement approach to the traits (or states) of anxiety, depression and anxiety. *Journal of Projective Techniques and Personality Assessment, 31*, 39–48.

Zuckerman (paternal) ancestors, left to right: great-grandfather, grandfather, father

Pilder (maternal) ancestors: grandfather and grandmother

Marvin and his beloved Vespa motor scooter in New York City

Marvin's arrest as a protester in Long Beach, New York

Marvin Zuckerman, 74, at retirement, 2002

The retiree on the Delaware Beach, in 2003, contemplating his next book

Index

Page numbers in italic indicate figures.